Saffron Republic

Saffron Republic examines the phenomenon of contemporary Hindu nationalism or 'new Hindutva' that is presently the dominant ideological and political-electoral formation in India. There is a rich body of work on Hindu nationalism, but its main focus is on an earlier moment of insurgent movement politics in the 1980s and 1990s. In contrast, new Hindutva is a governmental formation that converges with wider global currents and enjoys mainstream acceptance. To understand these new political forms and their implications for democratic futures, a fresh set of reflections is in order. This book approaches contemporary Hindutva as an example of a democratic authoritarianism or an authoritarian populism, a politics that simultaneously advances and violates ideas and practices of popular and constitutional democracy.

Thomas Blom Hansen is the Reliance-Dhirubhai Ambani Professor of Anthropology at Stanford University.

Srirupa Roy is Professor of Political Science at the Centre for Modern Indian Studies, University of Göttingen.

METAMORPHOSES OF THE POLITICAL: MULTIDISCIPLINARY APPROACHES

The Series is a publishing collaboration of Cambridge University Press with The M. S. Merian–R. Tagore International Centre of Advanced Studies 'Metamorphoses of the Political' (ICAS:MP). It seeks to publish new books that both expand and de-centre current perspectives on politics and the 'political' in the contemporary world. It examines, from a wide array of disciplinary and methodological approaches, how the 'political' has been conceptualized, articulated and transformed in specific arenas of contestation during the 'long twentieth century'. Though primarily located in India and the Global South, the Series seeks to interrogate and contribute to wider debates about global processes and politics. It is in this sense that the Series is imagined as one that is regionally focused but globally engaged, providing a context for interrogations of universalized theories of self, society and politics.

Series Editors:
- Niraja Gopal Jayal, formerly at Jawaharlal Nehru University, New Delhi
- Shail Mayaram, formerly at Centre for the Study of Developing Societies, Delhi
- Samita Sen, University of Cambridge, Cambridge
- Awadhendra Sharan, Centre for the Study of Developing Societies, Delhi
- Sanjay Srivastava, University College London, UK
- Ravi Vasudevan, Centre for the Study of Developing Societies, Delhi
- Sebastian Vollmer, University of Göttingen, Germany

ICAS:MP is an Indo-German research collaboration of six Indian and German institutions. It combines the benefits of an open, interdisciplinary forum for intellectual exchange with the advantages of a cutting-edge research centre. Located in New Delhi, ICAS:MP critically intervenes in global debates in the social sciences and humanities.

Other Titles in the Series
- *The Secret Life of AnOther Indian Nationalism: Transitions from the Pax Britannica to the Pax Americana* • Shail Mayaram
- *Debt, Trust, and Reputation: Extra-legal Finance in Northern India* • Sebastian Schwecke
- *Properties of Rent: Community, Capital and Politics in Globalizing Delhi* • Sushmita Pati
- *Women, Gender and Religious Nationalism* • Edited by Amrita Basu and Tanika Sarkar

Saffron Republic

Hindu Nationalism and State Power in India

Edited by
Thomas Blom Hansen
Srirupa Roy

CAMBRIDGE
UNIVERSITY PRESS

Shaftesbury Road, Cambridge CB2 8EA, United Kingdom

One Liberty Plaza, 20th Floor, New York, NY 10006, USA

477 Williamstown Road, Port Melbourne, vic 3207, Australia

314 to 321, 3rd Floor, Plot No.3, Splendor Forum, Jasola District Centre, New Delhi 110025, India

103 Penang Road, #05–06/07, Visioncrest Commercial, Singapore 238467

Cambridge University Press is part of the University of Cambridge.

It furthers the University's mission by disseminating knowledge in the pursuit of education, learning and research at the highest international levels of excellence.

www.cambridge.org
Information on this title: www.cambridge.org/9781009100489

© Cambridge University Press 2022

This publication is in copyright. Subject to statutory exception and to the provisions of relevant collective licensing agreements, no reproduction of any part may take place without the written permission of Cambridge University Press.

First published 2022
Reprint 2024

Printed in India by Avantika Printers Pvt. Ltd.

A catalogue record for this publication is available from the British Library

ISBN 978-1-009-10048-9 Hardback

Cambridge University Press has no responsibility for the persistence or accuracy of URLs for external or third-party internet websites referred to in this publication, and does not guarantee that any content on such websites is, or will remain, accurate or appropriate.

CONTENTS

List of Tables and Figures		vii
Acknowledgements		ix
List of Abbreviations		xi
1.	What Is New about 'New Hindutva'? *Thomas Blom Hansen* and *Srirupa Roy*	1

Rule

2.	New Hindutva Timeline: September 2013–October 2020 *Ashwin Subramanian*	25
3.	Normalizing Violence: Lessons from Hindu Nationalist India *Amrita Basu*	59
4.	Hindutva Establishments: Right-wing Think Tanks and the Mainstreaming of Governmental Hindutva *Srirupa Roy*	72
5.	New Hindutva and the 'UP Model': An Interview with Neha Dixit and Nakul Sawhney *Srirupa Roy* and *Thomas Blom Hansen*	107

Articulation

6.	The Making of a Majoritarian Metropolis: Crowd Action, Public Order, and Communal Zoning in Calcutta *Ritajyoti Bandyopadhyay*	130
7.	Social Segregation and Everyday Hindutva in Middle India *Thomas Blom Hansen*	158

CONTENTS

Inclusion

8. '*Mitakuye Oyasin* – We Are All Related:'
   Hindutva and Indigeneity in Northeast India
   Arkotong Longkumer 181

9. From Castes to Nationalist Hindus: The Making of
   Hinduism as a Civil Religion
   Suryakant Waghmore 199

10. When Hindutva Performs Muslimness:
    Ethnographic Encounters with the Muslim Rashtriya Manch
    Lalit Vachani 219

Violence

11. Violence after Violence: The Politics of Narratives
    over the Delhi Pogrom
    Irfan Ahmad 251

12. Development: India's Foundational Myth
    Mona Bhan 275

13. *Pratikriya*, Guilt, and Reactionary Violence
    Parvis Ghassem-Fachandi 284

Contributors 306

Index 308

TABLES AND FIGURES

Tables

4.1	Indian right-wing think tanks	78
4.2	Think tank mission statements	81
4.3	India Ideas Conclave – Snapshot of participants	91
4.4	India Ideas Conclave – Themes	93
6.1	A fifty-year trend of Hindu–Muslim population ratio in Calcutta, published by the Census of 1951	141

Figures

6.1	1946 Riot Map 1: North Calcutta (in the language of the police, 'Northern Division')	133
6.2	1946 Riot Map 2: 'Central Division'	134
6.3	1946 Riot Map 3: 'Southern Division'	135
8.1	RSS *shakha* in Pashigat, Arunachal Pradesh, May 2018	184
10.1	Indresh Kumar interviewed by ANI at the Rashtriya Ulema Sammelan (5 May 2019)	233
11.1	Screengrab of a viral video during the Delhi pogrom showing five severely injured men lying on a street while	

TABLES AND FIGURES

	being beaten by men in police uniform and forced to sing the national anthem. All the injured were Muslim; one of them, Faizan, died on 27 February, two days after the incident	265
11.2	A handicraft shop gutted during the anti-Muslim pogrom in New Delhi, late February 2020	266
13.1	Shrine caretaker at Chinthariya Pir Dargah, Spring 2019	297

ACKNOWLEDGEMENTS

We are grateful to the Merian-Tagore International Centre of Advanced Studies 'Metamorphoses of the Political' (ICAS:MP) and the Centre for Modern Indian Studies at the University of Göttingen for supporting a workshop on 'Understanding New Nationalisms' in January 2019. This volume is an outcome of that workshop. Discussions with the workshop contributors Ravi Ahuja, Ed Anderson, Angana Chatterji, Ravinder Kaur, Razak Khan, Badri Narayan, Aditya Sarkar, Tanika Sarkar, Subir Sinha, Nikita Sud, Peter van der Veer, and Rupa Viswanath have greatly enriched our work. We would also like to thank Ashwin Subramanian for his invaluable research support and Debjani Mazumder, Publisher, ICAS:MP, for steering the project to completion.

ABBREVIATIONS

ABVP	Akhil Bharatiya Vidyarthi Parishad
AFSPA	Armed Forces Special Powers Act
AIMIM	All India Majlis-e-Ittehadul Muslimeen
AIMPLB	All India Muslim Personal Law Board
AMU	Aligarh Muslim University
ASI	Archaeological Survey of India
BC	Backward Classes
BJP	Bharatiya Janata Party
BMAC	Babri Masjid Action Committee
CAA	Citizenship Amendment Act
CBI	Central Bureau of Investigation
CPI(M)	Communist Party of India (Marxist)
CRPF	Central Reserve Police Force
DU	Delhi University
FIR	first information report
GST	goods and services tax
ICCS	International Center for Cultural Studies
IIT	Indian Institute of Technology
INC	Indian National Congress
IPC	Indian Penal Code
JMI	Jamia Millia Islamia

ABBREVIATIONS

JNU	Jawaharlal Nehru University
LAC	Line of Actual Control
LoC	Line of Control
MLA	Member of Legislative Assembly
MP	Member of Parliament
MRM	Muslim Rashtriya Manch
NCRB	National Crime Records Bureau
NDA	National Democratic Alliance
NGO	non-governmental organization
NHPC	National Hydroelectric Power Corporation
NIA	National Investigation Agency
NPR	National Population Register
NRC	National Register of Citizens
NRI	non-resident Indian
NSA	National Security Act
OBC	Other Backward Classes
PSA	Public Safety Act
RBI	Reserve Bank of India
RIWATCH	Research Institute of World's Ancient Traditions Cultures and Heritage
RSS	Rashtriya Swayamsevak Sangh
SC	Scheduled Castes
ST	Scheduled Tribes
TMC	(All India) Trinamool Congress
UAPA	Unlawful Activities Prevention Act
UIDAI	Unique Identification Authority of India
UPA	United Progressive Alliance
VHP	Vishwa Hindu Parishad

1

WHAT IS NEW ABOUT 'NEW HINDUTVA'?

Thomas Blom Hansen and *Srirupa Roy*

This collection of essays examines the phenomenon of contemporary Hindu nationalism or 'New Hindutva' in India, the ideology that orients the popularly elected national government of the Bharatiya Janata Party (BJP, Indian People's Party) that has been in power since 2014. There is a rich body of academic work on Hindu nationalism, but its main focus is on the insurgent mass mobilizations that roiled the country in the 1980s and 1990s. In contrast to this era of *mandir* (temple) politics, new Hindutva is a governmental formation with considerable institutional heft that converges with wider global currents and enjoys an unprecedented level of mainstream acceptance.

Contemporary Hindu nationalist politics is also significantly different from earlier versions in both form and substance. For instance, economic and foreign policy projects and aspirations are as important to Hindu nationalists today as are their efforts to shape and transform cultural and religious identity along Hindu majoritarian lines. Expanding beyond the regional arena of north Indian Hindi heartland politics, regions in the south, east, and northeast of the country have emerged as central theatres of Hindutva political action. The politics of caste has assumed a new and intense significance for Hindu nationalist mobilization and electioneering. Finally, cellular and individualized forms of vigilante action have emerged alongside older cadre-based, centralized, and mass organizational forms to advance the violent politics of Hindutva in the twenty-first century.

To understand these new political forms and their implications for democratic futures, a fresh set of reflections is in order. The essays in this volume address contemporary Hindutva as an example of a *democratic authoritarianism* or an *authoritarian populism*, that is, a politics that simultaneously advances and violates ideas and practices of popular and constitutional democracy. The democratic context of Hindutva as an electorally acclaimed and now apparently mainstream political project is our key concern. What are the causes and consequences of the rise of Hindutva, and of avowedly non-democratic Hindu nationalist organizations like the Rashtriya Swayamsevak Sangh (RSS, National Volunteer Organization), in an intensely competitive electoral democracy?

Understanding Hindu Nationalism

The 1990s saw a surge of scholarly interest in the rise of Hindu nationalism. Reflecting the socio-political and academic *zeitgeist*, these interventions shared several common features. First, the bulk of late twentieth-century scholarship has approached Hindu nationalism in politically instrumentalist terms, as a deliberate and politically organized project of social engineering and collective identity formation. Countering essentialist arguments that assertions of Hindu group identity in Indian public life were eruptions of timeless religious passions, multiple authors defined *fin-de-siècle* Hindu nationalism as a project of collective mobilization and ideological engineering that reflected thoroughly modern political aspirations and calculated power plays by historically situated political actors (Basu 2015; Brass 1997, 2003; Hansen 1999; Jaffrelot 1996).

These evaluations were influenced both by current events, with Hindu nationalist ascendancy linked to the successful strategic manoeuvres of political parties like the BJP and its leaders, and by the dominant theoretical paradigms of the time. For instance, the shift towards constructivist approaches and the rejection of an 'ancient atavisms' mode of analysis for Indian politics was aligned with post-colonial theory and its intellectual critiques of orientalism (Ludden 1996; Van der Veer 1994; Breckenridge and Van der Veer 1993). Efforts to establish the modernity and political rationalities of Hindu nationalism bore the imprint of contemporaneous modernity critiques that urged for a reconsideration of modernity's normative and spatial–temporal contours. Moving sharply away from ideas of a salutary European modernity, the violence and exclusion of Hindu nationalism was seen to reflect modernity's thriving presence in the postcolony (Madan 1987; Nandy 1988).

Next and as the term itself indicates, the scholarship of the 1990s drew attention to the specifically nationalist dimensions of efforts to create an 'imagined community' of the Hindu nation. The primary focus was on the culturalist and identitarian stakes of the Hindutva project (Anderson 1983; Chatterjee 1993; Pandey 1999). 'Supply-side' and 'demand-side' perspectives respectively examined the ideological and organizational strategies of Hindu nationalist actors and institutions, and the beliefs and choices of ordinary citizens who subscribed to the Hindutva cause (Andersen and Damle 1987; Basu et al. 1993; Kakar 1996; see also Berenschot 2012). For both, Hindu nationalism was about ideological persuasion. Its primary aim was to cultivate sentiments of collective identification and cultural belonging; to affirm a Hindu self against a feared and hated Muslim other (Sarkar and Butalia 1995; Kumar 2016).

The enabling link between Hindu nationalism and the problem of communalism – a term that described the deep collective identifications with politically constructed formations of Hindu and Muslim religious community – was another prominent theme. In these accounts, the Hindutva project was a post-colonial variant of the colonial 'construction of communalism' (Pandey 1990; Tambiah 1996). Finally, the scholarly debates of the 1990s also invested Hindu nationalism with a decidedly insurgent charge. It was defined as an oppositional and often violent mobilization of the imagined Hindu nation against the institutional order of the state establishment and the Muslim other that the secular Indian state was accused of favouring and 'appeasing'. In this phase of scholarship, the Hindu nation and the Indian state were presented as fiercely antagonistic formations. Mirroring and reinforcing an enduring opposition between communalism and secularism that had structured Indian political thought and practice for many decades, the rise of Hindu nationalism in the 1990s was seen to imperil the survival of secularism.

In the early decades of the twenty-first century, a differently oriented set of scholarly reflections has gained ground. Reflecting the political successes of Hindutva as it transformed from an insurgent mobilization to a governing formation that has captured state power at both sub-national (regional state) and national levels, scholars have expanded their attention beyond the Hindu nation to the vision for a Hindu state. In recent years, the substantial work on the cultural and ideological activities of various Sangh Parivar organizations (Kanungo, Reddy, and Zavos 2012; Katju 2017; Menon 2011; Narayan 2008, 2021; Thachil 2014) have been supplemented by scholarly engagements with the policy and governance dimensions of Hindutva statecraft, electoral strategies of the BJP, the Sangh's political party, and the distinctive leadership style of the longest serving BJP Prime Minister, Narendra Modi (Basu 2015; Ganguly 2015; Sitapati 2020). Several recent publications have been authored by Hindu nationalist sympathizers, who have enhanced the political affairs and current events turn of contemporary writing on Hindu nationalism with their insider accounts of manoeuvres and political machinations within Hindutva organizations (Ganguly and Dwivedi 2019; Jha 2019; Mahurkar 2017; Sinha 2020).

The present volume continues this engagement with questions of statecraft and governance that we raise at a time when Hindu nationalism has been institutionalized and normalized as the ideology of the ruling national political party for two successive electoral cycles. A recent volume, *Majoritarian State*, has traversed similar ground, tracking Hindutva's 'moment of arrival' and its modulation from a nation-making to a governmental/statecraft project (Chatterji, Hansen, and Jaffrelot 2019). Many contributions to that work remain focused on the Hindu nationalist movement, and they map the distinctive manoeuvres and practices of Hindu nationalist organizations themselves. This volume, by contrast, focuses on the broader historical and social–political contexts and fields where Hindutva is embedded. We track the interplay of Hindutva forces and many other competing forces, institutions, and actors. We examine how the gradual embedding of the ideology of Hindutva across multiple societal and political domains has upended earlier assumptions about the stark opposition between a 'normal' Indian secular democracy and the Hindutva exception.

Populists in Power

The problem at hand is not unique to India. In recent years, authoritarian and populist governments have formed within constitutional (and in many cases, liberal) democracies in many different parts of the world (Kyle and Gultchin 2018; Mounck 2018; Müller 2016; Snyder 2017). As with the Indian BJP under Prime Minister Narendra Modi, leaders like Donald Trump, Recep Erdoğan, Viktor Orbán, Rodrigo Duterte, and other strongmen around the world have not directly annulled democracy in order to come to power. Rather, they have used democracy's normal and normative resources, relying, for instance, on the continued functioning of key democratic procedures such as elections, and on laws and institutions authorized by their respective constitutions (Scheppele 2018).

Once populists are in power, these practices of democratic and constitutional deployment continue. From Brazil to the Philippines, Turkey to the United States, authoritarian populist governments, many under individual strongmen leaders, hollow out and transform democratic regimes from within, effecting a molecular transmutation or modulation of the existing system rather than a sudden and frontal assault. Simply put, populists in power gradually morph rather than abruptly kill constitutional democracy. The use of terms like 'backsliding' to describe the transformational effects of authoritarian populist regimes on existing constitutional democracies conveys the elasticity of the processes involved. The entangled formations that result defy any rigid separation of authoritarian and democratic forms and moments (Bermeo 2016; Crewe and Sanders 2020; Mair 2013; Waldner and Lust 2018).

Instead of a binary switch or a tectonic shift, we have a sliding back and forth and a blurring of antinomian registers; democracy and authoritarian populism, liberalism and illiberalism exist in uneasy simultaneity rather than in a linear chronology of succession. The rhetoric of democracy and affective-moral appeals to the power of the people do not disappear but, in fact, are heightened and intensified in the age of authoritarian populism. We appear to confront a paradox: the time of liberal democracy's greatest threat is equally the time of democracy's greatest value as a discursive apparatus and rhetorical currency of political legitimation (Canovan 1999; Levitsky and Ziblatt 2018). Explaining the causes and consequences of this apparent paradox of authoritarian populism's 'long march through institutions' (Ahmad 2020) is an important purpose of this book.

The chapters are organized around four keywords that describe the four distinctive attributes of new Hindutva: *rule, articulation, inclusion,* and *violence.*

Rule

Departing from movement Hindutva's affective projects of social and individual identity formation, governmental Hindutva is centrally concerned with the dry business of institutions. Since forming the government in 2014, the BJP and the Sangh Parivar (the Hindu nationalist family of organizations) have engaged in practices of institutional capture, creation, and bypass at national and state levels. All of these involve the use of existing and constitutionally sanctioned instruments of rule; the intensification of tendencies inherent in normal democratic government; and the circulation of established idioms of public legitimation and justification (neoliberal efficiency, anti-corruption, and anti-elitist democratization are among the legitimation vocabularies that governmental Hindutva draws upon). In other words, governmental Hindutva does not reject as much as it repurposes and innovates upon constitutional democracy from within.

For instance, the practice of institutional capture that has attracted considerable media attention since 2014 is essentially about the BJP using its parliamentary majority – won through largely free and fair elections – to exercise the constitutionally sanctioned authority of executive appointment. Like all its predecessors, the new BJP government after 2014 filled a large number of important state offices with its own people – individuals who conformed to some preferred set of criteria (more on this later). These included cabinet ministries, gubernatorial offices, cultural, research, and educational institutions, and technocratic, regulatory, investigative, and watchdog state agencies, such as the National Institution for Transforming India (NITI Aayog), the Securities and Exchange Board of India (SEBI), the

Election Commission, the Central Information Commission, the Auditor-General, the Central Vigilance Commission, the Central Bureau of Investigation, and the public broadcaster Prasar Bharati. Significantly, several of these, such as the Election Commission, the Central Information Commission, and the Comptroller and Auditor General are check-and-balance institutions invested with powers of oversight and veto over the exercise of governmental power. Controlling these 'institutions of accountability' facilitated a process of 'executive aggrandizement' or the unconstrained exercise of power by the national executive (Bermeo 2016).

The judiciary and the bureaucracy were also targeted for personnel changes by the new BJP regime. One of the first legislative attempts of the BJP government in August 2014 concerned the National Judicial Appointments Commission (NJAC). Although it was ultimately unsuccessful, the measure aimed to replace the existing collegium system of judicial appointments where judges themselves determined the composition of the Supreme Court and high courts with a system in which the national executive would play a decisive role. In terms of bureaucratic appointments, the new BJP government paid special attention to the staffing of the prime minister's office, and, like all other governments before it, brought in new officers of its choosing to serve as principal secretaries and close aides to the prime minister.

While these were intra-bureaucracy transfers that conformed to existing civil service rules and conventions of seniority, in subsequent years the BJP also appointed several outsiders to senior bureaucratic positions. In 2018, the central government announced a new scheme of 'lateral entry' into the civil services that brought nine new joint secretaries from outside the tightly specialized ranks of elite civil service to key ministries. In July 2020, the government proposed to hire another 400 directors and deputy directors to head state agencies under this scheme. Although lateral entry was a significant departure from the existing insular system of elite bureaucracy, the main public justifications that were offered for the innovation remained on familiar terrain. Lateral entry was justified in terms of private-sector meritocracy and efficiency, using arguments that had been endorsed by non-BJP governments in the past with similar vigour.

In sum, if Hindutva ideologues have been able to capture the levers of power in significant political, cultural, and educational institutions in India, they have done so through established means. If the present scenario of RSS ideologues in high office and saffron-clad monks as chief ministers of major states seems unprecedented, the road to this unfamiliar destination is not entirely new; it is paved, in fact, by the discretionary powers of executive appointment that the existing system of constitutional democracy readily makes available. Because of its large electoral majority and the lack of an effective parliamentary opposition, the BJP government has been able to use these powers in an unconstrained way, and has made many more appointments, and done this far more swiftly, than its predecessors. For instance, while it is common practice for the ruling national party to appoint some state governors based on their party affiliations, the BJP has taken this to the logical extreme and appointed party people to gubernatorial positions in all but three Indian states as of 2018.

What is new as well is the overt ideological calculus that determines the appointment of individuals to governmental positions. Considerations of party politics and patronage have influenced appointments made by previous governments as well. But the present Hindutva regime relies almost exclusively on ideological and loyalty criteria. Positions are filled on the basis of a shared Hindutva worldview and personal loyalty to Prime Minister Narendra Modi. This has often meant that professional qualifications are overlooked. Several Hindutva ideologues and loyalists who have been appointed to key positions in educational and cultural institutions in recent years have been patently unqualified for the job. One example is the appointment of a television serial actor (Gajendra Chauhan) to head the Film and Television Institute of India (FTII), known for training several generations of world-renowned filmmakers, that sparked angry protests by the FTII student body in 2015.

In another significant difference that underscores the distinctive ideological nature of appointments to state institutions under the current Hindutva regime, the appointment process is overseen by a singular extra-governmental organization, the RSS, the force behind the Sangh Parivar (Nag 2017; Sampal 2020). The role of the RSS as a penumbral authority in the contemporary regime, a shadowy and unaccountable presence that insists on its non-political identity even as it facilitates an organized ideological *gleichschaltung* or a coordinated homogenization across multiple state institutions, is one of the distinguishing features of governmental Hindutva. This has several implications for the practice of democratic politics in India. For instance, the exercise of tacit forms of extra-governmental influence has heightened the political importance of intermediaries that link state, society, party, and the RSS. The creation of new mediating institutions and networks bridging state and social spaces is an important component of the new regime. Right-wing think tanks and individuals like Ram Madhav, a senior RSS leader who is also a key figure in the national organization of the BJP, are powerful players in national politics today. They adroitly mediate between the diverse power centres of the Sangh Parivar, party, state, and capital that conjointly constitute and shape political order in contemporary India.

The penumbral influence of the RSS also means that Hindutva agendas are diffused widely through different kinds of governmental spaces. Changes are enacted through a broad array of legal and policy measures that range from renaming cities, changing the colour of Uttar Pradesh's (UP's) public buses to saffron, and increasing budgetary allocations for Sanskrit education, to the designation of 25 December as 'good governance day' in 2016, a measure that effectively annulled the commemoration of Christmas as a national holiday by requiring all employees and students of central educational institutions to show up to work and school. Mirroring the diffused and flexible logics of Sangh social mobilizations, the advance of governmental Hindutva has taken a tentacular form as well. Hindutva has inserted itself within multiple legal and policy domains to carry forward its ideological project by any means necessary.[1]

Along with these practices of institutional capture and creation, concerted efforts of institutional bypass are also quite central to the project of Hindutva rule. As we have already seen, placing pliant and ideologically committed individuals at the helm of several key monitory or check-and-balance institutions cleared the way for the unfettered exercise of executive power in the service of Hindu *rashtra* after 2014. The BJP government has also systematically whittled down parliamentary opposition and eroded parliamentary practices and procedures that were designed to foster democratic deliberation and encourage the representation of diverse opinions. Examples of parliamentary bypass include relying on ordinances rather than legislative enactments that require parliamentary discussion; using money bills to get around the scrutiny of the Rajya Sabha (upper house of parliament) where the BJP is in a minority position (money bills do not require Rajya Sabha assent); rejecting the long-standing parliamentary convention of referring bills to parliamentary standing committees where opposition parties can make a legislative contribution; and discontinuing well-known deliberative and dialogic parliamentary practices such as division votes and parliamentary question hour.

Efforts of institutional bypass have extended beyond the state to the domain of civil society. The BJP regime has targeted many of the autonomous monitory institutions that aim to check the excesses of state power. Since its electoral victory in 2014, the BJP government has pursued efforts to curb and control media and civil society criticism with great vigour. It has used a variety of direct and indirect measures from income tax raids on media owners and the freezing of bank accounts of human rights organizations, to the criminalization and imprisonment of activists under non-bailable 'black laws' of anti-terrorism and colonial-era sedition laws.[2]

To a large extent, these practices of institutional bypass are enabled by the constitutive 'gaps and ambiguities' of democracy itself. Indian democracy, like many other formal democracies around the world, invests considerable discretionary power in the national executive.[3] This in turn has engendered an emphasis on convention and customs. Elected governments conventionally rely on unwritten codes of 'institutional forebearance' and conform to the normative rather than literal contours of their power. They do not do what they are formally capable of doing (Levitsky and Ziblatt 2018). The stability and reproduction of the democratic system has rested on the creation and management of this gap between effective and potential authority: democracy functions as a system of reserve or unexpended power, we might say.

Governmental Hindutva, however, rejects these norms and conventions and makes full use of its discretionary authority to transform and dismantle democratic institutions, acting 'as per rule' all the while, making literal and maximum use of its constitutionally authorized powers. This may be the ultimate irony of the authoritarianism-within-democracy formation of rule, and what makes the task of critique and resistance complex and fraught: 'that it depends, ultimately, not upon [the] bogeymen of democracy – not on demagoguery, populism, or the masses – but upon the constitutional mainstays we learned about in high-school civics' (Robin 2020).

The section on 'Rule' opens with Ashwin Subramaniam's timeline of governmental Hindutva, a detailed annotated reckoning with the policies, laws, crises and critical events that have taken place since the BJP took office in the summer of 2014. The next two chapters track how Hindutva has been normalized as a resource of rule. Through a discussion of the new modalities of state-sponsored violence since 2014, Amrita Basu draws attention to the 'webs of complicity between state, political parties, and civil society' that routinize violence as a governmental tactic. The networked relations and mainstreaming efforts of Hindutva are also the central foci of Srirupa Roy's chapter on the rise of right-wing think tanks over the past decade. Belying Hindutva's angry anti-establishment rhetoric, she shows that 'right-wing think tanks are centrally invested in the creation of a governing elite, and they work with and expand rather than demolish existing formations and networks of elite power in order to achieve this aim'. Shifting attention from the exceptional violence of the Hindutva project to the discourses of 'civilizational power' and the organization of international conclaves by right-wing think tanks that are attended by a wide array of national and global elites, the chapter draws attention to 'the wider enabling conditions of normal democratic rule that also sustain the Hindutva project'. Chapter 5, an interview with journalist Neha Dixit and filmmaker Nakul Sawhney, gives us a close-up portrait of the everyday practices of governmental Hindutva in UP where a militant Hindu ideologue, Ajay Bisht/Yogi Adityanath, is in power. Dixit and Sawhney show us how the model of 'Yogi Raj' has normalized anti-minority violence by portraying minority areas as intrinsically criminal and anti-national, in need of extraordinary measures such as violent raids, mass-arrests, and the lengthy incarceration of suspects.

Articulation

Like other religious majoritarianisms and authoritarian populisms across the world that have taken root in electoral democracies, Hindu nationalism is entangled with older social and political formations. Much of the support for Hindu nationalism used to come from a number of regions in India, and from certain upper caste and middle-class social environments, where Hindu nationalist values and anti-minority sentiments over decades have sedimented into a shared, majoritarian common sense. This process of sedimentation of Hindutva as a shared sentiment, however vague, did not always translate into electoral victories for the BJP. However, this sedimentation of key elements of Hindutva in diverse domains has had a number of other less perceptible effects. As the project of Hindutva has grown and deepened, its rather 'thin' core tenets (such as 'India is a Hindu homeland and Muslims are invaders') have allowed it to diversify, morph, and co-articulate with a large number of regional histories and specific circumstances.

In the 1980s, the sociologist Stuart Hall developed the notion of 'articulation' to capture a process whereby distinct cultural forms and ideological constructs become mobile and floating signifiers that are associated with a range of different social, economic, and cultural circumstances and forces (Hall 1993). Racial fear and racial pride, gendered frames, and nationalist fantasies depend on such mobile and floating signifiers and enduring tropes, Hall argued, capable of being expressed and given meaning and emotional charge in a wide variety of circumstances. In the Indian context, the very notion of Hindutva is indeed articulated as a forceful response to at least three mobile, floating and adaptable elements of long standing: (*a*) Fear of Muslims as a demographic threat, a source of non-vegetarian pollution, and a threat of violence. (*b*) Fear of 'western culture' and the breakdown of conventional sexual and gender norms. (*c*) Upper caste fears of the rise of the numerous lower caste communities in public life and education, jeopardizing the 'natural' dominance of upper caste Hindu men in all aspects of Indian society. Thinking with the process of articulation illuminates the distinctive organizational form of new Hindutva. Replacing the familiar model of a pre-planned master-minded project of Hindu nationalism that is controlled and orchestrated by a central node, Hindutva now partakes in many forms of assemblage politics. New Hindutva advances through a contingent, decentralized, and flexible series of actions and events that are shaped by localized contexts and imperatives and yet (re-)produce a Hindu majoritarian social order.

Instead of viewing Hindutva as an exception, a complete break with a secular–democratic past, an emphasis on articulation thus affords a consideration of unexpected and perverse continuities, affinities, and resonances between contemporary Hindu nationalist politics and older forms of democratic politics in India. Two chapters in this section on 'Articulation' focus explicitly on how Hindutva becomes co-articulated with deeply entrenched spatial, social, and economic boundaries and segmentations. Ritajyoti Bandyopadhyay investigates the gradual spatial and social segregation of Hindu and Muslim communities in Calcutta in the twentieth century. Always a Hindu-majority city in a Muslim-majority province, the tensions between the two communities were indelibly changed by the systematic and widespread killings, displacements, and loss of livelihood during the riots in August 1946. This resulted in deep and enduring segregation along community lines, a process that was reinforced with the massive influx of Hindus following Partition in 1947. Tracing the history of barely reported riots in subsequent years, Bandyopadhyay argues that Calcutta turned into a 'majoritarian city' at this point: '... a state of affairs where violence toward the minority is routinized as a self-reproducing system – a society where lynching envelops riot as the dominant form of physical violence'.

Thomas Hansen traces two interrelated processes of physical segregation of communities and deepening segmentation of economies and livelihoods in the old Deccan city of Aurangabad. Once an important administrative node in the Hyderabad State, Aurangabad experienced a rapid economic growth and a demographic transformation that turned it into a Hindu-majority city from the 1980s. The militant Hindu right organization Shiv Sena made Aurangabad a major base, turning it into one of the most 'riot-prone' cities in the country, marked by deep and antagonistic segregation of communities. Aurangabad's history of violence and communal antagonism has also structured its booming industrial growth and expanding labour markets since the 1980s. Virtually all major industries are owned by Hindu business families, and almost all attractive jobs in the city are held by Hindus in a deeply unequal labour market segmented along lines of religion and caste. This has further deepened the marginalization of Muslims in social, economic, and spatial terms, locally castigated for their 'backward' and conservative attitude, unable to forget the past glory of the Nizam's regime. This social and spatial isolation of Muslims has also consolidated the idea of Hindus as modern, entrepreneurial, and forward-looking, making it possible for Hindutva to emerge as a dominant common sense among many Hindus in the city.

Inclusion

Hindu nationalism has long been understood as an exclusionary political and social project. It creates and cultivates a normative distinction between good Hindu selves and a range of hated/feared others, from religious and caste minorities to political ideologies such as communism. With the consolidation of the BJP and RSS's hold on political and institutional power, a new logic of inclusion has gained prominence among Hindu nationalists. Efforts to incorporate and include a variety of previously excluded social groups such as Dalits and even Muslims are now part of the outreach policy of Hindu nationalist organizations. Fuelled by a new sense of political and cultural confidence, the defensive tenor of Hindutva that blamed India's weakness on foreign aggressors has now given way to a more full-throated embrace of an expansive idea of Akhand Bharat, a greater India and a greater Hindu civilization. As in other domains, these efforts demonstrate a new ideological and strategic inventiveness and expansive flexibility.

After its founding in 1964, the Sangh organization Vishwa Hindu Parishad (VHP)'s first missionary efforts were in India's northeast as a response to India's humiliating defeat at the hands of China in 1962. The rationale for VHP was explicitly to strengthen India's borders and to strengthen the presence of Hinduism in a region with a strong Christian presence rocked by several armed insurgencies against the Indian state. Today, this earlier defensive attitude has given way to an assertive embrace of indigeneity, the land (*bhumi*), and 'Mother Earth' as common ground between India's Hindu majority and the tribal and indigenous communities in the northeast. As Arkotong Longkumer shows in his chapter, RSS organizers in Arunachal Pradesh and elsewhere in the region counter Christian influence in the region by promoting the idea that ancestor worship and the mother goddess are the origins not just of indigenous and 'pagan' belief systems, but the original foundation of Hinduism as well.

Suryakant Waghmore explores an RSS-sponsored educational organization, Tapas, that promotes education of children from poor and lower caste backgrounds. He argues that the defence of the caste system among older upper caste leaders of RSS notwithstanding, organizations like Tapas works systematically to create 'caste-free spaces' where the caste hierarchies of everyday Hinduism are replaced by a deference to national heroes and the senior leadership of the RSS. Waghmore suggests that while an older secular ethos tried to encourage toleration between ethnic and caste communities, RSS and affiliates seek to replace a caste-ridden 'everyday Hinduism' with Hindutva as a new, 'thin' and patriotic 'civil religion' that projects itself as a caste-blind 'nationalist Hinduism', hospitable to all Hindus regardless of caste and birth.

While Muslims continue to play a pivotal role in Hindu nationalism as the all-important external and internal enemy, the new confidence of the Hindu nationalist movement has more recently given rise to a strong distinction between 'bad' and anti-national Muslims, and 'good' and patriotic Muslims. Lalit Vachani explores how the RSS-sponsored organization Muslim Rashtriya Manch (MRM) is trying to provide a platform for 'patriotic' Muslims who recognize and embrace the notion of India as a Hindu nation and homeland. Although MRM has a negligible grassroots footprint among ordinary Muslims, the organization's many public events and carefully staged performances of pro-Hindutva Muslims, and Muslim clerics without 'hatred in their hearts', serve nonetheless as an illustration and projection of a possible Muslim future in a Hindu India: as an enthusiastically patriotic minority, eager to please and affirm their role as loyal allies of what Longkumer in his new book calls 'The Greater India Experiment' (Longkumer 2020). These RSS performances of 'preferred Muslimness' have the media, the RSS rank and file, and the wider Hindu publics as their intended audience, Vachani argues. Despite the language of outreach, Muslim citizens, it turns out, are not the intended target audience of the MRM project.

These chapters highlight how Hindutva's success as a populist political formation sustained by electoral democracy has expanded and changed the project of Hindutva. Political power has neither diluted nor 'mellowed' Hindutva as many analysts had projected when Modi rose to power in 2014. Rather, it has enabled its ideological project to expand, adapt, and articulate as an overarching civilizational project. Hindutva does not 'tolerate' social, cultural, and religious minorities as the official secularism of old. It seeks to encompass them, absorb them, and define them as first and foremost Indian, as *bharatiya*.

Violence

Violence and the ubiquitous 'threat' from the Muslim enemy have always been key elements of the larger Hindutva project. The RSS was initially formed as a 'self-defence' organization, and the rhetoric and practices of the RSS and affiliates are to this day suffused with violent imagery and tropes. However, violence has never been praised or owned by the RSS in the way Shiv Sena has used direct attacks as its signature. Even largescale atrocities against minorities such as the 2002 pogrom in Gujarat were framed as a 'natural reaction' (Ghassem-Fachandi 2012), or as a morally justified form of spontaneous 'Hindu anger' beyond the control of any organized force. This pattern continued after BJP's electoral victory in 2014, albeit in a slightly different form. A generalized 'Hindu anger' was now enacted as decentralized and seemingly spontaneous acts of vigilante violence against Muslims suspected of transporting and selling beef, or as lynching of individual Muslims for no apparent reason. These violent acts were perpetrated by people who had no formal links to the BJP or the government, leaving RSS activists of many stripes free to endorse these actions as symptoms of a seething and ever-present desire among Hindus to punish those who insult the nation's honour.

This raises the question of how such supposedly ubiquitous Hindu anger has been gradually naturalized and taken for granted. Let us briefly turn to the long-standing debate on the nature of communal riots in independent India in order to understand this process of naturalization of anger and the desire for violent retribution. Virtually every major riot in India since the 1960s has been a concerted attack on Muslims by organized members of the majority community. As Megha Kumar has shown, the massive riot in Ahmedabad in Gujarat in 1969 was an organized attack on Muslim neighbourhoods. The style, the sexual violence, and the rabid anti-Muslim rhetoric of 1969 were largely repeated in subsequent riots in 1985 and again, most infamously, in the pogrom of 2002 (Berenschot 2012; Ghassem-Fachandi 2012; Kumar 2016). The literature on communal violence is rich and diverse: political scientists have studied the relationship between the staging of communal riots, electoral performance, and consolidation of political power (Basu 2015; Brass 1997, 2003; Wilkinson 2004). Others have explored the larger context of conditions and cleavages that make riots more likely to occur (Chibber 1999; Varshney 2002). Anthropologists and others have taken particular interest in the experiential dimensions of riots, among both victims and perpetrators (Das 1990; Ghassem-Fachandi 2012; Hansen 2001; Kakar 1996; Roy 1994; Tambiah 1996). The common thread running through these debates is the focus on the riot itself as an articulation of political interest, social competition, institutional bias, social dynamics within movements and crowds, as well as the complex of fear, enjoyment, and exhilaration that seem to drive rioters. The objective of many of these studies has been to explain why and when riots occur, to explore the circumstances and actors that propel them, and to understand their effects on electoral outcomes.

Incidents of communal riots always have an intense presence in public discourse where they are seen as 'law and order failures' that are routinely used to criticize the performance of local governments, or to transfer law enforcement officials. In public debates and among activists, officials, journalists, and scholars, communal riots have emerged as the most central indicator of the level of tension between Hindus and Muslims in particular, and indeed an indicator of the general level of tension between different religious and ethnic communities. The problem, however, is that the staging of a riot or pogrom does not necessarily tell us much about what drives ethno-religious cleavages in a city or area, and whether such tensions may have significant political and electoral consequences. As has been demonstrated by much of the scholarship, riots are complex occurrences, in part planned and directed, but also shaped by multiple contingencies and local events beyond the control of political activists and operatives who are active on the ground. Starting and participating in a riot are always high-risk political enterprises that can work to the advantage of those staging attacks but can also backfire.

WHAT IS NEW ABOUT 'NEW HINDUTVA'?

More importantly, riots may have local causes, but they are much more than an expression of tension and enmity in one city, or single locality. The long-term and trans-local ideological effects of riots are also much more consequential than is often evident from the literature cited above. As has been shown for Gujarat, the long-term consolidation of the BJP and the ideology of Hindutva in the state went hand in hand with the spatial segregation of Hindu and Muslims. Decades of physical threats and attacks on Muslims led hundreds of thousands to seek physical safety in Muslim-majority areas, while Hindus in these areas have tended to relocate to Hindu-majority areas (Field et. al. 2008; Jaffrelot and Gayer 2011). This process was not limited to areas that had experienced riots but was much more generalized because the ideological effects of riots – deepened suspicions and fears of the other community – are multiple, deep, and trans-local. Rumours and stories, including stock items such as the threats of 'Muslim mobs', or Muslims roaming the city with the intent of seducing or abducting Hindu women, tend to reinforce and rekindle the long-standing and remarkably stable repertoires of prejudices, stereotypes, and rumours that have persisted over many decades.

Such trans-local ideological effects of riots have in recent decades been multiplied by the proliferation of social media platforms that at an unprecedented speed circulate rumours, doctored videos, and gruesome footage of violent acts. The intensity of this circulation of images and generally 'fake news' about attacks or perceived threats in various parts of the country has by now greatly accelerated the process whereby riots and violent incidents anywhere can become 'nationalized', to use Stanley Tambiah's term (Tambiah 1996), and spark protests thousands of miles away. The deepening segregation of communities and trans-localization of Hindu–Muslim enmities, wherever they occur, have also paved the way for the emergence after 2014 of the figure of the 'abstract Muslim', a ubiquitous enemy figure who can be attacked, lynched, and tortured anywhere by any patriotic Hindu. The victims of these crimes seem random – truck drivers accused of transporting beef, a young man with a skull cap on a train, a day labourer – but the motivations and imputed audiences for these attacks are uniform: to become a celebrated patriotic hero, a *deshbhakt* (devotee of the nation), however short lived, on countless social media platforms that are popular among Hindu nationalist activists and millions of others.

With the formation of BJP's government in UP headed by Yogi Adityanath in 2017, a new configuration of violence began to emerge. Under what has become known as 'Yogi Raj', the BJP in UP, and Adityanath's trusted men and militants from the Gorakhnath Math, embarked on a more ambitious attempt at a takeover of the state apparatus, police, and security forces in UP. The state had become notorious in recent decades for its extensive campaign of unaccountable 'encounter killings' of suspected criminals, a very large number of which happened to be Muslim (Venugopal 2020). As Neha Dixit and Nakul Sawhney describe in their interview in this volume, this capture of the state by Adityanath and allies soon resulted in systematic harassment and illegal arrests of opponents of the government. Following the massive protests against the Citizenship Amendment Act (CAA) at the end of 2019, the UP police unleashed a reign of terror on Muslim neighbourhoods across the state, arresting, torturing, and detaining Muslim men on the flimsiest of pretexts. The UP police and courts are no longer enforcing the law but systematically violating the law by acting as extensions of the chief minister's will and whim, exacting vengeance on the Muslim community and opponents of Hindutva.

A similar attempt at capture of the police power of the state by RSS and affiliates can be seen in Maharashtra where attacks by Hindutva activists on Dalit celebrations at Bhima Koregaon in 2018 sparked massive Dalit protests across the state. The Dalit protests were met with overwhelming force by the police, and a few months later a range of Left and Dalit activists and intellectuals were detained and falsely charged with being 'urban naxals', supposedly secretive and 'anti-national' organizers of these protests and other activities undermining the Indian state (Phadke 2019). Following the 2019–20 protests against the CAA, Hindutva activists instigated deadly attacks on Muslim neighbourhoods in northeast Delhi, clearly framed as a vengeance against the many Muslims who had come out in the streets protesting the CAA. Following what seems to be the new script of Hindutva state power in India, the Delhi police took no action against elected BJP officials who had openly incited the violence and instead charged various Muslim community leaders with instigating the violence that Irfan Ahmad (this volume) and most observers describe as pre-meditated attacks on Muslim areas.

The earlier Hindutva narrative of violence being the inevitable and spontaneous effect of a naturalized Hindu anger is, in other words, gradually being supplanted by a more assertive narrative of justified vengeance and punishment of the enemies of the nation, disobedient minorities and others, as Ahmad observes. In the hands of new Hindutva, state violence is no longer just 'law-preserving' but instrumental and constituent as a new form of 'law-making' (Benjamin 1996). The new Hindutva order is, however, law-making without new laws: it mostly revolves around dismantling and altering existing legal and political norms and frameworks. It disregards existing legal protections of individuals and communities, activates repressive security laws (mostly enacted by the Congress regime), and promotes majoritarian solutions to vexed issues (such as the status of the Babri Masjid site).

Another example is the repealing of Article 370 of the Constitution that since 1950 has guaranteed a special status for Kashmir. In her piece in this volume, Mona Bhan argues that the justification of this move is framed in openly 'settler colonial' terms as an overdue incorporation of Kashmir into the sovereign Hindu nation. Since 2014, the BJP government has generally pushed for a more flexible application of the domicile laws, in order to enable traders, bureaucrats, and others who have migrated to 'restricted areas' (such as Kashmir and Ladakh, or tribal areas protected by the Sixth Schedule of the Indian Constitution) to obtain permanent domicile status. In 2016, protests broke out across Jharkhand against a change in the domicile laws that would allow non-native residents who had lived in the state for more than thirty years to obtain a domicile certificate (*The Hindu* 2016). In 2020, the Government of India introduced new domicile laws in Jammu and Kashmir. The new laws allow non-native residents to obtain domicile after fifteen years, or less if possessing advanced educational qualifications or if related to officials of the union government (Khan 2020). This has generated fears that the BJP seeks to enable a gradual policy of 'Hindu colonization' by letting non-Kashmiris purchase land and occupy dominant positions in the newly incorporated union territory's government and economy.

Throughout the country, this new regime of constituent violence is most visible in the open attacks on Muslims, the celebration and justification of attacks, lynching, and pogroms as a manifestation of a new, aggressive, and unapologetic Hindu. In his piece in this volume, Parvis Ghassem-Fachandi (2012) argues that the aftermath of the pogrom in Gujarat in 2002 was paradigmatic of this new regime of 'perverse permission':

> Hindus were to emerge from the pogrom free to choose violence, free of the superego's torturous grip. Modi transformed the ambivalence many Gujaratis felt for this figure into a form of Hindu righteousness and indignation.

This new and constituent violence against Muslims has gone further and deeper in Gujarat than any other state in India. Here, Muslims are more isolated and marginalized than ever before, pushed together in dense slums and urban enclaves, dispossessed of many properties and robbed of any legitimate public presence in cities and villages across the state. Hindu victory is total but some of Ghassem-Fachandi's interlocutors feel that something has been broken and lost. Ghassem-Fachandi narrates the extraordinary story of Kalubhai, an ordinary Hindu man, who is frantically building a shrine to a local Muslim *pir* who in a dream had demanded that a shrine be built. His family and neighbours seem to accept that the spirit of the long dead *pir* must be placated: 'It is hard to avoid the conclusion that Kalubhai speaks against all odds with the voice of a collective superego, a voice demanding the recognition of a trans-generational guilt vis-à-vis Muslims.'

The most poignant aspect of the story of Kalubhai may be that for him, and other of Ghassem-Fachandi's interlocutors, Muslims are no longer much of a physical and social presence in Gujarat today. They have mainly been relegated to a past from where they may come back to haunt their former neighbours. That may encapsulate something essential about the future of the Hindu India that RSS and its affiliates are envisioning. This view of Muslims as a form of anachronistic presence that needs to be overcome is also reflected in recent changes to the 1968 Enemy Property Act. The 1968 act enabled the Government of India to put properties of families who had left for Pakistan under the authority of the Office of the Custodian of Enemy Property. In 2017, the act was expanded so that all Muslim families whose more distant relatives may have left for Pakistan now potentially face confiscation of their properties, at the discretion of the Office of the Custodian. This legislation converted alienable land of 'enemies of the state' into national property, held by the Custodian in perpetuity. With the amendment in 2017, any property owned by a relative of someone who had left for Pakistan could be declared enemy property and thus the property of the nation. As a result, the number of properties held by the Custodian of Enemy Properties has risen from a little over 2,000 in 2010 to more than 15,000 in 2017, a number that is still rising (Doval 2017). Further, it allowed the Custodian to sell off properties, supposedly to non-Muslims deemed to be proper members of India's sovereign people (Umar 2019).

Modulations and Moving Targets

A brief note on the necessarily selective character of the volume is in order. We do not aim to provide a synthetic and comprehensive survey of every detail and development of Hindu nationalist rule over the past decade. Constraints of time and space mean that we have excluded several significant aspects of the new Hindutva project, for example, the 'mediatization' of new Hindutva and the heavy reliance on media and communication technologies by the BJP and the broader Sangh organizations in recent years; the role of the Hindutva diaspora and its distinctive brand of 'long-distance nationalism' in securing the electoral success and global legitimation of the BJP regime; the economic policies of the Hindu right and the often convergent interests of Indian and global capital and Hindutva organizations; and the strategies of 'southern Hindutva' that reap electoral dividends in states such as Karnataka that have historically been at far remove, both culturally and spatially, from the northern Hindi 'cow belt' milieus in which Hindutva has traditionally thrived.

Missing too are the ongoing modulations and moving targets of Hindu nationalism. From the early months of 2020, the political and social upheavals of the COVID-19 pandemic have continued to batter India and they are extracting an unimaginably high death toll as this volume goes to press. Just as the flames of riots and pogroms haunted an earlier generation of scholarship on movemental Hindutva, the burning fires of mass cremations shadow our attempts to grapple with its governmental moment. Across the world, the COVID-19 pandemic has illuminated and sharpened existing social fractures and strengthened the authoritarian muscle of state power, and India is no exception. Through its practical and narrative management of the pandemic, the BJP regime has advanced many of its political and ideological commitments to a majoritarian, Hindu-first vision of India, whether by blaming Muslim religious gatherings as 'super spreader' events (the myth of 'Tablighi Corona' that was propagated in 2020) or through myriad small acts of everyday discrimination, such as the placement of Hindu and Muslim COVID patients in separate hospital wards (Ghosh and Dabhi 2020; Slipowitz 2020).

But this present crisis also illuminates a number of unexpected details about Hindutva and state power that merit further and sustained reflection. First, the present crisis has made it abundantly clear that the primary objective of Hindutva governance is to exercise ideological and narrative control in a way that constantly portrays the BJP and its leadership in the most favourable light and stamps out any dissent. The fudging of all numbers (of infections, tests, deaths, and so on), the inadequate and bungled mobilization of resources to fight the pandemic, and Modi's premature declaration of 'victory' over the virus at the World Economic Forum in January 2021 are all elements of this strategy of narrative control.[4] Similar strategies of image manipulation were mobilized around the calculation and presentation of India's gross domestic product (GDP) and other economic indicators in 2015–16 as a part of the BJP's attempt at presenting India as an attractive destination for international capital and investment. Second, BJP's insistence on conducting electoral rallies and holding state elections in April 2021, as well as supporting massive religious festivals such as the Kumbh Mela, indicates that the imperatives of constantly renewing an emotional bond with the electorate and the so-called 'ordinary Hindus' far outweigh any governmental rationality around public health, livelihoods, or protection of vulnerable segments of the population.

At the time of writing in May 2021, India is living through the second month of the worst outbreak of the pandemic that has been seen anywhere in the world. Thousands of bodies are abandoned at riverbanks and dumped in rivers, hospitals are ill-equipped to deal with the enormous surge in critically ill patients, and the vaccine rollout is slow and woefully inadequate. It is evident that the most basic functions of the state – to offer a minimum of protection to citizens and residents from calamities and violence – have failed. The BJP's national leadership has been reluctant to act decisively, instead leaving the management of the pandemic to state governments, evidently hoping that this may shield Modi and the central government from being blamed for the ongoing loss of life and livelihood. But the BJP's lacklustre performance in a number of state elections in April 2021 suggests that COVID-19 may ultimately force a political and electoral reckoning that strategies of narrative redirection cannot counter. More than any other political force, new Hindutva has fashioned Indian politics into an emotional drama running on fear, anger, and resentment. This makes the BJP government vulnerable the day the emotional wave turns against them.

Notes

1. While many of the measures taken by the BJP seem to have a mainly ideological and cosmetic character without transforming the functions of the state, some parts of the anti-Muslim agenda of the RSS have resulted in more lasting legal changes. The Citizenship Amendment Act (CAA) is one of the clearest examples. Unlike the previous amendments to the 1955 Citizenship Act that had gradually established blood and descent as the basis of citizenship, the CAA used religious community as a basis for eligibility for citizenship, a provision that specifically excluded Muslims. The Act grants the option of citizenship to non-Muslim refugees/migrants from Bangladesh, Pakistan, and Afghanistan ostensibly on the compassionate ground of their presumed persecution as religious minorities in their native countries. Clearly, the law reflects the long-standing objective of defining India as a homeland for Hindus and other religious communities considered 'native to India'. Defining any non-Muslim from the wider region as belonging to the 'Hindu homeland' also reflects the RSS' long-standing vision of the entire subcontinent as Akhand Bharat, that is, 'greater India'.

2. Interestingly, none of this has required new legislation. BJP has simply availed itself of the extensive legal frameworks, police powers, and emergency provisions that were put in place by successive Congress governments since the 1960s, including Mrs Gandhi's Emergency rule from 1975 to 1977 (see Hansen 2021; Jaffrelot and Anil 2020; Prakash 2019).

3. The gap between parliamentary politics and the bureaucracy is unusually wide in India. It is rooted in the colonial apprehension of any elected native representative or legislative organ, and the attempts by the late colonial civil service to concentrate power at the 'white' top of the bureaucracy. Decades of Nehruvian reformist and modernizing zeal turned the bureaucracy into the main instrument of reforming and disciplining backward and recalcitrant citizens, a process that only added to this gap and further entrenchment of discretionary authority within the bureaucracy. In the hands of a regime invested in a particular ideological project of Hindutva, discretionary authority has turned out to be very useful in protecting rogue elements and vigilantes associated with the BJP, for example (see the section on 'Violence' later).

4. Modi's speech at the World Economic Forum, Davos, can be viewed here: https://www.youtube.com/watch?v=z7p5kDtH-mc (accessed on 15 May 2021).

References

Ahmad, A. 2020. *Liberal Democracy and the Extreme Right*. Hyderabad: Navatelangana Publishing House.

Andersen, W., and S. Damle. 1987. *Brotherhood in Saffron: The Rashtriya Swayamsevak Sangh and Hindu Revivalism*. Delhi: Vistaar Publications.

Anderson, B. 1983. *Imagined Communities*. London: Verso.

Basu, A. 2015. *Violent Conjunctures in Democratic India*. Cambridge and New York: Cambridge University Press.

Basu, T. et al. 1993. *Khaki Shorts and Saffron Flags: A Critique of the Hindu Right*. Delhi: Orient Longman.

Benjamin, W. 1996. *Selected Writings, Volume 1: 1913–1926*. Edited by M. Bullock and M. Jennings. Cambridge: Harvard University Press.

Berenschot, W. 2012. *Riot Politics: Hindu–Muslim Violence and the Indian State*. New York: Columbia University Press.

Bermeo, N. 2016. 'On Democratic Backsliding'. *Journal of Democracy* 27(1): 5–19.

Brass, P. 1997. *Theft of an Idol: Text and Context in the Representation of Collective Violence*. Princeton, NJ: Princeton University Press.

———. 2003. *The Production of Hindu–Muslim Violence in Contemporary India*. Seattle: University of Washington Press.

Breckenridge, C., and P. Van der Veer (eds.). 1993. *Orientalism and the Postcolonial Predicament: Perspectives on South Asia*. Philadelphia: University of Pennsylvania Press.

Canovan, M. 1999. 'Trust the People! Populism and the Two Faces of Democracy'. *Political Studies* 47(1): 2–16.

Chatterjee, P. 1993. *The Nation and Its Fragments: Colonial and Postcolonial Histories*. Princeton, NJ: Princeton University Press.

Chatterji, A., C. Jaffrelot, and T. Hansen (eds.). 2019. *Majoritarian State: How Hindu Nationalism Is Changing India*. London: Hurst and Company.

Chibber, P. 1999. *Democracy without Associations: Transformation of the Party System and Social Cleavages*. Ann Arbor: University of Michigan Press.

Crewe, I. and D. Sanders (eds.). 2020. *Authoritarian Populism and Liberal Democracy*. Cham, Switzerland: Palgrave Macmillan.

Das, V. 1990. *Mirrors of Violence: Communities, Riots and Survivors in South Asia*. New Delhi: Oxford University Press.

Doval, N. 2017. 'The Casualties of the Enemy Property Act'. *Mint*, 18 July. https://www.livemint.com/Politics/6i2xVa95WhvvYlI3E0fAZP/The-casualties-of-the-Enemy-Property-Act.html (accessed on 15 May 2021).

Field, E. et al. 2008. 'Segregation, Rent Control, and Riots: The Economics of Religious Conflict in an Indian City'. *American Economic Review* 98(2): 505–10.

Ganguly, A and S. Dwivedi 2019. *Amit Shah and the March of BJP*. Delhi: Bloomsbury.

Ganguly, S. 2015. 'Hindu Nationalism and the Foreign Policy of India's Bharatiya Janata Party'. 2014–15 Paper Series No. 2, Transatlantic Academy, Washington, DC.

Ghassem-Fachandi, P. 2012. *Pogrom in Gujarat: Hindu Nationalism and Anti-Muslim Violence in India*. Princeton, NJ: Princeton University Press.

Ghosh, S., and P. Dabhi. 2020. 'Ahmedabad Hospital Splits COVID Wards on Faith, Says Govt Decision'. *Indian Express*, 17 April. https://indianexpress.com/article/coronavirus/ahmedabad-covid-19-coronavirus-hospital-ward-6363040/ (accessed on 15 May 2021).

Hall, S. 1993. 'Culture, Community, Nation'. *Cultural Studies* 1(3): 349–63.

Hansen, T. 1999. *The Saffron Wave: Democracy and Hindu Nationalism in Modern India*. Princeton, NJ: Princeton University Press.

———. 2001. *Wages of Violence: Naming and Identity in Postcolonial Bombay*. Princeton, NJ: Princeton University Press.

———. 2021. *The Law of Force: The Violent Heart of Indian Politics*. New Delhi: Aleph Books.

Jaffrelot, C. 1996. *The Hindu Nationalist Movement in India*. New York: Columbia University Press.

Jaffrelot, C., and L. Gayer (eds.). 2011. *Muslims in Indian Cities: Trajectories of Marginalisation*. Delhi: Oxford University Press.

Jaffrelot, C., and P. Anil. 2020. *India's First Dictatorship: The Emergency, 1975–77*. London: Hurst Publishers.

Jha, P. 2019. *How the BJP Wins: Inside India's Greatest Election Machine*. Delhi: Juggernaut Books.

Kakar, S. 1996. *The Colors of Violence: Cultural Conflict, Religion and Violence*. Chicago: University of Chicago Press.

Kanungo, P., D. Reddy, and J. Zavos (eds.). 2012. *Public Hinduisms*. New Delhi: Sage Publications.

Katju, M. 2017. *Hinduising Democracy: The Vishva Hindu Parishad in Contemporary India*. New Delhi: New Text.

Khan, G. 2020. 'Explainer: All You Need to Know about Jammu and Kashmir's Domicile Law'. *Economic Times*, 23 July. https://economictimes.indiatimes.com/news/defence/explainer-all-you-need-to-know-about-jammu-and-kashmirs-domicile-law/articleshow/77122595.cms?from=mdr (accessed on 15 May 2021).

Kumar, M. 2016. *Communalism and Sexual Violence in India: The Politics of Gender, Ethnicity and Conflict*. London: I.B. Tauris.

Kyle, J. and Gultchin, L. 2018. *Populism in Power around the World*. London: Tony Blair Institute for Global Change.

Levitsky, S., and D. Ziblatt. 2018. *How Democracies Die*. New York: Penguin Random House.

Longkumer, A. 2020. *The Greater India Experiment: Hindutva and the Northeast*. Stanford: Stanford University Press.

Ludden, D. (ed.). 1996. *Making India Hindu*. New York: Oxford University Press.

Madan, T. N. 1987. 'Secularism in Its Place'. *Journal of Asian Studies* 46(4): 747–59.

Mahurkar, U. 2017. *Marching with a Billion: Analysing Narendra Modi's Government at Midterm*. Delhi: Penguin Random House.

Mair, P. 2013. *Ruling the Void: The Hollowing Out of Western Democracy*. London: Verso.

Menon, K. 2011. *Everyday Nationalism: Women of the Hindu Right in India*. Philadelphia: University of Pennsylvania Press.

Mounck, Y. 2018. *The People vs. Democracy*. Cambridge, MA: Harvard University Press.

Müller, J-W. 2016. *What Is Populism?* Philadelphia: University of Pennsylvania Press.

Nag, K. 2017. 'The RSS Remote Control Is Clearly Visible in the Appointment of Adityanath as UP CM'. *The Wire*, 21 March. https://thewire.in/politics/narendra-modi-sangh-parivar-yogi-adityanath-rss-uttar-pradesh (accessed on 15 May 2021).

Nandy, A. 1988. 'The Politics of Secularism and the Recovery of Religious Tolerance'. *Alternatives* 13: 177–94.

Narayan, B. 2008. *Fascinating Hindutva: Saffron Politics and Dalit Mobilisation*. New Delhi: Sage Publications.

———. 2021. *Republic of Hindutva: How the Sangh Is Shaping Indian Democracy*. New Delhi: Penguin.

Pandey, G. 1990. *The Construction of Communalism in Colonial North India*. New Delhi: Oxford University Press.

———. 1999. 'Can a Muslim Be an Indian?' *Comparative Studies in Society and History* 41(4): 608–29.

Phadke, M. 2019. 'It's Been a Year since the First "Urban Naxal" Arrests and Accused Are Still Waiting for Bail'. *The Print*, 6 June. https://theprint.in/india/its-been-a-year-since-the-first-urban-naxal-arrests-accused-are-still-waiting-for-bail/246338/ (accessed on 15 May 2021).

Prakash, G. 2019. *Emergency Chronicles: Indira Gandhi and Democracy's Turning Point*. Princeton, NJ: Princeton University Press.

Robin, C. 2020. 'The Gonzo Constitutionalism of the American Right'. *New York Review of Books*. 21 October. https://www.nybooks.com/daily/2020/10/21/the-gonzo-constitutionalism-of-the-american-right/ (accessed on 7 July 2021).

Roy, B. 1994. *Some Trouble with Cows: Making Sense of Social Conflict*. Berkeley: University of California Press.

Sampal, R. 2020. 'RSS Influence over Govt Institutions Grows with New IIMC and Prasar Bharati Appointments'. *The Print*, 10 July. https://theprint.in/india/rss-influence-over-govt-institutions-grows-with-new-iimc-prasar-bharati-appointments/457680/ (accessed on 15 May 2021).

Sarkar, T. and U. Butalia (eds.). 1996. *Women and Right Wing Movements: Indian Experiences*. London: Zed Books.

Scheppele, K. 2018. 'Autocratic Legalism.' *University of Chicago Law Review* 85(2): article 2.

Sinha, S. 2020. *Vajpayee: The Years That Changed India*. New Delhi: Penguin Random House.

Sitapati, V. 2020. *Jugalbandi: The BJP before Modi*. New Delhi: Viking.

Slipowitz, A. 2020. 'Why We Should Be Worried about India's Response to Coronavirus'. *Freedom House Perspectives*, 13 April. https://freedomhouse.org/article/why-we-should-be-worried-about-indias-response-coronavirus (accessed on 15 May 2021).

Snyder, T. 2017. *On Tyranny: Twenty Lessons from the Twentieth Century*. New York: Tim Duggan Books.

Tambiah, S. 1996. *Leveling Crowds: Ethnonationalist Crowds and Collective Violence in South Asia*. Berkeley: University of California Press.

Thachil, T. 2014. *Elite Parties, Poor Voters: How Social Services Wins Votes in India*. Cambridge and New York: Cambridge University Press.

The Hindu. 2016. 'JMM to Protest Jharkhand Proposed Domicile Policy'. 9 April. https://www.thehindu.com/news/national/other-states/jmm-to-protest-jharkhands-proposed-domicile-policy/article8453616.ece (accessed on 15 May 2021).

Umar, S. 2019. 'Constructing the "Citizen Enemy": The Impact of the Enemy Property Act of 1968 on India's Muslims'. *Journal of Muslim Minority Affairs* 39(4): 457–77.

Van der Veer, P. 1994. *Religious Nationalism: Hindus and Muslims in India*. Berkeley: University of California Press.

Varshney, A. 2002. *Ethnic Conflict and Civic Life: Hindus and Muslims in India*. New Haven: Yale University Press.

Venugopal, V. 2020. 'Nearly 37% of Those Killed in Encounters by UP Police in Past Three Years Are Muslim'. *Economic Times*, 12 August. https://economictimes.indiatimes.com/news/politics-and-nation/nearly-37-of-those-killed-in-encounters-by-up-police-in-past-3-years-are-muslims/articleshow/77511147.cms (accessed on 15 May 2021).

Waldner, D., and E. Lust. 2018. 'Unwelcome Change: Coming to Terms with Democratic Backsliding.' *Annual Review of Political Science* 21: 93–113.

Wilkinson, S. 2004. *Votes and Violence: Electoral Competition and Ethnic Riots in India*. Cambridge and New York: Cambridge University Press.

RULE

2

NEW HINDUTVA TIMELINE
SEPTEMBER 2013–OCTOBER 2020

Ashwin Subramanian

The following timeline is meant to be indicative and does not claim to capture every event of significance in India since 2014. The focus is on events that pertain (either directly or indirectly) to the actions of the Bharatiya Janata Party (BJP)–led central government and the political climate it has cultivated since winning the Lok Sabha elections in 2014.

The events mentioned in this timeline are drawn from media reports published in various English-language newspapers and online news outlets including (but not limited to) *The Hindu, Indian Express, Times of India,* BBC, NDTV, *Outlook India, Caravan, The Wire, Scroll.in,* and *Live Law.* I have also relied on reports prepared by organizations such as the Working People's Charter, Hate Crime Watch, People's Union for Civil Liberties (PUCL), and PRS Legislative Research and an edited volume titled *Dismantling India: A 4 Year Report* (Dayal, Dabiru, and Hashmi 2018), among others, for information on legislation passed by the central government, Supreme Court verdicts, and human rights and civil liberties investigations between 2014 and 2020.[1]

7 September 2013: Communal violence breaks out in Muzaffarnagar and Shamli districts of Uttar Pradesh (UP) after a year-long campaign by BJP leaders and local units accusing Muslim youth of engaging in 'love jihad', that is, marrying young Hindu women with the sole intention of converting them to Islam. The campaign succeeds in polarizing the local community, pitting Jats against Muslims. There are officially sixty-two deaths (of which forty-two are Muslims), and the violence displaces thousands of Muslims to refugee camps. Several incidents of sexual violence (and rape) against Muslim women are also reported.

16 May 2014: The sixteenth Lok Sabha election results are declared and the BJP-led National Democratic Alliance (NDA) is victorious. The NDA wins a total of 336 out of the 543 contested seats in India's lower house (Lok Sabha). Narendra Modi of the BJP is sworn in as the fifteenth prime minister of India on 26 May 2014. The BJP's campaign rhetoric focuses on the promise of *achhe din* (good days) and a corruption- (and Congress-) free India – crucially though, the BJP benefits from the polarization of local communities in the aftermath of the Muzaffarnagar riots of 2013 that helped to consolidate the Hindu vote across north and central India.

July 2014: The Union Ministry of Human Resource Development (MHRD) appoints Y Sudershan Rao as the chairman of the Indian Council of Historical Research (ICHR). Rao is closely affiliated to the RSS-linked Akhil Bharatiya Itihas Sankalan Yojana (All India Organization for the Compilation of (Indian) History). The ICHR appointment is the first in a series of efforts that have taken place since 2014 to 'saffronize' India's higher educational (and independent research) institutions.

August 2014: The Parliament passes the National Judicial Appointments Commission (NJAC) Act, which replaces the existing collegium system of appointing judges to the Supreme Court and the high courts with an NJAC Commission (set up by the central government) comprising the Chief Justice of India (CJI), the two most senior Supreme Court judges, the union law and justice minister, and two 'eminent persons' from civil society selected by the prime minister, leader of the Opposition, and the CJI. Critics see this as a move by the BJP government to dilute the independence of the judiciary. The NJAC Act sparks a protracted confrontation between the central government and the judiciary, and is resolved only in 2015.

15 August 2014: In his Independence Day speech, Prime Minister Modi announces the launch of the Pradhan Mantri Jan Dhan Yojana (Prime Minister's Scheme for Universal Financial Inclusion), a government scheme aimed at increasing financial inclusion in India by allowing poor Indians to open zero-balance bank accounts that they can operate through their mobile phones. The scheme has the (indirect) effect of making the Aadhaar biometric identification card compulsory, as the government links the direct cash/benefit transfers to Aadhaar-linked bank accounts. The prime minister christens the scheme 'JAM' (Jan Dhan–Aadhaar–Mobile) trinity.

28 September 2014: Prime Minister Modi addresses a mega rally of diaspora or non-resident Indians (NRIs) at Madison Square Garden in New York. An estimated 19,000 attend in person, and millions more watch televised and web-streamed versions of this highly publicized event. The United States had earlier denied Modi a diplomatic visa for his alleged involvement in the 2002 Gujarat riots, but revoked the ban after his victory in the 2014 Lok Sabha elections. Modi's appearance in the symbolic centre of the iconic American city conveys a triumphant message about his international re-legitimation and signals the global ambitions of the new Indian government.

2 October 2014: Prime Minister Modi launches the Swachh Bharat Abhiyan (Clean India Mission) to achieve universal sanitation coverage by constructing individual household and community-owned toilets to eliminate open defecation in the country. The central government also imposes a Swachh Bharat Cess of 0.5 per cent on all taxable services to fund the Clean India Mission. The scheme, however, does little to address the issue of manual scavenging – in July 2019, the Ministry of Social Justice and Empowerment estimated that a total of 54,130 manual scavengers (most of whom are Dalit and belong to India's lowest castes) operate across 170 districts in eighteen states.

19 October 2014: State legislative assembly elections are held in eight states across India, and the BJP sweeps to victory in Maharashtra, Jharkhand, and Haryana.

27 October 2014: The MHRD decides to discontinue the teaching of German in place of Sanskrit in central Kendriya Vidyalayas. The ministry's decision has the effect of making Sanskrit compulsory on the basis of a 2001 order that mandated a three-language formula (English, Hindi, and Sanskrit) in all Kendriya Vidyalayas.

29 November 2014: Judge Brijgopal Loya of the special CBI court is mysteriously found dead in the Ravi Bhavan, VIP guesthouse in Nagpur. Judge Loya was attending to the Sohrabuddin Sheikh encounter killing case, in which the main accused was Amit Shah, India's home minister and senior BJP leader. The forensics report of Loya's death as caused by a heart attack remains disputed and allegations of bribery emerge, claiming that Judge Loya was offered a huge bribe to deliver a verdict favourable to the BJP accused in the Sohrabuddin case.

1 December 2014: A fire engulfs the St Sebastian Church in northeast Delhi, decimating much of the church property. Subsequently, the pastor of the church alleged the involvement of Hindu right-wing groups in the 'fire accident'.

1 January 2015: The union cabinet passes a resolution to replace India's Planning Commission, the state technocracy that had overseen economic planning since Independence, with a new statutory body – the National Institute for Transforming India (NITI Aayog). The NITI Aayog is set up as a multi-tiered body chaired by the prime minister, a chief executive officer (CEO), a governing council of state chief ministers, and technocratic experts. Unlike the Planning Commission, which devised five-year national economic plans and decided allocations for states on plan expenditure, the NITI Aayog is mandated to develop a 'national agenda', promote 'cooperative federalism', serve as a think tank, and provide key strategic inputs on policy matters.

1 January 2015: Priya Pillai, an activist with Greenpeace India, is prevented from boarding a flight to London where she was to attend a meeting on the rights of forest-dwelling communities affected by coal mining. The government claims that Pillai's activism presents a negative image of India abroad.

16 February 2015: Govind Pansare, a veteran communist leader and anti-Hindutva activist, is assassinated by two men on a motorcycle outside his residence in the Kolhapur district of Maharashtra. Investigations (and raids) conducted by the Maharashtra Anti-Terrorism Squad (ATS) in 2018 reveal that Pansare's alleged assailants, Vinay Pawar and Sarang Akolkar, are members of the Hindu right-wing outfit Sanatan Sanstha. The two have been absconding since 2015, although other members of the Sanatan Sanstha have been arrested.

10 February 2015: The BJP experiences a major setback in the Delhi legislative assembly election, as the Aam Aadmi Party (AAP) headed by Arvind Kejriwal secures an absolute majority by winning sixty-seven of the seventy seats in Delhi.

2 March 2015: Baldev Sharma, a former editor of the RSS mouthpiece *Panchjanya*, is appointed as the chairman of the National Book Trust.

13 March 2015: A seventy-one-year-old nun is allegedly gang-raped by a gang of robbers at a convent school in Ranaghat (West Bengal). The West Bengal State Minorities Commission Chairperson, Professor Maria Fernandes, suspected the assault to be motivated by the issue of *ghar wapsi* (religious reconversion of Christians to Hinduism).

22 March 2015: A mob comprising members of the Hindu Dharma Sena vandalize a church in Jabalpur (Madhya Pradesh), alleging that Church authorities were 'converting' tribals to Christianity. The tribals (or *adivasis*) were from the Mandla district, where a church was set ablaze by unidentified people in September 2014.

28 March 2015: The Rafale deal initiated during the United Progressive Alliance (UPA)–II regime is scrapped by Prime Minister Modi during a visit to France in 2015. Under the conditions of the earlier deal, India was to secure a total of 126 Rafale fighter jets, 18 of which were to be purchased in 'fly-away condition' from France, and the remaining were to be built by the Indian firm Hindustan Aeronautics Limited (HAL) in collaboration with France's Dassault Aviation.

However, during his visit to France, Modi announces a new deal worth INR 59,000 crores, under which Dassault India is to supply thirty-six fighter jets to India while investing 50 per cent (or about INR 30,000 crores) in any firm engaged in defence production in India. Crucially though, even as documents reveal that Dassault had signed agreements with close to seventy-two firms to fulfil its obligations, the bulk of the investment is directed to a joint venture between Anil Ambani's Reliance Aerostructure and Dassault. The Rafale deal would be challenged in the Supreme Court in 2018.

30 March 2015: The Coal Mines (Special Provisions) Act, 2015, receives Presidential assent – the act opens India's nationalized coal mining sector to private players and sets terms for the auction and sale of coal mines/blocks.

April 2015: The union government cancels the licenses of nearly 9,000 foreign-funded non-governmental organizations (NGOs) on charges of failing to file taxes properly. The Ford Foundation, among other NGOs, is placed on a government watchlist, while the bank accounts of Greenpeace India are suspended.

11 May 2015: The Right to Fair Compensation and Transparency in Land Acquisition, Rehabilitation and Resettlement (Second Amendment) Bill is introduced in the Lok Sabha. It eases the process of land acquisition by allowing the government to exempt five categories of projects – defence, rural infrastructure, affordable housing, industrial corridors, and infrastructure including public–private partnerships – from social impact assessment, restrictions on acquisition on multi-cropped land, and consent from owners. The bill has been referred to a Joint Parliamentary Committee and is also under scrutiny from the Supreme Court as of July 2021.

12 May 2015: Tathagata Roy, a BJP politician and RSS member, is appointed as the Governor of Tripura. The central government appoints several other RSS–BJP veterans as governors of various Indian states, including Vajibhai Bala (Karnataka), Kalyan Singh (Rajasthan), and Keshri Nath Tripathi (West Bengal), among others.

12 June 2015: Students at the Film and Television Institute of India (FTII), Pune, begin an indefinite strike protesting the Information and Broadcasting Ministry's appointment of Gajendra Chauhan as chairman of the institute. Gajendra Chauhan is a BJP member and was famous for playing the role of Yudhishtir in the television adaptation of the Hindu epic Mahabharata. A group of forty students protesting Chauhan's appointment were '*lathi*-charged' (a forcible police technique of crowd dispersal) and detained by the Pune Police.

15 June 2015: The union government launches the 'Smart Cities Mission' with a budget allocation of INR 48,000 crores. Under the mission, 100 cities across

India are selected for transformative urban development and promised a massive disbursement of funds. As of January 2019, only 1.83 per cent of the allocated funds had been utilized.

30 August 2015: M. M. Kalburgi, a Kannada scholar, is shot by a man in his residence in Dharwad, Karnataka. The assailant is suspected to be a member of the right-wing Sanatan Sanstha outfit, also allegedly involved in the murders of Govind Pansare and Narendra Dabholkar (assassinated in 2013) in Maharashtra. Similar tactics are later used to assassinate Gauri Lankesh, a Kannada journalist, in 2017.

August 2015: The New Delhi Municipal Council (NDMC) renames Aurangzeb Road in Delhi as Dr A. P. J. Abdul Kalam Road – in a stated effort to 'correct the mistakes made in our history', and to replace the 'cruelty' associated with Mughal emperor Aurangzeb with former Indian president Dr Kalam's 'love for the nation'.

16 September 2015: Mahesh Rangarajan, the director of the Nehru Memorial Museum and Library (NMML), resigns after the union culture minister, Mahesh Sharma, alleges 'irregularities' in Rangarajan's appointment by the previous Congress government. The central government had earlier announced its decision to convert the NMML into a museum dedicated to all of India's prime ministers and not just to Nehru.

28 September 2015: Mohammad Akhlaq (fifty) is lynched to death by a Hindu right-wing mob in UP's Dadri for allegedly slaughtering a cow. The mob also seriously injures his son Danish. In subsequent months, numerous such incidents by self-styled cow-protection vigilante groups take place across north and central India. The mobs cite injury to Hindu religious sentiments and invoke the prohibitions of cow-protection laws in many states while threatening and murdering dairy farmers and cattle traders, most of whom are Muslims. 'Cow smuggling' features as the common allegation across all these cases. Between 2015 and December 2018, there are reports of at least forty-four people killed across twelve Indian states, thirty-six of whom are Muslims. Human Rights Watch finds evidence of police collusion with right-wing cow vigilantes across multiple states.

7 October 2015: The University Grants Commission (UGC), a statutory body under the MHRD, announces its decision to cancel all fellowships granted to MPhil and PhD students who have not taken the National Eligibility Test (NET). Students allege that the government's decision is implicitly aimed at opening India's higher educational institutions to privatizing forces and launch protests ('Occupy UGC') in several universities across the country, including the national capital.

NEW HINDUTVA TIMELINE

15 October 2015: A constitutional bench of the Supreme Court upholds the collegium system of appointing judges to the Supreme Court and the high courts, and strikes the NJAC down as unconstitutional.

6 November 2015: The central government orders Greenpeace India to shut down operations, and cancels its license to operate in the country, citing financial fraud and falsification of data. The Madras High Court subsequently intervenes and places the government order on hold.

8 November 2015: The *mahagathbandhan* (grand alliance) comprising the Janata Dal (United) [JD(U)], Rashtriya Janata Dal (RJD), and the Indian National Congress (INC) emerges victorious in the Bihar state elections. Nitish Kumar of the JD(U) is sworn in as the chief minister of Bihar for the fifth time. The opposition alliance between the JD(U), RJD, and the Congress proves to be short-lived, and the JD(U) aligns with the BJP in July 2017.

17 January 2016: Rohith Vemula, a Dalit PhD scholar at the University of Hyderabad, commits suicide after intense harassment by university administration officials. Vemula and four others were suspended from the university hostel after the union minister for labour and employment, Bandaru Dattatreya, alleged that the university was being used by 'anti-national' and 'casteist' groups and the university administration singled out Dalit students who had been involved in campus activism. Vemula's suicide sparks students' protests across the country and draws international attention from scholars and civil society activists. Over 300 scholars, activists, and writers from around the world condemn the actions of the Hyderabad University administration, demand the suspension of Vice Chancellor Appa Rao Podile, and call for a judicial enquiry into the role of ministers in the central cabinet (Smriti Irani and Bandaru Dattatreya) in inciting violence against Dalit students.

13 February 2016: Jawaharlal Nehru University (JNU) Students' Union president Kanhaiya Kumar is arrested by the Delhi Police under sedition charges and placed in Tihar Jail. The Hindu nationalist student organization Akhil Bharatiya Vidyarthi Parishad (ABVP) alleges that Kanhaiya (and other students such as Umar Khalid and Anirban Bhattacharya) are involved in 'anti-national' activities and raised 'anti-India' slogans at a protest meeting organized on campus. On his way to attend a hearing, Kanhaiya is physically attacked at the Patiala House Court in Delhi by robed lawyers professing allegiance to the BJP and Sangh Parivar. He is eventually released from Tihar on 2 March. The events in JNU spark protracted student protests against the ABVP and government repression in several university campuses across India. The protests resonate well beyond campus spaces, seeding numerous national and international solidarity actions with the protesting students.

16 February 2016: Former Delhi University professor S. A. R. Geelani is arrested under sedition charges for co-hosting an event at the Press Club of India commemorating the hanging of Afzal Guru (convicted in the 2001 Parliament attacks). He is imprisoned at Tihar Jail and is eventually released on 19 March 2016. Geelani had earlier been imprisoned (and tortured) for twenty-two months during the previous tenure of the BJP coalition government (between 2001 and 2003) for his alleged role in the 2001 Parliament attacks, for which he was sentenced to death. The Delhi High Court acquitted him of all charges in 2003 and released him from prison. Geelani passed away due to a cardiac arrest on 24 October 2019.

3–16 March 2016: The union minister of finance, Arun Jaitley, introduces the Aadhaar (Targeted Delivery of Financial and other Subsidies, Benefits, and Services) Bill as a 'money bill' in the Lok Sabha. The bill (passed into law on 16 March 2016) makes the Aadhaar (unique identification) number mandatory for availing government subsidies – including cash transfers for schemes such as the Pradhan Mantri Jan Dhan Yojana, pensions, Mahatma Gandhi National Rural Employment Guarantee Scheme (MNREGS), and so on. The decision to introduce the Aadhaar Bill as a money bill circumvents the legislative assent of the Rajya Sabha, where the BJP-led NDA does not have a majority. The bill is enacted as a law on 16 March. The constitutional validity of introducing the Aadhaar Bill as a money bill and the overall validity of the Aadhaar scheme in light of privacy and data protection issues were subsequently challenged in the Supreme Court and resolved two years later in 2018.

18 March 2016: Two Muslim cattle traders, Mohammed Mazlum Ansari (thirty-five) and Mohammed Imteyaz Khan (twelve), are killed in the Latehar district of Jharkhand in eastern India. Their bodies are found hanging from a tree, and the police do not file charges against the alleged accused, Vijay Prajapati, a local cow vigilante group leader, despite eyewitness evidence identifying him as one of the perpetrators.

14 April 2016: Ram Bahadur Rai, a senior journalist and former organizing secretary of the ABVP, is appointed as the president of the Indira Gandhi National Centre for the Arts.

1 May 2016: Modi launches the Pradhan Mantri Ujjwala Yojana (Prime Minister's Scheme for Free LPG Connections) to provide free cooking gas (LPG) connections to families living below the poverty line, aiming to replace the environmentally unfriendly use of wood and coal that is particularly prevalent in rural areas. By January 2019 the government claims to have provided LPG connections to over

60 million families, but close to 12 million beneficiaries are unable to afford LPG cylinder refills.

2 May 2016: The Mines and Minerals (Development and Regulation) Amendment Bill is passed in the Indian Parliament and allows for the transfer of mining leases granted in auction to private individuals, pending approval by state governments.

May 2016: The union finance minister, Arun Jaitley, introduces an amendment to the Foreign Contribution (Regulation) Act, 2010, in the Finance Bill (2016) by redefining what constitutes a 'foreign source', in effect letting both the BJP and the Congress off the hook for accepting donations from the Vedanta multinational corporation. The Delhi High Court had found both parties guilty of accepting foreign contributions in 2014.

19 May 2016: The BJP wins the Assam state elections by aggressively campaigning on a xenophobic, anti-'illegal migrant' platform. However, the BJP is not successful in the state elections of Tamil Nadu, West Bengal, and Kerala this year.

June 2016: Lawyers' Collective, an NGO founded by human rights lawyer Indira Jaising, is barred from receiving foreign funds for six months and has its license suspended by the central government. The government similarly suspends Teesta Setalvad's NGO, Sabrang, citing financial irregularities. Both Indira Jaising and Teesta Setalvad were actively involved in seeking justice for the 2002 Gujarat riot victims.

18 June 2016: The Reserve Bank of India's (RBI's) governor, Raghuram Rajan, resigns citing 'personal reasons'. In the lead-up to his resignation, Rajan (appointed by the previous Congress-led coalition government) was viciously attacked by BJP leader Subramaniam Swamy for not being 'mentally fully Indian'. The government appoints Urjit Patel as the new RBI governor in September.

11 July 2016: Seven members of the Dalit Sarvaiya community are assaulted by more than forty men belonging to the upper caste Darbar community in Una, Gujarat. Four of the Dalits were stripped and flogged with sticks and iron rods, while being filmed. Following severe criticism, the Gujarat state government promised compensation and justice to the victims, but no action has been taken till date, five years after the incident.

July–August 2016: Jignesh Mevani, a thirty-year-old Dalit lawyer and activist, organizes a rally of over 20,000 individuals demanding justice for the victims of the Una violence. Mevani rallies Dalits in Gujarat, demands land redistribution in the state, and urges the establishment of special courts to deal with cases of atrocities against Dalits.

28 July 2016: The Rajya Sabha passes the Compensatory Afforestation Funds Act, 2016. The act is passed despite opposition from environmental and *adivasi* (indigenous) groups who claim that it bypasses consent from village councils and other forest dwellers to carry out plantation activities in protected forest lands.

September 2016: The central government approves the Haryana government's decision to rename the city (and district) of Gurgaon to Gurugram. The renaming of Gurgaon was undertaken by the Haryana government with the stated aim of restoring the city's cultural heritage and links to Guru Dronacharya, a mythological figure from the Hindu epic Mahabharata. Gurugram literally translates to 'Guru's village'.

29 September 2016: The Indian Army announces that it has conducted 'surgical strikes' against militants across the Line of Control (LoC) in Pakistan-administered Kashmir and claims to have destroyed seven 'terror launchpads'.

15 October 2016: Najeeb Ahmed, a student of JNU, mysteriously disappears from the campus. The case is transferred to the Central Bureau of Investigation (CBI), amid false allegations from sections of the media that Najeeb is linked to Islamist extremist groups. As of October 2021, he remains missing.

8 November 2016: At 8 p.m. Indian time, Prime Minister Modi announces a sudden and immediate policy of 'demonetization' – touting it as a 'surgical strike' against 'black money' and 'corruption' – by withdrawing all INR 500 and 1,000 currency notes from circulation with immediate effect (that is, from midnight, or four hours after the prime minister's address). The sudden and dramatic decision to withdraw INR 500 and 1,000 currency notes (that constitute 86 per cent of all cash in circulation) adversely impacts the socio-economically marginalized classes who depend on daily wage cash payments. There are long queues of people outside ATMs waiting to withdraw money or to exchange the defunct currency notes.

18 December 2016: The central government cancels the foreign funding license of Gujarat's oldest Dalit rights organization, Navsarjan Trust.

11 January 2017: A Supreme Court bench comprising Justices Arun Mishra and Amitava Roy dismissed interim appeals seeking an investigation into the Sahara–Birla papers. These documents were seized in the course of a CBI investigation of two Indian corporations, the Sahara Group and the Birla group, and allegedly reveal details of payments that were made to a number of India's senior politicians – including Prime Minister Modi when he was the chief minister of Gujarat.

NEW HINDUTVA TIMELINE

27 January 2017: Members of the Karni Sena – a Hindu right-wing outfit – assault Bollywood movie director Sanjay Leela Bhansali in Jaipur. The group claims that his film (*Padmavat*) depicts Rani Padmini – a Rajput queen and protagonist of the sixteenth-century Avadhi epic poem *Padmavat* – in bad light and calls for a complete ban on the release of Bhansali's film. The Karni Sena and its splinter groups also set ablaze a public transport bus in Haryana, a roadside eatery in Madhya Pradesh, and threaten to cut off actor Deepika Padukone's (who plays Rani Padmini in Mr Bhansali's film) nose.

March 2017: Under the Finance Bill, 2017 (also introduced as a money bill), 'electoral bonds' are made available for purchase from the State Bank of India, allowing individuals and companies to anonymously purchase bonds in multiples of INR 1,000, 1 lakh (100,000), 10 lakh (1 million), and 1 crore (10 million), and donate to any registered political party.

1 April 2017: Two hundred cow vigilantes attack dairy farmer Pehlu Khan and his sons Irshad and Arif in Behror *tehsil* in Rajasthan's Alwar district. Pehlu Khan was transporting cows purchased for milk production. Despite repeatedly pleading with the vigilantes and showing them papers of his legal purchase, he is mercilessly beaten and dies in a hospital two days later. The police do not press charges against the accused and do not probe their links to the Hindutva organization Vishwa Hindu Parishad (VHP), despite oral evidence from Pehlu Khan and his sons.

February–March 2017: Elections are held in five Indian states – Punjab, Goa, Uttarakhand, UP, and Manipur – and the BJP is victorious in all but Punjab. In UP, an ultra-right-wing Hindu leader, Yogi Adityanath, is sworn in as chief minister. Adityanath is the founder of the Hindu militant outfit Hindu Yuva Vahini, and under his administration, UP sees a massive rise in 'police encounter killings'.

7 March 2017: Dr G. N. Saibaba, a professor at Delhi University (DU), is sentenced to life imprisonment under the Unlawful Activities (Prevention) Act (UAPA) by the District and Sessions Court in Gadchiroli, Maharashtra, for his alleged Maoist links, and for his likely involvement in 'anti-national activities'. Saibaba is 90 per cent disabled and suffers from various health ailments. The court also hands out life imprisonment sentences to three others – Prashant Rahi, Hem Mishra, Pandu Pora Narote, and Mahesh Kareman Tirki – while one other individual, Vijay Tirki, is sentenced to ten years in jail. On 28 July 2020, the Nagpur Bench of the Bombay High Court rejected Saibaba's bail application.

10 March 2017: The Enemy Property (Amendment and Validation) Bill, 2016, is passed by the Indian Parliament – the act empowers the central government to sell and dispose of the properties of Pakistani and Chinese nationals (within Indian territory) confiscated during the 1962, 1965, and 1971 conflicts. Such properties are designated as 'enemy properties'; the act further expands the definition of 'enemy' to include even those whose heirs are legally Indian or citizens of other countries that are not designated as 'enemy' by the Indian government.

March–April 2017: Farmers from Tamil Nadu gather in the Jantar Mantar area of New Delhi to protest against the growing agrarian crisis in the state. The protestors use novel ways to demonstrate by half-shaving their heads (and facial hair), hanging skulls on their necks (depicting the suicides of several others due to the mounting debt crisis), and stripping in front of the prime minister's office (PMO). They demand an INR 40,000-crore drought relief fund, loan waivers, and pensions from the central government.

May 2017: Braj Kumar Bihari replaces Sukhdeo Thorat as the new chairman of the Indian Council for Social Science Research (ICSSR). Braj Kumar is the founding member of Astha Bharati, a Hindu nationalist organization dedicated to 'India's unity and integrity'. One of the major aims of this organization is to 'culturally' integrate India's northeast with mainland India.

5 May 2017: Members of the dominant caste Thakur community attack the Dalit settlements of Shabbirpur village in the Saharanpur district of UP. Dalit residents allege that the local police failed to control the mob, which set fire to fifty-five Dalit houses and injured several women and children.

9 May 2017: The local police deny permission for a protest by a Dalit organization, the Bhim Army led by Chandrasekhar Azad 'Raavan', against the violence perpetrated by the Thakur community in Shabbirpur village. Violence breaks out between the police and members of the Bhim Army. Some vehicles are set ablaze and a police post is damaged. The police arrest Azad and other members of the Bhim Army in June 2017.

11–20 June 2017: A seventeen-year-old girl goes missing from the Mankhi village of UP's Unnao district and is later found to have been gang-raped by Kuldeep Singh Sengar, a BJP MLA, his brother Atul Singh, and their associates. Despite registering multiple complaints, the local police (and the state government) take no action against Sengar and his associates for over a year.

5 June 2017: The CBI conducts a raid at the residence of Prannoy Roy and Radhika Roy, founders of the national news organization NDTV, for allegedly causing a loss to a private bank. The channel terms the raid a 'witch-hunt' and an attempt to curb press freedom and muzzle media criticism of the government. The

Ministry of Information and Broadcasting had imposed a one-day ban on NDTV Hindi earlier in the year.

6 June 2017: Farmer protests erupt in parts of Madhya Pradesh and Maharashtra against agrarian distress; in Madhya Pradesh's Mandsaur district, five farmers are killed in the protests. The protestors specifically cite the detrimental effects of demonetization on the farming community, which they claim has disrupted cash supply in India's villages and destroyed the rural economy.

June 2017: Indian troops confront their Chinese counterparts in Doklam after the latter are seen with construction equipment in the region. Doklam is a contested region between China and Bhutan.

1 July 2017: The Goods and Services Tax (GST) comes into effect. Touted as a major tax reform, the GST imposes a single central indirect tax on consumers on a variety of commodities under different tax rates (ranging from 0.25 to 28 per cent). The introduction of the GST regime is seen by non-BJP ruled states as an attack on India's federal structure, by making state governments entirely dependent on the GST council for funds.

July 2017: An amendment to the Child Labour Prevention Act reduces the number of companies identified as 'hazardous' from eighty-three to only those listed in the Factories Act that pertain to mining and explosives. The amendment also permits children to work in family enterprises after school hours.

25 July 2017: Ram Nath Kovind, a Dalit BJP leader from UP, is sworn in as the fourteenth president of India.

8 August 2017: The World Watch Monitor, an international organization that tracks attacks on Christians across the world, reports that the attacks on Indian Christians – mostly by Hindu right-wing groups – for the first half of 2017 is almost as many as the total number of attacks on Christians in the country in 2016. A total of 410 incidents were reported in the first six months of 2017 – including two cases of murder, eighty-four incidents of violent assault, thirty-seven incidents of social boycott of Christians for not 'reconverting' to Hinduism.

21 August 2017: The Directorate of Revenue Intelligence (DRI) mysteriously drops ongoing proceedings against the Adani Group for tax evasion. The Adani Group is a multinational conglomerate with investments in key public utility sectors (energy, infrastructure, defence, aerospace, and so on), real estate, and financial services. Gautam Adani, founder of the Adani Group, is a friend of Prime Minister Modi. During the 2014 Lok Sabha campaign, Modi (then chief minister of Gujarat) used the Adani Group's chartered flight services for his campaign trips on several occasions.

28 August 2017: India and China mutually agree to a ceasefire regulation in the Doklam area. Several soldiers on both sides are injured, although the exact numbers are disputed.

22 August 2017: The Supreme Court of India declares the Islamic practice of instantaneous *triple talaq* (divorce) unconstitutional and in violation of the fundamental right to equality before the law under Article 14 of the Indian Constitution.

5 September 2017: Kannada journalist and activist Gauri Lankesh is shot dead by assailants in her Bengaluru residence (in Karnataka). The assailants are suspected to be members of the militant Hindu right-wing outfit Hindu Yuva Sena. Investigations reveal that the murders of Gauri Lankesh, Govind Pansare, M. M. Kalburgi, and Narendra Dabholkar were carried out by members of Hindu right-wing outfits with links to the Sanatan Sanstha. There has however, been no trial (or conviction) in the Gauri Lankesh case as of July 2021.

23 October 2017: Rakesh Asthana, an Indian Police Service (IPS) officer of the Gujarat cadre, is made a special director in the CBI by the central government. Asthana had previously investigated the burning of the Sabarmati Express at Godhra (Gujarat) in 2002. Asthana's appointment is challenged in the Supreme Court by lawyer (and public interest litigation, or PIL, activist) Prashant Bhushan, who claimed that the serving director of the CBI, Alok Verma, was not consulted in Asthana's appointment, and furthermore that there were allegations of bribery against Asthana. The Supreme Court dismissed the petition against Asthana in November 2017.

2 November 2017: Chandrasekhar Azad is booked under the National Security Act (NSA) by the UP Police. Two other members of the Bhim Army had been booked under the NSA in the previous month.

10 November 2017: Umar Khan, a farmer in the Alwar district of Rajasthan, is shot to death by a cow vigilante group for transporting cattle. The Alwar police allege that Umar Khan is a cow smuggler and arrest two of his fellow farmers, Tahir and Javed, who were seriously injured by the cow vigilante group.

November–December 2017: The BJP is victorious in both the Himachal Pradesh and Gujarat state elections. In Gujarat, Jignesh Mevani, the leader of the protests against Dalit violence in Una (2017) secures victory in the Vadgam constituency, contesting as an independent candidate.

31 December 2017: On the eve of the 200th anniversary of the colonial-era battle of Bhima Koregaon, many prominent activists gather in the city of Pune at a commemorative event (the Elgar Parishad) and take a pledge against communal bigotry propagated by the BJP and the RSS.

1 January 2018: Violence perpetrated by the Hindu right-wing group Samasta Hindu Aghadi breaks out at the Bhima Koregaon commemoration event, leaving one person dead and several others injured.

2–3 January 2018: Protests organized by Dalit groups across Maharashtra are brutally suppressed by the Maharashtra Police and Hindu right-wing outfits, leading to the death of a sixteen-year-old Dalit, Yogesh Prahalad Jadhav.

8 January 2018: Despite mounting evidence of Hindu right-wing involvement in instigating the violence at Bhima Koregaon and in other parts of Maharashtra, the Pune Police act on a complaint filed by Tushar Damgude, a self-proclaimed nationalist, and allege that 'Leftist groups with Maoist links' are responsible for the violence, and are additionally involved in a plot to assassinate Narendra Modi. Initially raids and investigations are carried out against the organizers of the Elgar Parishad before multiple high-profile arrests of prominent activists are made in June 2018.

10–23 January 2018: An eight-year-old Muslim girl is raped and brutally killed in the Kathua district of Jammu and Kashmir (J&K). The girl's body is found only on 17 January and provokes angry protests from the local Gujjar Muslim community. The Crime Branch arrests two J&K special police officers for their alleged involvement in the abduction and rape of the child. Local Hindutva groups form the Hindu Ekta Manch to defend the accused in the Kathua rape case (all Hindus), and the Jammu Bar Association calls for the case to be transferred to the CBI – a move supported by BJP leaders in the state and in the central government. Prime Minister Modi remains silent on this issue, just as he was silent on the Unnao rape case from the previous year.

12 January 2018: Four senior judges of the Supreme Court of India – Justice Chelameswar, Justice Ranjan Gogoi, Justice Kurian Joseph, and Justice Lokur – address a press conference, calling for the integrity and independence of the Supreme Court (and the judiciary) to be preserved for the 'survival of ... democracy'. The press conference laid bare their differences with the CJI, Dipak Misra, particularly on the issue of his alleged 'selective' allocation of cases in the court. Specifically, the judges were of the view that a petition pertaining to Judge Brijgopal Loya's death under mysterious circumstances (in November 2014) ought to have been referred to a senior bench of the Supreme Court.

February 2018: The BJP displaces the Communist Party of India (Marxist) (CPI[M]) government headed by four-term incumbent Manik Sarkar in the Tripura state elections. In Nagaland, the BJP secures victory in a coalition with the local National Democratic Progressive Party (NDPP).

February 2018: Arvind P. Jamkhedkar is appointed as the chairman of the ICHR after Y. Sudershan Rao resigned in late 2017. Jamkhedkar, an Indologist by training, announces that the ICHR will undertake inter-disciplinary research in an effort to 'reconstruct the past'.

21 February 2018: Kapil Kapoor, a former professor at the Centre for Linguistic and English Studies and the Special Centre for Sanskrit Studies at JNU, is appointed as the chairman of the Indian Institute of Advanced Studies (IIAS), Shimla. The central government had earlier appointed Makarand Paranjape (also from JNU) as the director of the IIAS in 2017. Both Kapoor and Paranjape are known to be critics of the Left and sympathizers of the current BJP regime.

24 February 2018: After nearly a year of governmental inaction on the case, the Unnao rape survivor's mother approaches the chief judicial magistrate and files a formal criminal complaint (in the form of a first information report [FIR]) against Kuldeep Singh Sengar.

March 2018: The Draft National Forest Policy is released by the Ministry of Environment, proposing the use of 'degraded forest areas' (less than 40 per cent tree canopy density) for private plantations and for projects under public–private partnerships. This covers over 34 million hectares of India's forest lands.

8 March 2018: The Supreme Court delivers a judgment on the controversial Hadiya case in which a Hindu father challenged the marriage of his daughter to a Muslim man of her choosing and her subsequent conversion to Islam. Setting aside an earlier ruling by the Kerala High Court, the apex judiciary upholds the legality of Hadiya's marriage and her right to freely choose both religion and life partner. However, in upholding a timeworn distinction between 'free' and 'forced' conversion, the Supreme Court's ruling allows the National Investigation Agency (NIA) to continue investigating allegations of forced conversions (to Islam) by 'well-oiled network(s)' in Kerala.

13 March 2018: A PIL is filed in the Supreme Court seeking an inquiry into the rationale for the central government's decision to procure thirty-six Rafale fighter jets from France for the Indian Air Force (IAF). The PIL also seeks a financial disclosure after annual reports of the manufacturer, Dassault Aviation, report India's total cost of procuring thirty-six fighter jets as double the amount that was quoted by the Indian government in Parliament. The petitioners also question the preferential terms set for Anil Ambani's Reliance Defence – a company they argue is heavily debt-ridden and has no experience in manufacturing aircraft and defence equipment.

20 March 2018: The Supreme Court provides immunity to serving officials accused of atrocities against scheduled castes and scheduled tribes, and rules that no public servant can be arrested after a complaint is filed against him/her under the Scheduled Castes and the Scheduled Tribes (Prevention of Atrocities) Act. The ruling provokes nationwide protests in which nine people are killed and several hundred are detained by the police across north and central India.

3–13 April 2018: On their way to a court hearing, the Unnao rape survivor's father is attacked by the accused's brother Atul Singh and his accomplices. The police proceed to arrest the man who was attacked, rather than the attacker, on charges of possessing illegal firearms. He later dies in custody on 9 April. A post-mortem report points to evidence of custodial torture. The Unnao rape case gains national attention after the rape survivor attempts to commit suicide by self-immolation outside Chief Minister Adityanath's residence in Lucknow on 8 April. After the Allahabad High Court transfers the case from the UP Police to the CBI on 10 April, Kuldeep Singh Sengar is arrested on 13 April – he is, however, not suspended from the BJP.

18 April 2018: In connection with the Bhima Koregaon violence, the Pune Police raid the homes of seven activists who participated in the Elgar Parishad meeting including Rona Wilson, Surendra Gadling, Sudhir Dhavale, Harsali Potdar, Jyoti Jagtap, Ramesh Ghaichor, Dipak Dhengle, and several members of the cultural and music troupe Kabir Kala Manch.

5 May 2018: The chapel inside Delhi's St Stephen's College is vandalized and defaced with Hindutva slogans and symbols. The words 'Mandir yahin banega' ('The temple will be built here') are found written on the door of the chapel, and the Cross outside the chapel is defaced with the Hindu swastika, and the words 'I'm going to hell' written on it.

18 May 2018: The Janata Dal (Secular) (JD[S]) in alliance with the Congress emerges victorious in the Karnataka state elections. The government headed by H. D. Kumaraswamy will, however, be dissolved within a year after nineteen members of the alliance submit their resignations to the House Speaker and the BJP emerges as the single largest party in the House with 105 seats.

6 June 2018: Sudhir Dhavale, Surendra Gadling, Mahesh Raut, Shoma Sen, and Rona Wilson are arrested under the UAPA for allegedly disrupting communal harmony and instigating violence during the Elgar Parishad, and for having 'Maoist links.'

18 June 2018: Mohammad Qasim is beaten to death by a mob on the suspicion of cow slaughter in the Hapur district of UP.

3 August 2018: The Scheduled Castes and the Scheduled Tribes (Prevention of Atrocities) Amendment Bill is introduced in the Lok Sabha by the minister of social justice and empowerment, Thaawarchand Gehlot, to reverse the Supreme Court judgment that had led to considerable national protest earlier in the year (March 2018). The amendment is passed by the Rajya Sabha on 9 August.

7 August 2018: S. Gurumurthy, a co-convener of the RSS affiliate Swadeshi Jagran Manch, is appointed by the union cabinet as a part-time, non-official director on the RBI's central board for four years.

28 August 2018: The Pune Police raid the homes of nine activists (including scholar Anand Teltumbde's residence) in Delhi, Mumbai, Hyderabad, Ranchi, and Goa, in continued pursuance of their 'Elgar Parishad conspiracy' case. Five activists – Sudha Bharadwaj, Gautam Navlakha, Vernon Gonsalves, Arun Ferreira, and Varavara Rao – are placed under house arrest.

14 September 2018: Chandrasekhar Azad 'Raavan' is released from prison after eighteen months in jail under the National Security Act (NSA) in connection with the Saharanpur violence in May 2017.

26 September 2018: A Supreme Court constitution bench headed by the Chief Justice Dipak Misra upholds the constitutional validity of the Aadhaar scheme (and act), albeit with provisions. The court rules that Aadhaar cannot be made mandatory for opening bank accounts and directs the central government to ensure greater data protection laws. Justice Chandrachud is the lone dissenting voice on the bench and challenges the passage of the Aadhaar Act as a money bill in Parliament in 2016.

28 September 2018: The Supreme Court, in a four–one majority verdict, rules that women between the ages of ten and fifty must be allowed into Kerala's Sabarimala temple, negating the temple authority's customary prohibition of 'menstruation-age' women into the religious space.

31 October 2018: Prime Minister Modi inaugurates the 182-metre-tall Sardar Vallabbhai Patel statue (or 'Statue of Unity') in Gujarat, billed as the tallest statue in the world.

October 2018: Out of 126 contracts made available to private companies (and public–private partnerships) to set up piped natural gas networks and fuel stations across India, the Adani Group secures twenty-five contracts – the largest number to be awarded to a single private entity in the bidding process.

October–November 2018: Five activists – Sudha Bharadwaj, Varavara Rao, Anand Teltumbde, Arun Ferreira, and Gautam Navlakha – are imprisoned under the UAPA. The Supreme Court dismisses a PIL filed by the academician Romila Thapar (and others) challenging the validity of the arrests in a two–one majority opinion. Justice Chandrachud in his dissenting opinion challenges the veracity of the evidence and questions the ability of the Maharashtra Police to conduct a fair investigation.

23–24 October 2018: The central government places the director of the CBI, Alok Verma, and the special director, Rakesh Asthana, on forced leave. In the preceding days, the CBI had raided its own offices and had also filed an FIR against Asthana on charges of bribery – who instead argued that it was Verma accepting the bribes. Verma challenged the government's order in the Supreme Court on 24 October, which the court eventually found illegal in January 2019. Asthana was later appointed as the director-general of the Border Security Force (BSF) in August 2020.

November 2018: The UP government approves renaming of Faizabad and Allahabad as Ayodhya and Prayagraj, respectively. In July 2018, the UP government had renamed the Mughalsarai Railway junction as the Deen Dayal Upadhyay Junction – Deen Dayal Upadhyay was an RSS *pracharak* and president of the Jan Sangh (a political party that was a forerunner to the BJP).

11 December 2018: The BJP is defeated by the Congress in Madhya Pradesh and Rajasthan state elections. In March 2020, the Kamal Nath–led Congress government in the state faces a severe political crisis with the resignation of over twenty MLAs, and the BJP returns to power in the state.

14 December 2018: The Supreme Court delivers its verdict in the Dassault Rafale procurement case and dismisses charges of governmental irregularities. A review petition on the verdict is filed by the senior lawyer (and prominent PIL activist) Prashant Bhushan and former union ministers Yashwant Sinha and Arun Shourie, who claim that the court was misled by the government.

8 January 2019: The 124th Constitutional Amendment Bill is introduced by the minister of social justice and empowerment, Thaawarchand Gehlot, to provide for a special reservation of 10 per cent for 'Economically Weaker Sections' of the population (whose families have a gross annual income of below INR 8 lakh per annum) who are not already covered under other categories of affirmative action (or reservations) in jobs and admissions in educational institutions. The amendment is criticized for trying to change the criterion for reservations set by the Supreme Court in the Indra Sawhney verdict in 1992. The bill is passed into law on 9 January in the Rajya Sabha.

10 January 2019: The Assam Police register sedition charges against anti-corruption activist Akhil Gogoi for speaking against the Citizenship Amendment Act (CAA) at a public meeting. Academician Hiren Gohain and former journalist Manjit Mahanta are also charged with sedition.

31 January 2019: India's unemployment rate reaches its highest in forty-five years, touching 6.1 per cent in the 2017–18 financial year – one year after demonetization. Two members of the National Statistical Commission, including the acting chairperson, P. C. Mohanan, resign after the central government delays the publication of the National Sample Survey Office (NSSO) employment survey data. Dismissing the unemployment statistics, the central government maintains that it has created more jobs.

14 February 2019: Forty-nine Central Reserve Police Force (CRPF) personnel are killed in a suicide attack allegedly by militants of Jaish-e-Mohammed in Pulwama (in Kashmir). The Indian government accuses Pakistan of supporting terrorism and revokes Pakistan's Most-Favoured Nation (MFN) trade clause.

26 February 2019: In response to the attack in Pulwama, the IAF carries out air strikes against a Jaish-e-Mohammed terror camp in Balakot.

27 February 2019: Wing Commander Abhinandan Varthaman of the IAF is captured by Pakistani troops after his aircraft was shot down inside Pakistan occupied Kashmir (PoK). He is later released by Pakistan on 1 March in a live telecast that is watched by millions of Indians. Varthaman is hailed by Prime Minister Modi and the mainstream media as a true national hero, and his 'safe return' is billed as a success of Indian diplomacy and proof of India's ability to prevail over Pakistan.

March 2019: The Adani Group – despite its inexperience in airport management – is granted all six contracts made available by the union government for modernizing airports in Guwahati, Ahmedabad, Jaipur, Lucknow, Thiruvananthapuram, and Mangaluru. During the first term of the Modi government, the Adani Group secured a total of fifteen major contracts related to defence, logistics, and power in many of the countries that Modi had visited during his trips abroad. These include the controversial 2014 Carmichael mine project in Australia that has been accused of serious financial irregularities, tax evasion, and environmental harm.

7 April 2019: A mob in the Biswanath district of Assam assaults sixty-eight-year-old Shaukat Ali on the suspicion of selling beef in the local market and proceeds to force-feed him a piece of pork. The mob also accuses him of being an illegal Bangladeshi migrant.

23 May 2019: Campaigning on a strongly nationalist platform and citing events such as Pulwama and the Balakot air strikes, the BJP-led NDA coalition retains power in the central government by winning an absolute majority of 353 seats in the seventeenth Lok Sabha elections. The BJP wins 303 seats (increasing its share from 282 in the 2014 elections), and Narendra Modi continues as India's prime minister for a second term. The BJP also retains power in Arunachal Pradesh, securing a victory in the state elections (held alongside the Lok Sabha elections).

21 June 2019: The Muslim Women (Protection of Rights on Marriage) Bill, 2019, is introduced in the Lok Sabha by the minister of law and justice, Ravi Shankar Prasad. The bill makes the declaration of *triple talaq* a cognizable, non-bailable offence with up to three years of imprisonment.

5 July 2019: During the budget proceedings, the union finance minister, Nirmala Sitharaman, announces a privatization or 'disinvestment' target of INR 1.05 lakh crores, with the government seeking to reduce its stake in public sector enterprises (PSEs) to below 51 per cent. These include undertakings such as Air India, Oil and Natural Gas Corporation (ONGC), Bharat Petroleum Corporation Limited (BPCL), Bharat Sanchar Nigam Limited (BSNL), and Life Insurance Corporation (LIC), among others.

2 August 2019: The Unlawful Activities (Prevention) Amendment Bill is passed in the Indian Parliament. Under the new amendments, the central government is empowered to designate any individual a terrorist if they are found guilty of committing/being involved in/preparing for/promoting an act of terror. Further, the central government is also authorized to list any individual as a terrorist in the official gazette, even before the charges of terrorism are proved in a court of law.

5 August 2019: Union Home Minister Amit Shah introduces two parliamentary resolutions abrogating the status of Article 370 (and Article 35A) that provide for the special status of J&K in the Indian constitution. In effect, the two resolutions annul the autonomy of J&K. The Jammu and Kashmir Reorganization Act, 2019 (passed on 6 August), splits the state into two union territories, J&K and Ladakh, which are to be administered directly by the central government. Communication services are suspended in the region, and several individuals are booked under the Public Safety Act (PSA) and confined to house arrest and preventive detention. This includes prominent political leaders of the state such as Omar and Farooq Abdullah of the Jammu and Kashmir National Conference, Tehreek-e-Hurriyat leader Syed Ali Shah Geelani, and the BJP's alliance partner in the state, Mehbooba Mufti of the Jammu and Kashmir People's Democratic Party. Farooq and Omar Abdullah are released from detention only in March 2020, while Mehbooba Mufti is released in October 2020.

31 August 2019: The final version of the National Register of Citizens (NRC), a population registry, is published for the state of Assam leaving out a total of more than 1.9 million people – approximately 6 per cent of the state's population. In an unanticipated development for the ruling BJP, a substantial proportion of those who are left out are Hindus. There is mounting criticism and angry opposition to the government, and growing fears that subsequent editions of the NRC enacted in other states will have the same adverse effect on Hindus, the core constituency of the BJP.

17 September 2019: The Sardar Sarovar Dam in Gujarat is filled to its full capacity, leading to the submergence of nearly 192 villages, affecting over 30,000 families – most of whom are still awaiting compensation.

22 September 2019: Modi addresses an audience of 50,000 along with American President Donald Trump at the 'Howdy Modi!' rally organized in Houston, Texas.

24 October 2019: The BJP emerges as the single-largest party in the Haryana state elections and forms the government by securing a post-poll alliance with the Jannayak Janta Party (JJP) and a few independent MLAs. The BJP's Manohar Lal Khattar is sworn in as chief minister of Haryana. In Maharashtra, however, despite securing a victory with alliance partner Shiv Sena, the BJP is unable to form the government. Subsequently, the Shiv Sena forms an alliance with the Congress and the Nationalist Congress Party (NCP), and Uddhav Thackeray (of the Shiv Sena) is sworn in as chief minister on 28 November.

9 November 2019: A five-judge constitution bench of the Supreme Court – led by CJI Ranjan Gogoi – delivers a unanimous verdict in the decades-long Ramjanmabhoomi (birthplace of Ram) case. The court holds that the disputed land in Ayodhya – site of the demolished Babri mosque that Hindu nationalists claim is the actual birthplace of the god Ram – does indeed belong to Ram Lalla (Lord Ram). The court also directs the central government to set up a trust to oversee the construction of a Ram temple at the site, and to allot a separate 5-acre plot to the Sunni Waqf Board for the construction of a mosque.

14 November 2019: The Supreme Court upholds its verdict in the Rafale fighter jet procurement case, dismissing review petitions challenging its December 2018 verdict.

19 November 2019: A five-judge constitution bench of the Supreme Court allows review petitions challenging its September 2018 verdict that allowed women between the ages of ten and fifty to enter the Sabarimala temple in Kerala.

20 November 2019: Union Home Minister Amit Shah announces in the Rajya Sabha that the NRC exercise recently concluded in Assam will be conducted across India.

11 December 2019: The CAA is passed in the Indian Parliament, leading to widespread protests against its perceived discriminatory intent. The CAA provides citizenship status for persecuted religious minorities that include Hindus, Sikhs, Buddhists, Jains, Parsis, and Christians from Afghanistan, Bangladesh, and Pakistan, but excludes Muslims (and Jews) from its named list of minorities. Civil society activists fear that in conjunction with the NRC and the National Population Register (NPR), the amendments to the citizenship laws have the potential to deny citizenship to large numbers of Indian Muslims. The NPR is a list of all individuals who have lived in India for more than six months, irrespective of their nationality, while the NRC purports to be a list of all citizens in India, compiled from the data collected under the NPR.

December 2019: UP registers the highest death toll among all Indian states in the protests against the CAA. The UP Police cracks down on several anti-CAA protest sites and raid several Muslim neighbourhoods and establishments. Police violence is particularly severe in Meerut and Muzaffarnagar, where the injured (some of whom are minors) are denied admission to hospitals, tortured in custody, and refused legal aid.

December 2019: The central government passes the Coastal Regulation Zone Notification, 2019, opening up India's coastline for enhanced commercial activities. The regulation was passed without consulting India's coastal communities and allows for construction on the previously protected 200-metre no-development zone in rural (coastal) areas.

15 December 2019: The Delhi Police storm the Jamia Millia Islamia university campus using tear gas and batons (*lathi*-charge) on students protesting against the CAA. The police also vandalize the university's library, reading rooms, and classrooms. Several students are injured – one of them suffers a serious head wound – and close to a hundred students are detained by the police and eventually released the following day. Earlier in the day, Prime Minister Modi, addressing a rally in Jharkhand, blamed the Congress for organizing the protests against the CAA and said protestors spreading violence could be identified 'by the clothes they wear', a thinly veiled dog whistle about Muslims and their visible sartorial markers (*hijab*, skull caps, and so on).

14 December 2019: Despite a severe cold wave in north India, nearly 200 women begin a peaceful sit-in protest against the CAA in the Shaheen Bagh area of Delhi. The protestors are soon joined by university students, civil society activists, and others who set up volunteer medical and food camps in the area. Several BJP leaders – including Union Minister of Law and Justice Ravi Shankar Prasad – accuse the protestors of Shaheen Bagh of offering a platform to the 'Tukde Tukde Gang' (that is, anti-national elements who wish to 'break India').

15 December 2019: The UP Police crack down on the students at Aligarh Muslim University using tear gas and stun grenades, and by firing bullets. Close to a hundred students are picked up by the police, and another hundred are injured in the violent police action. Students at the university were holding a protest vigil against the police action in the Jamia Millia Islamia campus (on 13 and 15 December).

15 December 2019: Anti-corruption activist and peasant leader Akhil Gogoi is arrested by the NIA for protesting against the CAA. Gogoi is charged under the UAPA and for 'waging a war against the nation'. Subsequently in January 2020, he is also charged with sedition along with two others, Hiren Gohain and Manit Mahanta. Gogoi was granted bail in March 2020 but was immediately arrested by the NIA again. He was eventually granted bail on 2 October 2020, and announced the formation of a political party, Raijor Dal (People's Party), to contest in the Assam state assembly elections scheduled for 2021.

20 December 2019: The UP Police unleash violence in the Muslim-majority neighbourhoods of Khalapar and Mehmood Nagar in Muzaffarnagar. The police fire live bullets – in addition to using tear gas and *lathi*-charging protestors – killing one person, Noor Mohammed. Residents of these neighbourhoods claim that the police were joined by members of the BJP, Bajrang Dal, and the RSS, who proceeded to loot money and jewellery from several houses.

30 December 2019: The central government picks out a hundred railway routes for private carriers to operate 150 passenger trains every year. Later in January 2020, the Indian Railways announces that its production units will soon be privatized in a modernization drive and private companies will be allowed to manage around

750 railway stations across the country. The All India Railwaymen's Federation (AIRF) launched a nationwide strike in September 2020 against the privatization of the Indian Railways.

5 January 2020: A mob of masked men enter the JNU campus and hostels with iron rods, sticks, acid, and glass bottles, attacking students and faculty members protesting the university administration's proposed fee hike. The JNU student union president, Aishe Ghosh, is severely injured from a head wound, while close to fifty others (both students and staff) are rushed to nearby hospitals with injuries. Despite evidence emerging of the ABVP's involvement in the attacks, the Delhi Police name the injured Aishe Ghosh as a primary suspect in inciting violence in the campus.

25 January 2020: Sharjeel Imam, a JNU student, is charged with sedition by the Assam (BJP coalition) government for delivering a speech at the Aligarh Muslim University against the CAA. He is arrested on 28 January from the Jehanabad area in Bihar.

28 January 2020: Authorities of the Shaheen Education Institute in Bidar, Karnataka, are booked under sedition charges after students at the primary school performed a play criticizing the CAA. Students between the ages of nine and twelve are called in four times for questioning by the Karnataka Police, and a student's mother and a teacher are arrested for organizing the play which allegedly insulted Prime Minister Modi.

January 2020: Bhushan Patwardhan, vice-chairman of the UGC, takes additional charge as the chairman of the ICSSR. Dr Patwardhan is a biomedical scientist specializing in research on Ayurvedic medicine.

8 February 2020: Arvind Kejriwal and the AAP retain power in Delhi by securing sixty-two of the seventy available seats in the state elections. The AAP secures victory over the BJP despite the latter's claims of Kejriwal's involvement with 'anti-national' elements (such as the protestors at Shaheen Bagh).

10 February 2020: Students from the Jamia Millia Islamia university are violently dispersed by the Delhi Police for conducting a peaceful protest march (against the CAA) on their way to the Parliament. A fact-finding team of the National Federation of Indian Women led by activist Aruna Roy later reports that nearly forty-five individuals (fifteen women and thirty men) faced sexual assault by the police.

17 February 2020: The Union Ministry of Culture claims to have spent INR 643.84 crores on the promotion of Sanskrit in the last three years, while allotting only INR 29 crores on the promotion of the other five classical Indian languages – Tamil, Telugu, Kannada, Malayalam, and Odia.

20 February 2020: The central government shifts the Bhima Koregaon investigation to the NIA.

20 February 2020: The Bengaluru Police charge Amulya Leone, a nineteen-year-old student, with sedition after she shouted 'Pakistan Zindabad' (Long live Pakistan) at a protest rally in Bengaluru. She is finally released on 11 June after being imprisoned for nearly four months.

24–26 February 2020: Parts of northeast Delhi witness large-scale communal violence and rioting. In the lead up to the violence, BJP leader Kapil Mishra delivers an ultimatum to the Delhi Police to clear anti-CAA protest sites (such as in Jaffrabad and Chand Bagh) or else face the consequences of his supporters taking direct action against the protestors. On 24 February, Hindu right-wing mobs attack anti-CAA protest sites, and despite the imposition of preventive curfew, numerous shops and mosques are burnt on 25 February. The Delhi Police – complicit in the violence perpetrated by Hindu right-wing mobs on the preceding days – clear protest sites on 26 February. The Delhi violence leaves over fifty people dead (thirty-nine of whom are Muslims) and close to 200 others injured.

24–25 February 2020: As violence continues in Delhi, US President Donald Trump and Prime Minister Modi address an audience of 125,000 in Ahmedabad, Gujarat, in the 'Namaste Trump' rally organized to mark the US president's first visit to India.

4 March 2020: The Supreme Court refuses to entertain social activist Harsh Mander's petition against BJP leaders Anurag Thakur, Parvesh Verma, Kapil Mishra, and Abhay Verma for hate speeches leading to the Delhi communal violence. Instead, it admits Solicitor General Tushar Mehta's allegations of hate speech against Mander.

11 March 2020: A 'Group of Intellectuals and Academicians' (GIA) submits a forty-eight-page 'fact-finding' report titled *Delhi Riots 2020: Report from Ground Zero – The Shaheen Bagh Model in North-East Delhi: From Dharna to Danga* to the minister of state for home affairs, Kishan Reddy. The report claims that the Delhi 'riots' were instigated by an 'Urban-Naxal-Jihadi' network, which seeks to replicate such violence 'targeting Hindu communities and localities' in other parts of the country.

13 March 2020: Kuldeep Singh Sengar – the prime accused in the Unnao rape case – and his brother Atul Singh are handed a ten-year prison sentence on charges of murder by Delhi's Tis Hazari Court.

16 March 2020: President Ram Nath Kovind nominates former CJI Ranjan Gogoi to the upper house (Rajya Sabha) of the Parliament. Justice Gogoi led the proceedings over the Ramjanmabhoomi case, in which the Supreme Court delivered a unanimous verdict declaring the site of the demolished Babri Masjid as belonging to Ram Lalla in November 2019. Justice Gogoi was accused of sexual harassment by a former Supreme Court staffer in April 2019, who also alleged that she was dismissed from service and harassed by the police. Claiming that the sexual harassment accusations were part of a 'bigger plot' to 'deactivate the office of the CJI', and as an attack on the 'independence of the Judiciary', Justice Gogoi had dismissed the allegations against him in a specially constituted three-member bench of the Supreme Court in April 2019.

16 March 2020: The Rajya Sabha passes the Central Sanskrit Universities Bill, 2019 (now an Act), converting three deemed-to-be Sanskrit universities into Central universities – the Rashtriya Sanskrit Sansthan (Delhi), Shri Lal Bahadur Shastri Rashtriya Sanskrit Vidyapeetha (Delhi), and the Rashtriya Sanskrit Vidyapeetha (Tirupati, Andhra Pradesh).

March 2020: A Tablighi Jamaat (evangelical Islamic organization) event is held in New Delhi and is attended by several individuals from both within and outside India. The congregation is immediately blamed by sections of the nationalist media – and by the home minister of state, Kishan Reddy – as the primary cause of spreading the COVID-19 virus in India. Hindu right-wing outfits refer to this as 'corona jihad', and the central government blacklists the visas of over 2,000 Tablighi members in June 2020.

22 March 2020: A day-long 'Janata Curfew' (people's curfew) from 7 a.m. to 9 p.m. is imposed in India to stop the spread of coronavirus. Along the lines of the dramatic demonetization announcement of November 2016, the curfew is announced in a sudden televised address by Prime Minister Modi broadcast on national television.

24 March 2020: Prime Minister Modi abruptly announces a twenty-one-day national lockdown in an effort to curb the spread of COVID-19. Hastily announced, the lockdown provides only a four-hour notice to everyone in the country before transport (and other services) are halted, leaving millions of migrant workers stranded without work, food, and housing in India's cities. Eventually this leads to a mass exodus of migrant workers walking extremely long distances to their villages amid a severe food crisis – hundreds of them die on these journeys, while others are brutally repressed by local police authorities.

2 April 2020: Meeran Haider, a PhD student at the Jamia Millia Islamia, is arrested by the Delhi Police for allegedly inciting large-scale communal violence in the city in February 2020. Two other students at the university – Safoora Zargar and Asif Iqbal Tanha – are arrested later in the month, while former JNU student Umar Khalid is booked under the UAPA on 21 April.

8 April 2020: Despite the nationwide lockdown, the Supreme Court declines interim relief to the activists arrested in the Bhima Koregaon case. Gautam Navlakha (on temporary bail) and Anand Teltumbde are taken into custody by the NIA.

10 April 2020: Safoora Zargar, a student of the Jamia Millia Islamia, is arrested by the Special Cell of the Delhi Police for her alleged role in instigating the Delhi violence (in February). Zargar, pregnant at the time of her arrest, is released from prison only on 23 June on 'humanitarian grounds', after the Delhi Police opposed her bail pleas on three separate occasions.

11 April 2020: The UP government accuses the digital news site *The Wire* and its founder-editor Siddharth Varadarajan for misinformation and for publishing distorted news about Yogi Adityanath. The UP Police issue a summons to Varadarajan, driving all the way to Delhi from Ayodhya in the midst of the national lockdown in what is seen by the Editor's Guild of India as an 'act of intimidation'.

18 April 2020: The Delhi Police charge former JNU student Sharjeel Imam with sedition and allege that his speech instigated riots in the Jamia Millia Islamia university area in December 2015.

May 2020: UP, Madhya Pradesh, and Gujarat announce their decision to suspend existing labour laws in order to reboot the economy and attract industrial investment.

17 May 2020: Prime Minister Modi announces an INR 20 lakh crore economic package with the aim of building an 'Atmanirbhar Bharat' (Self-reliant India) – the amount is, however, highly exaggerated, and includes previously committed financial outlays by the Reserve Bank of India (RBI) to provide INR 8 lakh crores in liquidity.

21 May 2020: Asif Iqbal Tanha, a student of the Jamia Millia Islamia and a member of the Student Islamic Organization (SIO), is arrested by the Delhi Police for allegedly inciting violence and in northeast Delhi in February 2020.

23 May 2020: Two Pinjra Tod ('Break the Cage', a collective of women university students) activists, Devangana Kalita and Natasha Narwal (both students at JNU), are arrested by the Delhi Police for participating in a sit-in protest against the CAA at Jafrabad (Delhi) in February 2020. They are granted bail by the Duty Magistrate before being arrested again by the Special Investigation Team (SIT) of the Crime Branch on charges of murder, rioting, and criminal conspiracy. Kalita is arrested for a third time by the Delhi Police on 1 June under charges of unlawful assembly and rioting at Daryaganj (in Delhi) and is sent to judicial custody. Devangana Kalita, Natasha Narwal, and another student – Asif Iqbal Tanha – were granted bail by the Delhi High Court on 15 June 2021, and released from Tihar jail on 17 June 2021.

29 May 2020: A seventy-page report titled *Delhi Riots: Conspiracy Unravelled*, prepared by a six-member committee headed by a former judge of the Bombay High Court (Justice Ambadas Joshi), is submitted to the Union Home Minister Amit Shah. This report makes claims similar to the GIA report submitted in March to the central government and blames the Delhi violence on an 'Urban-Naxal-Jihadi' network.

14 June 2020: Bollywood actor Sushant Singh Rajput, a native of Bihar, commits suicide in his home in Mumbai. His death is soon turned into a political tug-of-war between the BJP and the Shiv Sena in Mumbai, with the BJP accusing the Mumbai Police (and the Shiv Sena) of mishandling the investigation. In the following weeks, arrests and investigations (by the National Narcotics Control Bureau [NCB]) of several high-profile Bollywood stars are carried out amid accusations of nepotism and drug use in the industry.

15–29 June 2020: Indian and Chinese Army troops are engaged in clashes along the Line of Actual Control (LAC) in Ladakh. Twenty Indian soldiers are killed in the clashes. In response, the Indian government bans fifty-nine Chinese software applications (termed a 'digital strike'), claiming that they present a national security threat to the country.

21 July 2020: The NIA opposes jailed activist Varavara Rao's bail plea. Rao tests positive for COVID-19 in jail and is also said to be suffering from a neurological disorder. The NIA claims that Rao is seeking to take advantage of his age and of the global pandemic in order to seek bail.

28 July 2020: An associate professor of English at Delhi University, Hany Babu, is arrested by the NIA in connection with the Elgar Parishad case and is sent to judicial custody until 21 August.

29 July 2020: The union cabinet approves the Draft National Education Policy (NEP) 2020 – the first draft of the NEP had come under criticism in May 2019, after political parties had criticized the emphasis (and imposition) of Hindi in school curricula in non-Hindi states. The Draft NEP 2020 aims to replace the existing school structure in India, change school curriculum to focus on 'key concepts and ideas', and provide students (in senior schools) with increased flexibility in the choice of subjects. Among other reforms, the NEP also aims to follow a three-language formula, with emphasis on instruction in the regional language (or mother tongue) for the first few years of schooling, and Sanskrit (and foreign languages) for the secondary and senior levels; improve teacher training; and increase gross enrolment ratio (GER) in higher education institutions to 50 per cent by 2035. The NEP also renames the Union Ministry of Human Resources and Development as the Ministry of Education.

31 July 2020: Lukman Khan, a cattle trader, is nearly beaten to death by a cow vigilante group in Gurugram (formerly Gurgaon). The local police are captured on video standing by without trying to prevent the mob's violence.

31 July 2020: India's gross domestic product (GDP) shrinks by 23.9 per cent in the first quarter of the financial year due to the COVID-19 lockdown.

5 August 2020: Amid the national lockdown and the rising COVID-19 cases in the country, Prime Minister Modi participates in a Ram Mandir Bhoomi Pujan (foundation stone ceremony for the Ram temple) in Ayodhya. The ceremony is also attended by UP chief minister, Yogi Adityanath, and RSS chief, Mohan Bhagwat.

10 August 2020: The union government allows commercial coal mining and lists the mining rights of forty coal mines for offer in auctions.

17 August 2020: Rakesh Asthana, the former CBI special director, is appointed as the director-general of the BSF – he also holds the additional charge of the post of director-general, NCB.

22 August 2020: The Bombay High Court dismisses FIRs filed against twenty-nine foreigners charged for violating the conditions of their tourist visas by attending the Tablighi Jamaat event in March 2020. The court rules that the foreigners have been made 'scapegoats', blames the media for vilifying the foreigners, and observes that the action against Tablighi members was malicious in nature, intending to serve as an indirect warning to Indian Muslims that 'action in any form and for anything' can be taken against them.

September 2020: Amid damning reports of India's rapidly shrinking GDP, the BJP uses Sushant Singh Rajput's death as a rallying call to voters in Bihar – a state set for elections later in October–November – by running a campaign titled '#JusticeforSushantSinghRajput' on Twitter.

7 September 2020: The NIA issues summons to Partho Sarathi Ray, a Kolkata-based molecular biologist, K. V. Kurmanath, a journalist with *The Hindu*, and K. Satyanarayana, a professor at the English and Foreign Language University (EFLU), Hyderabad, in the ongoing Elgar Parishad and Bhima Koregaon investigation. Both Kurmanath and Satyanarayana are sons-in-law of jailed activist Varavara Rao, and had their homes raided earlier in 2018 by the Pune Police.

13 September 2020: Former JNU student Umar Khalid is arrested by the Special Cell of the Delhi Police under the UAPA and sent to ten days of custody for his alleged role in the Delhi violence (in February 2020). A Delhi court later extends his custody until 22 October. A day later, the Delhi Police also summoned documentary filmmakers Rahul Roy and Saba Dewan in connection with organizing anti-CAA protests.

14 September 2020: A nineteen-year-old Dalit woman is gang-raped and tortured by four upper caste Thakur men in Hathras (Uttar Pradesh). The victim provides oral testimony to the Uttar Pradesh Police on 22 September, before succumbing to her injuries on 29 September.

16 September 2020: G. Kishan Reddy, the minister of state for home affairs, states that 3,005 cases were registered under the UAPA in the years 2016, 2017, and 2018, respectively. Of the 3,005 cases, chargesheets have been filed only for 821 cases.

20 September 2020: The Farmers' Produce Trade and Commerce (Promotion and Facilitation) Act, the Farmers (Empowerment and Protection) Agreement of Price Assurance Act, and the Farm Services and the Essential Commodities (Amendment) Ordinance are introduced in the Indian Parliament – two of these bills are passed through a 'voice vote' in the Rajya Sabha. Under a voice vote, the Speaker (or in this case, the Deputy Chairman) seeks a response from members of the House in terms of 'ayes' or 'noes', and decides on the success of a motion depending on which side is louder (if 'aye', then the motion is passed). Crucially, this process circumvents the standard procedure of having members of Parliament vote on any legislation. Farmers' groups claim that these laws bypass the existing Agricultural Produce Market Committees (APMCs) and the Minimum Support Price (MSP) regime for agricultural commodities, and will instead allow private entities to dictate agricultural commodity prices. Protests against these laws are particularly intense in the states of Punjab and Haryana. On 26 September, the Shiromani Akali Dal quit the BJP-led NDA alliance in protest against the passage of the farm bills.[2]

24 September 2020: A Supreme Court bench dismisses Sudha Bharadwaj's bail plea application on medical grounds – the bail application was filed in reference to Sudha Bharadwaj's deteriorating health condition (and the possible risk of contracting COVID-19 in prison).

27 September2020: The Lok Sabha clears three labour codes – Industrial Relations Code, Code on Social Security, and Occupational Safety, Health and Working Conditions Code Bills, 2020. The government claims that the new labour codes will increase the ambit of social security provisions to cover vast sections of India's informal workers, including intra-state migrant workers and gig workers. Critics point out that labour unions and state governments were not consulted in the process of drafting the new labour codes, and that the legislations increase the vulnerability of India's informal labour force by granting extended discretion to employers to provide social security and to terminate workers' employment.

29 September 2020: Amnesty International India announces the closure of its India offices and the retrenchment of all its staff after its bank accounts are frozen by the central government. The organization had called for an inquiry into the abuses of the PSA in Kashmir since the abrogation of Article 370 and had recently published a report on the complicity of the Delhi Police in the February riots.

30 September 2020: The body of the Hathras rape victim is not handed over to her family and is instead cremated by the UP Police in an overnight clandestine operation.

1 October 2020: Amid widespread criticisms of their handling of the Hathras rape case and the nature of the 'cover-up' cremation afterwards, the UP Police claim that the nineteen-year-old Dalit woman from Hathras was not raped.

5 October 2020: Siddique Kappan, a New Delhi–based correspondent for several Malayalam news outlets, is arrested in Mathura (UP) while on his way to Hathras and charged with sedition under the provisions of the UAPA for allegedly raising funds for terrorist activities and inciting communal hatred. In October, India is also ranked 142 (out of 180 countries) on the World Press Freedom Index, released by Reporters Without Borders.

5 October 2020: The UP Police register an FIR against Bhim Army chief, Chandrasekhar Azad, and 400 others for violating section 144 of the Criminal Procedure Code (that prevents the gathering of five or more people). Azad was on his way to Hathras to meet the family of the nineteen-year-old rape victim. The police also prevent other activists, media personnel, and politicians from opposition parties (such as the Congress) from visiting the victim's family in Hathras.

7 October 2020: The Supreme Court rules that public places cannot be occupied indefinitely in reference to the protests against the CAA in Delhi's Shaheen Bagh.

13 October 2020: Stan Swamy, an eighty-three-year-old Jesuit priest and tribal activist, is the latest person to be arrested by the NIA in the Bhima Koregaon case. The NIA chargesheet accuses Swamy of having Maoist links and of organizing an 'armed militia' to take on the central government. Swamy's repeated bail plea attempts on health grounds are opposed by the NIA. He passes away on 6 July 2021 at the Holy Family Hospital in Mumbai, aged eighty-four.

16 October 2020: The Delhi Police assault Ahan Penkar, a staffer at the *Caravan* magazine, in the Model Town Police Station for reporting on the alleged rape and murder of a Dalit girl in north Delhi. Earlier in August 2020, three *Caravan* journalists – Shahid Tantray, Prabhjit Singh, and a woman staffer – were beaten (and the woman was sexually harassed) by a Hindu right-wing mob, while the Delhi Police stood by passively.

17 October 2020: India is ranked 94 out of 107 countries in the recently released Global Hunger Index (GHI), 2020. According to the GHI report, nearly 14 per cent of India's population is undernourished, and India has a child stunting rate of 37.4 per cent.

21 October 2020: In the ongoing Elgar Parishad case, the NIA charges the arrested activists, including Anand Teltumbde and Varavara Rao, of undertaking (and organizing) arms training in the forests of central India with Maoist groups and for trying to 'reinvent Dalit militancy' in India.

21 October 2020: The Punjab State Legislative Assembly passes a resolution rejecting the Centre's contentious farm bills. Hours later, news reports suggest that the Chhattisgarh and the Rajasthan governments are also seeking to introduce resolutions against the Centre's farm bills in the near future.

29 October 2020: Several locations (and NGO offices) in Kashmir and Delhi are raided by the NIA under suspicion of diverting funds to 'secessionist and separatist activities' in Jammu and Kashmir.

31 October 2020: The total number of coronavirus positive cases in the country rises to 8,137,119. Globally, India is the second-worst coronavirus-hit country, after the United States. India's fatality rate is the third highest in the world with a total of 121,641 recorded deaths so far.[3]

Notes

1. Acknowledgments: I thank Srirupa Roy and Lalit Vachani for alerting me to important events/incidents that had escaped my attention in an earlier version of this timeline. Thanks are also due to Rasika Ajotikar for her timely help in translating the Hindi terms mentioned in this timeline.

2. Following nearly a year of sustained protests by farmers from Punjab, Haryana, and UP, PM Modi announced the withdrawal of the three farm laws on 19 November 2021. Despite the announcement, the Samyukta Kisan Morcha (SKM) – one of the leading organizations in the protests – has vowed to continue the struggle until the central government legally guarantees the MSP regime (and meets other demands).

3. At the time this chapter goes to press (by end 2021), India's officially reported coronavirus case tally stands at 34,578,749 with a total of 111,897 active cases and 468,574 reported deaths. The country was in the grips of the second wave of the pandemic during April–May 2021, and recorded over 300,000 daily cases between 21 April 2021 and 18 May 2021. In this period, the country faced a critical shortage of medical supplies, hospital beds, medical oxygen and vaccines, and received foreign aid from the USA, UK, Russia, France, and China, among other countries. The drastic spike in daily cases coincided with the recently concluded legislative assembly campaigns and elections held in April in five states – West Bengal, Assam, Kerala, Tamil Nadu, and Puducherry. Prime Minister Modi and members of his and various opposition parties chose to aggressively campaign and address large gatherings of people despite scientific warnings of an impending second wave as early as March 2021. In addition to the elections, the Government of India also approved the staging of the Kumbh Mela – a Hindu religious festival – in Haridwar (Uttarakhand) in April, in which an estimated 70 lakh people participated.

3

NORMALIZING VIOLENCE
LESSONS FROM HINDU NATIONALIST INDIA

*Amrita Basu**

Hindu nationalist violence has a long ancestry, but its modalities have changed. If in the past the Rashtriya Swayamsevak Sangh (RSS) and its affiliates engineered 'riots' by spreading rumours and aggravating local tensions, they no longer need to do so. In the current political environment and amidst the massive growth of social media, the mere suspicion that a Muslim or Christian is violating Hindu social codes is justification for violence. While in the past, the Bharatiya Janata Party (BJP) fostered Hindu–Muslim tensions prior to elections to influence their outcomes, it now does so more frequently and less predictably. Hindu nationalist violence has increasingly become both routinized and normalized.

As a result, the targets of hate violence have grown. Although they are generally religious minorities, they have come to include students, intellectuals, and human rights activists who challenge religious orthodoxy and government policy. They include Dalits who challenge upper caste domination, as they did in Bhima Koregaon, Maharashtra, in January 2018, when they celebrated the defeat of an upper caste Hindu ruler 200 years ago. They include women who sought to enter the Sabarimala temple in Kerala to assert their equality in matters of faith after the Supreme Court authorized them to do so in 2018. They include students from Jamia Millia Islamia, Aligarh Muslim University, and Jawaharlal Nehru University (JNU).

Most existing scholarship on ethnic violence, including my own, has focused on politically motivated group violence, or what is commonly termed a 'riot'. The concept of 'riot' implies a certain unspecified threshold of violence with respect to the number of people injured and killed, and the amount of property destroyed. However, the term 'riot' has always been flawed because it ignores the pattern since the 1990s of well-planned Hindu nationalist attacks on Muslims. It has become even less useful amidst the normalization of Hindutva violence since the BJP was elected to national power in 2014.

Documenting recent developments in India, I argue that we need to devise new ways of conceptualizing violence that recognize its significance, independent of the scale of any single incident; appreciate the links between laws, public policy, and physical assault; and identify the webs of complicity between the state, political parties, and civil society. This entails appreciating multiple forms of violence and systematic forms of humiliation and coercion by dominant groups that are designed to subjugate, denigrate, silence, and intimidate people on the basis of their identities and beliefs. I include in my account of violence hate speech that is violent in itself and designed to provoke physical attacks. Although I recognize the forms of violence that are embedded in social practices and cultural institutions but do not result in physical assault, this is not the focus of my analysis.

Scholars have long been preoccupied with how ordinary people can engage in extraordinary acts of violence. For Hannah Arendt (1994), the most brilliant analyst of this phenomenon, 'The essence of totalitarian government, and perhaps the nature of every bureaucracy, is to make functionaries and mere cogs in the administrative machinery out of men, and thus to dehumanize them'. Accordingly, Arendt argued, Adolf Eichmann came to see his role as one of the chief architects of the Holocaust as not just normal and routine but ethical and imperative.

Extending Arendt's argument about the normalization of violence beyond totalitarian states, some scholars regard it as central to nation and state making. For example, Gyanendra Pandey (2006, 8) writes, 'violence, a "complex social fact", is a general and continuous aspect of the modern state, spinning out across multiple institutionalized landscapes with political, economic, religious, and moral implications'. Similarly, for Zygmunt Bauman and Leonidas Donskis (2016), modern life is associated with what they term 'adiaphora', a form of moral blindness that places certain acts or categories of human beings outside the universe of moral obligations. Other scholars explore the processes that normalize violent outcomes (Kalyvas 2006; Haleem 2020).

Although myriad parties, movements, and states seek to normalize violence in the contemporary period, populists and religious nationalists are especially effective in doing so. Right-wing populists equate the people with religious and ethnic majorities and seek to unify them by targeting subjugated racial and ethnic minorities. Populist leaders often normalize their promotion of ethnic and racial hatred by claiming that they embody the will of the people and are acting at the people's behest. What makes Narendra Modi distinctive is that since becoming prime minister, he has refrained from openly enjoining the masses to engage in violence.

Thus, violent attacks on religious minorities appear to emanate spontaneously from below. At the same time, Modi has promoted militant government leaders and civil society organizations that espouse violence and BJP state and national governments have passed laws that normalize violence.

Religious nationalists normalize violence by providing ethical justification for it. Claiming that the Hindu majority has been victimized by religious minorities who threaten their numerical superiority and religious beliefs, they depict popular violence by Hindus as courageous and morally righteous. Aggressors who think of themselves as victims are apt to deny and thus normalize the violence they engage in. The intertwining of legal, political, and religious–ethical injunctions to violence provide impunity for those who lynch Muslims for supposedly killing cows and consuming beef or for marrying Hindu women.

This normalization of violence has several important implications. It enforces upper caste Hindu dominance and aligns Hindu nationalism with Indian nationalism. It also issues a warning and threat to religious minorities, Dalits, women, and critics of the regime. And yet, if targeted violence has become increasingly normalized, it has not silenced peaceful dissent.

Hindu Nationalist Violence: From Vajpayee to Modi

Compared to the BJP-dominated National Democratic Alliance (NDA) government that occupied power in 1999–2004, the current BJP government is more committed to creating a Hindu nation-state. It is able to achieve its ideologically driven agenda because of its authoritarian style of governance. It has employed legal and extra-parliamentary means to promote Hindu dominance at the regional and national level while repressing peaceful opposition to its policies.

The most serious violence under the first NDA government (1999–2004), in Gujarat in 2002, claimed around 1,000 lives. The scale of the violence reflected the combined strength of Hindu nationalist forces and their success in defeating, repressing, and co-opting left, secular, and lower-class and caste movements, amidst the capitulation of the opposition Congress party to Hindu nationalism. The NDA government failed to stop the escalation of violence by declaring president's rule, suspending the state government, and ruling by decree (as Article 356 of the Indian Constitution authorizes).

Although Narendra Modi – the then chief minister of Gujarat – was not ultimately prosecuted, continued suspicions of his complicity will probably deter a recurrence of such violence in his home state. However, if the number of 'riots' has declined, politically motivated hate crimes have grown. Compared to the first NDA government, this regime has closer ties to the RSS, which disseminates views that promote violence, and is less constrained by coalition parties. The RSS supported Modi throughout his career and was responsible for his ascendance in Gujarat and nationally. RSS appointments to the Cabinet and to major academic and cultural institutions have significantly increased under the Modi-led BJP government (Kanungo 2019). The growing popularity of the RSS signals the normalization of an ideology that promotes violence, while the BJP's connections to the RSS demonstrate growing state support for this ideology.

RSS-affiliated organizations have increasingly espoused and precipitated violence. The Bharatiya Gau Raksha Dal (Indian Cow Protection Group) organizes vigilante groups that attack Muslims and sometimes Dalits, whom it accuses of consuming beef and killing cows. The RSS-affiliated youth organization, the Akhil Bharatiya Vidyarthi Parishad (ABVP), has organized a series of attacks on Indian students and faculty who criticize government policy. In February 2016, when students at JNU organized a protest against state repression in Kashmir, the ABVP alleged that their speeches were anti-national and encouraged the police to raid the university and arrest opposition student leaders, including student union president Kanhaiya Kumar. Though Kumar was released for lack of evidence against him, no government officials condemned the police violence and the arrests. The ABVP continued to attack activists and charge them with sedition, including at an Amnesty International meeting in Karnataka in August 2016, and at Jai Narain Vyas University in Jodhpur and Ramjas College in Delhi University in February 2017. The police did nothing to stop the attacks and did not file charges against any of the assailants (Shafi 2017; *South Asia Citizens Web* 2017).

Hindutva activists have increasingly employed social media to propagate hatred, further contributing to the normalization of violence. They post bigoted anti-minority views on social media, distort and invent news stories, and mobilize their followers to engage in violence, among other platforms through WhatsApp, which over 230 million Indians use. Soma Basu's study of 140 pro-BJP WhatsApp groups, in which several members of BJP IT cells and BJP legislative assembly members are participants, found that a quarter of their messages contained anti-Muslim messages. Home Minister Amit Shah has openly encouraged the public to support the BJP by making 'real or fake ... messages go viral' (S. Basu 2019).

The government has increasingly engaged in surveillance, censorship, incarceration, and assaults on critics of religious orthodoxy and government policy. It has curbed dissent by invoking laws that punish threats to national stability, such as sections 124A (outlawing sedition) and 120B (outlawing criminal conspiracy) of the Indian Penal Code (IPC). Although convictions are unusual, the police frequently harass government critics by arresting them under the anti-sedition law. According to the Indian Home Affairs Ministry's National Crime Records Bureau

(NCRB), 332 people were arrested for sedition from 2016 to 2018 (Yadav 2020). In October 2019, the state of Bihar charged forty-nine people with sedition for writing Prime Minister Modi an open letter expressing concern over the increase in anti-minority hate crimes and mob violence (Human Rights Watch 2020). Protests against the government's new citizenship laws triggered more sedition charges, as the state brands protestors anti-national (*India Today* 2020; *The Wire* 2020).

The government's suppression of dissent and of progressive civil society organizations, combined with its promotion of the RSS, normalizes hate speech and Hindu nationalist ideology. While strengthening Hindutva civil society groups, the government has undermined autonomous civil society organizations that defend marginalized communities and human rights. The Home Ministry has revoked the licenses of around 10,000 non-governmental organizations (NGOs) on grounds that they have violated the provisions of the Foreign Contributions (Regulation) Act, 2020. Although various laws proscribe hate speech on the basis of religion, ethnicity, and culture, hate speech and hate crimes are on the rise and are rarely prosecuted. Far from opposing the hate speech of its ministers and members of Parliament (MPs), the national government has ignored or even rewarded them. Within this political climate, repetitive and targeted acts of violence have become increasingly common. The government's failure to condemn such violence adds to the impunity with which Hindu nationalists redefine the boundaries of citizenship and nationhood.

Gathering accurate data on hate crimes is exceedingly difficult. News media that had been tracking religiously motivated hate crimes have ceased to do so. Although the NCRB has published reports on violent crimes since the 1950s, in 2017 it withheld information about violence against minorities and political dissidents (Schultz et al. 2019). However, Deepankar Basu (2021) has compiled reliable information on the growing incidence of what he terms religiously motivated hate crimes since the BJP was elected in 2014. Drawing on data from the Citizen's Religious Hate Crime Watch and the Election Commission of India's website, Basu finds that the BJP's electoral victory in 2014 was directly responsible for a rise in religiously motivated hate crimes, from 22 in 2009–13 to 195 in June 2014–18, representing a 786 percent increase. During this time, hate crimes declined against Christians and Sikhs, but increased against Muslims – from 36 to 83 per cent. Basu finds that hate crimes were greatest in the ten states where the BJP had won a high share of the popular vote as a result of weakened law enforcement by BJP state governments.

The following section discusses the responsibility of national and state governments, local administrators, BJP leaders, and Hindutva civil society groups for violence against Christians, Muslims, and women. It discusses violence surrounding laws on religious conversion and beef consumption, and the 'love jihad' campaign policing interreligious relationships. Hindutva-inspired civil society activists and pro-BJP local and state administrators are responsible for this violence. Uttar Pradesh's Chief Minister Yogi Adityanath and Prime Minister Modi bear particular responsibility for the violence against Muslims and women, the former for actively encouraging it and the latter for refusing to condemn it.

State–Societal Linkages

Hindu nationalists have engaged in extensive violence against India's Christian minority. Their rumours that Christians are forcibly converting Hindus have provided the pretext for vandalizing and destroying churches, and assaulting, abducting, and murdering priests and nuns. Perpetrators of these attacks do not need to prove that Christians are engaging in forcible conversions. Their aim is to warn Christians that their religious identities make them suspect. Hindu nationalist organizations have also organized *ghar wapsi* (homecoming) campaigns to 'reconvert' Christians and Muslims to Hinduism. What they term reconversion erroneously assumes that all Muslims and Christians were forcibly converted out of Hinduism and must be converted back into it. Underlying this campaign is the assertion of Hindu domination and a refusal to recognize and affirm religious pluralism.

BJP state governments have fostered distrust of Christians by passing the so-called Freedom of Religion legislation, prohibiting conversion to Christianity. Five state governments have passed laws which require converts out of Hinduism to inform the district magistrate and require community members to inform the police and administration if they suspect that pastors, nuns, and clergymen are proselytizing.

The complicity between state and national governments is also evident in beef lynchings. For example, when a mob brutally assaulted dairy farmer Pehlu Khan and four others in Alwar, Rajasthan, in April 2017, the police did not arrest the assailants. The police filed charges against Khan's family although the family had documents certifying that the cows were for dairy production (Angad 2017). BJP minister of parliamentary affairs, Mukhtar Abbas Naqvi, initially denied that the attack occurred. Later, BJP home minister (current defence minister), Rajnath Singh, defended the assailants.

Narendra Modi is indirectly responsible for beef-ban-related violence. During the 2014 national election campaign, he attacked the Congress Party for introducing a 'pink revolution' that resulted from increased cow slaughter. He delivered fiery speeches on the subject during the 2015 Bihar state election campaign. In the 2015 Dadri lynching, a group of men murdered Mohammad Akhlaq in his home because of rumours that he had slaughtered a cow and consumed beef. Modi waited eight days before addressing the Dadri lynching and even then denied government responsibility for this and other such incidents. Neither that statement nor the one he issued shortly thereafter stopped the wave of attacks on Muslims who were accused of consuming beef and killing cows. Modi spoke up again after a video went viral showing a group of Hindu men brutally beating several Dalit youths who were skinning a cow carcass in Una, Gujarat, in July 2016. Modi criticized the actions of cow vigilante groups but ignored the fact that BJP state governments have strengthened ties between the police and these groups. Just days after his speech, the Haryana government created a police task force in each district to detect cow smugglers and licensed cow protection groups to assist the police (Raj 2016).

BJP state governments have legitimated vigilante violence. Twenty-four of India's twenty-eight states have regulations prohibiting either the slaughter or the sale of cows, mainly at the behest of BJP state governments. When sworn in as chief minister of Uttar Pradesh in 2017, Yogi Adityanath ordered the shutdown of slaughterhouses, as the BJP had promised in its election campaign.

Several NDA officials have supported a beef ban. In May 2017, the Ministry of Environment banned the sale of cows and buffaloes for slaughter across India. The following month the national government issued regulations requiring people selling livestock to produce a written guarantee that cattle would not be slaughtered.

A particularly insidious Hindutva campaign alleges that Muslim men are engaging in so-called love jihad, that is, coercing Hindu women into romantic relationships, converting them to Islam, and abusing them. The campaign entails several levels of institutional complicity. Informants in courts tell Hindutva activists when an interfaith couple is getting married so activists can file contrived rape and kidnapping charges against the Muslim man and fabricate documents stating that the woman is a minor. The local administration and police, which includes RSS members, often support these groups. Key BJP and NDA government leaders have supported the love jihad campaign, particularly before elections.

Rumours of cow slaughter and love jihad have led government officials to engage in increased surveillance of the private sphere to determine what people are eating and who they are marrying. Some BJP state governments have taken absurd measures to determine whether beef is being consumed. However ineffective these tests may be, they send out important messages about what people should eat, what faith they should adopt, who they should love, and what they should believe.

The Deepening of Populism and Religious Nationalism: 2014–2020

Modalities of Hindutva violence are influenced by the populist and religious nationalist character of the current regime. The BJP's success rests on continual populist-style mobilization, often by violent means, to secure and expand its base. In this respect, the BJP government has a decisive advantage over many other populist regimes because it has strong, enduring ties to a network of RSS-affiliated civil society organizations. As the regime has become more populist and authoritarian, it has become increasingly intolerant of political dissent. The commitment to strengthening executive power and dismantling autonomous representative institutions – while strengthening civil society organizations that support the regime – is a hallmark of populist regimes, as is the suppression of criticism.

Modi's leadership style is both populist and religious nationalist. With claims that better days lie ahead, Modi has lofty ambitions: to end corruption, return power to the people, and improve India's global standing. Like other populists, Modi opposes political and cultural pluralism and draws a sharp distinction between 'the people' and elites. In keeping with his religious nationalist commitments, he identifies Hindus as the people and Muslims as anti-national outsiders. Modi's populist and religious nationalist commitments have deepened while he has been in office. In contrast to the 2014 election campaign, in which he emphasized economic issues, his 2019 election campaign was xenophobic and anti-minority. He repeatedly provoked fears about illegal migration and threats to national security by terrorist groups in Pakistan. The government's decision to launch air strikes on Pakistan in response to a terrorist attack that killed Indian soldiers in Jammu and Kashmir in February 2019 played a major role in the BJP's election and Modi's increased popularity. In this and other instances, Modi has spoken of a threat to not merely Hindu identity but also Indian identity, by conflating opposition to the current government's policies with being anti-Indian and anti-Hindu.

The government's policies since its re-election in 2019 stem from its populist-style centralization of power and its religious nationalist attempts to promote Hindu dominance. In August 2019, it revoked Article 370 of the Constitution which allowed Jammu and Kashmir to form their own state legislature and create their own laws. To encourage non-Kashmiris, primarily Hindus, to purchase land and settle in the region, it revoked Article 35A which protected Kashmiris' rights to land ownership and permanent residency. Following this sudden decision, the state deployed tens of thousands of Indian troops to the region, arrested opposition politicians and public figures, closed down telephone networks and the Internet, and banned travel to and from Kashmir. The government's actions have curtailed opportunities for the peaceful expression of dissent and increased the likelihood of violent opposition to its policies.

In 2019 the government published an updated version of the National Register of Citizens (NRC) for Assam, excluding the names of approximately 2 million people, many of them Muslims, who have lived in India for decades. Those who are unable to produce documentation of citizenship before Foreigners Tribunals (which is impossible for many displaced and impoverished people) will be sent to government detention centres with deplorable conditions (T. Hussain 2020). Members of these tribunals describe being under pressure from the government to declare Muslims non-citizens; former members believe they were fired for not doing so (Singh and Raj 2020).

Within months of the BJP's re-election, the Indian Parliament passed the Citizenship Amendment Act (CAA), which provides undocumented immigrants from Pakistan, Bangladesh, and Afghanistan an accelerated path to citizenship – unless they are Muslims. The Act further reduces the period of time required for naturalization for Hindu, Sikh, Buddhist, Jain, Parsi, and Christian immigrants who arrived in India before 31 December 2014 from Muslim-majority neighbouring countries. There is clearly a link between the CAA and the government's actions in Assam. The CAA enables Bengali Hindu migrants in Assam who were excluded from the NRC to become citizens. The Cabinet also approved funding for a National Population Register which will include a question about parents' birthplaces, suggesting that people whose citizenship the government questions will have to establish their Indian lineage. This legislation empowers government functionaries to profile Muslims and requires that Muslims – and only Muslims – document their citizenship.

The government's response to protests against the amendment of citizenship laws has often been violent. The police arrested and injured thousands of students who protested the citizenship laws at two predominantly Muslim universities, Jamia Millia Islamia and Aligarh Muslim University, in mid-December 2019. Less than three weeks later, the police, and allegedly the ABVP, assaulted student and faculty protesters at JNU in New Delhi. In Uttar Pradesh, fact-finding reports provide evidence of the police failing to protect innocent people, issuing arrests on false charges, and engaging in violence against protesters, including seemingly targeted attacks against Muslim children (Bhattacharya 2020). An umbrella body of about seventy organizations issued a report contending that Chief Minister Adityanath was responsible for the violence (*Sabrangindia* 2019).

As Hindutva violence has become normalized, it is less constrained by fear of international opposition. Indeed, it unfolded in New Delhi in February 2020 when Modi welcomed Donald Trump to New Delhi. That month, BJP leader Kapil Mishra instigated violence against anti-CAA protesters, leading to targeted anti-Muslim attacks in northeast Delhi in which fifty-three people, two-thirds of whom were Muslim, were killed. Hindu vigilante groups stormed and destroyed Muslim homes, burned mosques, and attacked Muslims with impunity from the police (Gettleman et al. 2020). Police records did not make note of Mishra's hate speech (Jain, Shukla, and Sanyal 2020).

The government now uses the term 'riots' to refer to peaceful protest against CAA. In April, the Delhi police engaged in widespread arrests of protesters whom it accused of instigating 'riots'; in many cases they failed to inform them of their legal rights or to notify their families of the arrests (Yamunan 2020). Meanwhile, they exonerated the Hindutva groups who attacked the protesters (Gettleman and Abi-Habib 2020).

The national lockdown due to COVID-19 has intensified state repression, surveillance, and anti-Muslim violence. Claiming health concerns, the police have detained and assaulted doctors, arrested people who left their home for groceries, and prevented NGOs from providing hospitals with ventilators, which they desperately needed (B. Hussain 2020; Mir 2020). Although the Supreme Court urged officials to empty prisons because of coronavirus, the police continue to detain journalists, students, and other activists on flimsy charges. The government's new contact-tracing application raises privacy and surveillance concerns (Clarance 2020). Propaganda on social media that accuses Muslims of intentionally spreading coronavirus – '#CoronaJihad' – has led people to boycott Muslim vendors and hospitals to refuse treatment to Muslim patients. Rather than condemning this anti-minority violence, the government has blamed Muslims for it. For example, while banning Muslim gatherings on grounds that they spread the virus, it has permitted Hindu religious gatherings to take place (Varadarajan 2020).

The BJP government's endorsement of targeted violence, particularly against religious minorities, combined with its growing centralization of power and suppression of dissent, demonstrates the dangerous imbrication of right-wing populism and religious nationalism. Modi embodies and performs both traditional Hindu values and the perspective of the 'common man' against the elite. The abrogation of Article 370 and the enactment of the CAA and NRC seek to redefine citizenship along populist and religious nationalist lines. The BJP's depiction of the Indian people excludes not only immigrants but also religious minorities and dissidents whom it depicts as anti-national. The normalization of hate speech and Hindutva ideology deepens linkages between populism and religious nationalism, as the BJP is able to claim that Hindu nationalism expresses the popular will.

Conclusion

This chapter illuminates the modalities and causes of Hindutva-initiated violence in contemporary India. Compared to pre-planned 'riots', organized from above, multiple, decentralized acts of violence appear to reflect a groundswell of Hindutva sentiment. Hate crimes unnerve and intimidate because their timing, location, and targets are unpredictable. They are not confined to 'riot-prone' regions and have multiple victims. While the major targets are Christian and Muslim minorities, they also include Dalits and women who allegedly violate upper caste social codes. Much as the BJP seeks Dalit electoral support, Hindu nationalism is at its core an upper caste project.

The effect of this modality of violence is to normalize attacks on minorities and political dissidents. A single murder, such as that of Mohammad Akhlaq, or single instance of police violence, such as against JNU student leader Aishe Ghosh, has demonstration effects. The individuals who are targeted serve as examples of what can happen to others who hold the same identities and views. Hindutva violence signals that Muslims and political dissidents do not have equal citizenship rights, including security and equality before the law. Perpetrators of hate crimes are unlikely to be punished and victims unlikely to be compensated. Hindutva violence has significant consequences for refashioning identities by seeking to define what it means to be a Hindu, a Muslim, a moral woman, and a good citizen. The message to Muslims is that they cannot be safe in India unless they adhere to Hindu norms; to Hindu women, that their place is in the home, not in the university, streets, or even temple, and that they should marry only men of their faith; to Dalits, that their assertion of pride in challenging upper caste dominance is an affront to Hindus. Politically motivated hate crimes have implications not only for those who are attacked verbally, physically, and legally, but for the entire society.

Rather than challenging deeply cherished democratic ideals, Modi has cleverly deployed them by ostensibly opposing established elites in the name of returning power to the people. The perversion of 'people power' is most evident in BJP leaders' failures to stop hate crimes. Modi's ability to provide easy answers to popular grievances reflects the long-term failure of Indian democracy to adequately address poverty, inequality, and minority well-being. Thus, a viable alternative to the BJP must challenge the material and institutional structures that foster myriad forms of inequality and violence. It must reinterpret 'power to the people' to entail secular, inclusive, peaceful, and genuinely democratic politics.

Note

* I am grateful to Srirupa Roy and Thomas Hansen for inviting me to the workshop in Göttingen, where I received helpful feedback from them and other conference participants.

References

Angad, A. 2017. 'Alwar Attack: Gau Rakshasa Killed a Dairy Farmer, Not Cattle Smuggler'. *Indian Express*, Mewat, 7 April. https://indianexpress.com/article/india/alwar-gau-rakshaks-killed-a-dairy-farmer-not-cattle-smuggler-4601434/ (accessed on 30 November 2021).

Arendt, H. 1994. *Eichmann in Jerusalem: A Report on the Banality of Evil*. New York: Penguin Group (first published in 1963).

Basu, D. 2021. 'Majoritarian Politics and Hate Crimes against Religious Minorities: Evidence from India, 2009–2018'. *World Development*, 146, 1 October. https://www.sciencedirect.com/science/article/abs/pii/S0305750X21001522 (accessed on 1 December 2021).

Basu, S. 2019. 'Manufacturing Islamophobia on WhatsApp in India'. *The Diplomat*, 10 May. https://thediplomat.com/2019/05/manufacturing-islamophobia-on-whatsapp-in-india/ (accessed on 30 November 2021).

Bauman, Z., and L. Donskis. 2016. *Liquid Evil*. John Wiley & Sons.

Bhattacharya, A. 2020. 'A Dangerous Pattern of Police Violence in Uttar Pradesh Has Been Masked by Clever Propaganda'. *Scroll.in*, 4 February. https://scroll.in/article/951187/a-dangerous-pattern-of-police-violence-in-uttar-pradesh-has-been-masked-by-clever-propaganda (accessed on 30 November 2021).

Clarance, A. 2020. 'Aarogya Setu: Why India's Covid-19 Contact Tracing App Is Controversial'. BBC News, 15 May. https://www.bbc.com/news/world-asia-india-52659520 (accessed on 1 December 2021).

Gettleman, J., and M. Abi-Habib. 2020. 'In India, Modi's Policies Have Lit a Fuse'. *New York Times*, 1 March. https://www.nytimes.com/2020/03/01/world/asia/india-modi-hindus.html (accessed on 1 December 2021).

Gettleman, J., S. Yasir, S. Raj, and H. Kumar. 2020. 'How Delhi's Police Turned against Muslims'. *New York Times*, 12 March. https://www.nytimes.com/2020/03/12/world/asia/india-police-muslims.html (accessed on 1 December 2021).

Haleem, I. (ed.). 2020. *Normalization of Violence: Conceptual Analysis and Reflections from Asia*. London: Routledge.

Human Rights Watch. 2020. 'India: Events of 2019'. In *World Report 2020*. https://www.hrw.org/world-report/2020/country-chapters/india (accessed on 1 December 2021).

Hussain, B. 2020. 'Fighting Covid-19 – And Repression – in Kashmir'. *Foreign Policy in Focus*, 14 April. https://fpif.org/fighting-covid-19-and-repression-in-kashmir/ (accessed on 1 December 2021).

Hussain, T. 2020. '"How Is It Human?": India's Largest Detention Centre Almost Ready'. *Al-Jazeera*, 2 January. https://www.aljazeera.com/news/2020/1/2/how-is-it-human-indias-largest-detention-centre-almost-ready (accessed on 1 December 2021).

———. 'Heat on Sharjeel Iman: Sedition Cases Filed against Anti-CAA Activist in Six States'. *India Today*, 28 January. https://www.indiatoday.in/india/story/heat-on-sharjeel-imam-sedition-cases-filed-against-anti-caa-activist-in-six-states-1640742-2020-01-27 (accessed on 1 December 2021).

Jain, S., S. Shukla, and A. Sanyal. 2020. 'Delhi Riots Chargesheet Skips Hate Speeches by BJP Leaders'. NDTV, June 9. https://www.ndtv.com/delhi-news/delhi-riots-chargesheet-skips-hate-speeches-by-bjp-leaders-2243342 (accessed on 1 December 2021).

Kalyvas, S. N., 2006. *The Logic of Violence in Civil War*. Cambridge: Cambridge University Press.

Kanungo, P. 2019. 'Sangh and Sarkar: The RSS Power Centre Shifts from Nagpur to New Delhi'. In *Majoritarian State: How Hindu Nationalism Is Changing India*, edited by A. P. Chatterjee, T. B. Hansen, and C. Jaffrelot, 133–49. London: Hurst.

Mir, T. 2020. 'India Is Using the Pandemic to Intensify Its Crackdown in Kashmir'. *Washington Post*, April 30. https://www.washingtonpost.com/opinions/2020/04/30/india-is-using-pandemic-intensify-its-crackdown-kashmir/ (accessed on 1 December 2021).

Pandey, G. 2006. *Routine Violence: Nations, Fragments, Histories*. Stanford University Press.

Raj, S. 2016. 'Indian State to License Cow Protection Groups to Aid Police'. *New York Times*, 11 August. https://www.nytimes.com/2016/08/12/world/asia/indian-state-to-license-cow-protection-groups-to-aid-police.html (accessed on 1 December 2021).

Sabrangindia. 2019. 'Fact Finding Report Reveals Excesses by Meerut Police against Muslims.' 28 December. https://www.sabrangindia.in/article/fact-finding-report-reveals-excesses-meerut-police-against-muslims (accessed on 1 December 2021).

Schultz, K., S. Raj, J. Gettleman, and H. Kumar. 2019. 'In India, Release of Hate Crime Data Depends on Who the Haters Are.' *The New York Times*, 24 October. https://www.nytimes.com/2019/10/24/world/asia/india-modi-hindu-violence.html (accessed on 1 December 2021).

Shafi, S. 2017. 'Nationalist Group ABVP Accused of Delhi Campus Violence'. *Al Jazeera*, 27 February. https://www.aljazeera.com/features/2017/2/27/nationalist-group-abvp-accused-of-delhi-campus-violence (accessed on 1 December 2021).

Singh, K. D., and S. Raj. 2020. '"Muslims Are Foreigners": Inside India's Campaign to Decide Who Is a Citizen'. *New York Times*, 4 April. https://www.nytimes.com/2020/04/04/world/asia/india-modi-citizenship-muslims-assam.html (accessed on 1 December 2021).

South Asia Citizens Web. 2017. 'India: Protect Universities and Academic Freedom from Threat of Violence and Intimidation – Say Human Rights Groups'. 22 February. https://www.scholarsatrisk.org/academic-freedom-media-review-archive/ (accessed on 1 December 2021).

The Wire. 2020. 'Woman Says "Pakistan Zindabad … Hindustan Zindabad" at CAA Protest, Booked for Sedition'. 21 February. https://thewire.in/politics/amulya-leona-bengaluru-caa-protest-sedition-owaisi-waris-pathan (accessed on 1 December 2021).

Varadarajan, S. 2020. 'In India, a Pandemic of Prejudice and Repression'. *New York Times*, 21 April. https://www.nytimes.com/2020/04/21/opinion/coronavirus-india.html (accessed on 1 December 2021).

Yadav, A. 2020. 'How India Uses Colonial-era Sedition Law against CAA Protesters'. *Al-Jazeera*, 21 January. https://www.aljazeera.com/news/2020/1/21/how-india-uses-colonial-era-sedition-law-against-caa-protesters (accessed on 1 December 2021).

Yamunan, S. 2020. 'Delhi Violence Arrests: Courts Must Ensure Police Are Not Using Lockdown to Undermine Basic Rights'. *Scroll.in*, 23 April. https://scroll.in/article/959985/delhi-violence-arrests-courts-must-ensure-police-are-not-using-lockdown-to-undermine-basic-rights (accessed on 1 December 2021).

4

HINDUTVA ESTABLISHMENTS
RIGHT-WING THINK TANKS AND THE MAINSTREAMING OF GOVERNMENTAL HINDUTVA

Srirupa Roy

In 2014, the Bharatiya Janata Party (Indian People's Party, BJP for short), the political wing of India's ethnomajoritarian Hindu nationalist movement that aims to redefine the country as a 'Hindu-first' nation, won the general elections and formed the government with a clear majority of 282 out of 543 parliamentary seats. Five years later, the BJP further consolidated these electoral gains. Defying the anti-incumbency pattern of Indian politics in which political parties are ousted from power in successive elections by a disillusioned electorate (Roy and Sopariwala 2019), the BJP returned to power in the 2019 elections with an increased tally of 303 parliamentary seats.

The BJP's ascent to national power since 2014 marks a major change in the political life of Hindu nationalism, from a mobilizational politics of insurgent opposition to a governmental politics of rule. While the former has been the familiar form of Hindu nationalist politics for close to a century, the latter is a new development that is less than a decade old.[1] Reflecting this chronology, the main focus of the vast and rich scholarship on Hindu nationalism, or Hindutva, is on its 'movemental' aspects, that is, the practices of agitational politics, popular mobilization, and the strategies of ideological reproduction that recruit individuals and groups to the cause of Hindutva. Moving beyond this protest movement framework, this chapter explores the relatively uncharted terrain of 'governmental Hindutva', a formation that reflects both the vision of cultural and religious homogenization that the Hindu nationalist movement has promoted for close to a century and a more recent political–institutional vision of India as a majoritarian 'ethnic democracy' with a strong unitary state governed by authoritarian populist strongmen leaders (Jaffrelot 2019; Peer 2017). What are the modes and effects of this transition from nationalist mobilization to authoritarian populist governance? What changes when Hindu nationalism is the currency of rule and not protest?

Going beyond existing accounts of deinstitutionalization and anti-elitism as the necessary and main consequences of populists in power (Crewe and Sanders 2020; Kyle and Gultchin 2018; Mounck 2018; Varshney 2019), I argue in this chapter that parallel processes of *institutional innovation and elite formation* are equally central to the project of governmental Hindutva. As we will see, when populists come to power, they create new kinds of institutions and intermediaries (agents, structures, networks, as well as spaces) and configure a new ruling class that is no less establishment and elite than the old.

My focus is on the elite formations of governmental Hindutva and the specific institutional innovation of the 'right-wing think tank' that has gained considerable political prominence in recent years, coinciding with the BJP and Hindutva's ascent to national power.

Think tanks combine academic and professional–administrative knowledge and experience: they are usually staffed by a combination of academics with intellectual interests in applied and policy research, and retired bureaucrats, diplomats, and military officials. The declared role of these non-state institutions is to create and foster 'epistemic communities' (Haas 1992) of research knowledge and expertise to advise and inform governmental policymaking (McGann and Weaver 2002; McGann 2016). Formally established as institutional conduits between knowledge, policy, and public constituencies, the role of think tanks goes well beyond their designated functions of providing technocratic expertise and public outreach, to the active creation of the informalized networks of power connecting state and non-state, domestic and international interests. India's right-wing think tanks do this too and their networked power formations advance the governmental Hindutva project in three significant ways.

First, they *normalize* Hindutva ideology by discursively translating Hindutva themes into recognized and 'mainstream' terms of governance and statecraft. Second, they *mediate and connect* Hindutva actors to existing institutional spaces of decision and rule, and network Hindutva elites with their counterparts from state, military, business, media, academic, and international organizations. Belying Hindutva's angry anti-establishment rhetoric, right-wing think tanks are centrally invested in the creation of a governing elite, and they work with and expand rather than demolish existing formations and networks of elite power in order to achieve this aim. Third, their specific mode of societal engagement, which combines publicity and visibility with secrecy and opacity, works to *veil and insulate* the narrow interests and political–ideological vision that, in direct violation of formal democratic commitments to the public good, are shaping and driving Indian statecraft today. What results is the insertion of the Hindutva project into the existing institutional and discursive terrain of Indian democratic government.

The relative smoothness and ease of the process is a sombre reminder that the 'old' and 'new' Indias of democratic norm and Hindutva exception may be more connected than oppositional. Challenges to Hindutva will need to reckon with these proximities and entanglements as well, looking beyond the internal logic of Hindu nationalism at the wider enabling conditions of normal democratic rule that also sustain the Hindutva project.

Right-wing Think Tank Worlds

Lineages and contexts

In contrast to other democracies, the United States foremost among them, think tanks have not played a very significant role in the policy worlds of post-independence India (McGann 2018; Stahl 2016),[2] where policy-making was largely the preserve of elite government actors such as senior diplomats and bureaucrats.[3] This changed towards the end of the twentieth century as the Indian state launched a concerted program of economic liberalization, opening up the protectionist and planned Indian economy to the unfettered forces of domestic and global capital. State as well as societal and economic elites invested in a common effort to replace the Nehruvian national project of state-led development and its rhetorical commitments to socialist welfare with triumphalist assertions of India's arrival on the global stage as a free market democracy (Kaur 2020). The 'command polity' of Nehruvian *étatisme* gradually but surely gave way to a dispersed and networked sovereignty that blurred boundaries between state and society and legitimized non-electoral forms of political authority (Jenkins 1999; Harriss and Corbridge 2000; Kohli 2010; Sinha 2019). Individuals and institutions located outside the worlds of electoral politics came to exercise power in the name of the people. Media, civil society, corporate actors, the apolitical middle classes, and the judiciary now claimed the mantle of democratic representation and promised to overhaul the corrupt and messy system of electoral politics and restore power to the people (Roy forthcoming, 2016; Baviskar and Ray 2011).

Think tanks were among the new institutional actors that exercised extra-electoral and networked power in the post-liberalization political field of millennial India and advanced the new national imagination of a rising India with global power ambitions. Located mostly in the capital city of New Delhi, they were linked to a diverse set of stakeholders that included the Observer Research Foundation (ORF) founded by the Dhirubhai Ambani family in 1990 and receiving the majority of its funding from their multinational corporation, Reliance Industries (Sarkar 2019); the Ananta Aspen Centre, a collaborative venture of the Aspen Institute of the United States and the Confederation of Indian Industries (CII) set up in 2004; Brookings India, established as a branch of the US-based Brookings Institution in 2013;[4] and Carnegie India, the Indian node of the Carnegie Endowment for International Peace's international network, set up in 2016 (Khan and Köllner 2018; Srivastava 2011).[5]

Several millennial think tanks were also associated with the Sangh Parivar or the Hindu nationalist 'family' of organizations and to the Sangh's nodal body, the Rashtriya Swayamsevak Sangh (National Volunteer Corps, RSS). The first Sangh-affiliated think tank, the Deendayal Research Institute (DDRI), was set up in 1968 as a New Delhi–based policy research institution that applied Hindu nationalist ideology to policy questions of the time. However, reflecting the political and electoral marginality of Hindu nationalism, DDRI's influence and public recognition were quite limited.[6] It was only in the early twenty-first century, in the time of ascendant Hindutva, economic liberalization, and a new era of 'mediatized politics' where the rapid growth of commercial news media outlets brought a new visibility to particular kinds of national political events and actors, that the Hindutva think tank gained public and political traction.

Between 2000 and 2011, nine think tanks were established with active Sangh assistance and involvement. Two of these have subsequently gained international recognition as entries in the Think Tank Index, an annual ranked list of global think tanks.[7] Their establishment reflected and advanced Hindu nationalism's bid for electoral success and governmental power. As the BJP racked up electoral victories in state as well as national elections and even formed the ruling national coalition on two occasions between 1996 and 2004, it was evident that Hindu nationalism sought state as much as social power – it trained its sights on *raj* as well as *samaj*. Along with their agenda of social transformation, of remaking Indian social order in Hindu majoritarian terms, Hindu nationalist organizations aimed to capture state power through electoral means, by contesting and winning elections. Like the Hindu nationalist political party, the think tank was a specialized organization of the Sangh family that addressed these goals of electoral success and state capture.

To achieve these goals, it was not enough to rely solely on languages and practices of insurgent popular mobilization. Demonstrating Hindutva's establishment credentials was also a key priority, that is, proving the ability of Hindutva institutional actors to play by and succeed within the existing rules of the political establishment. The new think tanks with their capital city presence and dense web of connections with the bureaucratic, political, and media establishment served as important institutional vectors of this effort. These connections would transect Hindutva and non-Hindutva spaces, networking individuals from Hindu nationalist organizations with their professedly non-Hindutva counterparts in a shared project of advancing and protecting the national interest. Reflecting the importance of these establishment connections, think tanks used more general terms such as 'right wing', right of centre', or even 'nationalist' to define themselves, and avoided more ideologically specified labels that tied them directly and exclusively to Hindutva and Sangh worlds.

Following the BJP majority victory in the 2014 elections, right-wing think tanks came to exercise visible authority and influence in governmental circles (Kartikeya 2017, 2018; Malhotra 2017; Sengupta 2014; Shah 2014). A revolving door system of appointments saw individuals from particular think tanks appointed to senior leadership positions in government that were closely associated with the prime minister's office (PMO), the institutional locus of the centralized executive authority that distinguishes the BJP regime. These included the founder-director of the Vivekananda International Foundation, Ajit Doval, who was appointed to the position of National Security Advisor, and Nripendra Misra, another senior Vivekananda International Foundation staffer who was appointed to the high-prestige position of Principal Secretary in the PMO.[8]

The revolving door also facilitated a movement in the opposite direction, from government into think tank spaces. In recent years, numerous Sangh leaders from the BJP and RSS, many among them cabinet ministers and parliamentary representatives, have joined the governing councils and advisory boards of think tanks and several have served in apex leadership roles as presidents and directors of these organizations. Examples include Vinay Sahasrabuddhe, the president of the India Foundation and national vice president of the BJP; Swapan Dasgupta, a director of the India Foundation, advisory board member of the Syama Prasad Mookerjee Research Foundation, and BJP parliamentary representative (Rajya Sabha); Ram Madhav, India Foundation board member, RSS senior volunteer, and BJP national general secretary; Rakesh Sinha, director of the India Policy Foundation, RSS ideologue, and BJP parliamentary representative (Rajya Sabha); and Swaminathan Gurumurthy, chairman of the Vivekananda International Foundation, RSS ideologue, and leader of the Sangh's economic front, the Swadeshi Jagran Manch.

With their career paths traversing and connecting state and social worlds, these individual power brokers have expanded policy making and governance decisions beyond the closed circles of bureaucratic and political authority. The think tanks with which they are associated such as the Vivekananda International Foundation, the India Foundation, the Public Policy Research Centre, the Syama Prasad Mookerjee Research Foundation, and the Forum for Integrated National Security have been gathered into the ambit of statecraft and serve as important institutional spaces of policy determination.

Public events hosted by these think tanks feature prominently in the capital city's political events calendar. At these events, senior figures from the national policy establishment (for example, ministers, bureaucrats, parliamentarians) engage in various forms of staged dialogue with 'eminent' interlocutors drawn from media, academia, other think tanks, and the mostly capital-city-based cohort of retired bureaucrats, diplomats, and officers of the armed forces. Often, they feature international visitors to India (for example, government officials, leaders of international organizations, senior academics) in conversation with their Indian counterparts, and facilitate what some have described as 'Track 1.5 diplomacy' between official and non-official representatives of different countries. Let us take a closer look at the distinctive actors, practices, and interests that populate and contour the social and political worlds of the right-wing think tank.

Terminology

At the outset, a clarification of terminology is in order. As noted earlier, 'right-wing' is an emic term that is used by representatives of the organizations themselves and by other supporters of Hindu nationalism.[9] Following this usage, I apply three selection criteria to define the universe of Indian right-wing think tanks. The first has to do with the public profile and recognition of the institution as a think tank in media coverage and scholarship. The second relates to what we might call the translational or mainstreaming commitments of think tanks. All the institutions listed below have multiple, and documented, institutional links to the Sangh Parivar. However, they deliberately avoid explicitly Hindutva idioms and repackage and translate Hindu nationalist ideologies into the registers of ideologically unmarked or general discourses of policy and statecraft that have normative status and political legitimacy.[10]

The third selection criterion is ideological content. Right-wing think tanks actively promote a set of ideological themes that range from free market principles of economy and commitments to social conservatism and religious majoritarianism (indirectly, via discourses of cultural preservation and traditional authenticity), to the political ideal of a strong and unitary state. Different think tanks in the right-wing ecosystem subscribe to different variants and combinations of these themes and their ideological intensities vary as do their specific policy visions. All do not explicitly identify as right wing, although a fair number do. Nevertheless, all the think tanks listed below endorse a common antagonism and even antipathy to 'left-wing' and 'western' ideas such as socialism, communism, secularism, and liberal individualism.[11]

Is the institution recognized and referenced as a think tank in media coverage and scholarship? Does it have documented linkages to Sangh Parivar organizations and leadership? Does it avoid direct Hindu nationalist identifications? Do its events and publications endorse anti-left and anti-liberal ideological positions? Affirmative answers to all four questions yield the following list of ten institutions.

Table 4.1 Indian right-wing think tanks

Name	Location	Year of establishment
Deendayal Research Institute (DDRI)	Delhi + others	1968
Image India Foundation (IIF)	Delhi	Early 2000s
India First Foundation (IFF)	Delhi	Early 2000s
Forum for Integrated National Security (FINS)	Pune, Mumbai + others	2003
India Policy Foundation (IPF)	Delhi	2008
SP Mookerjee Research Foundation (SPMRF)	Delhi	2008
Vivekananda International Foundation (VIF)	Delhi	2009
India Foundation (IF)	Delhi	2009
Public Policy Research Centre (PPRC)	Delhi	2011
Jammu Kashmir Study Centre (JKSC)	Delhi + others	2011

Source: Public websites of the listed think tanks.

Organizational locations and connections

Right-wing think tanks share two broad organizational similarities. The first is their metropolitan location and physical presence in the capital city, the seat of national government. Nine out of the ten think tanks on our list have their main offices in the capital city of New Delhi, and the only one with its national headquarters in another city (Mumbai), the Forum for Integrated Security, also has a Delhi office. In addition to the physical location of office buildings, the institutional leadership of right-wing think tanks also draws quite heavily on Delhi-based political elites and establishment insiders, further enmeshing these institutions in the circuits of national governmental power.

Most right-wing think tanks have retired senior bureaucrats, diplomats, and military officers serving in various capacities, for example, as senior advisors, board members, research fellows, directors, and presidents.[12] Politicians and incumbent government officials are quite centrally involved as well. In 2020, they occupied seventeen out of eighty-one (20 per cent) senior leadership positions at right-wing think tanks.[13] Networks also extend beyond the worlds of national government and high politics to connect think tanks to wider establishment formations.[14] As we will soon see, social and economic elites with public profiles such as senior journalists, media owners, entrepreneurs and CEOs, bestselling authors, and spiritual leaders are regularly invited to be speakers and chief guests at think tank events.

Second, right-wing think tanks are tightly integrated with Sangh Parivar organizations and ideologies. The saffron connection exists at multiple levels. As noted earlier, almost all the think tanks have senior Hindutva leaders in leadership positions. Their events routinely feature Hindu nationalist leaders and ideologues as speakers and 'distinguished guests'. The RSS head, Mohan Bhagwat, and senior leaders Suresh 'Bhaiyyaji' Joshi, Krishna Gopal, and Dattatreya Hosabale; Hindutva ideologue Subramaniam Swamy; and BJP ministers Amit Shah, Ravi Shankar Prasad, Nirmala Sitharaman, M. J. Akbar, Piyush Goyal, Suresh Prabhu, Sushma Swaraj, and Arun Jaitley are among those who have participated in think tank events in recent years.

There are also close and dense discursive affinities between think tanks and the wider organizational ensemble of Hindu nationalism. The research topics and publication themes pursued by these institutions echo and endorse many of the core beliefs of Hindu nationalism. Recent seminars and conferences organized by think tanks have addressed topics such as Ram Janmabhoomi, the status of Kashmir, and the Citizenship Amendment Act (CAA)[15] that are the prime focus of Sangh organizations. On numerous occasions, right-wing think tanks have served as venues and instruments of Hindutva experimentation and rehearsal. Several legislative and policy interventions that the BJP government has pursued since coming to office[16] were first elaborated to wider public and policy constituencies in the seminars and publications of various right-wing think tanks. For example, the Jammu Kashmir Study Centre and the India Foundation organized discussions and debates on the constitutional status of Article 370 and Article 35A several years before the BJP government annulled these provisions and ended the political autonomy of the state of Jammu and Kashmir in August 2019.[17]

Another momentous legislative action of the BJP government, the passage of the CAA in 2019 that introduced religious criteria into the determination of Indian citizenship, was prefigured and rehearsed in similar ways. Thus, already in 2013, discussions hosted by the India Foundation had flagged the plight of Hindu refugees from Pakistan and the responsibility of the Indian state to protect religious minorities from neighbouring countries.[18] Six years later, the CAA's offer of naturalization pathways to refugees from all religious communities except Islam would fulfil this demand.

Not only a space of rehearsal and experiment, the right-wing think tank has also been a theatre for Hindutva's governmental performances, a stage where Hindutva statecraft presents itself to public constituencies. Government officials from the incumbent BJP regime frequently communicate policy decisions at think tank events. Debates organized by think tanks on particular topics, with speakers whose views mirror official perspectives, are opportunities to present the government's point of view in an indirect, non-propagandist way. The passage of the 'triple *talaq*' bill of 2019, a controversial piece of legislation that instrumentalized women's rights to enact changes in Muslim personal law, was one such opportunity. As an unnamed BJP leader recounted to journalists Srijan Shukla and Neelam Pandey (2019):

> Passing the Triple Talaq bill was a major milestone for the government ... But the opposition was criticising it for being anti-Muslim. At this point, the government, as well as the party, felt that greater awareness was required and a public lecture should be conducted ... rather than asking the minority or the law ministry to organise an event on Triple Talaq, the Home Minister and BJP president Amit Shah felt it should be done by an outside agency and which is why the Dr Syama Prasad Mookerjee Research Foundation was asked to organise it.

In the context of the BJP regime's concerted cutback in formal press interactions – prime minister Modi has not held a single press conference since 2014 – these think tank events attract considerable media attention, and the speeches of state representatives are reported as official policy positions. Right-wing think tanks are thus effectively constituted as institutional extensions of the state.

Agendas and activities

What exactly do think tanks do? As Table 4.2 shows, the ten institutions on our list use broad and general terms to define their main purpose. Despite their many connections to the Sangh, right-wing think tanks deploy vocabularies of nationalism and patriotism in their mission statements and avoid any mention of linkages and affinities to Hindutva worldviews. Thus, the main mission of the Forum for Integrated National Security (FINS) is to 'build a strong, secure and prosperous nation through a united and awakened society'. The Syama Prasad Mookerjee Research Foundation defines itself in similar ways, as a 'forum which facilitates the convergence of ideas, positions and visions that aspire to strengthen the nation and preserve her unity and integrity and contribute towards her progress and integral development'.

Table 4.2 Think tank mission statements

Name	Mission statement
DDRI	To bring about total transformation and development of society through people's initiative and performance
Image India	NA
India First	NA
FINS	Analyse and evolve policies and solutions on national security with a three-pronged approach of initiate – interact – influence by engaging all stakeholders related with integrated national security
	Walking and Talking National Security
	Build a strong, secure and prosperous nation through a united and awakened society
IPF	Rigorous study and research to help our society objectively analyse the past, understand the present, and anticipate the future
SPMRF	Wisdom with valour brings glory to the nation
	Forum which facilitates the convergence of ideas, positions, and visions that aspire to strengthen the nation and preserve her unity and integrity and contribute towards her progress and integral development
VIF	Seeking Harmony in Diversity
	To become a centre of excellence to kick start innovative ideas and thoughts that can lead to a stronger, secure, and prosperous India playing its destined role in global affairs
IF	Analysis Advocacy Awareness
	Understanding contemporary India and its global context through a civilizational lens of a society on the forward move
PPRC	Constructively impacting policy formulation process with an emphasis on good governance practices, efficient implementation mechanisms and evidence-based policymaking, including policy audit and evaluation in the larger interest of the nation
JKSC	Our goal is to be recognized as a respected and a professional intellectual think tank in the country, providing the authentic information and bona fide data related to every aspect of the state of Jammu and Kashmir. The qualitative research and studies will intend to add value and improve the conditions and the lives of every state resident
	Endeavours to bring untouched facts and information out in the public domain.
	Highlights the rights of marginal groups in the state (women, SC, refugees)

Source: Public websites of the listed think tanks.

The deliberate avoidance of Hindutva affiliations is an attempt at nonpartisan institutional identification. Claiming technocratic authority by emphasizing the pursuit of objective scientific knowledge and the refusal of ideological frames and biases is not an unfamiliar strategic manoeuvre in think tank worlds. However, what sets apart the Indian right-wing think tank is its reproduction of nationalist and patriotic discourses. The passionate registers of their expression are at far remove from the tonally neutral conventions of scientific rationality. The Indian right-wing think tank defines its purpose and validates its existence through idioms of technopatriotism that ground claims of expertise in a distinctive combination of scientific knowledge and national devotion. Think tank experts not only have the right kinds of intellectual and professional knowledge and policy experience, but they also have the right kind of devotional attachment to the national cause. The cause as such is not explicitly specified – as we have seen already, in all the think tank mission statements the nation is an open and empty signifier referenced in very general terms. However, the activities that are pursued effect a slippage or conflation between the Indian and the Hindu, and align technopatriotism with devotion towards a specifically Hindu-first vision of the nation.

Turning now to think tank activities: the organization of events is a key priority for all think tanks. These include closed-door 'interactions' within and between different sets of national and international actors, small academic workshops and seminars on specialized topics, public lectures and book launches of invited guest scholars, and large, multi-day annual conventions branded as 'conclaves', 'forums', 'dialogues', or 'thinkfests', involving hundreds of guests who meet in plush venues in the full glare of media publicity. Research and publications comprise another prominent set of activities. All think tanks produce a large number of publications each year in both digital and print forms, for example, journals, monographs, occasional papers, white papers, and briefs, blogs, and newsletters. The majority of these are in-house publications, written by research fellows and scholars of the think tanks.[19] While some think tanks like the India Policy Foundation sell their publications, others distribute them without payment, and prioritize the public reach of their ideas. For instance, the Vivekananda Foundation not only publishes all its research in open-access digital formats, it also invests resources in digitizing the work of other authors to produce a carefully curated public canon of Indian texts.

Several think tanks also undertake training and pedagogical activities such as internships, junior fellowships, and certificate programs geared to early career researchers. The Kautilya Fellows Programme of the India Foundation, offered in partnership with the central ministry of External Affairs, is one example. Reflecting the translational commitments of right-wing think tanks to disseminate Hindutva ideologies through the discursive apparatus of mainstream nationalism, the fellowship combines a conventional workshop/master course on Indian foreign policy and public policy with 'a visit to Kumbh Mela in Prayagraj which is the largest religious congregation on earth'.[20]

Training and pedagogy takes non-academic forms as well, that emulate the socialization and indoctrination template of other Sangh organizations. For instance, FINS has organized 'border tours' and 'patriotic tourism' excursions in recent years that work to reproduce Hindutva ideologies through practical experiences. The FINS border tour initiative, *Sarhad ko Pranam* (Salutations to the Border) was organized in 2012 with a view to 'protect our nation-state from being bifurcated and dissected'. The program claimed to take 10,000 young people from different Indian states, many of them RSS volunteers, to locations along the 15,000-kilometre Indian land border where they would interact with soldiers and local residents to gain information and practice vigilance'.[21] A few years later, the organization also launched a program of patriotic tours or *yatras*. In 2014, FINS took eighty-five patriotic tourists to the Cellular Jail, the notorious colonial prison on the Andaman Islands where several iconic anti-colonial figures revered by Hindu nationalists were incarcerated.[22]

Research, publications, events, and training activities cluster around a common set of themes and policy areas that are invested with equivalent national value. Foreign policy, international relations and national security themes feature prominently in think tank programs, reflecting the influence of realist hard power paradigms and the preponderance of military, diplomats, and other foreign policy professionals in these epistemic spaces.[23] Other themes include history and culture, economy, and governance and politics. These are also invested with nationalist significance and framed as the equivalent counterparts of hard power; instrumentalized as resources and assets that, like defence capacities, must be cultivated in order to achieve India's dreams of global potency and recognition. In think tank publications, events, and training courses, the importance of cultural soft power receives special emphasis. Their vision of a strong state is as much about cultural assertion as it is about military and economic strength, and India's global ascent is linked to its successful use of soft, cultural or 'civilizational' power resources.

Let us take a closer look at this idea of civilizational power, which features prominently in right-wing think tank circles and is one of the main discursive tools for the mainstreaming and translation of Hindutva. As we will now see, civilizational power discourses modulate the ethnomajoritarian and antiliberal commitments of Hindutva ideology into publicly 'sayable' or permissible forms that are endorsed by wider political constituencies unconnected to the Sangh.

Mainstreaming Hindutva: Civilizational power

In March 2020, the India Foundation held its sixth India Ideas Conclave in Tent City, Gujarat, a resort of luxury tents adjacent to the Statue of Unity, the 182-metre-tall statue of nationalist leader 'Sardar' Vallabhbhai Patel built by the BJP government in 2018 and touted as the world's tallest statue. Addressing the conclave theme, 'Turning to Roots, Rising to Heights', the keynote speaker and Indian external affairs minister, S. Jaishankar (2020), observed:

> We are considering these matters against the backdrop of a larger canvas of a dialogue of civilizations. By doing so, we are rightly recognizing the importance of tradition, culture and faith as key variables in global affairs. That in itself is an evolution from the more sweeping and less granular, I should honestly say condescending postulates of globalism....
>
> India has to demonstrate an Indian Way, one that delivers at home, embraces the world, contributes its fullest and expresses comfortably what its people really are. [T]he world has much riding on its success in doing so.

Jaishankar's speech touches on all the main themes of the civilizational power discourse that pervades right-wing think tank worlds. Since its inception in the early twentieth century, Hindu nationalism has propagated ideas of India's civilizational greatness. Founding ideologues like V. D. Savarkar, M. S. Golwalkar, and K. B. Hedgewar defined India's nationhood in terms of the civilizational unity and continuity that fused territory, history, culture, religion, and people into a singular and organic national community enduring across time. But even as it draws on these older lineages, the idea of the civilizational that is deployed by contemporary right-wing think tanks and reproduced in Jaishankar's speech differs quite markedly from these communitarian imaginaries of civilization as the crucible of national identity and belonging. Perhaps the biggest divergence has to do with the geopolitical and policy frameworks of contemporary civilizational discourse that link the idea of civilization to global assertions of state power and denote it as a principle and instrument of international relations and geopolitical strategy (Acharya 2020; Coker 2019).

Influenced by Samuel Huntington's 'clash of civilizations' thesis of civilizational difference as the ground and axis of international politics,[24] civilization is defined as a specific kind of power resource and strategic policy instrument for states to build and assert a global presence. In Jaishankar's words, it is a 'key variable in global affairs', and moreover is one that requires careful cultivation and dedicated work, as the exhortatory terms of his speech suggest. In other words, contemporary civilizational discourse has a programmatic and prescriptive more than an analytical import. Moving beyond the causal explanation that civilization provides in Huntington's work (civilizational clash explains patterns of international conflict), contemporary right-wing think tanks in India define civilizational power in instrumental terms and present it as a policy recommendation and geopolitical doctrine or grand strategy.[25]

In this contemporary usage, civilizational power has four main attributes. First, it is selectively invested in certain states. Contrasted with the ubiquitous nation-state form that has dominated the world for well over a century, the civilizational state is defined as a rare entity that reflects a unique conjunction of particular kinds of historical, territorial, and demographic factors, namely historical depth and continuity, territorial expanse, and demographic diversity. India is glossed as such a conjunctive formation. Think tank discourses repeatedly stress the millennia of unbroken traditions,[26] the vast and varied territorial expanse, and the diverse populations that are integrated into peaceful coexistence by some ineffable yet enduring mechanism.

This definition of the civilizational state and civilizational power as an expression and function of coming together in difference – 'seeking harmony in diversity', as the motto of Vivekananda International Foundation puts it – diverges markedly from the homogenous imaginaries of the nation-state. Civilizational discourse makes much of this divergence, juxtaposing the long histories of expansive and tolerant civilizational power to the cultural uniformities of the nation-state form, seen as a recent and western invention that was imposed upon the world by the violence of imperial conquest. 'Much before the western political concept of nation and state, Indians have shared well-defined values of civilization and culture', proclaimed Ravi Shankar Prasad, Indian law minister and long-time RSS worker and BJP leader, at the India Ideas Conclave in 2020.

The west–non-west binary brings us to the second attribute of civilizational power, namely its constitutive anti-westernism and association with languages of victimhood and resistance. As Bruno Maçães, the Portuguese politician and scholar, observed upon his encounter with civilizational discourse during a recent visit to India, 'contemporary India is a wounded civilization asserting itself.... Civilizations are an alternative to the West' (2020). The project of recuperating civilizational power and restoring India's glory as a civilizational state is usually framed as one of resisting and undoing western dominance by moving beyond the oppressive strictures of a liberal nation-statist world order. Recall Jaishankar's description of the alternative world order configured by civilizational power as a welcome progression or 'evolution' from 'the condescending postulates of globalism' and normative western liberal order.[27] For Jaishankar, this evolution does not take place unbidden. Rather, it is a deliberate intervention that aims for a 'rebalancing'; a considered assertion of political agency by 'societies who were victimized for decades, if not centuries, by the West'. The assertion of Indian civilization to counter the 'age old' dominance of the west invariably takes a strident and even angry form of expression. As television anchor Arnab Goswami railed at the India Ideas Conclave of 2020, 'It is time to stop constantly seeking the approval of those who will not give you approval.... We don't need their certification, do we have the courage to say this?'

Third, civilizational power is a comparative and hierarchical concept. The figuration of India in civilizational terms is not only an assertion of distinction and uniqueness, it is also a claim about India's superior global status. Thus, in Jaishankar's speech, 'the Indian Way' is hailed as an exemplary 'demonstration' for a wider global audience; 'the world has much riding on its success'. For Ravi Shankar Prasad, Indian civilization with its 'linkage with the sacred' provides the solution that the western models of unbridled capitalism and 'totalitarian' communism have been unable to provide.[28] Indian genius, a familiar phrase in think tank discussions, reflects the hierarchical contours of civilizational discourse. Think tank events like the annual conclaves are occasions for asserting, often in high hyperbole, India's uniqueness and superiority on all fronts. For the prime minister of Bhutan in his 2014 conclave address, Indian civilization was the world's greatest civilization. The Dalai Lama concurred: 'the different ideas and philosophies that filled my brain come from India'.[29]

These claims of civilizational greatness position India as a leader on the world stage, with ready solutions to so many of the urgent problems bearing down on the troubled present. The high praise of pro-Hindutva academic David Frawley's call to 'preserve India's genius and reapply it to solve modern problems' and BJP external affairs minister Sushma Swaraj's confident proclamation that 'the civilizational legacy of India can provide a new way [and] be an antidote to the medieval barbarity being practiced by terrorist groups like the Taliban, IS, and Boko Haram' were declarations specifically crafted for the grand spectacle of the inaugural India Ideas Conclave in 2014.

But similar sentiments also pervade everyday think tank worlds. Publications and seminars routinely hail Indian versions of democracy, secularism, multicultural tolerance, and conflict resolution for their effectiveness and authenticity – they are examples of true tolerance, real democracy, lasting peace – and for being intrinsically better than western models. Celebrations of Indian *dharmocracy* as the unique configuration of a democracy based on 'moral authority',[30] of the four-fold caste order of *varnashramadharma* as an ideal social order,[31] and of the 'power of balance rather than the balance of power'[32] that has characterized the unique Indian approach to international relations, all construct Indian civilization as an invaluable resource not just for the contemporary nation, but for the entire world.

These encomiums are related to the final distinguishing attribute of civilizational power, namely the anodyne forms of its expression, and its associations with legitimate, socially and politically acceptable norms and values. For instance, speaking at the Indic Thoughts festival in 2017, BJP leader and RSS ideologue Ram Madhav declared that 'Indian thought is the most democratically evolved and most liberal in the world'. In a similar vein, Jaishankar in his keynote address to the India Ideas Conclave in 2020 defined the civilizational turn as a democratizing move that rejects 'elitist globalism' and 'take[s] power beyond the confines of the established elites'. India's civilizational power proves that 'a large democratic world exists beyond the west, one that gives democracy and pluralism a more universal appeal', he argued. Other examples abound, of how the call to civilizational awakening is invariably framed in terms of democracy, tolerance, harmony, peace – as an unobjectionable and indeed a compelling invitation that few can refuse or resist.[33]

This in turn draws attention to the semiotic gaps and glosses of the civilizational project and how the open-ended conception of civilization serves as ideological shorthand and translation. What is civilization: is it culture, ethnicity, religion, some combination of these, or something else altogether? How are civilizational boundaries determined? What kind of a category is the Indic and what defines the Indian way of life, a key term of civilizational discourse? The slippages and confusions that attend these questions allow multiple meanings to be layered upon the core idea of civilization, and formally disavowed sentiments to be tacitly communicated to wider publics. In the name of civilization, right-wing think tanks conflate the Indian, Indic, and the Hindu. According to Sanjeev Sanyal, the Principal Economic Advisor to the Indian government and a prominent author in Hindutva circles, Hindu thought traditions comprise the universe of 'Indian ways of thinking' and 'Indian schools of governance'.[34] Elaborating the sacred geography of 'our heritage', Ravi Shankar Prasad quickly and easily slides into the exclusive registers of Hindu space:

> [B]e it Kedarnath or Kanyakumari or Vaishno Devi or Rameshwaram, or the Adi Shakti sitting everywhere, or the way the Shankaracharya set up the four Maths, all have clearly concretized the idea of a civilizational and cultural India.[35]

The principle of civilizational difference is evoked to place Muslims outside Indian civilization, as inheritors of a different way of life. Sushma Swaraj's distinction between 'Indian civilization' and 'medieval barbarity' at the inaugural India Ideas conclave shows that Islam can be denied civilizational status altogether. The named groups of uncivilized 'barbarians' in her speech all just happen to be professing versions of Islamist ideology. In all these instances, standard tropes of Hindutva ideology such as the constitution of India as a Hindu-first nation and the intrinsic otherness of Muslims are disseminated implicitly via insinuations and 'dog whistles' to insider audiences. At the same time, the explicit idioms of civilizational *politesse* and the salutary visions of democracy, tolerance, secularism, and even liberalism that are formally embraced (recall Ram Madhav's comments cited earlier) engage and attract a wide range of Hindutva outsiders.

These dual registers of communication work together to translate Hindutva discourse and connect Sangh organizations to wider political and social constituencies. Even as they tacitly communicate core themes of Hindu nationalism, the formulations of civilizational discourse resonate beyond the immediate ideological worlds of Hindutva. For instance, the idea of Indian civilization as a global trailblazer aligns quite neatly with the mainstream national imaginaries of rising India that dominate our present. These are equally concerned with India's global recognition and status, and narrate similar triumphal arcs of India's victory on the global stage. Thus, echoing the think tank discourses on Indian genius and their efforts to establish India as the civilizational origin of all kinds of human and social innovations, commercial news media are quick to claim and celebrate the Indian origins of any prominent global figure, even notorious ones, from Nobel Prize winners and US vice-presidential candidates to embezzlers and conmen.

The think tank focus on the Indic, and the quest to illuminate a distinctive Indian way, also converges with contemporary intellectual and public cultural engagements with the indigenous and the vernacular, whether the case studies of resourceful Indian *jugaad* ('frugal improvisation') in business school curricula (Kaur 2016) or the burgeoning genre of 'pop mythology' bestsellers that package Hindu myths as civilizational truths and inheritances for their Indian audiences. Right-wing think tanks regularly draw in practitioners from these fields to participate in their events. For instance, recent India Ideas conclaves have seen mythological bestseller authors like Amish Tripathi and capitalists like Anand Mahindra[36] discuss civilizational themes with committed Sangh ideologues.

Civilizational discourse also fosters transnational connections. International speakers, from academics to heads of states, are regular participants in right-wing think tank events. Recent interlocutors at India Ideas conclaves have included the former heads of state of Jordan, the Netherlands, Slovenia, Bhutan; the former secretary general of the Organization of Islamic States; US Representative Tulsi Gabbard; Israeli ambassador to India Daniel Carmon; representatives of international think tanks such as Daniel Pipes (Middle East Forum), Sadanand Dhume (American Enterprise Institute), Daniel Twining (German Marshall Fund and International Republican Institute), Shamika Ravi (Brookings), and

Jean-Christophe Bas (Dialogue of Civilizations Research Institute). In 2019, the India Foundation was selected to be the official hub and interlocutor of an international network created by the Dialogue of Civilizations Research Institute, an international think tank founded by the Russian oligarch Vladimir Yakunin with the stated mandate of 'bring[ing] together diverse perspectives from the developed and the developing worlds in a non-confrontational and constructive spirit'.[37]

In sum, 'civilization' in the repertoire of right-wing think tanks is an open-ended umbrella term that brings together a diverse collection of actors with varied interests and stakes. The ambivalent meanings of civilizational discourse take Hindutva actors beyond their immediate ideological world and place them in polite company, recognized as legitimate and acceptable interlocutors by other sets of political, economic, and cultural elites within and beyond India.

These connections are forged through embodied encounters and interactions that take place in concrete locations. Think tanks have material infrastructures; Hindutva is mainstreamed and networked through tangible sets of actions, by people going to certain places and doing certain things. The annual convention or 'conclave' organized by right-wing think tanks that has been mentioned several times in the course of this chapter is one such place. The following section takes a closer look at this, at what we might describe, following Bruno Latour, as a key 'mediator' of the Hindutva project (Latour 2007).[38]

Networks and Opaque Publicities: The Conclave

Every year, Indian right-wing think tanks host events where political, economic, and cultural elites convene to discuss issues of pressing public and policy importance. Some of these are one-off or singular events, for example, the 'National Security Convention' that the Forum of Integrated Security's Jammu and Kashmir unit organized in Haridwar in 2010 and the Public Policy Research Council's 'Thinkathon for New India' in 2018. Others like the India Ideas Conclave of the India Foundation and the 'Samvad Global Hindu Buddhist Initiative' of the Vivekananda International Foundation are repeated at regular intervals.

These events are not limited to right-wing milieus. The think tank meeting calendar also includes the annual Raisina Dialogues organized by the ORF, the Ananta Aspen Centre's 'Ideas India' meetings, the annual Think20 Mumbai (T20 Mumbai) conference organized by Gateway House, and numerous events outside India as well. Since at least the middle decades of the twentieth century, meetings of 'private international policy groups' have been organized in different locations around the world (Carroll and Carson 2006; Friesen 2020; Ojala 2017; Pigman 2007; Rothkopf 2008). Meetings of the Mont Pèlerin Society, the

Bilderberg group, the Trilateral Commission, and the World Economic Forum in Davos are well-known annual gatherings of 'transnational elites', which offer a 'synthesis of public and private elements from states and societies of the capitalist world' (Carroll and Carson 2006, 53).

As many scholars have noted, these events serve as sites and instruments of 'international elite integration' (Carrroll and Carson 2006, 54). The opportunities for off-the-record interpersonal interactions, the use of specific kinds of communicative formats and modes of discussion and presentation, and the extensive media coverage and publicity relays of these high-profile events produce collective identification with a transnational elite identity. The right-wing think tank events organized in India also have an additional function, of legitimizing and 'credentialing' governmental Hindutva. In other words, they enable processes of elite formation, asserting and making visible the authoritative presence of Hindu nationalist actors within the political establishment, as members of the national 'power elite'.

Although populist themes of anti-establishment anger dominate the discourse of contemporary Hindutva organizations, their actual practices stray from these rhetorical commitments. Indeed, as the events organized by right-wing think tank show, Hindutva actors and organizations are quite centrally invested in claiming and demonstrating their proximity to and recognition by the very sets of actors routinely disparaged as the 'Lutyens elite'.[39] Conventions and conclaves are structured as carefully choreographed spaces of inter-elite interaction and conviviality, where a wide range of political, economic, and cultural elites can be seen to engage in collegial dialogue with their Hindutva counterparts on matters of mutual public concern. Ensuring the participation of recognized establishment figures from non-Sangh backgrounds – from prominent liberal public intellectuals to figures associated with the previous Congress regime – is a key priority.

Take for example the India Ideas Conclave organized annually by the India Foundation that features at least sixty speakers and over a hundred invited guests each year. All six editions of the conclave, the largest and most well publicized of Indian right-wing think tank events in India, have featured a wide range of 'eminent persons' from around the world, representing a broad spectrum of political–ideological commitments. The following tables summarize conclave themes and participation and provide an overview of the elite diversities that are carefully curated each year.

Table 4.3 India Ideas Conclave – Snapshot of participants

Government ministers + Executive	Arun Jaitley, Sushma Swaraj, Ravi Shankar Prasad, Suresh Prabhu, Nirmala Sitharaman, Piyush Goyal, Jayant Sinha, M. J. Akbar, Amit Shah, Venkaiah Naidu, Satyapal Singh, Hardeep Singh Puri
Parliament	Swapan Dasgupta, (Rajya Sabha), Chandan Mitra (Rajya Sabha), Rajeev Chandrashekhar (Rajya Sabha), Roopa Ganguly (Rajya Sabha), Harivansh Singh (Rajya Sabha), Jay Panda (Lok Sabha), Geetha Kothapalli (Lok Sabha)
State governments	Manohar Parrikar (Goa), Laxmikant Pareskar (Goa), Shivraj Singh Chouhan (MP), Archana Chitnis (MP), Himanta Biswa Sarma (Assam), Ajay Bisht/Yogi Adityanath (UP), Raja Shekhar Vundru (Haryana)
Other	Lokesh Chandra (Indian Council for Cultural Research), A Surya Prakash (Prasar Bharati), Lalitha Kumaramangalam (National Commission for Women), Shakti Sinha (Nehru Memorial), Jagadesh Kumar (Jawaharlal Nehru University), Sunaina Singh (Nalanda University), Rathin Roy (Niti Ayog), Shankar Saran (National Council for Educational Research and Training), Shamika Ravi (Prime Minister's Economic Advisory Council), Satish Marathe (Reserve Bank of India), Justice Permod Kohli, P. S. Narasimha (Additional Solicitor General), Sanjeev Sanyal (Prime Minister's Economic Advisory Council), Surya Prakash (Prasar Bharati)
Sangh (incl. BJP)	Ram Madhav, Subramaniam Swamy, Dattatreya Hosabale, Ashok Chowgule, Nupur Sharma, Suresh 'Bhaiyyaji' Joshi, Mohan Bhagwat, Krishna Gopal, Amit Malviya, Malavika Avinash, Sanjay Paswan
Other parties	Mufti Mohammad Sayeed (PDP), Mehbooba Mufti (PDP), Haseeb Drabu (PDP), Sajjad Lone (JKPC), Jaya Jaitley (Samata), Kumar Vishwas (AAP), Jayaprakash Narayan (Loksatta)
Civil service, Military	G. Parthasarathy (ex-ambassador), Veena Sikri (ex-ambassador), Gen. V. P. Malik
Religious	Sri Sri Ravi Shankar (Art of Living), Swami Dayananda Saraswati (Hindu Acharya Dharma Sabha), Sadguru Jaggi Vasudev (Isha Foundation), Maulana Mehmood Madani (Jamiat Ulema-e-Hind), Swami Tejomayananda (Chinmaya Mission), Dalai Lama, Sri M (Satsang Foundation)

Culture, Academic, Writers	Arvind Panagariya, Meghnad Desai, Amish Tripathi, David Frawley, Koenraad Elst, Dinesh Singh, Patrick French, Joe D'Cruz, Aatish Taseer, Amish Tripathi, Madhu Kishwar, Walter Andersen, Subhash Kashyap, Harsh Pant, Vivek Agnihotri, Rupa Subramanya, Hindol Sengupta, Zafar Sareshwala, Rajeev Srinivasan, Sirivenella Sitarama Sastry, Bharatbala, Minhaz Merchant, Badri Narayan, Pralay Kanungo, Manisha Priyam, Abhinav Singh, Makarand Paranjape, V. Ananta Nageswaran, Advaita Kala, Vikram Sampath
Media	Sultan Shahin, Amar Govindarajan, Tavleen Singh, Shekhar Gupta, Aroon Purie, Raj Chengappa, Ashok Malik, Kanchan Gupta, Nistula Hebbar, Shefali Vaidya, Arnab Goswami, Aarti Tikoo, Abhijit Majumder, Prashant Jha, Liz Mathew, Madhav Das Nalapat, Rahul Pandita, Abhijit Iyer-Mitra, Marya Shakil, Prafulla Ketkar, Shweta Singh, Raghavan Jagannathan, S. Prasannarajan, Sanjaya Baru
Economic	Vallabh Bhansali, Sumant Sinha, Milind Kamble (Dalit Indian Chamber of Commerce), Pratyush Kumar (Boeing India), Mohandas Pai, Yogini Deshpande, Grandhi Mallikarjuna Rao, Rajiv Lall, Anand Mahindra
International	Ekmeleddin Ihsanoglu (Organisation of Islamic Cooperation, ex-Secretary General), Ruud Lubbers (Netherlands, ex-Prime Minister), Abdelsalam al-Majali (Jordan, ex- Prime Minister), Chandrika Kumaratunga (Sri Lanka, ex-President), Alojz Peterle (Slovenia, ex-Prime Minister), Jigme Thinley (Bhutan, ex-Prime Minister), Sher Bahadur Deuba (Nepal, ex-Prime Minister), Pushpa Prachanda (Nepal, ex-Prime Minister), Zaki Nusseibeh (UAE, Cultural Advisor), Mohamed Nasheed (Maldives, ex-President), Naheed Farid (Afghanistan, Parliamentarian), Nyamdavaa Oidov (Mongolia, Ambassador), Daniel Carmon (Israel, Ambassador), Shaida Abdali (Afghanistan, Ambassador), James Tien (Taiwan, Trade Representative), Lobsang Sangay (Sikyong, Central Tibetan Administration), Dinesh Gunawardena (Sri Lanka, Minister), Carlos Magarinos (UNIDO, Director-General), Gunnar Stalsett (Norway, Bishop), Sadanand Dhume (American Enterprise Institute), Daniel Twining (German Marshall Fund), Daniel Pipes (Middle East Forum), Viktor Vekselberg (Skolkovo Foundation), Jean-Christopher Bas (Dialogue of Civilizations Research Institute),Tariq Ramadan (scholar), Tufail Ahmad (journalist), Tarek Fatah (journalist), Taslima Nasreen (writer)
Other	Laxmi Narayan Tripathi (transgender activist) Mohit Chouhan (music), Indian Ocean(music), Tana Bana (music), Lobsang Phuntsok (social work – Bhutan)

Source: India Ideas Conclave annual reports.

Table 4.4 India Ideas Conclave – Themes

Year	Location	Theme
2014	Park Hyatt Hotel, Goa	Integral Human Development
2015	Marriott Resort and Spa, Goa	Learning from Civilization
2016	The Lalit Golf & Spa Resort, Goa	India at 70: Democracy, Development, Dissent
2017	Grand Hyatt, Goa	Leadership in the 21st Century
2018	Andaz Hotel, Delhi	Citizen's Manifesto: Churn of Ideas
2020	Tent City – Statue of Unity, Gujarat	New India: Turning to Roots, Rising to Heights

Source: India Ideas Conclave annual reports.

Unsurprisingly, individuals in leadership positions within various Sangh organizations are a large and influential group at these events. Every conclave has featured high-ranking state officials and elected representatives from the BJP in prominent roles of keynote speaker, valedictorian, or chief guest. The RSS also has a strong presence at conclave events, with senior leaders such as Mohan Bhagwat, Dattatreya Hosabale, Krishna Gopal, and Suresh 'Bhaiyyaji' Joshi billed as lead speakers. Reflecting the Sangh's quick occupation of nodal state and parastatal institutions following the BJP's electoral victory in 2014, committed Hindu nationalist ideologues leading institutions such as the national public service broadcaster Prasar Bharati, Jawaharlal Nehru University, Indian Institute of Advanced Studies, the Nehru Memorial Museum and Library, and the Indian Council for Cultural Relations have also participated in these events in their dual capacities as state representatives as well as representatives of Hindutva.

The strong and visible presence of Sangh forces at the India Ideas Conclave defines it as an unmistakably saffron milieu. The range of institutions represented at these events, from right-wing think tanks to apex cabinet ministries and major national universities, attests to the wide extent of Hindutva's diffusion across establishment spaces. But the conclave is not a homogenous space of Hindutva assertion. Its functions of legitimation and networking are fulfilled through the visible participation of actors representing a diversity of institutional and political–ideological interests. Recognition and normative acceptance are also conferred by the presence of international participants, and each conclave has seen the active involvement of numerous dignitaries from outside India, such as present and former heads of state, leaders of international organizations, think tank counterparts, academics, journalists, and public intellectuals. As Table 4.3

shows, conclave speakers have included cultural and religious leaders from multiple faiths; intellectuals, writers, filmmakers, actors, and artists; media professionals; capitalists and entrepreneurs; politicians from rival political parties;[40] and civil society representatives and social workers. Among these are several individuals who are well known and self-identified as liberal and secular figures, including those who have spoken and written critically about the BJP and Hindutva such as the authors Patrick French and Aatish Taseer, the editor Shekhar Gupta, and academics Manisha Priyam and Pralay Kanungo.

Sessions on transgender activism and Dalit identity,[41] and cultural programs that feature activist music performed by the popular rock band Indian Ocean and the songs of the Bhakti poet Kabir, a celebrated icon of inter-religious coexistence, add to the intended design of the conclave (and of its institutional host, the right-wing think tank) as an open and tolerant space that welcomes and encourages the free expression of independent opinions and progressive worldviews. The invitations extended to prominent Muslim religious leaders, politicians, and authors perform a similar function of 'virtue-signalling' the conclave's tolerant and open-minded constitution as a reasonable, moderate, and altogether unobjectionable discursive space. The selection of discussion themes that are pitched at a high level of generality (see Table 4.4) and the choice of dialogic presentation formats such as 'conversation with ...', roundtables, and debates add to the impression of rational civility.

However, this remains at all times a selective civility that does not stray from the script of Hindutva ideology. As the preceding discussion of civilizational discourse has noted already, the general and anodyne rhetoric of right-wing think tanks conforms to and reproduces the normative ideals of Hindu nationalism, whether the identification of Indian civilizational greatness with the Hindu religion, or the othering of Islam as a global and national enemy. The choice of international guests and Muslim representatives who are well known for their critiques of Islam enables Islamophobic ideas to be advanced at the conclave in the form of authentic 'insider' auto-critiques by figures like Taslima Nasreen, Tarek Fatah, and Tariq Ramadan. Through their repeated declarations of preferential love for India, Nasreen and Adnan Sami, a Pakistani-origin singer who recently naturalized as an Indian citizen, also confirm the binary opposition between the fundamentalist Islam of Pakistan and Bangladesh and the tolerant Hinduism of India and perform Muslim choice and acceptance of Hindu-Indian sovereignty.[42]

The discussion so far has focused on the performative and visual aspects of the conclave: how curated diversity displays and dialogic performances of inter-elite interaction and recognition can further the translation and mainstreaming of Hindutva. Publicity is thus a key element of event design. Conclaves are spectacular events staged in luxury hotels in picturesque tourist destinations. Considerable efforts are extended to disseminate a preferred message about the grand success of the conclave to wider public constituencies within and beyond India. But this is not all. Conclaves involve considerable secrecy and opacity as well, and several key aspects of their organization remain hidden and murky. For instance, there is little public information about the financial sponsorship of conclaves. Who pay for these lavish events, and why? What are the funding sources of the India Foundation, the parent organization? These questions go unanswered (Ahmad 2019).

The absence of public information and accountability obscures the conflicts of interest that conclaves create. For instance, it was only through the dedicated work of an investigative journalist from *The Wire* news site (Chaturvedi 2017) that the sponsors of India Foundation events were revealed to include aerospace corporations from Israel and the United States (Magal and Boeing, respectively). But in the absence of any public information there can only be speculation about the nexus of interests that such events enable. In sum, the work of the conclave – and of its institutional host and organizer the right-wing think tank – is as much to publicize as it is to obscure the networks that thrive in its closed and shadowy worlds.

The opacities are aided by the informal character of the networks involved, which are often embodied in a single individual whose life and work transects multiple domains of power. The right-wing think tank ecosystem sees a few nodal individuals exercise a great deal of influence as 'connector' figures linked to multiple think tanks as well as to state and societal domains of power. Vinay Sahasrabuddhe is a prime example. A national vice president of the BJP, Sahasrabuddhe plays a senior leadership role in four different think tanks (Syama Prasad Mookerjee Research Foundation, India Foundation, India Policy Foundation, and Public Policy Research Foundation). His work also spans pivotal domains of state and social power: he is the president of the Indian Council for Cultural Relations, the apex state agency for 'external cultural policy', and a 'founder–functionary' of the Rambhau Malghi Prabodhini, an RSS organization (Sahasrabuddhe is a lifetime volunteer of the RSS).

Other, albeit less densely networked figures in the right-wing think tank field include A. Surya Prakash, associated with three think tanks as well as the national public broadcast authority Prasar Bharati; Swapan Dasgupta, a journalist, public intellectual and parliamentarian (member of the Rajya Sabha) who is involved with the India Foundation and the Syama Prasad Mookerjee Research Foundation; Kapil Kapoor, a former professor of Jawaharlal Nehru University, current chairperson of the Indian Institute of Advanced Studies, and senior leader of the India Policy Foundation and the Vivekananda International Foundation; and

Aniruddha Rajput, India's representative at the International Labour Conference (a United Nations organization) and a leader of the India Foundation and the Jammu Kashmir Study Centre.

These informal relations and opacities of rule are not unique to the right-wing think tank nor to the current moment of Hindu nationalist ascendance. As the introductory sections of this essay have noted, our story must move beyond the present to engage wider and older dynamics of state transformation and economic liberalization in India and the field of extra-electoral authority and networked power that they have constituted. Hindutva is not the only occupant of this field. Alongside the right-wing think tank are its counterpart institutions like the ORF, Carnegie India, Brookings India, Gateway House, and others that also engage in similar efforts of policy influence and political mediation.

All these institutions interact quite closely with each other. Although they are fuelled by diverse political and economic interests – arguably the Carnegie Endowment for International Peace and the Sangh Parivar have divergent stakes in the new India project – Indian think tanks participate in and sustain a shared elite community of expert influence. They attend one another's events and draw on a common pool of expertise and personnel. They advance common ideas about new India's global potency using similar modular formats of 'eminent' dialogue and debate before invitational publics.[43] They engage in similar practices of opaque publicities where the dazzle and glamour of important people in lavish settings veils the informal deals struck offstage in ways we do not and cannot know, and they collaboratively shape and sustain the networks of elite power that traverse Indian democracy today.

In sum, the right-wing think tank is part of an ecosystem that overlaps and intersects Hindutva and millennial capitalist projects; it is informed by both sets of imperatives. We need to look at these intersections as well, and at the wider enabling contexts of the immediate Hindutva moment. We can trace a crooked line that connects the 'porous state' (Sinha 2019) and its penumbral sovereignties that were formed in the latter decades of the twentieth century under the sign of economic liberalization, with the networked order of millennial Hindutva that governs our present.

Conclusion: *The Central Vista Elite*

The world of the Indian right-wing think tank offers three insights into the political character of governmental Hindutva, the dominant but analytically overlooked form of Hindu nationalism in contemporary India. First, governmental Hindutva is invested in institutional innovation and the creation of new infrastructures of rule. Contradicting the direct rule fantasies of populist discourse, authoritarian populism legitimizes the role and authority of intermediary institutions such as the right-wing think tank. Second, the closed and select circles of right-wing think tank worlds remind us that governmental Hindutva is a project of elite formation. Anti-elitism is the leitmotif of populist politics across the globe and Hindutva political discourse is no exception. Outrage and anger against the 'Lutyens elite' and the 'Khan Market gang'[44] suffuse the public discourse of Hindu nationalism. But this does not mean that governmental Hindutva is a non-elite formation. Anti-elitism is more a rhetorical device than a sociological and empirical fact.

The view into right-wing think tank milieus reveals that Hindutva establishment elites continue to derive their authority and their privileged immunities of power from the social hierarchies that have long constituted India's deeply unequal society. The overwhelmingly male, caste-privileged, Hindu-dominated worlds of right-wing think tanks call our attention to the formation of a Hindutva establishment that is structured and sustained by the cruel inequalities of power that populism rails against. To use the neologism of media commentator Aunindyo Chakravarty, 'Central Vista elites' are taking the place of Lutyens elites in the age of governmental Hindutva.[45] Chakravarty's neologism captures well the dual aspects of governmental Hindutva's elite formation project. At one level, the term highlights newness and substitution: Central Vista instead of Lutyens. At another level, it references the sociological fact of elite continuity: after all, the Central Vista is the geographic and symbolic core of Lutyens Delhi. These continuities and overlaps between old and new formations of power call into question the democratic claims of authoritarian populism and its promise of bringing power to the people. We can confront the normative sleight of hand and the slippage that is at its core, and ask who exactly the people are in the first place.

These questions lead to the third and final insight which relates to how we study Hindutva and other comparative instances of authoritarian populism. The existence and influence of institutions such as right-wing think tanks suggest a move beyond the prevailing frameworks of deviance and exceptionalism that structure existing discussions. The institutional infrastructures and elite manoeuvres of governmental Hindutva highlighted in this essay remind us that while there is much that is monstrous and directly violent about Hindu nationalist politics, there is much that is unexceptional and routinized as well. The relationship between these two registers of the norm and the exception should remain in focus. To understand the fit or articulation of Hindutva in Indian democracy, the ways in which it disperses within, inhabits, and relates to established patterns of democratic politics, is the task at hand.

Notes

1. There have been BJP governments in power at the state and local levels for several decades, and two previous instances when the BJP formed the national government in a coalition with other political parties, in 1996 for thirteen days, and from 1998 until 2004. However, it is only after the majority electoral victories of 2014 and 2019 that the party has free reign to establish its distinctive political vision of a Hindu nationalist India and the career of Hindutva national rule has taken off.

2. Two prominent Indian think tanks have engaged in foreign policy and international relations/strategic studies research and advocacy since the early decades of the Indian republic: the Indian Council of World Affairs (ICWA) and the Institute for Defence Studies and Analyses (IDSA), founded in 1943 and 1965, respectively. Both had strong institutional links to the Indian state from their inception. The vice-president of India and the minister of external affairs are the *ex-officio* presiding officers of the ICWA, and K. Subrahmanyam, a senior civil servant in the Defence Ministry and widely acknowledged as a leading figure in India's state security complex, served as director of IDSA from 1965 until 1975. In the field of development and social policy, there are several institutions that have performed policy research functions in India since the early post-colonial years. However, they have also engaged in other kinds of developmental and participatory research activities, or else have developed a more academic profile (for example, Centre for Policy Research, Centre for the Study of Developing Societies) and thus diverge from the conventional format of the think tank as an institution with an exclusive focus on policy formation.

3. At times, elected representatives have also engaged in policy formulation on subjects in which they have a direct and personal interest, for example, Jawaharlal Nehru's close involvement with foreign policy and economic planning policy, and Rajiv Gandhi's hands-on approach to technology and communications policy. For an analysis of Indian foreign policy formations, see Bajpai and Pant (2013) and Mattoo and Medcalf (2015).

4. In 2020, Brookings India was reconstituted as the Centre for Social and Economic Progress (CSEP), an independent public policy think tank.

5. Three defense-policy-focused think tanks associated with the different branches of the armed forces were also established in this period: the Centre for Air Power Studies, the Centre for Land and Warfare Studies, and the National Maritime Foundation.

6. DDRI was set up at a time of Hindutva's strategic modulation, when the goal of seeking power through the electoral system was a main priority (Fox 1987; Hansen 1999; Jaffrelot 1999). Seizing the political opportunity presented by the electoral defeats and leadership crises that had recently rocked the dominant Congress party, Hindu nationalists in the late 1960s invested their organizational energies in a political-electoral front and approach that sought to work through the existing political field, aligning and entangling Hindutva ideology with establishment discourses of mainstream political culture (Fox 1987; Hansen; 1999, Jaffrelot 1999). Set up as a research institute based in Delhi that would engage with political and governmental actors and institutions both within and outside the Sangh, the DDRI's agenda and programme reflected these

mainstreaming impulses. Many of the activities that the organization carried out in its early years were aligned with the reigning discourses of official nationalism. The 'rural uplift' program of creating self-reliant model villages that was launched in the late 1960s by Nanaji Deshmukh, the 1970 seminar on nuclear policy that made a strong case for Indian nuclearization, and the commemorative celebration of the life of the national leader 'JP' Jayaprakash Narayan organized in 1980 were all activities that endorsed and amplified accepted themes of Indian politics. Moreover, as the presence of the radical humanist and pioneering civil liberties activist lawyer V. M. Tarkunde as a speaker at the JP commemoration event showed, these events frequently involved a wide cross-section of individuals who did not profess Hindutva ideology, and contributed to the DDRI's self-positioning as a nonpartisan institution concerned with the wider national interest beyond party and ideology. See *Times of India*, 23 August 1970; 1 October 1980.

7 The complete title is the 'TTCSP Global Go To Think Tank Index Report'. Global and regional rankings of think tanks are published each year by the Think Tanks and Civil Society Program (TTCSP) of the Lauder Institute, a research institute at the University of Pennsylvania. Twenty-nine Indian think tanks feature in the latest edition of the index (2019). Of these, two are right-wing think tanks: The Vivekananda International Foundation and the India Foundation. The report is available at https://repository.upenn.edu/think_tanks/17/ (accessed on 30 September 2020).

8 For an in-depth account of the multiple networks mediated by Ajit Doval, the founder-director of the Vivekananda International Foundation, and by his son Shaurya Doval, a founder of the India Foundation, see the investigative reports by Donthi (2017a, 2017b) and Chaturvedi (2017). The Vivekananda International Foundation is a major institutional conduit that connects Hindutva ideologues to governmental positions. According to Srijan Shukla and Neelam Pandey's tally of individuals from the Vivekananda International Foundation who have been appointed to key government positions following the BJP victory in 2014, 'prominent appointments include S. Gurumurthy to [the] Reserve Bank of India's Monetary Policy Board, Anil Baijal as Delhi's lieutenant governor, V. K. Saraswat to the NITI Aayog, K. G. Suresh as the director general of the Indian Institute of Mass Communication, Arvind Gupta as deputy NSA, A. Surya Prakash as the chairperson of Prasar Bharti, and Arif Mohammed Khan as the governor of Kerala', see Shukla and Pandey (2019).

9 Writing about think tanks for the pro-Hindutva *Swarajya* magazine, journalist Rupa Subramanya noted, 'The creation of a non-left, non-politically correct, centre right ecosystem ... is slowly taking shape in India' (Subramanya 2016).

10 The table thus excludes organizations such as the Drishti Stree Adhyayan Prabhodan Kendra of Pune. This is also a policy-research-focused organization identified as a think tank and with demonstrated Sangh ties to its parent organization, the RSS. However, the public embrace of Hindutva ideology and explicit alignment with a Hindu *rashtra* (Hindu-majoritarian state) project means that it does not share the translational or mainstreaming commitments of its rightwing counterparts.

11 Anti-communist opinions are commonly expressed in these circles, whether denunciations of the 'totalitarian methods' of communist rule in the Soviet bloc or, closer

home, the follies of left state governments within India, most notably the Left Front regime that ruled West Bengal for more than two decades (2007–2011). Individuals like Deep Halder, a journalist who recently published an oral history of the Marichjhapi massacre of 1979 that indicts the Left Front government of West Bengal for its role in forcibly evicting and killing thousands of mostly Dalit refugees from Marichjhapi island in the Sundarbans delta region, are featured speakers at right-wing think tank events. The India Foundation and the Syama Prasad Mookerjee Foundation have hosted Halder's presentations in recent months, and he has also been invited speaker at the Pondy Lit Fest, an annual literary festival in Pondicherry organized by prominent supporters of Hindutva ideology (Makarand Paranjape, a self-described 'right' academic from Jawaharlal Nehru University was the founding curator of the festival). See Halder (2019).

12   The mix varies across think tanks, for example, FINS is heavily dominated by retired naval officers while retired diplomats feature prominently in the leadership ranks of the Vivekananda International Foundation.

13   Based on public data available for six think tanks on our list: India Foundation, Vivekananda International Foundation, Syama Prasad Mookerjee Research Foundation, Forum for Integrated National Security, India Policy Foundation, and Public Policy Research Centre.

14   These include academics (the leadership of the India Policy Foundation is almost exclusively comprised of academics), and entrepreneurs. One of the leading figures of the India Foundation is Shaurya Doval, a venture capitalist and son of Ajit Doval, the National Security Advisor and a founding director of the Vivekananda International Foundation.

15   To take just a few examples: in 2020 the India Ideas Conclave hosted a special session on Ramjanmabhoomi featuring Krishna Gopal of the RSS and Bhupendra Yadav of the BJP, the Syama Prasad Mookerjee Research Foundation organized seminars on the Citizenship Amendment Act and on 'Pakistan's Perfidy in Kashmir' (4 June and 9 May, respectively).

16   Right-wing think tanks have also primed the ground for the BJP in the run-up to elections by framing the intellectual and public cultural agenda around particular topics that legitimize the BJP's political claims. For instance, Snigdhendu Bhattacharya has recently documented how the Syama Prasad Mookerjee Research Foundation played an important role in the BJP's efforts to build its base in West Bengal during the 2019 elections. The Foundation held a series of events throughout the state that drew attention to the Bengali lineages of Hindu nationalism and attempted to dispel the view of Hindutva as a 'Hindi heartland' movement (Bhattacharya 2020).

17   According to news reports, the Jammu Kashmir Study Centre had prepared a legal challenge to Article 35A and organized panel discussions on the topic in the summer of 2015, four years before the government changed Kashmir's constitutional status (Rai 2015).

18   On April 10 2013, a panel discussion at the India Foundation on 'Human Rights Violations in India and Pakistan' broached the topic of 'atrocities against minorities'

in these countries, and presented India as a safe haven for these persecuted groups. 'Religious intolerance in our neighboring countries today has led to various atrocities against minorities including Hindus, Sikhs, Buddhists, Christians as well as against other factions within Islam itself'. India Foundation Seminar, 10 April 2013, https://indiafoundation.in/event-reports/panel-discussion-on-human-rights-violation-in-bangladesh-and-pakistan/(accessed on 30 September 2020).

19 There is an interesting division of labour that reflects the hierarchical structure of the think tank. Most list a series of high-profile 'distinguished fellows' with non-permanent affiliating arrangements with the institution (for example, honorary fellow, temporary/visiting fellow, advisor), and a smaller number of full-time paid research fellows, who are considerably younger and come from academic backgrounds, many directly from postgraduate programmes.

20 The website of the Kautilya Fellows Programme is available online at http://kfp.indiafoundation.in/ (accessed on 30 September 2020).

21 See FINS press release on 'Sarhad ko Pranam 2012', https://samvada.org/?p=13758 (accessed on 30 September 2020).

22 'Forum for Integrated National Security Fans Patriotism Through Tourism', *Times of India*, 31 January 2014, https://timesofindia.indiatimes.com/city/goa/Forum-for-Integrated-National-Security-fans-patriotism-through-tourism/articleshow/29623786.cms? (accessed on 30 September 2020).

23 This is a general tendency, which is not limited to India, nor to the right-wing think tank context.

24 Huntington's classical realist understanding of international relations sees global order as a space and condition of anarchy, riven by permanently antagonistic conflict of power between self-interested strategic actors unbound by any kind of ethical or universalist commitment. The cessation of war and conflict, should it come about, is linked to strategic calculations of self-interest rather than to moral-utopian ideals (Huntington 1996).

25 This is not a twenty-first century invention. We see a version of this discourse at the time of India's founding as well, when Nehruvian foreign policy innovations in the 1950s were also framed in terms of a civilizational logic. Thus, the Panchashila doctrine of peaceful coexistence was defined as the realization of a civilizational commitment, as embodied by the Buddhist-Ashokan practices from the third century BCE. Note that this idea also involved a sleight of hand or slippage between civilization, culture, and religion, with religious doctrine (in this case, Buddhist doctrine) supplying the content and meaning of civilization.

26 See, for instance, the remarks of RSS leader Dattatreya Hosabale at the India Ideas Conclave in 2014: 'the RSS is not introducing anything new, only reiterating what has been said and practiced for millennia'.

27 See also Bajpai 2018, 114–5 on how civilizational discourse in both India and China combines claims about 'civilizational entitlement and colonial occupation' with a sense of victimhood.

28 See Prasad's speech at the India Ideas Conclave 2020.
29 The Dalai Lama, India Ideas Conclave, 2016.
30 See India Foundation, 'Rethinking Democracy and Beyond (A Plea for Dharmocracy)', https://indiafoundation.in/articles-and-commentaries/rethinking-democracy-and-beyond-a-plea-for-dharmocracy/ (accessed on 30 September 2020).
31 According to BJP leader and RSS ideologue Ram Madhav, what we know of as the caste system today has no connection to the *varnashrama* system of the Hindu *dharmashastras*. The latter 'never sanctioned any caste hierarchy; nor did it allow any discrimination'. See Ram Madhav Varanasi, 'What Dalits Want', https://indiafoundation.in/articles-and-commentaries/what-dalits-want/ (accessed on 30 September 2020).
32 M. J. Akbar, India Ideas Conclave, 2016.
33 In this discourse, civilization is itself conceived of as an essentially democratic and inclusive formation that 'harmonizes difference', unlike the homogenizing tendencies of the nation-state and liberal universalism. See the speech of Jean-Michael Bas, the president of the Dialogue of Civilizations Research Institute, at the India Ideas Conclave of 2020, on how civilization 'provides a moral compass' and is a new way of constructing world order, rejecting a 'flattening universalism' for the 'sharing' and 'harmonization' of difference.
34 According to Sanyal, Kautilya, Shukracharya, Kamandak, and Brihaspati have authored the four schools of 'Indian governance'. See Sanyal at the India Ideas Conclave, 2020.
35 Prasad at the India Ideas Conclave, 2020.
36 The chairman of the Mahindra Group delivered the keynote at the India Ideas Conclave in 2020.
37 See https://doc-research.org/ (accessed on 30 September 2020).
38 Distinguishing between intermediaries and mediators, Latour defines the latter in relation to transformative agency: they 'transform, translate, distort, and modify the meaning or the elements that they are supposed to carry.' See Latour (2007, 39).
39 This colloquial term refers to sections of the Indian capital city that were designed by the colonial architect Edward Lutyens. A heritage-protected urban zone with large tracts of open green spaces and a marked absence of urban sprawl and pollution, Lutyens Delhi is where high ranking government officials, politicians, and wealthy elites reside. The term thus references the cultural, political, and economic elite of the country.
40 Political figures associated with the previous Congress regime that is publicly reviled by Hindu nationalists, for instance, Sanjaya Baru, the former media advisor to Prime Minister Manmohan Singh, are also regular conclave guests.
41 Milind Kamble, the founder of the Dalit Indian Chamber of Commerce, engaged the topic of Dalit identity in his speech to the India Ideas conclave in 2015. In 2017, the conclave hosted sessions on 'queer pitch' and transgender issues, and presented one of its annual awards to a transgender activist, Laxmi Narayan Tripathi.
42 Sami's speech at the India Ideas Conclave in 2020 emphasized not only his choice of Indian citizenship (and the fact that he was willing to give up his close connections to

the Pakistani ruling establishment in order to do so), but the superiority of India over Pakistan and all other countries.

43 These formats are popularized and disseminated outside the immediate think tank context as well, through other sets of corporatized and mediatized initiatives such as the annual international conclaves organized by commercial media organizations, and corporate sponsored cultural festivals such as the Jaipur Literary Festival and other 'litfests' that are regular events in the cultural calendar of Indian elites. The soundbite-friendly, made-for-media style of crisp public presentation delivered with casual ease, and the choreographed conversations staged as informal and candid chats between a collegial host and their guest seated on comfortable living room-style furniture that television talk show formats have popularized, also serve as enabling infrastructures.

44 This term was used by Narendra Modi in a media interview in 2019 and was swiftly popularized in Hindutva social media circuits as a disparaging description of establishment elites associated with the Nehruvian state project that has governed India since independence. Khan Market is an exclusive retail district in central Delhi that houses many expensive boutique stores, restaurants, and bars. The 'Khan Market gang' is deemed to be completely out of touch with the majority of Indians, both in terms of their shopping venues and the Western liberal values that they endorse. The term was first used in a newspaper column by senior journalist Ashok Malik in 2017, who has worked as a speechwriter for senior BJP leaders and has strong Hindutva affiliations.

45 Chakravarty uses this term to describe the dominant social classes that exercise social, political, and economic power in the contemporary era of Hindutva governance. For a rich and compelling account of the 'new power elite' in India that has emerged since the advent of economic liberalization in the 1990s, see Baru 2021. The Central Vista project is an ambitious, multi-billion dollar urban redevelopment initiative launched by the BJP government in 2019, that aims to radically change the existing layout and architecture of the colonial designed Central Vista, an expanse in the heart of central Delhi around which the main buildings of national government, from the Parliament to central ministries and the National Archives, are located. In a decision laden with symbolic significance, the Gujarat-based architecture firm HCP Design and its principal architect, Bimal Patel, have been selected to replace the heritage protected architectural vision of Edward Lutyens. See Chakravarty (2020).

References

Acharya, A. 2020. 'The Myth of the Civilization State: Rising Powers and the Cultural Challenge to World Order'. *International Affairs* 34(2): 139–56.

Ahmad, O. 2019. 'Who Funds Think Tanks and How Effective Are They in India'. *The Quint*, March 14.

Bajpai, K., and H. Pant (eds.). 2013. *India's Foreign Policy: A Reader*. Oxford: Oxford University Press.

Bajpai, R. 2018. 'Civilizational Perspectives in International Relations and Contemporary India–China Relations'. In *The 'Clash of Civilizations' 25 Years On*, edited by D. Orsi. https://www.e-ir.info/2018/04/26/civilizational-perspectives-in-international-relations-and-contemporary-china-india-relations/ (accessed on 16 November 2020).

Baru, S. 2021. *India's Power Elite: Class, Caste and a Cultural Revolution*. Delhi: India Viking.

Baviskar, A., and R. Ray (eds.). 2011. *Elite and Everyman: The Cultural Politics of the Indian Middle Classes*. Abingdon: Routledge.

Bhattacharya, S. 2020. *Mission Bengal: A Saffron Experiment*. Delhi: HarperCollins India.

Carroll, W., and C. Carson. 2006. 'Neoliberalism, Capitalist Class Formation, and the Global Network of Corporations and Policy Groups'. In *Neoliberal Hegemony: A Global Critique*, edited by D. Plehwe et al. Abingdon: Routledge.

Chakravarty, A. 2020. 'NEP Is the Last Nail in the Lutyen Elite's Coffin'. NDTV Blog. https://www.ndtv.com/blog/in-new-education-policy-modis-giant-move-vs-lutyens-delhi-2271516 (accessed on 30 September 2020).

Chakravartty, P., and S. Roy. 2013. 'Media Pluralism Redux: Towards New Frameworks of Comparative Media Studies Beyond the West'. *Political Communication* 30(3): 349–70.

Chaturvedi, S. 2017. 'Think Tank Run by Ajit Doval's Son Has Conflict of Interest Writ Large'. *The Wire*, 4 November.

Coker, C. 2019. *The Rise of the Civilizational State*. Cambridge, UK: Polity Press.

Crewe, I., and D. Sanders (eds.). 2020. *Authoritarian Populism and Liberal Democracy*. Cham, Switzerland: Palgrave Macmillan.

Donthi, P. 2017a. 'How Ties with the Think Tanks Vivekananda International Foundation and India Foundation Enhance Ajit Doval's Influence'. *Caravan Magazine*, 5 November.

———. 2017b. 'Undercover: Ajit Doval in Theory and Practice'. *Caravan Magazine*, September.

Fox, R. 1987. 'Gandhian Socialism and Hindu Nationalism: Cultural Domination in the World System'. *Journal of Commonwealth and Comparative Politics* 25(3): 233–47.

Friesen, E. 2020. *The World Economic Forum and Transnational Networking*. Bingley: Emerald Publishing.

Haas, P. 1992. 'Epistemic Communities and International Policy Coordination'. *International Organization* 46(1): 1–35.

Halder, D. 2019. *Blood Island: An Oral History of the Marichjhapi Massacre*. Delhi: HarperCollins India.

Hansen, T. 1999. *The Saffron Wave: Democracy and Hindu Nationalism in Modern India*. Delhi: Oxford University Press.

Harriss, J., and S. Corbridge, 2000. *Reinventing India: Liberalization, Hindu Nationalism, and Popular Democracy*. Cambridge, UK: Polity Press.

Huntington, S. 1996. *The Clash of Civilizations and the Remaking of World Order*. New York: Simon & Schuster.

Jaffrelot, C. 1999. *The Hindu Nationalist Movement and Indian Politics*. Delhi: Penguin India.

———. 2019. 'A *De Facto* Ethnic Democracy? Obliterating and Targeting the Other, Hindu Vigilantes, and the Ethno-State'. In *Majoritarian State: How Hindu Nationalism Is changing India*, edited by A. Chatterji, et al., 41–68. London: Hurst & Company.

Jaishankar, S. 2020. 'Address by External Affairs Minister at 6th India Ideas Conclave'. Ministry of External Affairs, Government of India. https://www.mea.gov.in/Speeches-Statements.htm?dtl/32440 (accessed on 30 September 2020).

Jenkins, R. 1999. *Democratic Politics and Economic Reform in India*. Cambridge, UK: Cambridge University Press.

Jha, P. 2015. 'India's Most Influential Think Tanks'. *Hindustan Times*, 16 August.

Kartikeya, C. 2017. 'India@70: How RSS Linked Think Tanks Are Helping It Capture Mindspace'. *Catch News*, 12 August.

———. 2018. '8 RSS Think Tanks That Are Competing for Intellectual Space in Delhi'. *Catch News*, 13 February.

Kaur, R. 2016. 'The Innovative Indian: Common Man and the Politics of *Jugaad* Culture'. *Contemporary South Asia* 24(3): 313–27.

———. 2020. *Brand New Nation: Capitalist Dreams and Nationalist Design in Twenty-First Century India*. Stanford: Stanford University Press.

Khan, K. and P. Köllner. 2018. 'Foreign Policy Think Tanks in India: New Actors, Divergent Profiles'. *GIGA Focus Asia* 1.

Kohli. A. 2010. *Democracy and Development in India: From Socialism to Pro-Business*. Delhi: Oxford University Press.

Kyle, J., and Gultchin, L. 2018. *Populism in Power Around the World*. London: Tony Blair Institute for Global Change.

Latour, B. 2007. *Reassembling the Social*. Oxford: Oxford University Press.

Maçães, B. 2020. 'The Attack of the Civilization–State'. *Noema Magazine*, 20 June.

Malhotra, J. 2017. 'The Growing Role of Government-approved Think Tanks'. NDTV, 1 March.

Mattoo, A., and R. Medcalf. 2015. 'Think Tanks and Universities'. In *The Oxford Handbook of Indian Foreign Policy*, edited by D. Malone, C. Raja Mohan, and S. Raghavan, 271–84.

McGann, J. 2016. *The Fifth Estate: Think Tanks, Public Policy and Governance*. Washington, DC: Brookings Institution Press.

McGann, J., and R. Weaver (eds.). 2002. *Think Tanks and Civil Societies*. New York: Routledge.

McGann, J (ed.). 2018. *Think Tanks and Emerging Power Policy Networks*. Cham, Switzerland: Palgrave Macmillan.

Mounck, Y. 2018. *The People vs. Democracy*. Cambridge, MA: Harvard University Press.

Nye, J. 2005. *Soft Power: The Means to Success in World Politics*. New York: Public Affairs.

Ojala, M. 2017. 'The Making of a Global Elite: Global Economy and the Davos Man in the *Financial Times* 2000–2011'. Unpublished Ph.D. dissertation, University of Helsinki.

Peer, Basharat. 2017. *A Question of Order: India, Turkey, and the Return of Strongmen*. New York: Columbia Global Reports.

Pigman, G. 2007. *The World Economic Forum: A Multi-Stakeholder Approach to Global Governance*. Abingdon: Routledge.

Rai, S. 2015. 'In First Direct Salvo, RSS Aims Legal Missile at J-K Special Status'. *India Today*, 10 July. https://www.indiatoday.in/india/story/parivar-poses-legal-challenge-jammu-and-kashmir-special-status-indian-constitution-281647-2015-07-10 (accessed on 30 September 2020).

Rothkopf, D. 2008. *Superclass: The Global Power Elite and the World They Are Making*. New York: Farrar, Strauss & Giroux.

Roy, P., and D. Sopariwala. 2019. *The Verdict: Decoding India's Elections*. Delhi: Penguin Random House.

Roy, S. 2016. 'Angry Citizens: Civic Anger and the Politics of Curative Democracy in India'. *Identities* 23(3): 362–77.

———. Forthcoming 2021. 'The Political Outsider'. In *The People of India: Politics in the Twenty-First Century*, edited by R. Kaur and N. Mathur. Delhi: Penguin Random House.

Sarkar, U. 2019. 'Readiness and Reliance'. *Caravan Magazine*, 1 March.

Sengupta, U. 2014. 'Drawing on the Right Brain'. *Outlook*. 24 November.

Shah, A. 2014. 'Right-wing Think Tanks Eat into Left's Mindspace'. *DNA*, 14 September.

Shukla, S., and N. Pandey. 2019. 'How the Right Is Tackling Left's Intellectual Hegemony in Delhi – One Think Tank at a Time'. *The Print*, 30 December.

Sinha, A. 2019. 'India's Porous State: Blurred Boundaries and the Evolving Business–State Relationship'. In *Business and Politics in India*, edited by C. Jaffrelot, A. Kohli, and K. Murali, 50–92. New York: Oxford University Press.

Srivastava, J. 2011. *Think Tanks in South Asia: Analysing the Knowledge–Power Interface*. London: Overseas Development Institute.

Stahl, J. 2016. *Right Moves: The Conservative Think Tank in American Political Culture since 1945*. Chapel Hill: University of North Carolina Press.

Subramanya, R. 2016. 'India Ideas Conclave: A Hugely Important First Step'. *Swarajya Magazine*, 22 November. https://swarajyamag.com/india-ideas-conclave-2014/india-ideas-conclave-a-hugely-important-first-step (accessed on 30 September 2020).

Varshney, A. 2019. 'The Emergence of Right-wing Populism in India'. In *Re-forming India: The Nation Today*, edited by N. Jayal. Delhi: Penguin Viking.

5

NEW HINDUTVA AND THE 'UP MODEL'
AN INTERVIEW WITH NEHA DIXIT AND NAKUL SAWHNEY

Srirupa Roy and *Thomas Blom Hansen**

NEHA DIXIT is an independent journalist working from Delhi, India. Her journalism revolves around the themes of Hindu nationalism, gender, and social justice in South Asia, and her work has been published in several leading media outlets including *The Wire, Al Jazeera, New York Times, Outlook,* and *Caravan*. Her published works are available online at http://neha-dixit.blogspot.com/. Neha has won numerous awards for her work, including the International Press Freedom Award (2019), the Kurt Schork Award in International Journalism (2014), the European Commission's Lorenzo Natali Media Prize (2011), and the Chameli Devi Jain Award for Outstanding Woman Journalist (2016).

NAKUL SAWHNEY is an independent documentary filmmaker. His work has largely focused on issues of human rights, gender, communalism, labour rights, caste, and social justice. Prominent films include *Izzatnagari ki Asabhya Betiyaan* (Immoral Daughters in the Land of Honour) and *Muzaffarnagar Baaqi Hai* (Muzaffarnagar Eventually). He founded and is currently running a film and media collective, ChalChitra Abhiyaan, based in western Uttar Pradesh.

Tell us about how you have engaged with Hindu nationalism in your work.

NAKUL: I think my involvement with Hindutva politics goes back to 2010 when I started working on *Izzatnagari ki Asabhya Betiyaan*, which is set in the Jat belt, largely in Haryana (Sawhney 2011). It's a film that looks at crimes and killings in the name of honour and the resistance by young women against self-styled caste authorities, the *khap panchayats*[1] which are passing diktats against self-choice marriages. When I look at it in retrospect, I think that the sort of Jat identity politics that was deeply anti-women and anti-Dalit created a fertile ground for Hindutva to flourish in west Uttar Pradesh (UP) and in Haryana as well.

I then worked on several other documentaries set in west UP.[2] *Muzaffarnagar Baaqi Hai* looks at the Muzaffarnagar massacre of 2013. The film explores the various social, political, and economic reasons and fallouts of the massacre. A film screening was attacked by the Akhil Bharatiya Vidyarthi Parishad (ABVP), the student wing of the Rashtriya Swayamsevak Sangh (RSS), on 1 August 2015 at Kirori Mal College in Delhi University. The film was subsequently screened in many parts of the country to oppose the disruption at Delhi University. Several other screenings were also stopped and attacked by right-wing goons and local police. Dalit scholar and activist Rohith Vemula had also organized a screening at Hyderabad Central University (HCU). Among the many reasons he was hounded by HCU administration was the screening of this film, which led to his eventual suicide in 2016. I am now part of a film and media collective called ChalChitra Abhiyaan, which operates from west UP.[3] We've been following several aspects that are related to the politics of Hindutva. Now with Yogi Adityanath in power as chief minister, we're looking at the most lumpenized form of Hindutva.

NEHA: The first time I did an in-depth report on the Hindu right-wing was during my visit to a Rashtra Sevika Samiti training camp in Aurangabad in 2012. It's the women's wing of the RSS and there I came face to face with the kind of indoctrination work that happens and the kind of training that is given to full timers, to go to various parts of the country and work in various capacities for the dissemination of the Hindutva ideology (Dixit 2013a).

After that I've done a couple of long reports on the Hindu right-wing, which include investigating charges of 'Love Jihad' against Muslims and writing about the incidents of sectarian violence and the kind of gender violence that this involves (Dixit 2014b). I've worked on the Muzaffarnagar riots and the kind of sexual violence that happens as part of the communal situation on the ground (Dixit 2103b, 2014a). I have also covered how the RSS is trafficking children from the Northeast and taking them away to Punjab and Gujarat for the purpose of indoctrination, so that is also a larger investigation (Dixit 2016). Most recently, I have looked at how forms of Hindutva have changed on the ground, and the situation in UP with the police controlled by the chief minister who is an ultra-right fundamentalist (Dixit 2018). Generally speaking, since the National Democratic Alliance (NDA) II came to power in 2014, Hindutva politics intersects with anything that one is reporting, whether it's gender, politics, or even sports for that matter.

NEW HINDUTVA AND THE 'UP MODEL'

In the course of your work in UP, have you observed any distinctive and new features of how Hindutva works today? Is there a 'UP model' of Hindutva that differs from the earlier 'Gujarat model'?

NAKUL: The first is the functioning of the police. During the Gujarat 'riots' of 2002, one saw the bias of the police and many people claimed that they worked according to instructions given by the state government. Today you see such biases playing out on a daily basis not just in UP, but in most parts of India or at least in north India. The scale at which those biases are playing out in UP is unparalleled. The functioning of the police in UP today is something that we've historically seen in what were declared to be 'disturbed states'. In the past, states like Kashmir, the northeastern states, and Punjab were declared disturbed states and draconian laws were implemented there, TADA being one example.[4] The police and paramilitary in these disturbed states played an extremely autocratic and partisan role. Today in UP, the police is functioning in a similar way.

Second – and here I'm mainly speaking about the sugarcane belt of west UP – we see vigilante Hindutva organizations becoming very visible in everyday life. There is an economic crisis here, and a lot of unemployment that you would expect would turn people against the government. But, instead, a lot of the unemployed youngsters are joining the ranks of various Hindutva organizations, like the Hindu Yuva Vahini, Bajrang Dal, Gau Raksha Samiti, and so on, and going around draped in saffron *gamcha*s. Barring Muslims and a Dalit caste (Jatavs), and a large section of Jats, there's an almost 100 per cent exodus of every other caste into the BJP. One will have to study the causes more deeply, but the growth of Hindutva is linked to the steady decline of what was once a very militant agrarian movement in west UP, and the decline of the Dalit party BSP (Bahujan Samaj Party), which had its strongest presence in west UP.

What are these young men who are draping themselves in saffron and joining these vigilante groups telling you? Why are they there and what attracts them? Is it a kind of enjoyment and entertainment? Is it a kind of compensation for other things? Is it camaraderie or is it just being busy doing kaam, doing something?

NAKUL: The aspect of enjoyment and belonging certainly matters, but we should look at this in the wider context of what is available to enjoy, to belong to. There are no alternate progressive cultural forums for these youngsters, no place where they can find a sense of identity or larger collectives that they could be part of. The only collectives that are available to them are what these very regressive right-wing organizations provide. The RSS and Hindutva organizations have created several such forums. Unfortunately, the opposition didn't think along those lines of cultural mobilization. How do the youth engage themselves culturally? There are no theatre clubs, film clubs, sports tournaments that should have been organized by mass organizations of the opposition parties. They don't exist, only RSS ones do. A lot of these unemployed kids have a difficult time. The mother is going to give you a dressing down about how we've invested so much in your education and you're not getting a job. The father comes back in the evening and gives you a dressing down about how he has slaved all his life to get you a decent education and you're not getting a job. These are the massive inferiority complexes also playing out, and these RSS organizations give them a false sense of confidence to counter this.

The propaganda machinery is also very strong today; the entire media is playing the role of RSS *pracharaks* (preachers). Many of the youngsters genuinely believe in the politics and rhetoric of Hindutva. Youngsters are convinced that they are doing the country a big favour. This macho bullying attitude is seen as some sort of a virtue, and they tend to enjoy it a great deal.

NEHA: I think that they've managed to institutionalize a lot of things that were earlier called 'fringe'. For example, one of the first things that Yogi Adityanath did after becoming chief minister was to institutionalize the 'Love Jihad' narrative of Muslim boys trying to make Hindu women fall in love with them, convert them, and carry out a kind of jihad. The Adityanath government launched a campaign to counter this, the 'anti-Romeo' vigilante squads formally sanctioned by the government, but there was a lot of backlash because they ended up attacking Hindu men as well, and so they had to actually take it back.[5]

Another example: the UP government has recently introduced a bill in the local assembly that says that if there is any kind of dissent or protest, the government will have the power to place criminal charges on the protestors and arrest them.[6] This needs to be seen in the context of the protests against the Citizenship Amendment Act (CAA) this past December (2019), especially in UP, when a lot of people were picked up for protesting and their properties were attached. A lot of these people were charged under the Unlawful Activities Prevention Act and the National Security Act. So, they have been invoking a 'war against the state' kind of charge against people who are mere dissenters. I have not heard of this happening before; this was the first time. The UP government also put the names of the protestors on hoardings on the street, calling them terrorists and anti-nationals. In the past, these kinds of practices would be carried out by Hindutva vigilantes or unemployed youth. Now it is a government practice.

Apart from this, as Nakul has said, the police has become a wing of the Hindutva government in UP. Between April 2017 and the present, there have been almost 1,500 police shootouts in UP and the government presents this data in an annual press conference each year, putting it out as an achievement. They are proud of it. In these 1,500 police shootouts, close to 170 people have been killed, but there has been no inquiry (Dixit 2019). Most people who have been shot, injured, or killed are either Muslims, Other Backward Classes (OBCs), or Dalits, so just looking at the kind of people who have been targeted shows the direct Hindutva agenda being played out through the police action.

People have been protesting. The United Nations, in fact, took cognizance in 2019 and sent notices to the Indian government that these were pre-planned killings and not chance encounters. Our own National Human Rights Commission has sent multiple notices to the UP government. But there has been no action. The propaganda machinery ensures that all of this is seen as criminals being killed, which is seen to be justified and normal. The UP government has also taken up the central government's template of attacking activists, lawyers, and journalists. It is charging journalists with criminal cases. In recent weeks, two journalists have been killed, in Ghaziabad and Ballia.[7] A journalist from Delhi was picked up by the UP police just four days ago, on the basis of a complaint filed by a Hindutva leader.[8] During the COVID lockdown they tried to summon the editor of *The Wire*, Siddharth Varadarajan, to Lucknow or Faizabad, to face charges for publishing a factual story about the UP government's actions during the lockdown.[9]

The Gujarat pogrom was a moment of high-visibility exceptional violence, whereas Neha is telling us about violence as a normalized routine part of everyday state practice. Is the routinization and acceptance of violence as part of state practice one of the distinguishing features of the UP model of new Hindutva?

NEHA: It's important to talk about the example of Dr Kafeel Khan. Several children died because of a lack of oxygen in a government hospital in Gorakhpur, Yogi Adityanath's bastion. Dr Kafeel Khan, one of the paediatricians, tried to spend his own money to get oxygen for the children and, in fact, saved many. But because his testimony was put out in the media, and he disclosed that government hospitals did not have enough resources, he was jailed under the National Security Act and his custody kept getting extended.[10] This is an example of the government's vindictive policies and how they are using exceptional laws like the National Security Act for something routine, to stop dissent and criticism. Another example of this is how the government filed a case of criminal conspiracy against a journalist in Mirzapur, just for reporting that government schools under the midday meal programme are serving students roti with salt instead of nutritious food. He was charged with a criminal act just for bare minimum reporting.

The Gujarat model is about Hindutva's makeover. The success of the Gujarat model has been attributed to the way in which Hindutva disguised and translated itself: how Modi remade himself as a development man, used the language of Gujarati asmita (Gujarati pride), attracted international investment and international recognition. In contrast, the UP model that you are describing is not about a makeover or sneaking Hindutva in through the back door, but an assertion of violence and power.

NAKUL: Absolutely, I think making Yogi Adityanath the chief minister was in itself a very clear announcement that we're not going to disguise anything else any longer. Of all their tall leaders, Adityanath presented the most crass version of Hindutva. So, it was very clearly a statement that they've made: Hindutva will not come disguised as anything else, under some rubric or rhetoric of development. I think also, if you look at how the anti-CAA protests were handled in UP, it's vastly different from what we've seen in other parts of the country, including other BJP-ruled states. In Muzaffarnagar, for example, there was some sort of an altercation between the police and the protesters. A lot of people claim that this was instigated by the police. This happens often: the police try to hijack the movement and then give it a violent form, and it gives them an excuse and it validates their violence.

The protesters went back to their houses. There is a big Muslim-majority ghetto in Muzaffarnagar called Khalapar that is colloquially referred to as 'mini Pakistan'. The police with the Rapid Action Force (RAF) and with people in civilian clothes in hundreds entered Khalapar that night. They stormed into several Muslim houses, ransacked them, broke everything that they could. A lot of people were very severely injured.[11] And all of this happened openly; there was no attempt at disguising it. Of course, they denied it, but there's plenty of evidence to prove that the police had done this, everybody knew that the police had done this. This was a strange 'riot situation'. Very often when there are riots targeting Muslims, the violence is carried out in areas where Muslims are in a minority. But what do you do in a Muslim-majority area? The violence is carried out by the police and RAF. Similar events have happened in Bijnor and Meerut, where people were killed because of police excesses. In Bijnor, forensic reports showed that one of the protestors was killed by a bullet from a police gun. In Meerut, four people were killed by police firing during the anti-CAA protests.[12]

NEW HINDUTVA AND THE 'UP MODEL'

In Kandhla, there's this protester who had sent out WhatsApp messages with information about the time and place of a CAA–NRC protest. He was arrested by the police and was in jail for about two weeks, and the SDM (sub-divisional magistrate) made sure he didn't get bail. There were many such arrests in Shamli district as well, and all these people were picked up under Section 151,[13] a charge for which you usually don't even make it to jail. But they were all in jail for a good two weeks. Someone had given a call for an all-India *bandh* (strike) against the CAA–NRC–NPR on 29 January. In Kandhla, many of us had done a very private and discreet campaign for the *bandh*. In a small town you know who the police guys and the LIU (local investigating unit) are – the people who are not officially in the police but who pass on information to them. We were able to bypass all of that and the police was caught off guard and there was a complete *bandh* in Kandhla township. That afternoon the SP (superintendent of police) of Shamli makes a statement at a press conference openly saying that any protest demonstrations against CAA–NRC–NPR will be dealt with very firmly. Now, they can impose Section 144 and say that nobody's allowed to protest.[14] But here they are saying something specific, that you can't protest against CAA–NRC–NPR, and they are saying this openly.

To give you another idea of how blatant this is: in Meerut a Dalit activist, Sushil Gautam, also gave a call for protesting against CAA–NRC–NPR. He was immediately picked up by the police and had to spend three odd days in jail. But while he was in jail, at the exact same spot while section 144 is still being imposed, the ABVP[15] held a pro-CAA protest and there was no action against them. So, the point is that it's not even just about violence; it's about being *blatantly* partisan.

Another example: There's a Muslim-majority village called Taprana in Shamli district, where there was an altercation between a mob and the cops who had gone there to arrest someone. This is a feudal macho kind of place where police altercations with Muslims and with Jats, Gujjars, and other dominant castes are not uncommon. The police left following the altercation, but then returned to the village and ransacked about thirty-five Muslim houses, broke everything that they could break, and left. Something like this was previously unheard of, but it's now a frequent occurrence.

We've filmed on at least two occasions in two different villages where something like this has happened, where the police have entered Muslim-majority villages, ransacked several houses, and left. This is becoming the new normal, and it's a scary kind of normal, and it's blatant. There are also no attempts to disguise the anti-Muslim attitudes of the police, the fact that they've become a wing or an extension of the ideological framework of Hindutva in general. You hear about this level of brutality in disturbed states, where there is free hand. This is the kind of free hand that they've got in UP today.

What you're saying about this pattern of violence reminds me very much of what I saw first-hand in Maharashtra following the Bhima Koregaon protests where police would do exactly the same thing.[16] They would enter Dalit homes and smash everything they could find. And they were not necessarily interested in arresting everybody but intimidating them: it was a campaign of intimidation. How does this play out with the BSP as a major force to be reckoned with in the area?[17] Is there also a kind of pushback against Dalit assertion? Is that something that is openly articulated or is it a more implicit dog-whistle kind of rolling back of an earlier regime of Dalit pride?

NAKUL: There's been an increase in violence against Dalits as well, not just by the police but by people from dominant castes, which could be Rajputs, Gujjars, and even Jats in some parts. When we spoke with Dalits who had been attacked, a lot of them told us that their attackers would say, *ab to humari upar bhi sarkar hai, neeche bhi sarkar hai*, we have a government above at the centre and below in the state, you know. They definitely feel a lot more emboldened.

The police played a role when the Bhim Army emerged as a force in west UP and especially in Saharanpur district. There were a lot of atrocities and police excesses committed on people who were either Bhim Army activists or suspected to be with the Bhim Army, and a lot of young Dalits were also arrested. But there has been massive pushback, which we have been privileged to see very closely through two Dalit movements: Bhim Army and the movement in Gujarat under Jignesh Mevani's leadership.[18] The BJP is now being very careful because the Hindutva agenda is to incorporate and appropriate Dalits as part of the larger Hindu fold. Physical attacks continue, but I have a feeling that the police has been given instructions to back off a little on that front. The attacks on Dalits are happening now at the level of policy, at an institutional level, for instance, the revocation of the Prevention of Atrocities (Scheduled Caste and Scheduled Tribes) Act',[19] and many other policies that are not being talked about.

For example, there is a very important scholarship that the UP government used to give to SC (Scheduled Caste) and ST (Scheduled Tribes) students irrespective of their marks in the 12th standard (school-leaving) examination.[20] Dalit students would get an almost 100 per cent scholarship to attend a private college. A lot of Dalits I know personally in west UP really benefited from that scheme. A lot of them said that they wouldn't have been able to get access to higher education had it not been for that government scheme. But the government tweaked this policy and said that the scholarship would not be given just on a caste basis to Dalits who came from economically weaker sections. Students also had to score more than 60 per cent in the school-leaving examinations in order to be eligible for the scholarship. Now this is a very high percentage, especially in the UP educational board. A lot of Dalits come from working-class backgrounds and don't have access to tuitions and so on, and government schools are anyway in shambles. So, the scholarship is not for all Dalits from economically weaker sections anymore; most are no longer eligible to apply.

Another change is that during the BSP regime, every time there were atrocities on Dalits, the police would act, and they would arrest the culprits. The cases would go on forever, but there was this fear of the police acting. Now, in a lot of atrocity cases, the police do nothing, and it's becoming virtually impossible to get people arrested, or to even file charge sheets or FIRs (first information reports).

How has the police been made the arm of Hindutva? Is it a process of ideological infiltration of police cadres? Is it about control from on top and then everybody just follows that chain of command? Does it reflect the communalization of the police forces?

NAKUL: I think it is a mix of various such factors. I think that there's also something else, which is that the police work for about sixteen–twenty hours a day. They're not getting enough leave; the UP government isn't filling in all the vacancies. So, this is a poor police force which is very overworked and underpaid, and it's a very angry and frustrated bunch of people with a lot of power. Along with everything else, I think we have to talk about genuine police reforms as well. I really feel that it's not enough to just blame the police.

It's kind of astonishing and depressing that all of these years of the BSP in power did not create an institutional legacy that could have acted as some kind of bulwark against what the Yogi government is doing today. What about transformation in administration during the BSP regime and the presence of more Dalits in local administration and police: Shouldn't that have made a difference?

NAKUL: That's not entirely true. Yes, a lot of institutional changes that should have happened did not happen. The BSP wasn't really looking at the detailed questions that confront Dalits; it was essentially about consolidating to vote and come to power, which undermined the need for movements and so on. So, I agree with you there. But it is also true that a lot of Dalits who are in the police today, at various ranks, are actually trying to play a sensitive role. There is a lot of pressure from on top, and there's only so much you can do. But there are actually Dalits in the police who have come from the BSP kind of training and are actually a lot more sensitive in handling situations. That is the only silver lining in the UP police today, at least in west UP.

How do you get out these stories of silver linings and alternative possibilities in the public domain? What are your thoughts on the role of media, both in propping up the Hindutva regime and in charting other avenues?

NEHA: Actually the 'propaganda model' explains the political atmosphere that we are in (Edward and Chomsky 2002). The role of the corporate houses is key: the kind of media owners we have are very much in love with the political parties in power, and they dominate television and web platforms. Media ownership completely controls and facilitates the propagation of the Hindutva ideology in many ways. For instance, recently there was an endless media conversation for almost a month and a half on the suicide of an actor, Sushant Singh Rajput. A kind of smokescreen is being created where nothing else is being discussed, whether it's the rise of COVID cases, the national education policy, or unemployment. Also, the corporate ownership of media has created a system where there is a lot of space for binary opinion journalism instead of ground reports or investigative reports that are far more complex, and actually pin down and provide evidence to hold the government accountable.

This is the first time in Indian history where a prime minister has not held a press conference in six years. A central cabinet minister, V. K. Singh, has coined the word 'presstitutes' for journalists who are asking questions, and the word has been normalized. This is also a time when attacks on journalists have increased. The latest Home Ministry report suggests that almost 1,700 journalists have been physically attacked in a span of one year, and these are conservative government figures. It's not like the press was not attacked earlier. There were always legal notices and cases. But there are differences today. First, the government now provides impunity to the people who physically attack the media, documentary filmmakers, journalists, etc. There is no action taken against these attacks and there is no conviction. Even in the case of Gauri Lankesh, who was killed in 2017, we've still not seen any conviction.[21]

This government has also started to criminalize journalism: they file law and order related cases against journalists, which means that a lot of self-censorship goes on. They don't need to engage in emergency-era censorship anymore; self-censorship fulfils the role. In newsrooms, stories are getting killed every day. There are standing instructions not to publish certain things about the prime minister and the home minister on the front page. For instance, the home minister was recently found to be COVID positive but there was barely any reporting around it. The government has also cornered news organizations by withdrawing government ads on several occasions.

Two weeks ago, three *Caravan* journalists were physically attacked in northeast Delhi while doing a follow-up story on the Delhi riots. They were literally held hostage by a mob, and the woman journalist was also sexually harassed. The police were not very proactive and it took the journalists the entire night of giving statements to finally file an official and therefore chargeable FIR and not just a written complaint.[22] During the Delhi riots, what happened was that for the first time in many years, journalists were made to recite the *Hanuman Chalisa*[23] to prove that they were Hindus while reporting. Some Muslim journalists had to be vouched for by their Hindu colleagues, who dissembled to shield them when confronting angry mob inquiries about their religious identity. This kind of pattern that is becoming normal now is really dangerous: the fact that even reporters reporting from the ground have to first think of their religion, that they can be lynched or killed for that. And the government obviously wants things to be like this.

NAKUL: At the local level, a strange economic model is at work that makes local media an extension of the state, publishing what the state says. Reporters are paid very little, and they make their money either by getting ads for the newspapers or by acting as mediators between people and the local *thana* (police station). So essentially, what they're getting are state versions.

A lot of the local news is entirely speaking the language of the local police and the administration. For example, after we covered the story about Taprana village where Muslim houses were attacked, the story became national news, and many national reporters went there to cover it. To counter this, the local SSP (senior superintendent of police) got all the local Shamli YouTube channels and news channels to publish a video from the police's point of view where they showed a cop who was injured and a destroyed police jeep and said that they were attacked.

One of the roles that we are being able to play is that finally at a very small level, some challenge to the state version is being put out, and sometimes it catches the attention of the national media. I'll give you another example. Shortly before the 2019 Lok Sabha elections, around 200 Muslim houses were burned down in a slum in Meerut. Fortunately, no one died. The Meerut police suddenly turned off the internet. This is a common occurrence in west UP: the police will get the internet suppliers to turn off the internet. No one covered the story in the media as a result. But we got to know about the events through a friend in Meerut who called us up. Our people went, filmed, and the next day it was up on ChalChitra Abhiyaan, and it again became national news because of us.

We actually function in a clandestine manner. The administration is very confused about who we are. I've had the local investigator call me and ask for more information on ChalChitra Abhiyaan, I ask them to send their request by email because I know that they generally don't use email. I don't know if my phone is being tapped, if we're being followed, but I'm assuming this is happening. I don't know how much of our digital footprint is being hacked. Working locally and taking on the state locally as journalists, as artists, as activists is literally playing with fire.

NEHA: We've heard of internet shutdowns in Kashmir, where 4G services have still not been restored.[24] But during the anti-CAA protests this also became a prominent action in UP. Aligarh did not have access to the internet for a long time, and many other places as well. Even in Lucknow in the second or third week of December 2019 they did not have internet for almost a week. As we were talking about, earlier these actions were restricted to troubled areas, but it's not that way any longer. If you protest against something that they don't like, the internet goes away.

Another thing to add about the role of media is the cinema that is being produced in the times of Hindutva. Many mainstream films are coming out with the Hindutva narrative, whether it is *Manikarnika*, *Tanhaji*, or *Uri*, the film on the surgical strikes. Films that are in line with the Hindutva narrative are put out as mainstream cinema, and they have a huge impact. This is also part of the propaganda machinery that we should look at.

What about your practice of independent journalism: Has it become more difficult for you to propose and report on certain kinds of stories over the past year?

NEHA: It's become very difficult. Very few organizations want to run investigative stories. It has also become a part of what you could call the 'privilege package': if I can afford to subsidize my story and report it, there may be one organization that is going to publish it. But most of the time news organizations that have money are the ones that are in sync with the government's agenda and ideology, so they are not going to publish it. And the few that are ready to publish, like *The Wire* or the *Caravan*, these places do not have the resources. They can publish, but they have no money to pay the reporters. And once legal cases are filed, do they have enough resources to take them on? This also plays a role in publication decisions: organizations may want to publish a story, but do they have the resources to fight it out?

I would also like to point out that the role of international media has not been very encouraging. They mainly want to publish opinion pieces from journalists in India and much of their reporting is done by people who are not from here, so they don't understand the politics. A certain kind of Western narrative is formed, which is very individualistic. So many stories put out in the international media are about the experiences of one person, a heroic journalist who has an adventure. This type of celebrity journalism does not really present the accurate picture. The people's voices that need to be put out are not the focus of the story. This has become a common practice, and it helps the right-wing agenda.

Moving now to the anti-CAA protests, why did the ferment emerge around the CAA and not around other things? We were taken aback by the mass mobilizations around this issue.

NAKUL: The government did a lot of things in quick succession: Ram Janmabhoomi, the Ayodhya–Babri Masjid verdict,[25] revocation of Article 370,[26] then the CAA.[27] I think they'd begun to push their luck too much; they kept pushing people to the wall. Had the CAA been spaced out a little bit, the protests may not have been as major. They overestimated themselves when they thought that they could get away with that kind of brutal police violence against the students of Jamia Millia Islamia.[28] It got a lot of media coverage because it happened in the national capital. A lot of those fence sitters who weren't entirely comfortable with the Modi regime but were willing to give him a shot were now forced to acknowledge that this Hindutva government wants to change India into a Hindu theocratic state. A lot of people had thought that Modi wouldn't be able to do it and were willing to give him a chance and focus on his development promises. I think this large section was shaken by the CAA, the quick succession of events, and then the attack on students at Jamia.

For the first time in six years, there were so many protests against the government, and the government was forced to take a step back. They had to retreat once earlier as well, in the face of the protests against the revocation of the SC/ST Atrocities Prevention Act.[29] They were pushed back for a second time on the CAA–NRC issue, and Modi had to finally go to Ramlila Maidan and announce that his government has never spoken about the NRC. Of course, this statement was a myth, there were lots of videos that people dug out of Amit Shah saying on multiple occasions NRC *aayega*, CAA *aayega*, CAA *aayega phir* NRC *aayega* (NRC will come, CAA will come, CAA will come and then NRC will come).

Nobody was expecting this scale of mobilizations. It was massive. It was led by Muslim women; it was a glorious movement, and it pushed the government back. I think that a government which functions with this degree of hubris and arrogance is now getting back at the people who were organizing these protests, with these relentless arrests and police harassment of activists in Delhi and during the lockdown.

These movements may not bring about tangible and immediate changes, but they lay seeds and ignite sparks that can blaze again, they lay infrastructures for the future.

In the course of your work have you seen certain things unfolding now, alliances and resistances – or maybe we don't even want to give it such a big word – that give you some hope about possibilities that may unfold in the future?

NAKUL: Traditional political parties in the opposition, at least in north India, have absolutely failed to take on the BJP politically. There are definitely new movements, new formations thinking afresh. You have organizations like Pinjra Tod that have sprung up in campuses.[30] Jignesh Mevani in Gujarat is an example, and you can find several others that are thinking differently, beyond the old communist left politics and the old, straitjacketed identity politics as well. We're also seeing a lot of new cultural experiments in different parts of the country, including the ChalChitra Abhiyaan. We are cultural but also do all kinds of other work.

People who were seen on the left at one time are now speaking a different language, talking about questions of identity and subaltern identities, more intersectional politics and gender. But not to the extent that these should be talked about, unfortunately even now. You also have so many people in the Dalit movement, who initially came from the old Bahujanwadi training[31] and are now changing the way they're thinking, for instance, now they are talking about privatization in a big way. In UP so many Dalit groups are talking about privatization because it's also directly about reservations and employment. They have seen how small sections of the previous generation of Dalits had benefited from government jobs, and privatization ends this opportunity. Material questions that were not so much a part of the Bahujan movement are becoming part of it today. It's no longer the Bahujan movement; I would say it's broadly the Dalit movement, which is taking on a different shape. I really feel that something new is emerging from here.

In the Muslim community also, there is a churning that we've never seen, at least in north India, before. We put up two videos on ChalChitra Abhiyaan, of the replication of Shaheen Bagh in Deoband in Saharanpur.[32] Deoband is the seat of the Jamiat Ulema-e-Hind and Darul Uloom, both very deeply conservative. It was amazing to see the replication of Shaheen Bagh there. So many Muslim women were out, challenging so many gender norms, and so many men of the town also came together to facilitate the movement. The leadership was in the hands of the women; men were not allowed in that park. It became a reverse *zenana*: it's usually the other way around – women are not allowed in public spaces.

So, I think something fascinating is emerging. It will take time to translate into an electoral opposition to the BJP, which is not going to happen overnight. I sense that there are going to be fascinating movements on a whole range of issues, from privatization to class to questions concerning Dalits to gender questions which you've seen through Pinjra Tod. Unemployment is also going to be a huge issue in the coming months. I think we will see the emergence of a new kind of progressive politics. I would be lying if I said I had a clear and vivid understanding of what exactly it will look like. I think the beauty of it will be its amorphous nature. It will not have the definite fixed structures of a CPM (Communist Party of India–Marxist) or a BSP. It won't be those straitjacketed, musty organizations; it will be far more vibrant. But it's going to be met with massive suppression and state repression. We are already seeing the signs of that.

I'll give you one more example of a new politics. During a calamity it is usually the conventional *sarkari* (governmental) NGOs (non-governmental organizations) or even the RSS that does a lot of relief work. But now during the lockdown and the COVID crisis for the first time I am seeing broadly progressive organizations heavily invested in relief work, distributing rations, starting free *mazdoor dhabas* (workers canteens). I really feel there's a new kind of investment in grassroots politics and in a different kind of grassroots politics.

NEHA: As Nakul has pointed out, several of the people who were part of the anti-CAA protest were fence-sitters who had suddenly got moved by the violence in Jamia and later in JNU (Jawahar Nehru University). The women who were coming out and participating had no clear ideology. As soon as the COVID lockdown happened, these same people, the same groups, quickly became relief supply groups. They started working towards supplying relief material to people. If you look at the figures, 69 per cent of the relief material provided to people was by civil society and not the government. So why did it increase so much? To me, it seems like an indicator that the situation has pushed people to come forward and be more active participants. It could be in the most basic way of coming together and collecting food. It happened across metropolitan and tier-II cities. There is now a kind of consciousness and motivation, and once you have been initiated into this public sphere, actively participating, I don't think that's going to go back anywhere. Shaheen Bagh and the other places we've talked about, all these women who have come out, all these children who have sat for protests for months and months, this is not going to go away. It will come out in some way, and it makes me hopeful. There will be a lot of bloodshed but there is no going back from this space.

NAKUL: Healthcare is also becoming a public issue for the first time. Some of it because of the AAP (Aam Admi Party) in Delhi, but now post-COVID, so many people are talking about healthcare. I am just adding to what Neha said. I think there's no going back.

The kind of intersectionality that you talked about is emerging organically. The people who were motivated around the CAA protests moved into relief work, which then morphed into something else.

NEHA: I have been part of the Vasant Kunj solidarity group. It's a mix of all kinds of people. The group suddenly came together to participate in the CAA protest. Then they were doing all this relief work. Then they also started drafting statements to the local MLA (member of legislative assembly) asking why domestic workers were not getting paid during the lockdown. They have just moved from one to the other to the other, and this movement and linkage is by people who didn't come with any definite set of political ideas.

The fact that the COVID crisis immediately followed Shaheen Bagh is happenstance, but the outcome is that the so-called communal question can no longer be the communal question alone. Fighting Hindutva seems to be about much more than defending secularism in these times.

NEHA: I fully agree. The problem has been that since 1992, it's not just the BJP that's made it a secularism versus communalism binary. People in the opposition, especially the Congress, and later unfortunately even the Left, Samajwadi Party, and BSP – everybody contributed. I think the only people who broke the binary after many years was the AAP that said look it's Hindutva versus social welfare, not communalism versus secularism. Unfortunately, they also shifted and surrendered to BJP and soft Hindutva. They blew up a beautiful chance. It really can't just be Hindutva versus secularism. It has to be Hindutva versus secularism which must also mean healthcare, employment, better lives – the entire range of things.

Notes

*   27 August 2020. Virtual conversation (Delhi/Göttingen/Palo Alto). We are grateful to Shashi Chandhok for her assistance with transcription and editing and to Ashwin Subramanian for research support.
1   A *khap panchayat* is a quasi-judicial body comprising a group of village male elders belonging to the locally dominant caste (such as the Jats in Haryana and some parts of UP) that deliberates on property disputes and enforces rules of caste endogamy by imposing strict punishments (flogging, outcasting members, and also sanctioning

'honour killings') on transgressing individuals in order to preserve the 'honour' of the village community (typically, of dominant caste men). The Supreme Court of India declared *khap panchayat*s illegal in March 2018, holding that it was unlawful for any external person/body to interfere in marriages between consenting adults. For details of the Supreme Court verdict on *khap panchayat*s, see Outlook Web Bureau (2018).

2 These include *Muzaffarnagar Baaqi Hai* (Muzaffarnagar Eventually), *Kairana, Surkhiyon ke Baad* (Kairana, After the Headlines), *Muavza* (Redressal), and various other short videos that can be seen on the ChalChitra Abhiyaan website.

3 See https://www.chalchitraabhiyaan.com/ (accessed on 13 October 2020).

4 The Terrorist and Disruptive Activities (Prevention) Act (TADA) – in force between 1985 and 1995 – was an anti-terrorism law in India that gave law enforcing authorities special powers to arrest/detain anyone suspected of being involved in 'terrorist' and 'disruptive activities'. These were, in turn, vaguely defined to encompass a variety of activities, and were used by both the central and various state governments against protestors. The law was allowed to lapse in 1995 in the face of mounting evidence of its misuse (for instance, custodial abuse, torture, etc.) by law enforcement authorities.

5 The 'anti-Romeo squads' are mobile police units created by the UP government (under Yogi Adityanath) in 2017 to patrol college campuses to ensure the safety of college-going women, and prevent sexual harassment or 'eve-teasing', the widely used euphemism in India. These squads were created in the context of widely circulating rumours of 'love jihad' – allegations that Muslim youth were seducing young Hindu women into marriage, to effect religious conversion (to Islam) – and were part of the BJP's election manifesto in the UP state assembly elections.

6 This government regulation, passed in response to the protests against the CAA in UP, requires 'vandals' to pay damages or face the seizure of their property, even before their guilt is proved. In addition to this decision, the UP government also pursued the tactic of placing public hoardings across major cities, such as Lucknow, identifying individuals who had (allegedly) participated in the protests against the CAA. The Supreme Court, following on the order of the Allahabad High Court, found this law unconstitutional, and ordered the government to remove these 'name and shame' hoardings. For a news report on the Supreme Court's decision, see Vaidyanathan and Pandey (2020).

7 Ratan Singh, a local journalist, was shot dead in the Ballia district of UP on 24 August 2020. The state police have claimed that the journalist's murder was due to an on-going 'property dispute' with his neighbour, and not because of his profession. Vikram Joshi, another journalist, was killed earlier in the year on 20 July, near his residence in Ghaziabad. For details of Ratan Singh's murder, see Scroll Staff (2020). For details of Vikram Joshi's murder, see Special Correspondent (2020).

8 The journalist referred to is Prashant Kanojia who was arrested by the UP police on 18 August 2020. The police claimed that Mr Kanojia had posted a tweet that 'disrupted communal harmony' based on a first information report (FIR) complaint registered at the Hazratganj police station. Mr Kanojia was previously arrested by the UP police in 2019 for making 'objectionable comments' against Chief Minister Yogi Adityanath. For details of Mr Kanojia's arrest, see Ara (2020b).

9   Two FIRs were filed against Siddharth Varadarajan by the UP government for 'creating or promoting enmity, hatred or ill-will between classes' with reference to an article published in *The Wire*, and also for tweeting 'unverified claims'. The UP police delivered the summons notice to Varadarajan during the national lockdown, driving down from Ayodhya (in UP) to Delhi. For details of the case against Varadarajan and *The Wire*, see, The Wire Analysis (2020).

10 Dr Kafeel Khan was arrested by the UP police for allegedly making a 'provocative' speech at the Aligarh Muslim University during the anti-CAA protests. Despite being granted bail, Dr Khan was not released by the police, and was instead detained under the provisions of the National Security Act (NSA). He was released on 1 September 2020 after the Allahabad High Court found his detention under the NSA untenable. For a timeline of Dr Khan's case, beginning with the oxygen shortage at Gorakhpur's government hospitals that tragically resulted in the deaths of more than a hundred children, see The Wire Staff (2020).

11 The attacks against Muslims in the locality of Khalapar, in Muzaffarnagar occurred on 20 December 2019. Residents of another Muslim-majority locality – Mehmood Nagar – were subject to brutal attacks by the state police on the very same day. For details, see Dhara (2019).

12 See the ChalChitra Abhiyaan report on this incident, available at https://www.youtube.com/watch?v=D3lKJOyA4sc&t=3s (accessed on 13 October 2020).

13 Section 151 of the Code of Criminal Procedure allows the Indian police to take 'preventive detention' measures by detaining an individual (or a group of individuals), without a warrant or orders from the magistrate.

14 Section 144 of the Code of Criminal Procedure empowers the executive magistrate of any state or territory within states to prohibit the gathering of five or more people, holding of public meetings, etc.

15 The Akhil Bharatiya Vidyarthi Parishad (ABVP) is a student organisation affiliated to the Rashtriya Swayamsevak Sangh (RSS). The ABVP has a student unit in most of India's higher educational institutions and has particularly been at the forefront of instigating (and inflicting) violence in university campuses (such as the Hyderabad Central University in 2015, the Jawaharlal Nehru University in 2016 and in 2020, etc.) against faculty members, and most often against left-wing student groups. Additionally, members of the ABVP have repeatedly interrupted documentary film screenings and lectures critical of the current central government.

16 On 6 June 2018, five activists (Sudhir Dhawale, Surendra Gadling, Mahesh Raut, Shoma Sen, and Rona Wilson) were arrested under the Unlawful Activities Prevention Act (UAPA), and subsequently others including Sudha Bharadwaj, Gautam Navlakha, Varavara Rao, Arun Pereira, and Vernon Gonsalves were arrested under the same law by the Pune Police. The arrested activists were accused of instigating violence during the annual commemoration of the Bhima Koregaon battle on 1 January 2018. A subsequent FIR filed against these activists accused them of having 'Maoist links', and of their involvement in a plot to assassinate Prime Minister Narendra Modi. The case is now under investigation by the National Investigation Agency (NIA), and some of the activists

(including Varavara Rao and Sudha Bharadwaj) remain under custody without trial even to this day. For a brief timeline of the events in the aftermath of the Bhima Koregaon violence, see *Peoples Dispatch* (2020). For a separate website that includes details of all the arrested activists, see https://free-them-all.net/ (accessed on 13 October 2020).

17 The Bahujan Samaj Party (BSP) was founded in 1984 by Kanshi Ram and is currently headed by Mayawati. The BSP is influenced by the non-Brahmin caste movements of the late nineteenth and early twentieth centuries and claims to represent the interests of India's non-upper caste groups such as Scheduled Castes (or Dalits), Scheduled Tribes, Other Backward Classes, and religious minorities (Muslims, for instance). The BSP president, Mayawati, briefly held office as the chief minister of Uttar Pradesh on three occasions (in 1995, 1997, and from 2002 to 2003) before securing the absolute majority to form the state government in the legislative assembly elections of 2007 and completed five years in office in 2012. The party currently has ten members of Parliament in India's lower house (Lok Sabha).

18 The Bhim Army is a Dalit organization founded by Chandrasekhar Azad 'Raavan' and Vinay Ratan Singh in UP's Saharanpur district in response to caste oppression (and violence) of Dalits by the locally dominant Thakur caste. Azad has been repeatedly persecuted by the UP state government under national security laws, and has also been arrested for his participation in the anti-CAA protests. Jignesh Mevani is a lawyer and social activist from Gujarat who rose to national prominence after leading a large protest rally against the flogging of seven Dalit men in Una (Gujarat) in July 2016. In December 2017, Mevani became a member of the Gujarat's state assembly, representing the Vadgam constituency. In the aftermath of the Bhima Koregaon violence, Mevani was charged by the Pune Police of 'creating communal disharmony, and for making "provocative speeches"'.

19 In March 2018, the Supreme Court of India ruled that no public servant could be arrested immediately after a complaint is filed against him/her under the SC/ST Prevention of Atrocities Act. The ruling prompted nationwide protests in which nine people were killed, and several hundreds were detained by the police, across north and central India. Facing widespread backlash by Dalit groups, the central government initially blamed its political opponents (particularly the Congress) for the protests, but eventually backtracked on its words, by hastily passing an amendment to the SC/ST Prevention of Atrocities Act to reverse the Supreme Court's decision in early August 2018. This was done due to the impending state legislative assembly elections in five states, including most crucially Madhya Pradesh (MP), Chhattisgarh, and Rajasthan – the central government's gamble of reversing the Supreme Court's order to pacify Dalit groups failed as the BJP succumbed to electoral losses in MP, Chhattisgarh, and Rajasthan.

20 In October 2019, the Yogi Adityanath–led UP government amended the post-Matric scholarship regulations for SC/ST students by making scholarships conditional on the achievement of a minimum 60 per cent grade percentage in the intermediate or 12th grade examinations. This scholarship was earlier available to all SC/ST students irrespective of their grades, and the amendment has triggered protests in several parts of UP by several Dalit organisations. For details, see the ChalChitra Abhiyaan report

at https://www.youtube.com/watch?v=p4c5ThRHjec&t=9s (accessed on 13 October 2020).

21 A staunch critic of the BJP, Gauri Lankesh was a journalist and activist based in Bangalore (Karnataka). She was shot dead by assailants – allegedly of the Hindu Yuva Sena, a militant right-wing outfit – outside her home on 5 September 2017. The Karnataka government is yet to set up a fast-track court to commence trial despite a chargesheet filed by the Karnataka Special Investigations Team (SIT) with evidence against seventeen of the eighteen arrested accused in November 2018. For details on the current status of the case, see Shantha (2020).

22 Three *Caravan* journalists – Prabhjit Singh, Shahid Tantray, and an unnamed woman staffer – were surrounded by a mob of about 100 people in the Subhash Mohalla area of Delhi on 5 August 2020. The journalists were physically assaulted, and the woman staffer was also sexually harassed as the mob demanded that they delete video footage of their interviews with local Muslim residents, and also of a tape that contained evidence of a local BJP leader physically threatening the journalists. For details of this incident, see Ara (2020a).

23 The *Hanuman Chalisa* is a devotional hymn authored by the poet Tulsidas. It comprises forty verses in the Awadhi language, devoted to Lord Hanuman (the monkey god in Hindu mythology, and devotee of Lord Ram).

24 4G services in Kashmir were restored on 16 August 2020, after almost two years.

25 On 9 November 2019 a five-judge Constitution bench of the Supreme Court of India, led by Chief Justice Ranjan Gogoi, passed a unanimous verdict in the long-standing Ramjanmbahoomi (Birthplace of Ram) dispute. The court's verdict held that the disputed land – upon which the Babri mosque once stood, until its demolition on 6 December 1992 by Hindu right-wing mobs – belongs to Ram Lalla (Lord Ram). Further, the court directed the central government to set up a trust to oversee the construction of a Ram temple at the site, and also directed the government to allot a 5-acre plot to the Sunni Waqf Board for the construction of a mosque in Ayodhya. For details, see Scroll Staff (2019).

26 On 5 August 2019, Union Home Minister Amit Shah introduced two resolutions in Parliament that abrogated the special status of Jammu and Kashmir under Article 370 of the Indian Constitution. Under Article 370, Jammu and Kashmir was allowed to draft its own state constitution and the legislative authority of Indian Parliament was consequently limited in the state. For an explanation of the legal manoeuvres involved in the sudden abrogation of Article 370, see Yamunan (2019).

27 The Citizenship Amendment Act, 2019, passed in the Indian Parliament on 11 December 2019 lays out revised rules for Indian citizenship. It provides citizenship status for persecuted religious minorities from Afghanistan, Bangladesh, and Pakistan, but crucially this list of 'persecuted religious minorties' does not include Muslims, and is restricted to Hindus, Sikhs, Buddhists, Jains, Parsis, and Christians. For details on the amendments to the Citizenship law, see Danyal (2019).

28 On 15 December 2019, the Delhi Police forcefully entered the Jamia Millia Islamia (a higher educational institution) campus, using tear gas and batons to disperse several of

the university's students protesting against the CAA. The police violence – captured on video – was particularly severe in areas that included the university's libraries and washrooms. More than seventy students were injured and rushed to nearby hospitals, while several hundreds were also detained by the police. For details, see HT Correspondent (2020).

29 See note 19.
30 Pinjra Tod (Break the Cage) emerged in 2015 as a movement of women students from colleges affiliated to Delhi University, Ambedkar University, and Jamia Millia Islamia, in response to discriminatory hostel regulations that prohibit women to step out at night (after 8 p.m., for instance). While the movement has since spread to other higher educational institutions in India and widened its focus to include a range of different concerns related to the intersectional inequalities confronted by young students, its activists have also come under the punitive eye of the Indian state. In May 2020, two Pinjra Tod activists – Devangana Kalita and Natasha Narwal – were arrested by the Delhi police for participating in the anti-CAA protests, and therefore for preventing public servants from performing their duties.
31 A reference to the ideological training and thought of the BSP (political party and movement) from the 1980s and 1990s that emerged to challenge the hegemony of dominant castes in the state. Initiated by BSP founder Kanshi Ram, the Bahujanwadi project largely focused on questions of Dalit and OBC caste representation in politics and government, and on the political empowerment of the community. Material questions relating to Dalits and the annihilation of caste were not as central.
32 For the video on the replication of Shaheen Bagh in Deoband, see ChalChitra Abhiyaan (2020a, 2020b).

References

Ara, I. 2020a. 'How Caravan Journalists Were Attacked While Reporting in North East Delhi'. *The Wire*, 12 August. https://thewire.in/media/caravan-reporters-attacked-north-east-delhi (accessed on 13 October 2020).

———. 2020b. 'UP Police Arrests Prashant Kanojia, Says Tweet on "Hindu Army" Leader "Disrupts Communal Harmony"'. *The Wire*, 18 August. https://thewire.in/rights/prashant-kanojia-arrested-tweets-uttar-pradesh-police-transit-remand (accessed on 13 October 2020).

ChalChitra Abhiyaan. 2020a. 'Women of Deoband Recreate Shaheen Bagh'. 17 March. https://www.chalchitraabhiyaan.com/women-of-deoband-recreate-shaheen-bagh/ (accessed on 13 October 2020).

———. 2020b. 'In Spite of 40 FIRs Deoband Women Stay Put'. 17 March. https://www.chalchitraabhiyaan.com/in-spite-of-40-firs-deoband-women-stay-put/ (accessed on 13 October 2020).

Danyal, S. 2019. 'Explainer: How Exactly Does India's Citizenship Amendment Bill Discriminate against Muslims?' *Scroll.in*, 5 December. https://scroll.in/article/944852/explainer-how-exactly-does-india-s-citizenship-amendment-bill-discriminate-against-muslims (accessed on 13 October 2020).

Dhara, T. 2019. 'In Muzaffarnagar, Police and Hindutva Groups Attack Muslims in an Attempt to Recreate 2013 Riots'. *The Caravan*, 29 December. https://caravanmagazine.in/politics/muzaffarnagar-police-hindutva-groups-attack-muslims-attempt-recreate-2013-riots (accessed on 13 October 2020).

Dixit, N. 2013a. 'Holier Than Cow'. *Outlook*, 28 January. https://magazine.outlookindia.com/story/holier-than-cow/283593 (accessed on 13 October 2020).

———. 2013b. 'Thread Bared'. *Outlook*, 30 December. https://magazine.outlookindia.com/story/thread-bared/288907 (accessed on 13 October 2020).

———. 2014a. 'Shadow Lines'. *Outlook*, 4 August. https://magazine.outlookindia.com/story/shadow-lines/291494 (accessed on 13 October 2020).

———. 2014b. 'Love Jihad': War on Romance in India'. *Al Jazeera*, 14 October. https://www.aljazeera.com/features/2014/10/14/love-jihad-war-on-romance-in-india (accessed on 13 October 2020).

———. 2016. 'Operation #BetiUthao'. *Outlook*, 8 August. https://magazine.outlookindia.com/story/operation-betiuthao/297626 (accessed on 13 October 2020).

———. 2018. 'A Chronicle of the Crime Fiction That Is Adityanath's Encounter Raj'. *The Wire*, 24 February. https://thewire.in/rights/chronicle-crime-fiction-adityanaths-encounter-raj (accessed on 13 October 2020).

———. 2019. 'Gun Law: The Unstoppable Rise of Indian Police Encounter Shootings'. *National News*, 10 January. https://www.thenational.ae/opinion/comment/gun-law-the-unstoppable-rise-of-indian-police-encounter-shootings-1.811634 (accessed on 13 October 2020).

Edward, H., and N. Chomsky. 2002. 'A Propaganda Model'. In *Manufacturing Consent: The Political Economy of Mass Media*, 1–36. New York: Pantheon Books.

HT Correspondent. 2020. 'A Blow-by-blow Account of Jamia Protest in Last 24 Hrs over Citizenship Act'. *Hindustan Times*, 7 August. https://www.hindustantimes.com/india-news/a-blow-by-blow-account-of-jamia-protest-in-last-24-hrs-over-citizenship-act/story-DKCtRz81fc673j4tVaFAWI.html (accessed on 13 October 2020).

Outlook Web Bureau. 2018. 'Supreme Court Says Khap Panchayats Illegal, No Assembly Can Interfere in a Marriage between Two Consenting Adults'. *Outlook*. 27 March. https://www.outlookindia.com/website/story/supreme-court-declares-khap-panchayats-illegal/310063 (accessed on 13 October 2020).

Peoples Dispatch. 2020. 'Bhima Koregaon Case: A Comprehensive Timeline'. 6 June. https://peoplesdispatch.org/2020/06/06/bhima-koregaon-case-a-comprehensive-timeline/ (accessed on 13 October 2020).

Sawhney, N. S. 2011. *Izzatnagari ki Asabhya Betiyan* [Documentary]. News Click, Magic Lantern Foundation.

Scroll Staff. 2019. 'Ayodhya Case: Supreme Court Verdict Paves Way for Ram Temple, Allots

Separate Space to New Mosque'. *Scroll.in*, 9 November. https://scroll.in/latest/943195/ayodhya-case-supreme-court-verdict-paves-way-for-ram-temple-allots-separate-space-to-new-mosque (accessed on 13 October 2020).

———. 2020. 'Uttar Pradesh: Journalist Shot Dead in Ballia District, Police Arrest Six Accused'. *Scroll.in*, 25 August. https://scroll.in/latest/971315/uttar-pradesh-journalist-shot-dead-in-ballia-family-counters-polices-property-dispute-claims (accessed on 13 October 2020).

Shantha, S. 2020. 'On Third Anniversary, Gauri Lankesh's Family Await Speedy Trial'. *The Wire*, 5 September. https://thewire.in/rights/gauri-lankesh-third-death-anniversary-trial-investigation (accessed on 13 October 2020).

Special Correspondent. 2020. 'Ghaziabad Journalist Vikram Joshi Dies of Bullet Injury'. *The Hindu*, 22 July. https://www.thehindu.com/news/national/other-states/journalist-shot-at-by-assailants-in-ghaziabad-dies/article32156594.ece#:~:text=Ghaziabad%20journalist%20Vikram%20Joshi%2C%20who,a%20private%20hospital%2C%20police%20said (accessed on 13 October 2020).

The Wire Analysis. 2020. 'FAQ: What Are the UP Police FIRs against The Wire Actually About?' *The Wire*, 19 April. https://thewire.in/media/faq-up-police-fir-siddharth-varadarajan (accessed on 13 October 2020).

The Wire Staff. 2020. 'A Timeline: The Cases against Dr Kafeel Khan and His Arrests'. *The Wire*, 2 September. https://thewire.in/rights/kafeel-khan-arrest-cases-timeline (accessed on 13 October 2020).

Vaidyanathan A., and A. Pandey. 2020. '"No Law to Support You", Says Supreme Court as UP Defends "Shame" Posters'. NDTV, 12 March. https://www.ndtv.com/india-news/no-law-to-support-you-supreme-court-observes-on-up-government-defending-name-and-shame-posters-2193569 (accessed on 13 October 2020).

Yamunan, S. 2019. 'Move to Scrap Special Status of Jammu and Kashmir Is an Unprecedented Attack on India's Constitution'. *Scroll.in*, 5 August. https://scroll.in/article/932869/move-to-scrap-special-status-of-jammu-and-kashmir-is-an-unprecedented-attack-on-indias-constitution (accessed on 13 October 2020).

ARTICULATION

6

THE MAKING OF A MAJORITARIAN METROPOLIS
CROWD ACTION, PUBLIC ORDER, AND COMMUNAL ZONING IN CALCUTTA

Ritajyoti Bandyopadhyay

Introduction

Throughout its colonial history, Calcutta had been a Hindu majority city at the heart of a Muslim majority province. Until the mid-twentieth century, despite the bitter rivalry, the city's Hindu and Muslim populations inhabited shared spaces even in neighbourhoods that had less than 10 per cent minority population. This character of the city began to transform in the inter-war decades, culminating in a decisive territorial marginalization and ghettoization of Muslims in Calcutta in the mid-twentieth century, following the Partition of India in 1947. At 'the stroke of midnight' on 15 August 1947, Calcutta emerged as the Hindu-majority capital city of the Hindu-majority state of West Bengal. The Partition and the streams of Hindu-Bengali refugee migration from East Pakistan transformed Calcutta into a 'refugee city' in successive decades.

The chapter tracks the ways in which Hindu–Muslim relationship unfolded in the city in the post-colonial era, which, I believe, continues to anticipate a politically self-conscious and coherent articulation of Hindutva in municipal politics in recent years. In many Indian cities, Hindutva over the decades has manifested as a powerful space maker which established majoritarianism as *common sense*.[1] City dwellers have learned to identify and rationalize their belonging to the city in the context of this majoritarian urban common sense. In Calcutta, the normalization of the majoritarian city presupposes a foundational violence that annulled the earlier communal distribution of space and property between the majority and minority communities and introduced a new order of things. The 'Muslim ghetto' is the product of both the cleansing force of the civil war of 1946 and the rationality of the market process that maintained and reproduced communal stakes in the real estate transactions of the post-colonial city in subsequent decades.

In this chapter, I closely analyse a communal civil war in 1946 and a relatively minor communal outbreak in 1950, and relate these mobilizations with growing communal segregation in Calcutta in the subsequent decades. The chapter has three sections. The first section presents a close reading of an interrogation of a police officer by a high-powered enquiry commission in 1946–47 and unravels a rather complex spatial relationship between the city's Hindus and Muslims in the pre-Independence era. The second section tracks a series of developments in the aftermath of Independence which led to the complete territorial defeat of Muslims in Calcutta and a gradual normalization of Hindu dominance over space and public discourse, and the way the histories of normalization in Calcutta have laid the groundwork for the contemporary rise of Hindutva in the city and the state as a normalized force. The third section chronicles some ethnographic vignettes aiming at a 'thick description' of how majoritarian common sense operates in our everyday urban life.

Certain observations about the current conjuncture drove me to undertake this historical inquiry. It can be inferred from the election data between 2014 and 2019 that the Bharatiya Janata Party (BJP) has, at last, become a noteworthy electoral force in West Bengal. While the right-wing party managed to secure only a couple of seats in the 2016 assembly elections, BJP candidates for the first time in electoral history secured the second position in three seats with 16.8 per cent vote share – the party's most remarkable performance to date, surpassing its previous best of 11.66 per cent in the 1991 general elections. In subsequent Lok Sabha by-polls, the party succeeded in pushing the the Communist Party of India (Marxist), or CPI(M), to the third position and registered a sizeable increase in its vote share. In the Uluberia by-poll (an industrial town in the Howrah industrial belt) for instance, the BJP received 23.29 per cent votes, a 12 per cent increase from 2014. In the 2019 Lok Sabha elections, the BJP surprised all election analysts by grabbing eighteen out of forty-two seats in West Bengal, securing a 40 per cent vote share. Calcutta remained with the ruling Trinamool Congress (TMC), but there were speculations that Calcutta's fall was just a matter of time. In the 2021 assembly elections, the TMC retained its hold over the Greater Calcutta region. The ruling party performed remarkably well in the urban areas of West Bengal, securing 50 per cent vote share, on average. In most of the urban constituencies, the BJP stood second and emerged as a substantial electoral force.

The working-class neighbourhoods of both Howrah and Calcutta have witnessed a sharp rise in the popularity of the BJP in recent years. A preliminary observation of the membership of different political parties in some of these neighbourhoods suggests a substantial presence of Dalits in the rank and file of the BJP. The rise of the BJP to electoral significance coincided with the eruption of mini, informal temples of Lord Rama and Hanuman on just about every vacant space in the city (and at times on streets and pavements). In addition, there appears to be a substantial mobilization of money in building imposing temple structures, especially in neighbourhoods traditionally known for hosting substantial Muslim populations, most remarkably in corporation wards 14, 15, and 16 in the north-east, 48 and 49 in the central-east, 78 in the south, and 73, 74, and 75 in the west. Often, these temples are the centres of provocative communal mobilization with massive sound systems attached to the sites.[2]

My local contacts in various neighbourhoods (most of them are street vendors with whom I have been working since 2006) informed me that many local clubs[3] have begun to switch their allegiance to the BJP covertly. They still hang Chief Minister Mamata Banerjee's cut-outs at the front gate, but consciously keep contact with the local BJP and Rashtriya Swayamsevak Sangh (RSS) functionaries. Certain clubs are overt in their support of the BJP and Hindutva, especially in central Calcutta (such as the Burrabazar area where the BJP has a traditional base) and in the refugee areas of the south and southwest where they actively collaborate with the RSS *shakha*s to organize the rituals of physical exercise for local children and youth. In short, the recent electoral success of the BJP is powered by the growth of its social and cultural organizations in the city and in various districts of the state in general.[4]

As the following sections will show, the growing Hindutva social, cultural, and political presence in the city in recent years is a historically sedimented process that has unfolded in Calcutta since at least the late-colonial era.

A Civil War and an Interrogation

Exactly a year before India and Pakistan attained freedom, Calcutta witnessed a major outbreak of communal tension, which assumed the dimension of a civil war. Dubbed the 'Great Calcutta Killings' in public discourse, the violence in the third week of August 1946 left about 15,000 dead and 100,000 injured, and rendered about 2,000,000 individuals homeless. The official estimate was, of course, much more conservative.[5]

The Calcutta Disturbances Commission was set up under a special act of the Bengal Legislature called the Bengal Act XIV of 1946 to 'enquire into the causes and the course of the disturbances in Calcutta between Friday, 16th and, Tuesday, 20 August of 1946 and into the measures taken to deal with them and to submit to the Government of Bengal a report of their findings'.[6] The president of the commission, the incumbent Chief Justice of India (CJI), was authorized to take evidence from the sources that he would deem necessary for the commission's deliberations. The commission remained incomplete in its proceedings and inconclusive in delivering a judgment. However, it gathered rich documentation of crowd action in a city that, for over a week, decimated public order. The commission interrogated several police and army officials of various ranks who oversaw the city when the civil war broke out.

One of the first things that the commission accomplished was to prepare a clear map demarcating 'predominantly Hindu localities, predominantly Moslem localities ... the border of the No-Man's land ... mixed localities ... aristocratic Moslem localities such as Park Circus ... four prominent bustees' in Kalabagan, Mehdibagan, Rajabajar and Watganj, and so on (Samaddar 2017, 60). The Advocate General of Bengal was entrusted with the responsibility to come up with such a map, which was anticipated to make the task of commission's fact-finding easier. The witnesses were asked to describe and mark their activities during the days of the riot on the map (Figures 6.1–6.3).

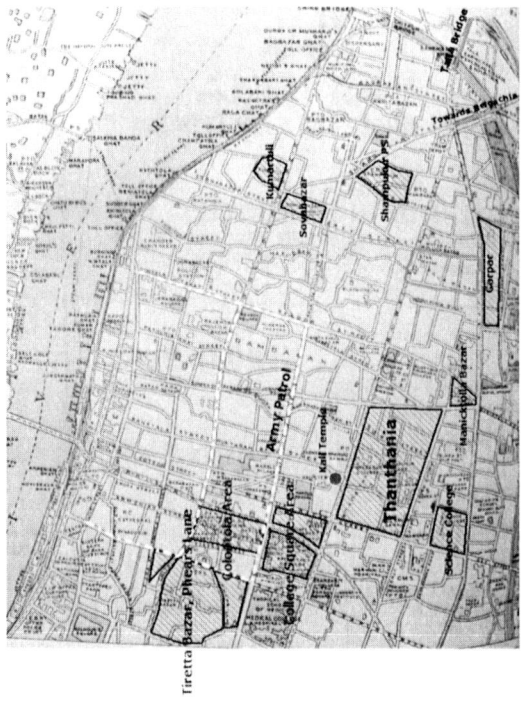

Figure 6.1 1946 Riot Map 1: North Calcutta (in the language of the police, 'Northern Division'). The map is extracted from *Thaker's Indian Directory 1945*, Thaker's Directories, Ltd (Calcutta: Thacker, Spink & Co., 1946).

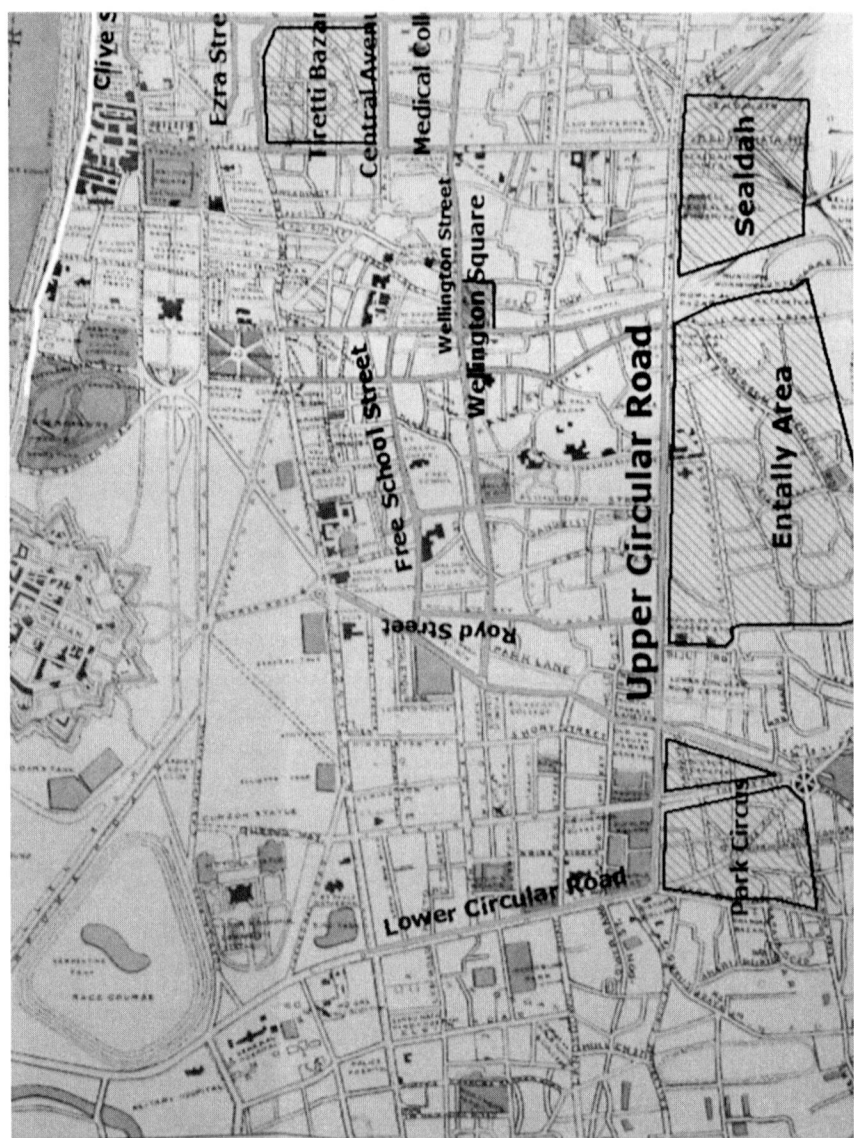

Figure 6.2 1946 Riot Map 2: 'Central Division.' The map is extracted from *Thaker's Indian Directory 1945*, Thaker's Directories, Ltd (Calcutta: Thacker, Spink & Co., 1946).

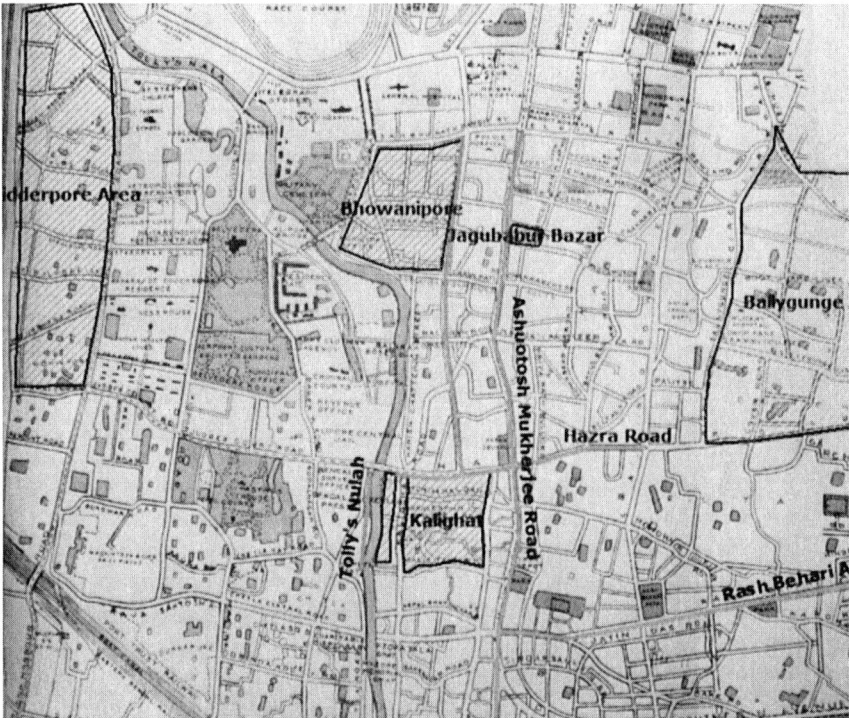

Figure 6.3 1946 Riot Map 3: 'Southern Division.' The map is extracted from *Thaker's Indian Directory 1945*, Thaker's Directories, Ltd (Calcutta: Thacker, Spink & Co., 1946).

In this context, we will follow the commission's interrogation of N. H. Khundkar, the officer-in-charge of the Burtolla Police Station (Figure 6.1), whose jurisdiction was bounded on the north by Grey Street–Ultodanga Road; on the east by Gouribere Lane–Halishbagan Street, then a little east of Upper Circular Road to the east of the Maniktala Market (Calcutta Disturbances Commission of Enquiry 1947). Khundkar answered as many as 1,706 questions (each question consisted of four–five related questions), making it one of the longest interrogations. What emerged from this three-day-long encounter on 14, 17, and 18 February 1947 was a complex sociology of the riot that called into question the existing paradigm of comprehending crowd action. It appears that the interrogators (commissioners B. A. Siddiky and B. Somayya) and Khundkar operated from two mutually incommensurable epistemic spaces and 'cut the world differently', even though they deployed very similar coordinates, units, and standards of measurement – street names, house numbers, geographic boundaries of communal distribution, demographic features of the jurisdiction, chronological reconstruction of events, sociological breakdown of the crowds, and so on – to understand what 'actually' happened in the first two days of the riot. Khundkar's extraordinary narrative of entangled relationships continued to frustrate any easy understanding of the 'cause and course of disturbances' that the commission was mandated to unravel. What followed at the end was a *crisis in comprehensibility* – as the failure of the commission as a regime of truth became apparent.

Let us first get a sense of the population in the jurisdiction of Burtolla *thana*. According to Khundkar's estimate, his jurisdiction had around 9 per cent Muslim population during the time of the riots:

B. A. Siddiky: Are they spread over the whole area in your jurisdiction, or are they in pockets?

Witness: They have got *bustee* areas, Muslim pockets here and there…

Siddiky: will you kindly name these pockets in your area?

Witness: One was in Ram Chand Ghosh Lane. Then in Musjidbari Street. It has got no particular name. This pocket is in Musjidbari Street. Then to the south of it is Ram Chand Ghosh Lane. Then there is one Muslim pocket there in Central Avenue. There is a mosque which bears a number of Musjidbari Street. At the crossing of Musjidbari Street and Central Avenue, there is a mosque, and near it, there are two or three houses. Three Muslim families used to live in the rooms attached to the mosque.

B. Somayya: There are no houses apart from the mosque?

Witness: No. Then Gulu Ostagar Lane. Here is also a Muslim pocket. There were big buildings and huts here; about eight houses. Then we come to near about Beadon Row. Hereabout was a mosque and attached to the side of the mosque, three or four Muslim families used to live in some rooms attached to the mosque. There were also two or three huts close by. Then we come to what is called Chidam Mudi Lane. Near about is a mosque. Nobody used to live here, but the *Mutawalli* and three or four families used to live at this place. This is called Blacquire Square. This is in Hari Ghose Street. It falls on Grey Street, and it comes out from Beadon Street. About this place, there was a mosque about halfway off. This is opposite Bhim Ghosh Lane. Here, there were no Muslim residents, but there were 2, 3 or 4 shopkeepers, Biri and cigarette sellers—Muslim shopkeepers. Then here is the police station and we are on Cornwallis Street. About this place, there is a mosque.

President: Just north of the police station?

Witness: Not exactly north, it is North West. Here we have got a big mansion, thereafter the residence of a Hindu gentleman. Then the mosque.

By the side of that mosque, in the rooms attached to the mosque, some Kabulis used to reside. Then this is Raja Raj Kissen Street, and this is Sahitya Parishad Street. These are two populous streets. Between these is Goabagan Cattle Market.

Somayya: Do any Muslims live there?

Witness: There are Muslim cattle dealers, and some Hindu cattle dealers live mostly this side on the Sahitya Parishad Street, and the north side live Muslims. On the north side of Raja Raj Kissen Street, there are some cattle huts cattle khatals they are called, almost close to Upper Circular Road. We have Muslims here.

Somayya: Scattered?

Witness: Almost compact, around the cattle market except on the south where the Hindu cattle dealers live. This we come to the crossing of Upper Circular Road and Vivekananda Road. This is not exactly opposite the crossing. Here we have a market called Maniktolla Market. There is a mosque and there are few residential huts as well as shops—Muslim shops. Here there was a Hindu shop also. This is called Nandan Bagan bustee, between Circular Road and Raja Dinendra Street.

Somayya: Is that all Muslim area?

Witness: No[,] mixed area. Muslims were very few, scattered all over. Here is a bustee at No. 76/1 Cornwallis Street, just west of the police station. This is a mixed area…

What is important in this conversation is the way in which Khundkar handled a set of seemingly objective demographic questions – how many of which community live where – arguably a series of census questions that could then be tabulated and analysed. Khundkar, in his turn, took the commissioners through a visual/pictorial and mostly qualitative description of his jurisdiction. Of course, he started with some census figures, but then the description increasingly relied on his identification of houses, buildings, shops, residential quarters, streets and lanes, and mosques – the way a resident would relate to the neighbourhood. Did he answer the questions posed? Yes and no. He gave a more complex description of the lived reality of communal distribution in his jurisdiction that defied the frame through which the members of the commission were visualizing the conflict. In other words, the members of the commission were trying to 'fix' the population into time, space, and ratio, while Khundkar was describing mobile geography, entangled realities of inter-communal, inter-ethnic, and inter-class sharing of space, and a set of mobile crowds that were attacking various portions of his jurisdiction and continuously switching location. Time and again, Khundkar's narrative would frustrate them.

The discussion continued for the whole day on 14 February 1947 in this circular manner. On several occasions, the commission wanted Khundkar to specify the 'composition of the crowds'. Thus, at one point Siddiky asked him: 'I mean of what class they were composed?' Khundkar replied: 'Of the Muslim mob, some were wearing Pyjamas, some lungis ... and of the Hindus, I saw young men, Bengali young men. Kalwars and low-class people on both sides.' (Calcutta Disturbances Commission of Enquiry 1947, 18) Here, it is noteworthy that Siddiky was a representative of the Muslim League in the commission and his intention was to project the comparative innocence and victimhood of the city's Muslim community. Thus, at one point he asked, 'By this could you judge that the mood of this Hindu mob was very bad?' To this Khundkar's said: 'The mood was bad on both sides. Equally bad.' Then, Siddiky anxiously asked Khundkar to give a 'pocket-by-pocket' breakup of the plight of the Muslims where they were attacked by Hindu mobs (Calcutta Disturbances Commission of Enquiry 1947, 22). He took up the instance of Musjidbari Street *bustee*: 'This one is not a *bustee* proper, but there are a few Muslims living here and there within a radius of a few yards. Is it not? (Calcutta Disturbances Commission of Enquiry 1947, 20)' Now Khundkar reiterated his earlier position and said: 'All the Muslims are living side by side.' (Calcutta Disturbances Commission of Enquiry 1947, 20) 'How many Muslims are living there?' 'There are about six *pucca* buildings and huts also', Khundkar answered (Calcutta Disturbances Commission of Enquiry 1947, 20). An anxious Siddiky asked Khundkar to give precise numbers: 'Did I not ask for a number?' 'May be 100', replied Khundkar. 'And would you tell us now what happened to these 100 Muslims of Musjidbari Street?' Khundkar replied: 'Nothing happened to them ...' 'Not a single Muslim was killed'? 'Not a single Muslim was killed because Hindus protected them' (Calcutta Disturbances Commission of Enquiry 1947, 21). Siddiky pointed out that, after all, the entire Muslim population was evacuated from the place for safety. Therefore, they lost their 'hearth and home. They might not have been killed to the last man' (Calcutta Disturbances Commission of Enquiry 1947, 21). Khundkar chose to remain silent.

The riot of 1946 took the dimension of a civil war in which the crowds sharpened religious boundaries in space and their strategic formations, in the form of mobile territories, travelling in the streets and claiming them. But, in so doing, the crowds dissolved all fears of mixing. Thus, time and again the affidavits and interrogations in the commission found a dense intermingling and liaison between *bhadralok* elements, the terrorists, the lumpenproletariat, and the *goondas* in the crowds. The police chased the crowds in order to disintegrate them into more easily recognizable mobs, which, in turn, retaliated by chasing the police patrol. This inherent mobility of the crowd–police dyad led to a sporadic and discrete response – the crowds would disappear and re-form a few yards away or elsewhere, keeping the police patrol on the move in different directions throughout the city, blurring the boundaries of formal jurisdictions between *thana*s. Khundkar would frequently be seen crossing his own jurisdictional boundaries to chase the crowds, adding another layer of difficulty for Their Lordships to reconstruct his mobility: '... You say at the junction of the Upper Circular Road and the Vivekananda Road you met the Deputy Commissioner North ... Is this within your jurisdiction?' Khundkar confirmed that it was outside his jurisdiction. 'Is his [Mr Manik Mullick's] residence within your jurisdiction?' Khundkar replied: 'No, that is not in my jurisdiction but is on the border' (Calcutta Disturbances Commission of Enquiry 1947, 13).

Throughout the proceedings of the commission on 14 February 1946, Khundkar continued to define his jurisdiction in terms of its 'borders' – the interfaces it had with other *thana*s. But how does one define this borderland? How does one tackle a situation when it bordered another territory? When Khundkar was asked this, he replied vaguely. 'From your evidence, I have gathered, Mr Khundkar, that incidents which took place on the borderline, should be dealt with by both the *thana*s. Is not that so?' Khundkar's replied bluntly: 'Those that occurred in my jurisdiction, it was my first duty to deal with them instead of asking the other police station to deal with it.' Do the boundaries emerging from a civil war neatly intercept the formal boundaries of the police stations? In the dialectic of boundary-breaking and boundary-preserving exercises, lines continuously flow with the mobile bodies that take the form of a crowd only by breaking and refunctioning these boundaries. Police chasing the crowds to maintain the boundary between two rival communities and the crowd chasing police to blur that boundary was, in fact, a recurring theme in Khundkar's deposition. Those were the points in which power and violence intercepted each other, simultaneously instigating and electrifying those who took part in this game.

The commission's session with Khundkar remained inconclusive for want of a common measure. When the commission sought census data on population, Khundkar could only find names of places, mosques, some houses, and a few huts. Their conversation exposed conceptual incompatibilities and hence the limits of communication. Khundkar's voice was recorded, but it was hardly heard. By the time Khundkar's affidavit was read, its 'context' had already ebbed away into 'archival compost'. The more he clarified his affidavit, the more it appeared incomprehensible to Their Lordships. Ultimately, the commission decided to end its deliberations without producing a report on its findings (Samaddar 2017).

Khundkar's sessions with the commission pointed to the fact that the Hindu–Muslim communal segregation of the city remained an unfinished endeavour, at least until the 1946 riot, despite a repeated convergence between the violence of city rebuilding and communal violence throughout the twentieth century. Janam Mukherjee (2015, 218) points out that the question of majority and minority community had localized characters – 'the prevailing territorial dynamic of *local* dominance'. There were Hindu-dominated neighbourhoods where some Muslims resided (more overwhelmingly so, given Calcutta was overall a Hindu-majority city) and vice versa. The contextual and localized nature of the territorial distribution of the Hindu and Muslim populations in the city also acted as a deterrent against communal riots. The riot of 1946 disturbed this equation fundamentally by 'de-housing' around 10 per cent of the city population over a few months. Still, until Independence, Muslims retained their territorial claim over some portions of the city. Independence was a game-changer for the Muslims in Calcutta. The riot of 1946 had intimate transactions with the foundational violence of the two nation-states. This was arguably the last time communal warfare took place in the city.

When Is the Majoritarian City?

We have seen in the previous section that even during the 1946 riots, it was difficult for the police officers working on the ground to zone-mark the pockets of the city as exclusively Hindu or Muslim. The neighbourhoods were mixed even in places where Muslims were in a clear minority in census terms. The creation of Pakistan and Calcutta's settlement with India, coupled with the disbandment of the Bengal Provincial Muslim League and a spectacular influx of refugees in the city, produced the objective material condition for the emergence of the majoritarian city. The upper caste refugees found leaders in all the established political parties of the day (a leadership capable of keeping the district-level mass leaders out of the core power structure of the ruling Congress Party and the Left opposition), while the Muslim leadership within the Congress lost ground in territorial reorganization and in the factional squabbles within the party structure. The Partition produced two new minority communities – the Hindus in East Pakistan and the Muslims in West Bengal (Bandyopadhyay 2012).

Five years after the August 1946 riot, the Census of 1951 published a fifty-year trend of Hindu–Muslim population ratio in Calcutta (Table 6.1).[7]

Table 6.1 A fifty-year trend of Hindu–Muslim population ratio in Calcutta, published by the Census of 1951

Year	Hindu Population	Muslim Population	Muslim Population as a percentage of the Hindu Population
1901	603,310	270,797	44.9
1911	672,206	275,280	41.0
1921	725,561	248,912	34.3
1931	796,628	281,520	35.3
1941	1,531,512	497,535	32.5
1951	2,125,907	305,932	14.4

Source: Census of 1951, Vol. VI, Part III, Calcutta City, p. XV.

The census figures register a decline of the Muslim population in Calcutta between 1941 and 1951 by 191,603 individuals. The West Bengal government registered a flight of 130,000 Muslims by 1951 because of the 'fear of disturbances' (Chatterji 2005, 229). According to an estimate, the Muslim population in Calcutta dropped from around 23 per cent in 1946–47 to around 12 per cent in 1951 (Kundu 2008). The 1961 Census found a near elimination of Muslims from certain wards of the city and a consequent rise of Muslim concentration in areas such as Park Circus, Ekbalpore, Bowbazar, Karaya, Narkeldanga, Beniapukur, and so on. M. K. A. Siddiqui concludes from the Census of 1961 that the Muslims were almost totally swept away from the northern, eastern, south-central, and south-eastern wards of the city (Siddiqui 1974, 16). Many of these wards also witnessed refugee resettlement throughout the 1950s.

Scholars such as Joya Chatterji (2005), Anwesha Sengupta (2015), and Sekhar Bandyopadhyay (2012) have recently drawn our attention to the various ways in which the near elimination and ghettoization of Muslims happened in the post-Partition years. Chatterji, arguably the pioneer in this field, showed how mosques, graveyards, and other properties under the Waqf Board were slowly but systematically occupied by the Hindu refugees. At times, such encroachments were coupled with communal violence.

These scholars referred to such an outbreak of communal violence in February 1950. The only credible surviving record of the carnage of 1950 in the public domain is a seven-page fact-finding report by Mridula Sarabhai. Wards 15 and 16 along with areas adjacent to Beadon Street, Amherst Street, and the working-class areas of the eastern frontier of the city bounded by Canal South Road in the north,

Tangra Road in the south, Palmer Bazar Road in the west, and New Tangra Road in the east[8] were severely affected by the February violence. Certain neighbourhood clubs in the affected areas were seen to be actively engaged in evicting Muslims and settling Hindu refugees in the vacant houses and hutments.[9] A section of the Congress workers, the RSS, and the Hindu Mahasabha activists were actively involved in this violence. Thus, RSS leader M. S. Golwalkar's presence in Burrabazar on 15 and 16 February was far from being a mere coincidence.[10]

A remarkable feature of violence during the trouble of 1950 was the proliferation of the cases of mob lynching of Muslims inside Muslim *mohallas* situated often in the margins of the city.[11] During her investigation Mridula Sarabhai encountered such a case at Ismail Street in Entally:

> The incident in Ismail Street coincided with the Prime Minister's visit to Calcutta on 6 March, 1950 ... on or about 8 March, I visited the place, saw the injured and heard the complaints of Hindus and Muslims. Hindus claimed that they were in the minority. It was the Muslims who were the aggressors. But the Muslims had another story to tell. From the type of devastation, one could not understand the Hindu claim ... It was quite apparent the persons who were sleeping were attacked. From the way, the doors and windows, even the lavatory doors, were broken one could see the place had been the victim of a consorted attack and all this in a Muslim Mohalla only.[12]

During the riot of 1950, some allegations came regarding the role of the police. An eyewitness, for instance, complained that a mob was led by people in khaki, 'giving the appearance of belonging to either the police or the military' (Bandyopadhyay 2012, 51). It was also alleged that the patrolling police parties intentionally delayed action and thus helped the Hindu mobs to do their job. The remarks of some of the prominent Muslim legislators in the assembly before and during the carnage also revealed a sense of insecurity among Muslims in the city. Already on 6 February 1950 – a couple of days before the carnage – S. K. Rafiq described the silent complicity of the administration in these various instances of violence:

> These troubles do not start at daytime; they always take place at night. And as usual, it takes time for the Police to arrive. The Police arrive not only one or two but sometimes three or four hours after the occurrence. Those who live near College Street and Mechuabazaar junction know how certain people, members certain community, tried to interfere with the *Kowali* which was being held in the market there, resulting in loss of properties and injuries to members of the minority community. (Sengupta 2015, 441–42)

The next day, another member of the House, Hussain Ara Begum, reported how Muslims in Maniktala, Narkeldanga, and Paikpara were intimidated and forced to quit their neighbourhoods.¹³ She claimed that being unable to trust the state machinery, Muslims in thousands fled to safer locations in their perception in Park Circus, Beniapukur, Narkeldanga, Zakaria Street, and Kidderpore (*The Statesman*, 1 July 1950).¹⁴ The jute mills and other factories in the industrial townships around Calcutta had to close production due to the flight of Muslim workers. Sekhar Bandyopadhyay (2012) says that during the riot days, about 25,000 Muslim refugees were squatting in and around the Park Circus Maidan (*The Statesman*, 1 July 1950).

By the third week of March 1950, these refugees were all gone. The British Consulate speculated that they had 'mostly migrated to Pakistan' (*The Statesman*, 1 July 1950, 55). According to the East Pakistani Press, about 1,100,000 Muslims crossed the international borders by 22 May 1950. While this must be an exaggeration, the official West Bengal figure of 437,612 was a rather conservative estimate. Joya Chatterji takes a nuanced position and believes that about a million Muslims left for Pakistan after Partition, and 70 per cent of them were from West Bengal (*The Statesman*, 1 July 1950).¹⁵

The riot of 1950 did not spare the city's elite Muslim population either. A Hindu mob targeted and set fire to the residence of the prominent Muslim League leader Abul Hasim who decided to stay in Calcutta after Partition, but this incident forced him to resettle in Dhaka. According to his son Badruddin Umar, several of their relatives followed the family and migrated to East Pakistan (*The Statesman*, 1 July 1950).

What is important to note in the instance of the riot of 1950 is the continuous, mundane, and unofficial nature of mob lynching of the members of the Muslim community in the city. Recall how both Rafiq and Begum referred to cases that occurred before the actual carnage on 8–10 February 1950. The Ismail Street case in Sarabhai's report, on the other hand, took place in early March 1950, nearly a month after the official carnage.

The violence of 1950 did not have a precise date of the beginning, and it certainly did not end with Nehru's subsequent visit to the refugee city. In the next one and a half decades, February 1950 became a norm rather than an exception. It is roughly estimated that between 1947 and 1977, around 40 riots took place in Calcutta and its surrounding areas, of which the one in January 1964 was significant in ravaging Muslim-dominated neighbourhoods in Amherst Street, Sealdah, Taltola, Entally, Beniapukur, and Beliaghata in the central-eastern parts of the city, Garia in the south, and squatter colonies along the Sealdah–Ballygunge rail track (Das 2000). The riots continued until 15 January 1964. According to one estimate, 8 lakh Muslims left for East Bengal from West Bengal and Assam (Kundu 2008). One direct impact of the sustained communal tension in the 1950s and 1960s was a growing crowding of Muslims of all classes in some of the pockets of the city, especially in Park Circus, Raja Bazaar, and in south-eastern fringes such as Tangra, Tiljala, and Topsia.[16]

Calcutta remained relatively free from major incidents of explicit communal fury during the period of the long Left Front regime in West Bengal (1977–2011). There were, however, numerous incidents of group violence as Calcutta began to expand eastward, grabbing slums and squatter colonies that hosted a substantial section of Muslim and Dalit populations along the rail track between the areas of Park Circus in the north and Bagha Jatin in the south.[17] Eventually, Bijon Setu (bridge/flyover) over the Ballygunge rail station, along with Sukanta Setu over Jadavpur rail station, became a prime vehicle of the eastward expansion of Calcutta, culminating in the massive Eastern Metropolitan Bypass project (started in 1973), which, in subsequent decades, led to a huge real estate boom and peri-urban growth in these neighbourhoods and the East Calcutta wetlands area, stretching from Salt Lake in the north, Garia in the south, the Dhapa dumping ground in the east, and the Eastern Metropolitan Bypass in the west. Urbanization in this area remained a matter of intense conflict, and it continued to keep the major political regimes in the past four decades well funded to run their everyday machinery (Roy 2002).

The expansion of the real estate market in the eastern fringe of the city further marginalized the working-class Muslim and Dalit populations of the city. The real estate operators lobbied aggressively with the government to shift the tanneries that employed thousands of Muslims and Dalits to areas further south and east in newly formed industrial hubs, citing grounds of pollution, and then proceeded to recycle these lands into new middle-class residential quarters. The slums that still existed in these areas lost their immediate livelihood contexts, forcing the residents to find employment elsewhere or in other sectors within the informal economy. The loss of proximity between life and labour made life more expensive and hence unsustainable in these slums which enabled a faster real estate transition in these fringe areas.[18] In 2011, during my ethnographic visit to the Muslim-dominated Gobra slum at the backyard of the National Medical College in Park Circus, I located several substantial gated middle-class housing enclaves amid a thickly populated slum area being named after prominent Hindu deities and things that conveyed Hindu sensibilities. I was told that these enclaves came up between 2000 and 2009.[19]

The Common Sense of a Majoritarian City

As the previous sections of the chapter have shown, Calcutta lost its complex feature of inter-communal sharing of space in the post-1946 years, as Muslims were pushed to certain exclusive pockets in the south-eastern and south-western pockets of the city, where their overall invisibility was compensated by the locally concentrated hyper-visibility of Muslim practices. The wealthy Hindu minority population in Garden Reach, Metiaburuj, and Park Circus began to desert their ancestral places and move to exclusively Hindu neighbourhoods between the 1970s and 2000s. A complex intertwining of the cultural othering of ghettos, real estate dynamics, and communal tension came to constitute the structural relationship between the majoritarian city and its minority ghettos.

The Left Front government was successful in checking the outbreak of communal riots for over three decades during its long reign between 1977 and 2011. However, it did little to address the structural imbalance between the majority and minority communities in terms of their access to social infrastructures, such as health, education, and employment. The Sachar Committee Report (2006) explicitly stated that the state of West Bengal had failed to provide basic resources for the uplift of its Muslim citizens. The literacy rate among Muslims in Calcutta was reported to be much lower in 2006 than during Independence in 1947 (Sattar 2018). The Left Front government also failed to eliminate the latent communalism that continued to inform the city's *bhadralok* world. In fact, it may be argued that the period of Left rule enabled latent majoritarianism by subsuming communal and caste contradictions into class issues. The government could not make the Muslims of the city feel secure about their futures. The spectre of riots continued to loom large among the city's Muslims. In sum, latent majoritarianism thrived during the Left rule which found a powerful political articulation after Narendra Modi came to power in 2014.[20]

Anasuya Chatterjee's in-depth ethnographic research in the Muslim-dominated Park Circus area documents this unequal structural relationship between the majority and the minority communities. A Hindu man who moved from Park Circus to a housing enclave near the Eastern Metropolitan Bypass reported to Chatterjee that 'Muslims ... are very dogmatic when it comes to religion. They think the neighbourhood belongs to them and they can do whatever they like ... it is difficult for Hindus to stay there ... Like many others we moved out at the first opportunity'. A number of Chatterjee's Hindu respondents (still residing in Park Circus) complained that Muslims lacked culture and a sense of the changing time: 'See how all of them, irrespective of "class" can live together ... That is because their sense of community feeling is so strong' (Chatterjee 2017).

Several Muslim men in Park Circus reported to Chatterjee that Muslims could not leave Park Circus for two reasons. First, the Muslims were frequently denied housing in Hindu-dominated neighbourhoods even when they had the capacity to afford housing in such neighbourhoods:

> Do you see the condition I live in? My sons feel ashamed to invite their friends home. We can afford to live in a much better place, but Hindus somehow don't like to live with us. We have searched for homes in many decent neighborhoods, but they either ask exorbitant rates or say they cannot rent out their homes to Muslims. (Chatterjee 2017, 157)

Second, Muslims felt safer being in Muslim ghettos as the memory of riots in Calcutta and elsewhere still haunted them:

> ... Muslims must live together ... I remember what happened in 1992–93. Hindus from Darapara (a nearby Hindu slum) came and attacked us with swords and lathis; they tried to burn down our houses. The police never come when you need them. Because our people were prepared, they could stand up to it. Even women knew that they should heat up oil and keep it ready to throw at the enemy. Together we could prevent them from entering our slum ... When Muslims live together people are forced to think twice before attacking them. (Chatterjee 2017, 151)

In fact, Chatterjee found that middle-class Muslims preferred to live close to the Muslim-dominated slum areas as they felt safer being under the protection of the Muslim working class. Thus, a lawyer told Chatterjee the following: 'Both rich and gentle-mannered middle-class Muslims know that they need these desperate slum-dwellers to protect them during communal riots. Middle class people are not capable of defending themselves; and they will not take to the streets when a riot breaks out' (Chatterjee 2017, 151).

These excerpts suggest that the memory of riots and the market economy of rent enforce each other in making ghettos durable. They further allude to the fact that social relationships between the majority and the minority communities are established during the major incidents of violence that have taken place at specific historical moments. Well after these events are over, even for people who have not directly experienced them, they serve as memories and warnings of the 'permanent warfare' between communities that can erupt at any time and must be kept at bay. For Muslims in the ghetto, peace is when war is fought elsewhere. Thus, one of Chatterjee's Muslim respondents says:

> Muslims to a large extent slowly overcame the fear of 1992 before Gujarat happened. The latter has really shaken the Muslims; look at what happened in Gulbarg Society [in Ahmedabad] ... it was said to be in a cosmopolitan area and home to affluent Muslims. It makes us think many times before purchasing a house/flat outside a Muslim area.

However, this remains an uneasy and differently violent peace. The segregated ghetto does not so much mean the end of communal violence as its displacement and transformation into other forms and modalities. Existing as an outcome of efforts to ward off and escape from large-scale, major violence, the Muslim ghetto marks and underwrites the *latent violence* of a majoritarian city. Let us take a closer look at this through a few ethnographic vignettes of how latent violence affects the lives of Muslims in present-day Calcutta.

Instance 1

In 2013, I interviewed several Muslim students studying in various colleges in the College Street area and Jadavpur University. Most of the students I met were from various districts of West Bengal, living in private boarding houses and as paying guests (known in Calcutta as 'PG'). All of them had a story to share regarding their difficulties with house-hunting. Usually, Hindu owners refuse to rent out their PG arrangements to Muslim students, I was told. Most of the respondents could find accommodation only in Muslim localities from Muslim landlords. One such student said that he found a PG arrangement in Park Circus though his college was in Jadavpur – nearly 5 kilometres away. A woman named Labani added a rather interesting twist to this narrative. She was in search of a PG arrangement in a refugee-dominated neighbourhood in south Calcutta. Upon hearing her name, the owner was convinced that she must be a Hindu girl and was glad to offer her a shared room. On the day of her move, Labani had to deposit a photocopy of her voter ID. The owner discovered that Labani's surname was 'Jangi'. This surname was unheard of among the Hindus, and it was extremely rare for even the Muslims. In addition, the word means militant in English. The landlady asked Labani to pack up and move out immediately.

I then followed the trail and met some PG owners in the Jadavpur University area, where I lived as a PG for a decade. I met Mr and Mrs Chatterjee, residents of Jadavpur Central Road. The couple was well known in the neighbourhood for their close friendship with a noted Revolutionary Socialist Party (RSP) leader. Mr Chatterjee's father was a prominent refugee activist of the 1950s. In many ways, the Chatterjees could be identified with the progressive, educated, and liberal *bhadralok* milieu of our times (that is, disavowal of caste and religious conservatism in *public* and its performance in *private*). After the marriage of their only daughter, they decided to start a 'PG' accommodation for boys. When asked if they had any Muslim students living in the PG, or whether they would like to accept a Muslim boy in the future, Chatterjees replied:

> You know, we do not believe in casteism or communalism. We will be extremely glad to have a cosmopolitan culture in our PG. But, the parents … you know, … They are from smaller towns. They lack urbanity. They

don't understand that intercommunal living is a part of good education ... Therefore, we have not so far accepted any Muslim boys. After all, everybody should consent to live together.

I went to many housing societies with the same question and received two types of answers: (*a*) 'we do not wish to live with the Muslims because they are culturally different' and (*b*) 'we have no issues, but we fear that our neighbours won't accept a Muslim family'. This is how the contemporary rental economy creates and reproduces the communal segregation of the city patterned by the earlier and more explicit violence of slum clearance and riots.

Instance 2

In the aftermath of the 1992 riots that broke out in different parts of the country in the aftermath of the Babri Mosque demolitions, the Calcutta Police rounded up several innocent Muslim young men from various slums in Topsia, Tangra, and Park Circus. When they were released after interrogation, they complained that the police had made them chant 'Jai Shree Ram'. My respondents from these slums repeatedly told me that they were always under special surveillance and were regularly summoned for interrogation whenever there was a crime in the city. Seabrook and Siddiqui draw our attention to the following press coverage:

> Ajijur Rahaman Sardar, son of Jamaluddin of Birmnagar, Majherpara Police Station, Bashirhat, District North 24 Parganas, was shown arrested on 22 June 2007. For: Attempted armed dacoity in Tiljala, Calcutta. Acquitted by the court for want of evidence in 2008.
>
> Ajijur Rahaman Sardar, son of Jamiruddin of Birmnagar, Majherpara Police Station, Bashirhat, District North 24 Parganas, was shown arrested on 29 June 2007, for alleged smuggling of RDX (explosive) into Lucknow on June 22–23, 2007. Status: lodged in Lucknow jail awaiting trial.

Seabrook and Siddiqui pursued the case a little further and found another narrative: 'While in the custody of police in Tiljala, Sardar was alleged to have smuggled explosives into Lucknow.' Such discrepancies in various narratives of the same event are rarely covered in the media (Seabrook and Siddiqui 2011, 79).

Take another similar instance. On 15 January 2008, *The Telegraph* carried out an article titled 'Cop Goof-up on Calcuttan'. In late 2007, Aftab Alam Ansari, a twenty-seven-year-old man, was arrested by the Calcutta Police on 27 December 2007 on charges of transporting explosives for the 'court blasts' in Uttar Pradesh (UP). On 23 November 2007, in a span of just twenty-five minutes, six bomb blasts occurred in Lucknow, Varanasi, and Faizabad, killing and injuring many people.

The Telegraph writes: 'The police had claimed that the 27-year-old Ansari had "single-handedly" carted the entire cache of explosives used in the chain blasts in Uttar Pradesh courts in November that killed 15 people' (*The Telegraph* 2008a).

On 26 December 2007, a group of CID officials, posing as the officials of the Unit Trust of India Mutual Funds, stormed into Aftab's home. Aftab was in his office, and his mother, Ayesha was at home. The officials claimed to be looking for Aftab for some bank matter. They asked Ayesha to furnish Aftab's photo, which she did. They then showed her a photograph of another man and asked her to identify him as her son Aftab, but Ayesha refused to identify him as her son. The officials carried a secret camera that took a detailed picture of their home. When Aftab arrived, he was greeted and encircled by some CID officers. That night, he was taken into informal custody in a flat near the airport. Aftab remembered:

> One officer said to me 'Your name is Muktar, alias Raju'. I said, 'That is not my name. My name is Ansari.' They beat me. 'No, no, you are a terrorist. You belong to HUJI, Harkat-ul-Jihad al-Islami. You are an active member and were the mastermind of the serial blasts in Uttar Pradesh ... where 28 people were killed'. (Seabrook and Siddiqui 2011, 81)

Despite Aftab's denial of his involvement in the terror act, senior IPS (Indian Police Service) officers hastily called a press conference. There, they announced with a conviction that the mastermind of the UP-court blast had been apprehended. The chief minister, who was also the police minister (and a politburo member of the CPI[M]) publicly expressed his happiness in the police department's alertness to apprehend such a 'prize catch'. Seabrook and Siddiqui have copiously documented the ordeal that Aftab and his mother faced in the next few days.

Aftab was subsequently transferred to Lucknow under the custody of the UP Police. Ayesha rushed to Lucknow in search of her son and found him nowhere, not even in jails. Subsequently, the UP Police became convinced that their efficient counterparts in Bengal had committed a mistake. The UP Police spokesman acknowledged the mistake. When asked if the guilty would be punished, he gave a vague reply: 'We will see later.' Aftab's release was delayed by another day because the court rejected the police plea for his release on grounds that it was 'wrongly worded'. *The Telegraph* carried this news the next day and wrote:

> The STF had been set on Aftab's trail by a claim by two arrested militants that the mastermind of the court blasts in the state called himself Aftab as well as Mukhtar, Raju and Bangladeshi. Mohamad Khalid and Tariq Quazmi, however, had mentioned no middle name or surname. (*The Telegraph* 2008b)

It may be noted here that Aftab's father was a retired state government employee, that they were not slum dwellers, and they came from a historically Hindu-dominated mixed class neighbourhood of Baranagar.

In a recent essay, Thomas Hansen reports similar observations from Mumbai. A former corporator from a Muslim-majority area told him:

> The police call this a 'notorious area'. Whenever anything happens, they come rushing in and arrest people, mostly charge-sheeters and notorious characters but also innocent boys ... Crying mothers would come to my office. I had to go to the police station at least three times a week to plea with them, to ask them to let these boys go. (Hansen 2019, 26)

Hansen calls this a 'regime of low intensity terror'. In a majoritarian city, ghettos enter the majority common sense as permanent exceptions. These neighbourhoods become the self-evidence of criminality. When Hansen asked a police official why such anticipatory measures were necessary, his reply confirmed this public common sense: 'Well, it is a security precaution. We are trying to find people who know something. These people have so many secrets, we know that ... When you let them sit like that for some hours, people crack, you see ... We get a lot of information this way' (Hansen 2019, 26).

A retired Muslim police inspector in Calcutta called Aziz (name changed) informed me that the police had installed extra *chowkis* (police posts) in Muslim slums in the aftermath of the 1992 riots. Initially, he thought that those were temporary installations. However, not only did the *chowkis* remain, but the number of such installations also continued to grow, especially in the early 2000s in the context of a series of bomb blasts in Indian cities. 'The Muslim neighbourhoods', he continued, 'were the ones where they first installed CCTV cameras ... This happened just before I retired.' He informed me that the British had a conscious policy to keep communal check-balance in the 'forces'. This, according to Aziz, was slowly reversed in the post-colonial decades. 'Now, you will hardly see Muslims in good numbers in any of the levels, in any of the branches.' He said that both the IB and the SB (intelligence wings) have seen a systematic exclusion of Muslim officials since 1992.

For the Hindu majority and the majoritarian state, the Muslim ghetto represents a site where preparations are underway for a decisive battle that could eventually reduce Hindus into a minority – the ghetto is the haven for radical ideas, Kashmiri terrorists, and Pakistani secret service interlopers. Thus, the establishment of a majoritarian city does not mean the end of the war. Indeed, the majoritarian city represents a condition when the majority becomes the image of the minority in which none, even the majority community, escapes the spectre of the threat of minoritization.

Instance 3

On 13 January 2020, I visited an Aadhaar Centre in Muslim-dominated Beniapukur in connection with another ethnographic research project. As I entered the premises, I saw a long queue of all age groups, from old ladies to children. I was puzzled since I knew that all the local residents of the area had already completed their Aadhaar formalities. Fearful of losing out in the 'identity race' set up by Aadhaar, they had enrolled themselves at the very inception of the scheme. Initially, I thought that the queue must have something to do with the passage of the Citizenship Amendment Act (CAA) 2019. Upon investigation, I learnt that this was a usual sight in that Aadhaar Centre, unconnected to the CAA. Numerous Muslim citizens came every day to the centre to get the spelling of their names corrected. Why? One Zeeshan told me that in four of his crucial identity documents – birth certificate, school certificate, voter ID, and Aadhaar – there were at least three versions of his name (Jishan, Zishan, Zeeshan). This ambiguity had caused him a lot of difficulties in all kinds of situations, and he was anxious to put an end to this. A perceptive old lady told me that *sarkari* (government) officials (predominantly Hindus) regularly found these Muslim names culturally alien to their regular vocabulary. They imposed what they thought would be the correct spelling of a name. The second clerk would find it difficult to accept the judgement of his predecessor and would 'correct' the spelling once again in the next document. The cycle goes on. The Aadhaar Centres in these neighbourhoods never cease to exhaust their utility.

What then is a majoritarian city? *The majoritarian city refers to a situation where violence towards the minority is routinized as a self-reproducing system* – a society where sporadic acts of lynching replace the large-scale riot as the dominant form of physical violence. It is a situation in which demographically heterogeneous neighbourhoods turn into pure and sanitized zones through the expulsion of minority elements, resulting in clear territorial demarcations of space, access, and resources in the city. However, while erasing minority traces, it renders certain practices associated with minority communities hyper-visible. In a majoritarian city, violence towards the minority community takes an everyday form through such mundane *sarkari* procedures as the Aadhaar name correction efforts we have just discussed. Every Muslim in Calcutta grows up with the fear of losing out and lagging. It is a strange blackmail of the norm (that the minority citizens must behave in a particular manner and conform to an imposed norm of 'good' citizen behaviour) that a majoritarian city or state imposes on its minorities. The burden of proof always lies on them.

As I have already indicated, the recent rise of electoral Hindutva in Calcutta is founded upon this already existing societal Hindutva – the majoritarian common sense – which expressed itself through communal zoning and territorialization of neighbourhoods. This formulation takes us to the idea of the city as a concentrated site of contentious politics. We have seen how communal identity formation involves a social war of taking ownership over the city streets during the riots. The street as the quintessential urban commons turns out to be an uneven terrain of the familiar and the unperceived, where negotiations about meaning and power can unfold.

Societal Hindutva is pervasive in Calcutta's political landscape, and it is not restricted to the BJP's aggressive electoral campaigns since 2014. The post-2014 years have witnessed a growth of the party's grassroots presence. Even though it failed to yield a decisive electoral victory for the BJP in Calcutta, it divided the political space into a communal axis. A more extensive social and economic history of the dispersal of various population groups in Calcutta over the twentieth century is needed to unravel the nature of societal Hindutva that facilitated the growth of electoral Hindutva in recent years.

Conclusion

This chapter has related the recent flourishing of Hindutva politics and sociality in Calcutta to a longer historical process that goes back to the late-colonial and the early post-colonial periods. The discussion on the 1946 and 1950 riots has shown how a particular kind of ghettoization of Muslims took place after the 'partitioned independence' that erased the colonial intermixing of populations. In other words, we have seen how communal conflicts between 1946 and 1950 established census legible and communally segregated neighbourhoods in Calcutta. After Independence, Muslims in India were reduced to a much smaller minority. In Calcutta, they became too weak to take on the Hindus of the city. That is why the character of the riot of 1950 was so different from that of 1946–47.

Moving beyond the moment of post-colonial founding, the chapter has also tracked certain pathways of majoritarianism that unfolded in Calcutta under a Left Front regime that was committed to a secularist ethos. I have argued that the normalization of communal zoning through a segregated real estate market, and the sustained criminalization of the Muslims through the latter half of the twentieth century leading into the twenty-first, produced a majoritarian urbanscape in spatial, social, and cultural terms.

Calcutta's majoritarian common sense grew consistently along with – perhaps even enabled by – various 'progressive' ideas of democracy and development under successive secular regimes. Rarely was there any large-scale communal conflict in the city following the major violence of the late-colonial and early post-colonial era. As the example of the Chatterjees in Jadavpur shows, the Hindu *bhadralok* in the city learned to publicly disavow communalism and majoritarian sentiments while nurturing them in their private spheres. Several of my Muslim friends told me how they were misidentified by others as Hindus and then subjected to casual Hindu jokes about Muslims.

This is not only, or merely, about slights and stereotypes. The majoritarian common sense operates as a form of tacit violence that affects everyday life practices and chances of Muslim populations of the city, and this has been the case well before the current electoral surge of Hindutva in the city. With the ascendancy of Hindutva as a nationally triumphant ideology and politics, these latent and tacit tendencies of majoritarianism and its attendant violence become more obvious and pronounced, coming out into the open in the public discourse and political-cultural practice of the city today.

Notes

1   I use this term in Gramscian sense as meaning 'the incoherent set of generally held assumptions and beliefs common to any given society.' See Hoare and Nowell Smith (1971, 323).

2   There are instances when such temples also received active patronage from the ruling Trinamool Congress (TMC). After assuming power in 2011, the TMC instrumentalized religious patronage for electoral mobilization by extending financial support to poor Muslim and Hindu clergymen and by allocating state funds to support neighbourhood clubs that organize Hindu festivals. The TMC's politics of religious patronage ended up contributing towards communal polarization when the Modi wave became palpable. To retain its Hindu votes at the face of Modi's explicit majoritarian rhetoric, the TMC began to patronize Hindu festivals and Hindu institutions even though it remained committed to its Muslim voters. It is said, 'there is nothing more unequal than the equal treatment of unequals'. Thus, all over India, there emerged a 'consensus' over soft and hard majoritarianism which is a defining feature of the 'Modi moment'. West Bengal failed to offer an exception to this rule. Note that I collected these ethnographic nuggets before the 2019 Lok Sabha (Parliamentary) elections in which the BJP's electoral performance surprised all election speculators. The electoral scenario in Calcutta swung in favour of the TMC in the 2021 assembly elections. However, my findings of the social roots of Hindutva in Calcutta remain unchanged.

3   Clubs are key male-dominated socio-cultural institutions in Calcutta that usually work at the level of neighbourhoods, or *paras*. They organize community festivals (both religious and secular) and set up and maintain social norms for neighbourhood residents. Often, the clubs engage in conflict resolution. From the late 1960s, clubs increasingly became closely entangled with local electoral politics. They were seen to possess an enormous capacity to mobilize popular opinion on civic issues. The Congress regime in Calcutta in the 1960s and 1970s brought the clubs under direct political patronage.

4   In an excellent recent study of the BJP's 'Mission Bengal', political journalist Snigdhendu Bhattacharya notes: 'About three dozen outfits belonging to the Sangh Parivar were active in Bengal, and nearly half of them recorded exponential expansion of activities

between 2010 and 2018.' Between March 2013 and March 2014, the number of RSS *shakhas* increased from about 820 to 1,010. 'Besides *shakhas*', notes Bhattacharya, 'there were 520 weekly gatherings called *milan* and 2,536 monthly gatherings called *mandali* in West Bengal.' See Bhattacharya (2020, 10).

5   The Riot of 1946 has been a well-researched topic. For a general understanding of the sequence of events before, during, and after the riot, see Chatterji (1995), Das (1991), Markovits (2007), Mukherjee (2015), Nazakato (2015), and Samaddar (2017). For testimonies and oral history accounts, see Sengupta (2006). For an exhaustive account of the movement of the police and military forces in the city, see Basu (2019).

6   Bengal Act XIV of 1946, The Calcutta Disturbances Commission of Enquiry Act, 1946.

7   Census of 1951, Vol. VI, Part III, Calcutta City, p. XV. Also cited in Chatterji (2005).

8   This area is also known for the city's China Town and tanneries, oil mills, hide warehouses, slaughterhouses, and petty waste-recycling units inhabited predominantly by Hindu Dalits and Muslims.

9   Such a case was reported in the Lalbagan area in the northern district of the city bounded by Nirod Behari Mullik Road in the north, Vivekananda Road in the south, Upper Circular Road in the west, and Canal West Road in the east, where one Lallbagan Seva Samiti (at Raja Dinendra Street) claimed to have resettled 650 refugee families in 229 vacant houses earlier occupied by Muslims. The Samiti received active encouragement from the northern district committee of the Congress Party. See Sengupta (2015).

10 See Chatterji (2005). Since the assassination of Gandhi in early 1948, the Hindu Mahasabha had maintained a low profile in the city, anticipating public outrage. Shortly after the assassination, a crowd had pelted stones at Mahasabha leader Syamaprasad Mookerjee's Calcutta residence on Ashutosh Mookerjee Road. In view of this, the Hindu Mahasabha decided to withdraw from political activities and concentrate on philanthropic work with the incoming Hindu refugees. However, its involvement – especially the role of one of its key functionaries in Calcutta, Ashutosh Lahiry – igniting the Hindu sentiment in the city before and after the 1950 riot could hardly be ignored. On 4 November 1949, Lahiry told in a press conference that the 'Moslem problem inside the Indian union' must comprise 'work of nationalizing the four crores of our Moslem brethren'. Right after the February riot, the Bengal unit of Hindu Mahasabha decided to raise a volunteer corps named Sanatan Bahini. By June 1950, the number of volunteers crossed 1,500. On 22 March 1950, N. B. Khare, the president of Hindu Mahasabha, visited Calcutta, and it was reported that he had asked Lahiry to create such a situation in Bengal so that the Indian Army was compelled to initiate an armed intervention in East Pakistan. It was, however, extremely hard to implicate Lahiry due to the lack of direct evidence of his alleged involvement in communal violence. See Brief History of Sri Ashutosh Lahiry; and History sheet of Shri Ashutosh Lahiry, GB, IB Records, S. No. 45/1920, F. No. 210/20, West Bengal State Archives. See Bandyopadhyay (2009, ch. 2) for a detailed account of Ashutosh Lahiry's activities during the riots of 1946 and 1950.

11 It is important to note that communal outbreaks since the 1950 event tended to concentrate only in the known Muslim areas, keeping the rest of the city out of their

impact. Thus, the 1964 carnage took place in pockets such as Taltala, Jotasanko, Kareya, Beniapukur, Amherst Street, Beleghata, Entally, Watrgunj, and Garden Reach. See Sengupta (2015, 445). Another point to be reckoned with is the fact that the geography of these disturbances clearly shifted to the margins of the city even though certain old epicentres appeared in the list of areas.

12 Mridula Sarabhai's Report on the Communal Situation and Riots in Calcutta in 1950, in Bagchi and Dasgupta (2009).

13 Mridula Sarabhai's Report on the Communal Situation and Riots in Calcutta in 1950, in Bagchi and Dasgupta (2009).

14 Also see Bandyopadhyay (2012).

15 During this riot, frantic property exchanges happened between Muslims willing to move to East Pakistan and the Hindu refugees. Contemporary newspapers published several such advertisements for property exchange. One such advertisement in a popular daily contained the following information: 'A Muslim businessman named Nuruddin Ahmed of 1-E, Anjuman Road, Kolkata sought to exchange or sale his running automobile business situated on one of the main roads of the city with an income of minimum 2/3 thousand per month along with attached garage and residential house with similar business in any towns of East Pakistan immediately' (Kundu 2008).

16 Take the instance of the Dhobiatala Camp near Dhapa garbage dumping station. Here, 48 riot-torn Muslim families were stationed in 1964. An estimate of 1992 shows that this camp had a population of 5,000 individuals of which 4,543 were Muslims, mostly earning a livelihood in local leather and soap manufacturing factories (Das 2000).

17 Between the 1970s and 1990s, this entire stretch attained tremendous notoriety for wagon breaking, smuggling, pickpocketing, dacoity, as well as mass massacres. On 30 April 1982, Bijon Setu witnessed a mass massacre, when a local mob burnt seventeen monks of the Ananda Margi sect alive on allegations of child-lifting. A little over a year earlier, *The Statesman* carried out a long investigative piece on the topic of group violence in Kasba and Panchanantala areas. The report found that most of the criminals residing in these slums were snatchers, highway robbers, and dacoits who operated elsewhere. These gangs were also known for smuggling rice and extorting money in the Dhakuria Bazar area. Gang wars over the spoils were very frequent. Another Panchanantala resident recounted a clash between the members of a gang over the spoils of a robbery near the 17A bus stand. The gang split: one went to the Congress (I) camp for protection and the other sought refuge with the CPI(M). One group had a hold over the Panchanantala Bustee, while the other had control over the slums of Jagannath Ghosh Road and Gobardanga. During the elections, the political parties frequently submitted themselves to these gangs: 'Leaders of a gang wield considerable authority over residents of their stronghold and can intimidate to vote for one political party. It is easy to enlist names of false voters in the voters list in slum areas. Authority over criminals facilitates such enlistment.' The middle-class residents of the nearby 'Banerjee Para' made frequent allegations that the local police had an 'understanding' with these gangs and the political leaders who protected these elements (*The Statesman* 1981).

18 An instance of this transition will suffice for our purpose. A Hindu–Muslim riot broke out in Calcutta in December 1992, in the aftermath of the Babri Masjid demolition. The Muslim areas of the Dhobiatola slum reduced to rubble. In his investigation of the 1992 riot, Suranjan Das found that certain real estate agents offered each household INR 20,000 to vacate their huts. See Das (2000).

19 Gobra slum attracted real estate players due to its locational advantage. It is well connected with Sealdah and Park Circus rail stations and with major urban streets such as Park Street, Shakespeare Avenue, Suhrawardy Avenue, A. J. C. Bose Road flyover, Circus Avenue, and Sir Syed Amir Ali Avenue.

20 Snigdhendu Bhattacharya estimates that during the Ram Mandir movement in 1991–92, the number of RSS *shakhas* operating in West Bengal was 1500. The 'high tide' of Hindutva continued until 2000. It was only in 2001 that the Left resolved to push the RSS back after facing electoral challenges from the TMC–BJP alliance in the western districts of the state between 1998 and 2000. By 2003, the number of *shakhas* had declined to 1,000 and when the Left exited from power in 2011, the number was further reduced to 800. See Bhattacharya (2020).

References

Bagchi, J., and S. Dasgupta (eds.). 2009. *The Trauma and Triumph: Gender and Partition in Eastern India*. Vol. 2. Kolkata: Stree.

Bandyopadhyay, S. 2012. *Decolonization in South Asia: Meanings of Freedom in Post-independence West Bengal, 1947–52*. Hyderabad: Orient BlackSwan.

Basu, A. 2019. 'Communal Riots and Urban Planning in Calcutta, 1918–1946'. Unpublished Master's Thesis, Department of Humanities and Social Sciences, IISER Mohali (under the supervision of R. Bandyopadhyay).

Bhattacharya, S. 2020. *Mission Bengal: A Saffron Experiment*. Noida: Harper Collins.

Calcutta Disturbances Commission of Enquiry. 1947. Proceedings from Friday, 14 February 1947, P. W. 13, Interrogation of Mr N. H. Khundkar, Officer-in-Charge, Burtolla Police Station, 5–46, (17 February 1947) 47–84, (18 February 1947) 85–104.

Chatterjee, A. 2017. *Margins of Citizenship: Muslims in Urban India*. New York and London: Routledge.

Chatterji, J. 1995. *Bengal Divided: Hindu Communalism and Partition, 1932–1947*. Cambridge: Cambridge University Press.

———. 2005. 'Of Graveyards and Ghettos: Muslims in Partitioned West Bengal, 1947–67'. In *Living Together Separately: Cultural India in History and Politics*, edited by M. Hasan and A. Roy, 222–49. New Delhi: Oxford University Press.

Das, S. 1991. *Communal Riots in Bengal, 1905–47*. New Delhi: Oxford University Press.

———. 2000. 'The 1992 Calcutta Riot in Historical Continuum: A Relapse into "Communal Fury"?' *Modern Asian Studies* 34(2): 281–306.

Hansen, T. 2019. 'Democracy against the Law: Reflections on India's Illiberal Democracy.' *Majoritarian State: How Hindu Nationalism Is Changing India*, edited by A. P. Chatterji, T. B. Hansen and C. Jaffrelot, 19–40. Noida: HarperCollins.

Hoare, Q., and G. Nowell Smith (eds.). 1971. *Selections from the Prison Notebooks of Antonio Gramsci*. London: Lawrence & Wishart.

Kundu, T. S. 2008. 'The Partition and the Muslim Minorities of West Bengal, 1947–1967'. *Indian Journal of Politics* 42(1 and 2): 78–113.

Markovits, C. 2007. 'The Calcutta Riots of 1946'. *Online Encyclopaedia of Mass Violence*. 5 November. http://www.sciencespo.fr/ceri/en/ouvrage/oemv (accessed on 18 June 2020).

Mukherjee, J. 2015. *Hungry Bengal: War, Famine, and Riots and the End of Empire*. Noida: Harper Collins.

Nakazato, N. 2015. 'Calcutta Disturbances: Colonial Administration, Riot Systems and Local Networks'. In *Calcutta the Stormy Decades*, edited by T. Sarkar and S. Bandyopadhyay, 267–319. New Delhi: Social Science Press.

Roy, A. 2002. *City Requiem Calcutta: Gender and Poverty*. Minneapolis: University of Minnesota Press.

Samaddar, R. 2016. *Ideas and Frameworks of Governing India*. New York and London: Routledge.

———. 2017 'Policing a Riot-torn City: Kolkata, 16–18 August 1946'. *Journal of Genocide Research* 19(1): 39–60.

Sattar, S. 2018. 'Social Exclusions and Muslims in Kolkata'. In *Lives of Muslims in India: Politics, Exclusion and Violence*, edited by Abdul Shaban, 226–49. New York and London: Routledge.

Seabrook, J., and I. A. Siddiqui. 2011. *People without History: India's Muslim Ghettos*. London: Pluto Press.

Sengupta, A. 2015. 'Becoming a Minority Community: Calcutta's Muslims After Partition'. In *The Stormy Decades*, edited by T. Sarkar and S. Bandyopadhyay, 434–58. New Delhi: Social Science Press.

Sengupta, D. 2006. 'A City Feeding on Itself: Testimonies and Histories of "Direct Action" Day'. *Sarai Reader*, 288–95. New Delhi: CSDS.

Siddiqui, M. K. A. 1974. *Muslims of Calcutta: A Study of Their Social Organization*. Calcutta: Anthropological Survey of India.

The Statesman. 1981. 'Where Political Patronage Sustains Gang Warfare'. 29 January.

The Telegraph. 2008a. 'Cop Goof-up on Calcuttan'. 15 January. https://www.telegraphindia.com/india/cop-goof-up-on-calcuttan/cid/627463 (accessed on 9 August 2020).

———. 2008b. 'Goof-up II Prolongs Aftab Agony – After Identity, Cops Get Name Wrong, Forcing Calcuttan to Spend Extra Day in Jail'. 16 January. https://www.telegraphindia.com/india/goof-up-ii-prolongs-aftab-agony-after-identity-cops-get-name-wrong-forcing-calcuttan-to-spend-extra-day-in-jail/cid/627427 (accessed on 9 August 2020).

7

SOCIAL SEGREGATION AND EVERYDAY HINDUTVA IN MIDDLE INDIA

Thomas Blom Hansen

Following the 2014 general election that brought Modi to power, enormous attention was paid by many commentators and analysts to the appeal of Modi to a young and restless electorate, particularly young men aspiring to jobs and recognition in a rapidly growing economy. It is true that the spectacular election campaign in 2014 moved the crucial few per cent of the vote in key states in north and central India that allowed the Bharatiya Janata Party (BJP) its unprecedented win of seats in Lok Sabha (Chibber 2014). Many of these gains, especially in Uttar Pradesh, were consolidated in 2019. It is also true that the BJP has been able to establish itself in new arenas, such as throughout the Northeast (Longkumer 2019).

However, the bulk of the electoral support for the BJP in both these election cycles came from regions and social milieus where the party and other organizations affiliated with the Rashtriya Swayamsevak Sangh (RSS) had already established a firm standing since the early 1990s. When we consider the characteristics of 'new' Hindutva, the main analytical challenge is to understand how the key tenets of Hindutva seem to have been consolidated into a form of everyday common sense and widespread sentiment, and how this has allowed the BJP to reproduce and further extend its support throughout the towns, cities, and villages of northern, central, and western India for more than three decades. Here, I will explore how the ideological frames of Hindutva have been coarticulated with other social processes and identity formations that mark everyday social life in much of northern and western India.

I shall explore such processes of coarticulation by looking at the long history of Hindu nationalist mobilization and consolidation in Aurangabad, Maharashtra,

SOCIAL SEGREGATION AND EVERYDAY HINDUTVA IN MIDDLE INDIA

a city known in the prose of the Indian police as 'riot prone' and a hotbed of Hindu communal activism since the 1980s when Shiv Sena made it its first major stronghold outside of Mumbai.

While Aurangabad may be unique with regard to its history of communal violence, it exhibits many of the same features as other growing cities in the Deccan region and western India. Aurangabad has trebled its population (estimated to be 2.1 million in 2018) in the past thirty years, just like Hyderabad (> 10 million), Bhopal (2.7 million), Nagpur (2.9 million), and Indore (3.1 million). All of these urban areas have seen steady growth in manufacturing and service industries, and they serve as major regional hubs of education and services. These are all historical cities, erstwhile centres of powerful Muslim and Maratha dynasties, with substantial Muslim populations that are today increasingly marginalized and almost entirely excluded from the modern industrial and service economies that define these cities.[1]

I did fieldwork in Aurangabad city and some villages in the surrounding district in 1991–92, and again in 2012, and for an extended period of time in 2017–18. I shall draw on this varied and longitudinal material and try to throw light on the embedding and institutionalization of Hindutva in the city in the following three different realms:

1. The reinterpretation of the city's and the region's history and historical memory as moments in a larger, if not perennial, conflict between Muslim invaders and a native Hindu population.
2. The demographic growth and transformation since the beginning of rapid industrial growth in the late 1980s that quadrupled the city's population and brought large numbers of Dalits and Other Backward Class (OBC) communities into the city's workforce. The rise of Hindutva in the city correlates closely with the reduced significance of the historically dominant Muslim population in the city and its economy, and the rise to public prominence of a new economic and political elite drawn from middle and lower caste backgrounds.
3. The process of social and spatial segregation of Muslims and Hindus in separate neighbourhoods, networks, and economies since the late 1980s.

Let me begin on a somewhat self-critical note. Like most others who studied the rise of Hindu nationalism in the late 1980s, I, too, was interested in exploring the ideological force of Hindutva. I was keen on showing that the RSS's claim to represent a larger Hindu tradition was a complete invention, one that nonetheless had the requisite agility and flexibility to encompass, absorb, and reinterpret a number of discrete and local histories and traditions, organizing them along a fault line between an aggressive and intolerant Islam on one side, and a pluralist, autochthonous, and all-encompassing Hindu culture on the other. Writing against the conventional determinist mode of understanding politics as a reflection of underlying class and caste dynamics, I argued that the rise of the RSS/BJP should be seen as an example of how ideologically driven movements could reconfigure social, political, and public life in a country as large and complex as India (Hansen 1999). This analysis applied well to the moment of Hindu nationalism's ascendance and breakthrough in the 1980s and 1990s but much less so to the long-term consolidation of this movement, and the sentiments it rode on, into what I called a 'communal common sense'. To understand this latter process, we need to consider Hindutva not so much as an invention or a break with the tradition of secularism that in India was mainly understood as a set of performative codes in public life rather than a deeper sense of active toleration (Hansen 2011). Instead, I suggest, the continued success of Hindutva rests on the sustained capacity for re-articulation and synthesis of a range of ideologies, institutional practices, and historical memories that are of very long standing.

From the 'City of Gates' to the Notorious City

Aurangabad's famous city walls and its fifty-two gates were completed during the seventeenth century, when the city served as the southern headquarters of the Mughal Empire, the base from where Aurangzeb waged campaigns against the Marathas and the Deccan sultanates. It soon became the first capital of the Nizam Asaf Jahi dynasty and flourished as a home to both the emerging Shia elite around the court and a sizeable number of absentee landlords, military commanders, scholars, and traders. With the consolidation of the Nizam's administration in Hyderabad, Aurangabad lost importance and became a relative backwater, a highly cultured, if staid, seat of administration and madrasahs surrounded by a vast rural hinterland populated by a largely Marathi-speaking peasantry. The typical village in Marathwada had less than 10 per cent Muslims, mostly small farmers and artisans, while social power was held mainly by Maratha landowners and, to a lesser extent, the more distant *jagirdars* – mostly Muslims – who collected taxes and served as officials of the Nizam's government.

A decade after the 'police action' that ended the Nizam's rule in 1948, the seven mainly Marathi-speaking districts of Marathwada were incorporated into the new state of Maharashtra in 1960. Since the British period, these districts had been portrayed as 'backward', estimated by the Planning Commission in the 1950s to be the poorest region in the entire country (Deshpande 1973). The administration in the new state launched a series of infrastructural and industrial development schemes that aimed at addressing what at the time was described as deep 'backwardness'. In 1990, an official of the Maharashtra Industrial Development Corporation, a young upper caste man from Pune, described Marathwada to me in the following terms:

SOCIAL SEGREGATION AND EVERYDAY HINDUTVA IN MIDDLE INDIA

This was a place where no development took place for generations. There was no industry, no modern universities ... even the technology was backward. The train line to Hyderabad was narrow gauge and very old. Under the Nizam's rule everything was stable, nothing changed but the people were poor, both Muslims and Hindus. The Nizam was the richest man in the world, but he and his ministers just hoarded money, nothing came back to the people ... We are changing all of that nowadays and the people want change ... [referring to the riots in the city] ... Naturally some people are angry at their old masters, many feel that their attitude [of Muslims, TBH] has not changed, that they still feel better than us.

Many of the city's educated and socially progressive segments, both Hindus and Dalits, had for decades been critical of the political style and legacy of what they saw as a socially conservative, 'feudal', and intransigent Muslim culture in the old city. This critique of 'feudal mindsets' was rooted in the movement for the liberation of Marathwada from the Nizam's rule, Marathwada Mukti Sangram (MMS), which had broad support among the upper caste Hindus and across Marathwada in the 1940s and 1950s. Prominent leaders such as Govindbhai Shroff and Swami Tirth campaigned for freedom, modern education, and land reforms, and were affiliated with the more progressive, socialist wing of the Congress. The theme of feudal oppression and historical exploitation of a Marathi-speaking peasantry had been equally central to the larger movement for a separate Maharashtrian state in the 1950s, Samyukta Maharashtra Samiti (SMS). Strongly supported by the left (and the cultural right), the SMS was slanted towards a strongly anti-feudal and anti-commercial rhetoric that had been pivotal to progressive politics and non-Brahmin populism in the Bombay Presidency since the late nineteenth century. For almost two generations, these movements had identified the Brahmin (*bhatji*) and the moneylender (*shethji*) as the main exploiters of a proud Marathi-speaking peasantry, the protagonist of the progressive, non-Brahmin movement in the state (Omvedt 2011). In Marathwada, there were much fewer Brahmins than in western Maharashtra, and the main adversaries were instead the figure of the 'Muslim landlord' and later the freebooting Razakar vigilante corps that had been given an almost free hand in the Nizam's territories in 1946–48 (Pernau 2000, 322–45). These anti-feudal sentiments were deeply embedded in the progressive and mainstream political vocabulary of Marathwada already in the 1940s. It is unsurprising that the institutional and social structures of the Nizam's dominions added a distinctly anti-Muslim dimension to progressive political discourse in the region.

In the 1980s, these historical tensions were re-articulated in new and dramatic ways. The city had seen serious caste violence between Dalits and caste Hindus in 1978 around the controversy about the renaming of the local university after B. R. Ambedkar, and later in 1987 around the publication of Ambedkar's *Riddles in Hinduism* (Guru 1991). During the early 1980s, Shiv Sena entered the Marathwada region, describing themselves as a 'Hindu fighting force', engaging both Muslims and Dalits in street fights, provoking smaller riots and conflagrations in the streets of the city and surrounding towns and villages for years, and eventually establishing a dominant political presence (Hansen 1996). Shiv Sena's electoral victory in the municipal elections in 1988 set off a serious confrontation between Hindus and Muslims that left dozens dead and hundreds injured.[2] The tensions intensified in the following years and culminated in severe and bloody riots following the destruction of the Babri Masjid on 6 December 1992. Most of the city was under curfew for several weeks. As it had been the case in 1988, killings, arson, and attacks spread to many major villages and *talukas* across the six districts of the Marathwada region.[3] These dramatic events precipitated a significant demographic shift in the city as Hindus and Dalits began to leave the old city for newer colonies in what became 'new Aurangabad', while Muslims from mixed areas in the city and from villages in the district sought refuge and safety in the Muslim-majority areas.[4]

From this relative obscurity, Aurangabad suddenly made headlines in 2010 when 150 Mercedes cars were sold to customers in the city in what amounted to the single largest luxury car deal in Indian history.[5] It turned out that the deal was organized as a public statement from the business community to the city administration: 'Aurangabad has everything and is an economic powerhouse, but investors are still scared of coming here due to its perceived negative image, which we decided to change forever,' Sachin Mulay, president of the Chamber of Marathwada Industries and Agriculture, told me in July 2012. One of the buyers added: 'I hope the deal serves as an eye-opener to the civic administration and they take steps to ensure quality infrastructure in the city.'

The vast majority of the Mercedes customers belonged to the city's small but powerful cluster of Marwari families, as well as Sindhi and Punjabi builders and industrialists who had all benefited from the spectacular industrial bonanza in the preceding two decades.

The population of Aurangabad went from 400,000 in the late 1980s to well above 2 million in 2018,[6] as many migrants from the adjacent districts were attracted to the more than 2,000 registered industrial units plus the substantial undergrowth of smaller service and ancillary industries that sprouted across the city in the 1990s and early 2000s.

Members of the city's economic elite hoped that this economic growth would spell the end of the isolation and provincial outlook in Aurangabad. 'We are an emerging metropolis but with a mentality of a small town,' a young engineer working at the Skoda plant told me in 2012. Most educated Hindus assert that the city's main problem remains the large impoverished Muslim population (around 30 per cent in 2019–20 – larger in absolute numbers than in the past but proportionally smaller than the majority it used to constitute up to the 1970s) and lower caste Hindus and Dalits residing in the older parts of the city. This population is generally regarded as uneducated and largely marginal to the new industrial economy that has drawn its workforce mainly from the surrounding towns and villages.

By contrast, the residents of 'new Aurangabad' – the industrial parks, the new residential areas developed by the state development corporations and private companies, and the new hotels and shopping centres set apart from the old city – see themselves as forward-looking, professional, and uninterested in the politics of the old. It is also a segment of the population that is largely new to the city, having moved from western Maharashtra, north India, Bengal, and Hyderabad, and whose main languages of interaction are Hindi and English. In the old city, the dominant languages are Urdu (at times spoken in the Dakhani dialect) and Marathi, which are separated by deep gulfs of suspicion, unintelligibility, and apprehension. Few Muslims speak Marathi beyond a few phrases, and hardly any Marathi-speaking Hindu reads or properly understands colloquial Urdu. There is no desire to bridge the gulf. As on the outskirts of the city, simplified Hindi is often the actual language of interaction. The language ideologies on both sides are strong and incommensurable, steeped in the constant rehearsals of historical conflicts, and unwilling to yield, except through the commercial and technocratic medium of English.

This is a pattern well known in other parts of India, where the populations of the old *qasbahs* and city centres are presented as residues of a myopic, conservative, and localized past beyond repair or redemption[7] (Jaffrelot and Gayer 2011). This equation of Muslims, historical urban centres, and 'backwardness' acquired a profound and pernicious effect in provincial cities such as Aurangabad.

The Communal Charge of History

Soon after the quest for renaming of Bombay was initiated in 1995, the Shiv Sena–BJP state government declared that it wished to rename Aurangabad as Sambhajinagar, after Sambhaji, the son of Shivaji. After extensive protests among the city's Muslim community, a commission of historians was asked to deliberate on the question. Their conclusion came less than a year later: the city was founded and named 'Khadkee' in the sixteenth century by Malik Ambar – an illustrious Deccan figure, an Ethiopian slave who was freed by the ruler of Ahmednagar and became one of the great and innovative commanders of the Deccan, pioneering most of the military techniques later perfected by Shivaji. If renaming were to happen, the commission said, it should be named after Malik Ambar.[8]

This, in turn, generated vociferous protests from Shiv Sena and also from conservative Muslims, who desired to retain a Persian legacy and a close link to the Urdu and Dakhani culture associated with Hyderabad. The issue has found no resolution but is still smouldering – as late as 2011, the Aurangabad Municipal Corporation decided in a vote to rename the city and its airport after Sambhaji, but the name remains unrecognized by the state government.

Instead, there has been a concerted effort to change and rename significant parts of the city. A relatively new square, Kranti Chowk, which was named to commemorate the 'liberation' of Marathwada from Nizami rule in 1948, features a huge equestrian statue of Shivaji erected in the 1990s. A few years later, as the city's main highway crossing this square was to be significantly expanded, Shiv Sena argued that it now had 'emotional value'. A huge flyover was built to curve on either side of Shivaji's statue, further boosting the visibility of the statue that is constantly illuminated by four stadium-quality floodlights. Nearby, at the newly created Savarkar Chowk, a big, shiny statue of this Maharashtrian hero was erected in 2002. The statue stands next to the old Qassab Mohalla, the butcher's area, which was partially cleared in the spring of 2012 and converted into land earmarked for commercial developments. However, a local municipal councillor told me in 2012 that the municipality was worried about whether any other community would move into this area: 'No Hindu wants to live there, but maybe we can get some of the foreign companies to lease the land.' Another innovation has been the conversion of an old museum of Mughal coins and weapons into a large museum entirely devoted to Shivaji.

In September 2017, on the anniversary of the beginning of 'Operation Polo' in 1948 – the so-called police action where the Indian Army forcibly incorporated the Hyderabad state into the Indian Union – a new monument was inaugurated in Aurangabad. It is a garden of sorts, made in shining marble and stone. The site was the very place where British troops had executed rebel troops in 1857, and it had also served as a place for public executions during a part of the Nizam rule. It was colloquially known as *kala chabutra*. At the centre of the new monument stands a gigantic flagpole, sprouting from a huge lotus, and the Indian tricolour is now visible across most of the city. The monument has three large plaques with inscriptions in Marathi and English. One celebrates the heroes of 1857 in a more generic sense, the second celebrates India's independence in 1947, and the third, which is the most popular with the visiting crowds, commemorates the liberation of Marathwada in 1948. The text depicts the events in 1948 as the culmination of a long struggle against the 'feudal forces' and the Razakars of the Nizam's state, and it mentions many of the local Hindu heroes – Swami Tirth, Govindrao Shroff, and others – all leading members of the Hyderabad State Congress. When the monument was inaugurated, the local newspapers were careful to mention one particular fact that had been heavily promoted by the city's officials: the very large flagpole of this new patriotic monument was 10 feet taller than the iconic minaret in Daulatabad, the ancient city near Aurangabad, built by the famous 'mad' sultan Tuqhlaq who had marched the population of Delhi south to build a new and less vulnerable capital in the Deccan in the fourteenth century (*Lokmat* 2017).

This plaque points to a larger narrative that has been gradually imprinted upon the city space of Aurangabad: the MMS liberated Hindus and began a new era of majority rule in the region. The Nizam of Hyderabad had banned the State Congress during several periods and their activities went underground throughout the 1940s (Pernau 2000, 225–95). Much of the information available from this period is based on the widely distributed hagiographical Marathi biographies of the leaders of the movement, as well as scattered oral history. Cast in a heroic and triumphalist mould, these narratives are kept alive by senior judges and administrators who were part of the first administration set up after the incorporation of Hyderabad into the Indian Union. Several of these elderly public figures were guests of honour at the inauguration of the monument in 2017 where they were felicitated and praised as 'freedom fighters' and exemplary patriots and *deshbhakts*.

A major part of these official narratives centre on the terror and rapes committed by the Razakar forces in the years leading up to 1948. There are also tales of Hindu families (mostly landowning) fleeing in 1947 to the border areas around the state, fearing that the horrors of Punjab would be played out here as well. Since there were few large, organized refugee camps, the estimates of 400,000 displaced Hindus come from volunteers, both Congress and RSS-affiliated groups. The estimates of the number of Muslims seeking refuge in the Hyderabad state during the same year are substantially higher (750,000) and more certain as the Nizam's administration set up camps and relief efforts across its territories in 1946–47.[9]

Throughout the latter part of 1947 and early 1948, the Hyderabad State Congress was distributing arms to (many RSS-affiliated) Hindu volunteers across the border territories and inside the Hyderabad state (Puroshottam 2014). There were regular cross-border raids and attacks on public buildings, officials, and infrastructure, mostly carried out in the Marathi-speaking Marathwada districts and borderlands where both Arya Samaj and the RSS wielded considerable influence (Sherman 2015, 23). In the Telugu-speaking regions, similar efforts were spearheaded by a young and upcoming Congress leader called Narasimha Rao.

In the official narrative of the standoff between the new republic and Hyderabad state, victory was sudden and decisive with the police action in 1948.[10] However, the full extent of the aftermath of the police action has only slowly and gradually emerged after having been buried and dismissed for several generations. The classified Sunderlal Report, written by Nehru's private secretary who was sent to

Hyderabad shortly after the police action, paints a bleak and dystopian picture of extensive violence, killings, and rapes of Muslims throughout the rural areas and small towns of the region, perpetrated by what he calls 'armed irregulars' (State Congress and RSS volunteers). It is estimated that more than 400,000 people left the region and their land, migrating to the cities and other parts of India perceived to be safer for Muslims.[11]

During the general political ferment in India from 1965 to the late 1970s, the Communist Party of India (CPI) and various socialist and radical movements gained a certain foothold and popularity in the city. They won considerable influence in the city council in the 1969 election and were able to exercise it for a number of years. One of the lasting outcomes was a new master plan for the city, strongly influenced by progressive and developmentalist visions of the age. It proposed radical widening of roads and revamping and upgrading the existing old city, including covering the many *nalas* dating from Malik Ambar's time, removing substantial parts of the city wall while preserving only select historical gates and monuments. The plan was, in the words of one of its original fathers, 'designed to shake up our sleepy feudal city and make it into a modern college town. That was our vision – educate the people, give them parks and lakes instead of dirty *nalas*, good buses instead of rickshaws, modern shops instead of dirty open-air markets'.[12]

The group of young progressives was mainly educated Hindus, mostly sons and daughters of the city's trading classes of Gujarati and Sindhi background. At the time, many of the city's local politicians were rumoured to align themselves with popular Muslim *pehlwans* and *dadas* who ran affairs in slums and the cramped lanes of the old city. Inevitably, the progressives reasoned that modernizing the city and creating a new and more just form of social order would entail overturning the old Muslim dominance. This discourse laid the ground for a broad consensus among many Hindus and Dalits around the intrinsic backwardness and hostility of Muslims to reforms and a modern outlook. This 'progressive' phase in the city's history is today mainly visible in a range of monuments celebrating the toil of farmers and workers and their emancipation from the oppression of the feudal past. These were mostly erected in the 1960s and 1970s and have subsequently been incorporated into the larger and hegemonic narrative of the region's liberation from the Nizam's regime in 1948.

As demonstrated by Eric Beverley in a recent book, the dominant picture of the Hyderabad state as a decaying feudal society was actively promoted by the British in their efforts to portray themselves as apostles of reason and compassionate government. The reality was, as Beverley shows, that especially the cities of the Hyderabad state were fairly dynamic and cosmopolitan since the late nineteenth century. Here an Urdu public flourished, Muslim intellectuals from across the world congregated, and the project of developing a vernacular modernity – Muslim, Urdu, and Dakhani – was taken very seriously (Beverley 2015).

In the spring of 2012, a new, activist city commissioner decided to dust off the master plan from the 1960s and implement it. Within a few months, more than 2,000 houses, mainly in Muslim areas in the old city, were declared 'unauthorized' and many were quickly demolished. The commissioner told me at the time that it had been a more effective implementation in Muslim areas because 'these people have taken out fewer stay orders in the high court'.

In the traditional Hindu areas in the old city, houses owned by politicians and influential families were spared as these families had taken out stay orders in court until a higher compensation could be negotiated. Smaller temples and some mosques had also been spared (and still stand like islands in the widened streets), while a number of historical Muslim schools and several smaller *dargah*s and mosques had been entirely or partially removed, including a *tazia* workshop dating from the eighteenth century.

For many Muslims, these draconian demolitions in 2012 were understood in the context of a much longer and deeper history of violence and dispossession that began in 1948 and had accelerated since the 1980s. The full extent of the aftermath of the police action and the scale of Muslim dispossession in the years that followed are only slowly and gradually emerging today.

There are few available records of these atrocities, land grabs, or the number of refugees as the region was under military administration for almost two years after the police action and many documents from the time remain classified or inaccessible. In the years following the military government, public administration was regrouped, and the former administrators of the Hyderabad state were 're-educated'. A young officer from the Indian Administrative Service (IAS) at the time, aged 101 when I met with him, told me in 2018:

'Those who had been involved in Razakar atrocities were prosecuted and dismissed. The rest was trained in the British administration style we used and then they got their jobs back'.

However, this officer and others who were involved at the time roundly dismissed the notion that there were large-scale casualties. Some even suggested that the Sunderlal Report (accidentally found and photocopied by an American scholar) was a forgery committed by foreigners. Scholars and students are slowly recovering stories and memories from Muslim families about displacement, theft of land, rapes, and killings. These are deeply buried in family histories as shameful events, a disaster that completely shook the old order. Many of the victims seem to have been minor landowning families – not the big *jagirdar*s and absentee landlords who belonged to the Hyderabadi elite that in large numbers relocated to Pakistan,

Canada, United Kingdom, and California (Leonard 2007) – but nonetheless local village elites of sorts by virtue of their landholdings.

Others were members of the police force and the army who were given land as a part of their pay and perks by the Hyderabad state. I met at least a dozen Muslim families who narrated that the grandfather was a policeman or government servant and 'came to Aurangabad in the 1950s'.

Some older people reluctantly narrated violent incidents they witnessed or atrocities that affected members of their wider family, but few would directly tell me stories of what happened to their own family. Most evidence of the events in 1948 remains circumstantial. I found, for instance, that many Sindhi Hindus settled in the Marathwada region in the early 1950s, mostly refugees from what had become Pakistan. A large part of the Punjabi community in the city are descendants of former military men who settled there after 1948. Most of these Sindhi and Punjabi families are major landowners and builders today. As I inquired into how they acquired such extensive land holdings, I often encountered responses such as, 'Oh, there was so much land because all these Muslims had gone to Pakistan.' Or, 'In Marathwada, the land was cheap and easy to buy. That is why we came here.' However, anecdotal evidence suggests that much of the land was forcibly acquired or handed over to these refugee communities by government authorities at the time. Local (Aurangabad and other Marathwada districts) land records from the period of the military government which ended in December 1949 remain sealed. Many of the administrative files from the Hyderabad state are also said to have disappeared.[13]

As a result of this systematic official erasure of the dramatic upheavals, displacements, and mass violence of 1948, Muslim memories of these events remain inchoate, subdued echoes of a past that no one wants to recover. The new, mainly Hindu, administrators from elsewhere were openly vested in portraying the police action as an act of liberation and historical justice (Sherman 2007). For the older Muslim elite, these events were a deeply humiliating defeat in terms of livelihood, social standing, and political power.[14] Yet, today, one finds considerable pride in the era of the Nizam's rule and a good deal of romanticization and nostalgia for the time when 'we Muslims lived with dignity here', as many Muslims told me. The recent electoral success of the Hyderabad-based All India Majlis-e-Ittehadul Muslimeen (AIMIM) in Marathwada and Aurangabad[15] owed much to their ability to tap into this disavowed memory that cannot find an acceptable discursive and representational form.[16]

The Social and Spatial Dynamics of Everyday Hindutva

The RSS had established networks throughout the Hyderabad state since the 1930s but these networks were generally confined to numerically very small Bania and

SOCIAL SEGREGATION AND EVERYDAY HINDUTVA IN MIDDLE INDIA

Brahmin communities in the region's towns and villages. In the 1950s, political power shifted dramatically from local Muslim landowners and elites to landowning Maratha families and Bania communities that had played a major role in the resistance to the Nizam's rule, both within the Hyderabad State Congress and in the cultural activism that had been promoted by Arya Samaj across Marathwada since the late nineteenth century. These communities had also been major beneficiaries of the often forced and violent redistribution of land and other assets previously held by the Nizam and the notables and *jagirdars* of the Nizam's realm. Marathwada has historically been characterized by relatively large Dalit communities, more than 20 per cent of the population in most districts, and a preponderance of lower caste Hindus, mostly smaller OBC communities, and Kunbi, Vanjari (landowning Scheduled Tribe, or ST, community), and Lingayats.

By the 1980s, on the back of large-scale infrastructural development by the state of Maharashtra since the 1960s, the Marathwada region began to see improved economic growth across many fields and rapid industrialization in cities like Aurangabad, Jalna, and Paithan. Large numbers of young men and their families flocked to the cities to work, attend colleges, and start small businesses. The majority of these new urbanites belonged to OBC and Dalit communities and were the first in their extended families to receive education and enjoy modest, disposable incomes. This new demographic reality completely changed the city's political life in the 1980s and 1990s. The city emerged as a hotbed of Dalit activism around Milind College (founded by Ambedkar in 1950), and there was a dramatic campaign to rename the local Marathwada University in the late 1970s. Many of these activists went on to play decisive roles in Dalit politics and activism across the state and the rest of India.

In the 1980s, Shiv Sena became a popular catalyst for both social aspiration and hyper-masculine vigilante-style street activism across Maharashtra (Hansen 2001), directing its anger against Muslims and the political establishment of the Congress party. In Aurangabad and elsewhere in Marathwada, Shiv Sena attracted many young men from the OBC communities, as well as a significant number of Dalits. Since the early 1990s, all the key leaders of Shiv Sena in Aurangabad and the wider region (Chandrakant Khaire, Pradeep Jaiswal, Sanjay Shirsat, and so on) were young men from OBC or Dalit communities who had launched their political careers as street fighters in the 1980s.

By contrast, the BJP had for decades attracted a more distinctly, albeit limited, upper caste constituency across the state and in Marathwada. To this day, most key leaders and the majority of local activists from the BJP and RSS in Aurangabad belong to upper caste communities (Bania, Brahmin, and Maratha). As the white-collar workforce and middle-class colonies have expanded in Aurangabad, the BJP has also expanded its networks and constituency. The current member of legislative assembly (MLA) for the BJP, Atul Save, is in his second term in a new constituency in 'new Aurangabad' – a vast area of new middle-class colonies that have emerged over the past twenty years south of the old city. Many of his followers would readily admit that he was elected not so much because of the BJP's or RSS's networks in the city (which are relatively weak and found only in traditional upper caste areas) but more on the strength of the reputation of his father, Morehswar Save, a legendary Maratha businessman and politician who joined Shiv Sena and was instrumental in the growth and consolidation of the party in the city and the region.

During its quarter-century hold on local political power in the city, Shiv Sena has consolidated its hold on mainly lower caste Hindu areas in the old city and lower-middle-class and slum areas with large numbers of Hindus. Today, the BJP dominates the new middle-class colonies, while the Hyderabad-based AIMIM has strong support in the evermore consolidated Muslim areas in the older parts of the city.[17] In the city's many and well-developed Dalit colonies that are adjacent to and often mixed with Muslim areas, one sees an interesting blend of loyalties to various Dalit parties, Shiv Sena, and AIMIM, which received a substantial number of votes in these areas in 2015. In the past decades, the city's large Dalit population (about 25 per cent of the total population) has emerged as the decisive 'swing voters', and Dalit activists have earned a strong reputation as effective organizers and disciplined local workers and 'vote-getters', a highly prized segment of 'political specialists' in the local political scene in the city (and the state as a whole) that are now recruited by all political formations.

This political consolidation of the BJP and Shiv Sena has been underwritten in important ways by significant changes in the spatial distribution of communities in the city since the 1980s. The violent clashes between Muslims and militant Hindus in the 1980s, and a succession of serious riots in 1988, 1990, 1992–93, took place mostly in and around the dense lanes of the old, walled city, traditionally Muslim but also home to substantial Hindu and Dalit communities. As colonies and informal settlements and slums began to develop in 'new Aurangabad' and around the edges of the city in the 1990s, many families – both Muslims and Hindus (including Dalits) – decided to relocate to these areas that were more clearly defined by one community than the old city. In 2017–18, I surveyed 600 households in three areas – a lower-middle-class area in new Aurangabad, a large slum area south of the old city, and an older area in the western part of the city that has changed from scattered slum settlements to a densely built-up middle-class area with distinct Dalit and Muslim colonies. Of those surveyed in the newer colonies, almost a quarter had relocated from the old city. Informants cited many reasons for their move: many were looking for more spacious dwellings at a lower price;

many said that the relationships between communities in the old city had turned from friendly to hostile. Almost everybody cited personal safety and the security of their families as the most important factor in their relocation. The effects of this gradual demographic shift are similar to the pattern across northern and western India: deeper and more systematic segregation along religious and caste lines and a greater internal socio-religious homogeneity within colonies and neighbourhoods (Gayer and Jaffrelot 2011). This shift has spatialized caste and community in unprecedented ways and has mapped political loyalties more clearly along spatial boundaries than was ever the case before. Socio-religious segregation has also changed and segregated everyday habits and predilections when it comes to leisure, consumption, and movement around the city. Many Hindus increasingly see the old city as a dangerous and undesirable area to visit, or even drive through, while most Muslims, and many Dalits, still see the dense markets and shops there as the natural space of leisure and socializing.

Community Capitalism and the Consolidation of Upper Caste Power

In the mid-1980s, several large industries began to relocate to Aurangabad and other sites in the Marathwada region. They were beneficiaries of generous tax breaks and cheap, almost free, land provided under the Marathwada Regional Development schemes devised in the 1960s and 1970s and paying full benefits in the 1990s. Bajaj's massive plant producing autorickshaws was the largest, and Videocon's facility producing white goods followed soon after. In the 1990s and early 2000s, companies such as Skoda, Foster Beer, MAN, Colgate, Siemens, Audi, Johnson and Johnson, Crompton, Wockhardt, and many others opened production facilities here.

By 2012, the Marathwada Chamber of Commerce listed 2,083 registered industrial units in the city. Based on my perusal of the names listed as owners in this record, I found that 95 per cent were owned by Hindus, mainly Bania and Maratha style names. Of the Hindu owners, more than half were Marwari style names controlling virtually all the major companies in the city. Of the remaining, sixty to seventy mainly small enterprises (3.5 per cent) were owned by Dalits, mostly neo-Buddhist Mahars.[18] I found only two Muslim-owned/controlled industrial enterprises: one is a branch of the global pharmaceutical company Wockhardt controlled by the Gujarati Korakiwallah family, and the other, also in the pharmaceutical field, has since moved to Paithan, south of Aurangabad. The owner, a member of an old elite family and holder of an American doctoral degree, told me in 2012 that he found the business climate and the interactions with local authorities to be 'persistently hostile to Muslims, and Muslim enterprises in particular'. There is only one Muslim-owned bank in the city, controlled by members of the wealthy Bohra community.

Barbara Harriss-White (2000) found a similar confluence of community institutions and patterns of business and private accumulation in Tamil Nadu in the 1990s and called it 'corporatist capitalism'. This reflects a deeply established tradition of how to do modern business in India that was legally entrenched in the emerging complexes of law and regulations – such as the trust as a dominant legal form, the Hindu Unified Family, and other nineteenth-century innovations – as Ritu Birla (2008) and Tirthankar Roy (2010) have shown. On the production side, since the eighteenth century, 'community capitalism' is a recognized model of how to establish and maintain artisanal production, as Douglas Haynes (2012) has shown in his work on small-town capitalism in India. Haynes further suggests that these community-based small-scale business practices provide a form of coherence and persistent model within what is known as the informal sector in India.[19] However, the links between the so-called organized sector and the informal sector are many and mediated by structures of caste and community-based affinity, as my next example shows.

Bajaj was the first major firm to relocate parts of their production facilities for autorickshaws to Aurangabad in the late 1980s. Soon the workforce grew to almost 10,000, and the company ran into prolonged disputes with local unions, the most vociferous of which was led by young and upcoming Shiv Sena leaders who had also established themselves as the dominant political force. In response to this challenge, the firm started to downscale its centralized shop floor operations and outsource the production of many of the technically simple parts that go into an autorickshaw. *Mistri*s and supervisors at Bajaj were offered attractive severance packages, including some of the machinery on long-term leases. Many went on to set up small production units in nearby towns and villages. This model expanded and dispersed the industrial workforce into the rural areas. Many of these small units grew and diversified, and emerged as versatile machine parts and electronics subcontractors that gradually became keyed into the rapidly expanding sector of auto-parts manufacturing in India. Almost all of these *mistri*s-turned-industrialists belonged to the dominant Maratha-Kunbi caste cluster and various smaller OBC communities. When recruiting qualified labour, they have also generally followed the same logic of the community – be it defined by caste or religion – as the fundamental unit of trust and accumulation. This preference for Hindus in general, and in particular communities who supported Shiv Sena, was expressed in no uncertain terms by local leaders. A former union organizer and a Dalit MLA, Sanjay Shirsat, was very clear when he described the process to me in 2018:

> When so many industries began to move to Aurangabad, we wanted to make sure that the good jobs went to Hindus. Most Hindus are hard-working and

SOCIAL SEGREGATION AND EVERYDAY HINDUTVA IN MIDDLE INDIA

> honest people, but Muslims tend to be in illegal activities and crime. We wanted to protect our people and these jobs, so we kept the Muslims out of these companies.

Until the early 2000s, the majority of workers in private industries was regular, permanent, and largely unionized – with a range of rights and entitlements. Narrative and anecdotal evidence suggests that the vast majority indeed was Hindu, drawn from middle castes – Maratha and upper OBC – although it is difficult to verify the precise proportion empirically.

Today, automation and rationalization of work processes have reduced the total number of workers, even as production volume and turnover have increased. During my interviews with industrialists and businesspeople in Aurangabad, most cited 'labour trouble' as a major motivation behind their investment in technology and their increased reliance on contract labour, often managed by third-party agencies, to run specific production lines within the factory space. An owner of a cluster of medium-sized manufacturing units put it succinctly:

> I have been to China a couple of times and I have seen Chinese workers. We don't have a work force like that. In India, management of labour is very difficult. I have cut back my staff to only 15–20 per cent of what it used to be, the rest is brought in by the labour contractors ... it is much better that way.

The supreme irony is that many of the labour contractors are former union organizers who are still known and trusted by the industrial workers. Today, they leverage their standing among skilled and unskilled workers to become suppliers of labour to logistics companies that manage production lines in many large manufacturing companies. In this part of India, as elsewhere, the age of the 'good job' – secure and with pension – is on the wane. That also has implications for the composition of the workforce. A former union organizer-turned-labour-contractor, a man from a dominant caste background, now nearing retirement, told me:

> When I was young getting a job in a big company was a dream for many – even the jobs at an assembly line, or operating a machine. Most of us had matric certificate. And we had more training on the job. We enjoyed life, we had good homes and our children were educated. Today, that is all changed. There are no trainings on the job, no pension and the pay is quite low. So we don't get the same quality of people anymore ... It is hard to put a good crew together of decent workers ... I get these SC fellows who complain or do politics, I get these lazy and arrogant Muslim fellows who cannot get up in the morning, some are drunkards or they take drugs. The best ones are the youngsters from the village, they don't complain and work hard – like we used to do.

The nostalgia for the good days of the 'honest Hindu worker' notwithstanding, this narrative points to two larger structural features of the labour market in Aurangabad, and by extension, probably other cities across India. First, an earlier growth in jobs in manufacturing has slowed down in India, and globally, with the advancement of automation technologies. New jobs in manufacturing require a high level of practical skills and formal training, features that are generally lacking in Indian workforce.[20] Second, as jobs in manufacturing and industry are changing from stable jobs to short-term, casual jobs with little security or benefits, the social composition of the workforce is also changing from the earlier preponderance of higher and middle caste Hindus to the more marginalized, less educated communities – OBCs, Dalits, STs, and, to a lesser extent, Muslims. The bias against Muslims in labour recruitment continues to be very pronounced, now perpetuated by the labour contractors, many of whom belong to dominant caste communities, and by the mostly Hindu Bania owners of industrial undertakings. Technicians, engineers, and managerial staff are almost all caste Hindus, often recruited from other parts of the state and the country. Many Dalits and Muslims that I interviewed claimed that recruitment practices were somewhat less discriminatory at the city's foreign-controlled companies. Young Dalits and Muslims showed a strong preference for these companies. A young Dalit engineer explained that the problem was that caste Hindus did not understand what a free-market economy entailed: 'Hindu companies always only employed their own kind ... We want a free market, real merit-based recruitment.'

A young Muslim engineer described his predicament:

> I studied engineering in Pune and had top marks in my exams. I tried for jobs at Bajaj, at Kirloskar, and other Indian companies but I was turned down each time. Finally, I got a job at Skoda ... today I work for a German logistics company that runs some of their assembly lines ... a German manager looked at my papers and offered me the job. He did not have a problem with my name.

The net result is that Muslims in Aurangabad are virtually excluded from the city's long economic boom and expansion since the late 1980s. My own ethnographic work and surveys conducted during 2017–18 confirm the bleak picture of the socio-economic situation of Muslims one finds in the Sachar Report and the more recent quantitative studies of Muslims in Maharashtra (Chief Minister's Study Group 2013). Muslims overwhelmingly work in small businesses or are self-employed in a variety of mostly small-scale trade and service occupations.

Dalits in Aurangabad have enjoyed steady improvements in educational attainment, and many families have seen very significant social mobility in the past decades. The very active Dalit movement in the city and the region has ensured that the SC quotas in the public sector, the municipal government, and the city's many educational institutions have been filled. As a result, many Dalit households in Aurangabad have several holders of tertiary degrees and usually at least one member with a permanent government job. Until the 1970s, the city's municipal administration used to be filled with Muslims at all levels from the peon to the senior officer. Today, Dalits along with caste Hindus fill virtually every significant post, while the number of Muslim officers is reduced to less than a handful.

Conclusion

As Hindu nationalism rose to prominence in the 1990s, its ideological force mapped on to older landscapes and histories of conflict and apprehension along religious lines across India. Since the 1960s, Aurangabad had been considered a 'hotspot' of communal tension, an image that was further entrenched during the 1980s when Shiv Sena's consolidation in the region created a near-permanent state of tension and conflict in the city and the adjacent districts.

While nationwide campaigns such as the Ram Janmabhoomi campaign to 'liberate' the birthplace of Lord Ram in Ayodhya had considerable impact in the city, it was still the historical matrix of enmity and suspicion in the wake of the rule of the Nizam, and the violence around the 'police action' in 1948 that fuelled local political imaginings and slogans. In Aurangabad and elsewhere in the Deccan, Hindu nationalists portray Muslims as bigoted and violent Razakars, the irregular vigilantes of the dying days of the Hyderabad state. This past reverberated during election campaigns where the Hyderabad-based Muslim party AIMIM established itself as a major political force in the city, a fact that helped an otherwise declining Shiv Sena to mobilize both Hindu fear and triumphalism vis-à-vis the perceived menace of a resurgent Muslim 'arrogance'. In short, a more generalized Hindu nationalist ideology was rewritten in the region according to an already dense communal grammar.

Similarly, the ideology of Hindutva has become deeply embedded in the physical segregations and institutional and economic structures of the city. The local economy was always segmented, but contrary to the expectations of many development economists and officials, the rapid industrial boom in the 1990s and 2000s in the region neither ameliorated nor addressed the deep social and cultural antagonisms. On the contrary, the economic boom primarily benefited a small segment of the local Bania trading communities. The recruitment of industrial labour happened explicitly along the lines of caste and community, excluding Muslims and, to some extent, Dalits from new and attractive jobs in manufacturing.

A similar pattern could be observed in the physical expansion of the city into new suburbs and residential areas, inhabited mainly by Hindus. Today, the city is more socially segregated along the lines of religious community and caste than it ever was during the decades marked by simmering tension and street violence. Older enmities, as well as new layers of Hindu nationalist ideology, were drivers of this process because they legitimized, and gave a new justification to, already existing fears, prejudices, and preferences. The case of Aurangabad, and many other growing cities across central India for that matter, demonstrates that one significant strength of Hindu nationalism as an ideology and a political project lies in its ability to flexibly adapt to local circumstances and existing predilections and to subsume local, historical narratives into an overarching national framework.

Notes

1 The population of Aurangabad is 51 per cent Hindus, 30 per cent Muslims, and 15 per cent neo-Buddhists. Corresponding figures for Bhopal are 69 per cent Hindus and 26 per cent Muslims; Hyderabad: 65 per cent Hindus and 30 per cent Muslims; Nagpur: 69 per cent Hindus, 12 per cent Muslims, and 15 per cent neo-Buddhists; and Indore: 80 per cent Hindus and 15 per cent Muslims. https://www.census2011.co.in/census/ (accessed on 10 May 2021).

2 https://www.indiatoday.in/magazine/indiascope/story/19880615-maharashtra-civic-poll-battle-in-aurangabad-inflames-communal-passions-797337-1988-06-15 (accessed on 10 May 2021).

3 Sherman (2015) has shown how Muslims were attacked in many villages in the region after the 1948 'police action' that incorporated the Nizam's territories into the new Indian republic. At the time, mosques and *dargahs* were destroyed and, in some cases, converted to temples. I have previously explored the dynamic of some of this violence, and the memory of the 1948 attacks, in three different villages near Aurangabad (Hansen 1996).

4 This process of social segregation in Aurangabad has been a central part of my recent field research in the city in 2017–18. I interviewed multiple Hindu and Dalit families who had relocated from the old city to areas in 'new Aurangabad' in the 1990s out of fear of being affected in fresh rounds of riots.

5 http://archive.indianexpress.com/news/benz-makes-history-as-aurangabad-gets-150-mercedes-cars-at-one-go/697775/ (accessed on 25 April 2021).

6 https://www.census2011.co.in/census/city/360-aurangabad.html. Recent estimates of the total population in the urban region vary between 2.8 million and 3 million. https://indiapopulation2019.com/population-of-aurangabad-2019.html (accessed on 21 March 2021).

7 The historical importance of thousands of *qasbah* towns spread across northern and central India from the fourteenth to the nineteenth century is difficult to overestimate.

For centuries, these towns were centres of learning, trade, and cultural refinement. In the nineteenth century, they became crucial sites of new forms of cultural and political modernity (Rahman 2015).

8   Interview with Dr Shaikh Ramzan, member of the commission, on 17 July 2012. For an account of Malik Ambar's life, see Ali (2016).

9   For an interesting discussion of refugees, violence, and rehabilitation before and after the 'police action' in 1948, see Sherman (2015, 19–53). For a detailed account of the political process leading to the incorporation of Hyderabad into the Indian Union, see Noorani (2014).

10 See, for instance, the official history published by the Ministry of Defence in 1972 (Prasad 1972) or the account by V. P. Menon, Union Minister of the States and veteran bureaucrat, who oversaw the integration of the princely states into the Indian Union (Menon 1956).

11 Sunderlal estimated that up to 40,000 individuals, mostly Muslim men, had been killed in the weeks following the police action. The full text of the Sunderlal Report is reproduced in Noorani (2014). Other documents and inquiries produced by civil servants and military commanders of the time seem to corroborate that the overwhelming proportion of these killings, land grabs, and destruction of mosques took place in the Marathwada region (Sherman 2015, 19–47).

12 Advocate Arun Kapadia (interviewed on 22 July 2012)

13 I gathered this information from the Marathwada regional office of the Maharashtra State Archives in Aurangabad. The archivists were visibly uneasy about even discussing land records from the late 1940s and early 1950s. Taylor Sherman shows that the rehabilitation efforts after the police action were heavily slanted in favour of Hindus. Most (Hindu) officials overseeing this were reluctant to see Hindu violence against Muslims as a crime and simply saw it as a 'natural reaction against centuries of Muslim rule' (Sherman 2015, 45).

14 By 1948, 85 per cent of all officers in the civil services of the Hyderabad state were Muslim. After the police action, thousands were terminated at a short notice and replaced with Hindus, mostly from outside the region. Some of these were appointees in a new 'supervisory system', shadowing the older departments with a mandate to reform and control them. This system was known as 'Dual Administration' and lasted until 1950. In 1952, many former Muslim bureaucrats joined the so-called Mulkhi agitation that protested the replacement of locals of the land (*mulkhis*) with people from outside (Sherman 2015, 90–118).

15 In 2014, AIMIM won an MLA seat in Aurangabad and many municipal seats in Aurangabad, Nanded, and other smaller towns and cities across the Marathwada region. In 2019, AIMIM won the Lok Sabha seat in Aurangabad.

16 During the widespread wave of violence and protests after the demolition of Babri Masjid in Ayodhya on 6 December 1992, several villages and *talukas* across the Marathwada region were scenes of what seemed like copycat attacks and destructions of *dargahs* and local mosques. This was one of the few regions in the country where violence occurred

outside major urban centres. The violence occurred in exactly the same districts that had seen extensive destruction of hundreds of mosques and *dargah*s in 1948. After the 'police action' of 1948, high-ranking administrators condoned the violence by claiming that these *dargah*s and *masjid*s had been forcibly converted from temples in the past. The events of 6 December 1992 gave local militant Hindus a chance to revisit this history and reiterate their 'original' claim to the land and various sites of worship.

17 The rise of AIMIM in Aurangabad was sudden and decisive. A local journalist, Imtiyaz Jaleel, became the party's MLA in 2014, the year after the party won 25 seats in the municipal corporation on a programme of Dalit–Muslim unity. In 2019, Jaleel won the city's coveted parliamentary seat, defeating Shiv Sena for the first time in twenty-five years.

18 Identifying caste on the basis of names is always complicated and imprecise. Identifying members of Dalit communities in Maharashtra by names is complicated by the fact that many Dalits, especially Mahars, have surnames that are also common among Marathas, the dominant caste in most of the state.

19 The Sachar Committee Report on living conditions among Muslims in India established that Muslims were less integrated into the organized sector than any other community in the country – only 8 per cent of Muslims reported that they were employed in the organized sector (Prime Minister's High-level Committee, Government of India 2006, 79–104). The report also established that Muslims are uniquely dependent on small businesses, casual labour, and self-employment. As a result, most Muslims work for, and with, other Muslims. This well-known pattern is often taken as proof of the 'introversion' of the Muslim community. However, as recently demonstrated by quantitative social science studies, the reliance on labour from within one's own family and community is generally pronounced among marginal and stigmatized communities across India (Iyer, Khanna, and Varshney 2013). This 'introversion' is pronounced at the upper end of the business world as well. A recent study of the composition of corporate boards of India's 1,000 largest firms (representing 80 per cent of the market capitalization at the Bombay Stock Exchange) demonstrated that 70 per cent of all board members belong to the same community as the founder(s) of the firm (Ajit, Donker, and Saxena 2012).

20 A new study points out that the Indian workforce comprises only 4.6 per cent of workers with formal skills (against 75 per cent in Germany, 24 per cent in China). Most of the skilled labour in India are classified as levels 1 and 2 (the highest is 4). Kaura and Khan (2020).

References

Ajit, D., H. Donker, and R. Saxena. 2012. 'Corporate Boards in India: Blocked by Caste?' *Economic and Political Weekly* 47(32): 39–43.

Ali, O. H. 2016. *Malik Ambar: Power and Slavery Across the Indian Ocean*. New York: Oxford University Press.

Beverley, E. L. 2015. *Hyderabad, British India, and the World: Muslim Networks and Minor Sovereignty, c. 1850–1950*. New York: Cambridge University Press.

Birla, R. 2009. *Stages of Capital. Law, Culture and Market Governance in Late Colonial India.* Durham, NC: Duke University Press.

Chhibber, P., and S. L. Ostermann. 2014. 'BJP's Fragile Mandate: Modi and Vote Mobilizers in the 2014 General Election'. *Studies in Indian Politics* 2(2): 137–51.

Chief Minister's Study Group Government of Maharashtra. 2013. *The Socio-economic and Educational Backwardness of Muslims in Maharashtra.* Mumbai: Government of Maharashtra.

Deshpande, P. 2007. *Creative Pasts. Historical Memory and Identity in Western India, 1700–1960.* New York: Columbia University Press.

Deshpande, S. H. (ed.). 1973. *Economy of Maharashtra.* Bombay: Samaj Prabodhan Sanstha.

Eaton, R. 2005. *Social History of the Deccan, 1300–1761.* Cambridge: Cambridge University Press

Guru, G. 1991. 'Dalit Killings in Marathwada'. *Economic and Political Weekly* 26(51): 2926–30.

Hansen, T. B. 1996. 'The Vernacularisation of Hindutva: Shiv Sena and BJP in Rural Maharashtra.' *Contributions to Indian Sociology* 30(2): 177–214.

———. 1999. *The Saffron Wave: Democracy and Hindu Nationalism in Modern India.* Princeton, NJ: Princeton University Press.

———. 2001. *Wages of Violence. Naming and Identity in Postcolonial Bombay.* Princeton, NJ: Princeton University Press.

Harris-White, B. 2000. *India Working: Essays on Society and Economy.* Cambridge: Cambridge University Press.

Haynes, D. 2012. *Small Town Capitalism in Western India: Artisans, Merchants, and the Making of the Informal Economy, 1870–1960.* Cambridge: Cambridge University Press.

Isaksen K. L. 2007. *Locating Home: India's Hyderabadis Abroad.* Stanford: Stanford University Press.

Iyer, L., T. Khanna, and A. Varshney. 2013. 'Caste and Entrepreneurship in India'. *Economic and Political Weekly* 48(6): 52–60.

Jaffrelot, C., and L. Gayer (eds.). 2011. *Muslims in Indian Cities. Trajectories of Marginalization.* London: Hurst and Co.

Kaura, N., and N. Khan. 2020. 'India Chasing a Fleeting Manufacturing Dream'. Observer Research Foundation, 7 June. https://www.orfonline.org/expert-speak/india-chasing-fleeting-manufacturing-dream-67451/ (accessed on 10 May 2021).

Longkumer, A. 2019. 'Playing the Waiting Game: The BJP, Hindutva, and the Northeast.' In *Majoritarian State: How Hindu Nationalism Is Changing India*, edited by A. Chatterji, C. Jaffrelot, and T. B. Hansen, 281–96. London: Hurst and Co.

Menon, V. P. 1956. *The Story of the Integration of the Indian States.* London: Longmans.

Noorani, A. G. 2014. *The Destruction of Hyderabad.* London: Hurst and Co.

Omvedt, G. 2011. *Cultural Revolt in a Colonial Society: The Non-Brahman Movement in Western India.* New Delhi: Manohar Publishers.

Pernau, M. 2000. *The Passing of Patrimonialism: Politics and Political Culture in Hyderabad, 1911–1948*. New Delhi: Manohar Publishers.

Prasad, S. N. 1972. *Operation Polo: The Police Action against Hyderabad 1948*. Delhi: Ministry of Defence, Historical Section, Government of India.

Prime Minister's High-level Committee, Government of India. 2006. *Social, Economic and Educational Status of the Muslim Community in India: A Report*. Delhi: Government of India.

Puroshottam, S. 2014. 'Destroying Hyderabad and Making the Nation'. *Economic and Political Weekly* 49(22): 29–33.

Rahman, R. M. 2015. *Locale, Everyday Islam, and Modernity: Qasbah Towns and Muslim Life in Colonial India*. New Delhi: Oxford University Press.

Rao, A. 2009. *The Caste Question: Dalits and the Politics of Modern India*. Berkeley: University of California Press.

Roy, T. 2010. *Company of Kinsmen: Enterprise and Community in South Asia 1700–1940*. New Delhi: Oxford University Press.

Sherman, T. 2007. 'The Integration of the Princely State of Hyderabad and the Making of the Postcolonial Indian State, 1948–56'. *Indian Economic and Social History Review* 44(4): 489–516.

———. 2015. *Muslim Belonging in Secular India. Negotiating Citizenship in Postcolonial Hyderabad*. Cambridge: Cambridge University Press.

INCLUSION

8

'*MITAKUYE OYASIN* – WE ARE ALL RELATED'
HINDUTVA AND INDIGENEITY IN NORTHEAST INDIA*

Arkotong Longkumer

Introduction

On 5 August 2020, Prime Minister Narendra Modi laid the foundation for the controversial Ram Temple in Ayodhya by performing *bhumi puja* (groundbreaking ceremony) amid a massive surge of coronavirus cases. According to various media accounts, soil and water were collected from different pilgrimage sites, which Lord Ram allegedly visited, unifying India through a sacred geography of myth and ritual (*North East Now* 2020). Members of the Rashtriya Swayamsevak Sangh (RSS) and the Dolloi, village chief of Jowai, Meghalaya collected soil and water from the River Myntdu according to the ritual of the indigenous Niamtre faith (Manosh 2020). Myntdu is not only a river sacred to the indigenous people, but it is also the place where the Jaintia rebellion started against the British led by U Kiang Nangbah (Manosh 2020).

According to the RSS *pracharak* Gaurav Tiwari, the Niamtre people of Meghalaya worship 'Ram and Lakhan (Lakshman)'. Since time immemorial, they naturalise the region's long mythological connection to Bharat (India) that includes Rukmini (allegedly from Arunachal Pradesh), Krishna's consort, and other figures from the Mahabharata (Longkumer 2020). The RSS believes soil and water to be integral elements upon which identities and histories are materialised. Varied responses were aired on Facebook about how this act of collecting soil and water plays on the larger Hindutva idea of cultural appropriation on the one hand and the argument that all indigenous faiths are, in some way, a part of the larger Hindu cultural and religious universe on the other. The natural features (mountains, rivers, soil, and land), places of pilgrimage, and ritual spaces act as material evidence that ground

181

the Northeast to Bharatvarsh through 'earth' (*bhumi*).¹ In fact, a Vivekananda Kendra worker in Arunachal Pradesh, Narendra Joshi (2000, 7), draws on V. D. Savarkar's notion of Hindutva to establish these connections:

> After all we can hide or destroy papers, stones, paintings or pothis, but we cannot hide the Himalayas, we cannot destroy Kailasa, Manasarovar and mighty rivers originating from there. Those divine mothers are originating from the same place, innocent of the political boundaries and the associated heinous divisions they have to witness as they come down to the ground realities. But even now, with all our great 'achievements', *we may perhaps negate the history [but] we cannot negate the geography of this region.* (Emphasis added)

The way place-making is evoked through the geography of mountains and rivers is consistent with how spatial imagination is understood in the Mahabharata. The well-known Indologist Sheldon Pollock reminds us that space is marked not by precision but by its indeterminacy, perplexity, and exoticism, 'where the culture of Sanskrit, and its message, a kind of political power, have application' (Pollock 1998, 16). Here, in the spirit of the Mahabharata, ritual sites precede modern administrative maps. One could argue that the RSS's emphasis to ground the nation through the natural elements of soil and water, unifying the country in the Ayodhya ritual by Narendra Modi, highlights its idea of 'Ek Bharat, Shreshtha Bharat' (One India, Great India). Away from political slogans, how does this process unfold – using the idea of earth as the basic principle upon which Hindutva as an indigenous principle is constructed? What are the mechanisms by which Hindutva actors forge 'unity' amid the differences and fragmentation to a region since India's independence?

This chapter explores these questions by asking how the Sangh Parivar (hereafter Sangh) has accommodated the notion of Hindutva to appeal to, and be included within, the concept of indigeneity. It allows the Sangh to construct, and make, certain worlds possible, 'worldings', as an active engagement with ideas and practices, showing how Hindutva is about a way of being in the world. One of the cornerstones of the rights of indigenous peoples propounded by the International Labour Organisation (ILO) in 1989, which influenced the United Nations Declaration on the Rights of Indigenous Peoples (UNDRIP), is around the idea of protecting indigenous 'ways of life … and [developing] their identities, languages and religions, within the framework of the States in which they live' (Niezen 2011, 5). Ronald Niezen argues that the ILO idea, and that of other transnational bodies working for indigenous peoples rights, is very much oriented towards 'their assimilation into the body politic of states as a response to the imperatives of development (including "spiritual development") and equality' (Niezen 2011, 6). It is important to note how this very discourse of 'ways of life' for indigenous peoples can take on a particular edge when dominant groups such as the Sangh can assimilate this narrative of indigeneity to argue that Hindutva too is 'a way of life'.[2]

I will draw on the works of the Research Institute of World's Ancient Traditions Cultures and Heritage (RIWATCH) based in Arunachal Pradesh and the International Centre for Cultural Studies (ICCS) based in Pennsylvania, US, and examine how their activities – ranging from organizing conferences on 'native spiritualities' to arranging student exchanges and research programmes – argue for connecting with various indigenous traditions around the world as a way of making certain worlds possible through the idea of 'nurturing roots', and based on the Lakota slogan 'Mitakuye Oyasin' (We are all related). In this way, I ask to what extent are the Sangh activists in Northeast India making Hindutva into a universal principle related to ideas of earth and soil.

Local Grounds, Global Networks

On a lovely summer morning in May 2018, my friends and I were invited to a Sangh *shakha* in Arunachal Pradesh. A day before, I had told the Bharatiya Janata Party (BJP) general secretary of the state (also an RSS member) that access to the RSS is difficult. I asked him if the reticence was partly to do with the fact that the organization had something to hide. He retorted by arguing that the RSS is transparent. Perhaps to demonstrate that his rhetoric was not bluster, I received an invitation from him the following evening to attend an RSS *shakha* in Pasighat, a few hours' drive from the capital, Itanagar, where we were based.

We arrived at a large place that resembled a school. Here, in this *shakha*, 120 young tribal boys from all over the state were being taught self-defence, about the Hindu nation and its key ideologies, and discipline through a rigorous twenty-day programme. The morning educational session was already underway when we arrived. We entered through the back entrance, just in time to catch the last session on global indigenous traditions (in English). Facing the stage were the prominent pictures of the founder of the RSS, K. B. Hedgewar (the founding *sarsanghchalak*, chief) and M. S. Golwalkar, the second *sarsanghchalak*, and a picture of Bharat Mata festooned with garlands (see Figure 8.1). A PowerPoint presentation was projected onto a small screen, displaying colourful images of indigenous traditions from around the world and emphasizing the need to preserve indigenous knowledge. Towards the end of the presentation, the instructor, Vikram,[3] asked the young boys to say 'Mitakuye Oyasin – We are all related'. The young boys repeated 'Mitakuye

Figure 8.1 RSS *shakha* in Pasighat, Arunachal Pradesh, May 2018
Source: Author.

Oyasin' in unison, conveying the message that they were related to the Native Americans and other indigenous peoples around the world.

After the session concluded, we were served a vegetarian lunch in the common kitchen. After lunch, Vikram and I walked around the compound where the *shakha* was held and sat in a quiet spot under a tree. Soon a young boy arrived to give us *prasad* (in Hinduism, *prasad* is food and water offered to a deity during *puja* (worship). It is believed to be consecrated by the deity and is later distributed to the worshippers. This made Vikram uncomfortable, as he had just been emphasizing that this *shakha* had nothing to do with Hinduism. The tension between Hindutva as a secular principle and Hinduism as a religious practice is a grey area that many have tried to untangle in the context of Hindu nationalism (see Longkumer 2017). This slippage is something that has occurred quite frequently in my interaction with Hindutva actors in the Northeast. I was aware of *prasad* and accepted it without a fuss, which pleased the young boy at least.

Culture, Nationalism, and Indigeneity

'Mitakuye Oyasin' is a phrase from the Lakota language, Vikram, who is trained in the Vivekananda Kendra, tells me. He adds that in Hinduism too, 'we say *Vasudeva*

Kutumbakam (the whole universe is one). So, we are related'. Upon researching about different native communities around the world, Vikram came up with an idea. 'We found that instead of doing research on different ethnic communities of Northeast India, why shouldn't we have a sort of a comparative and cross-cultural study between all native communities of the world?' That is how RIWATCH came into existence, he explains.

RIWATCH (with the motto 'Nurturing the Roots') is in Roing in the Lower Dibang Valley district of Arunachal Pradesh. It is a 'community-based research organization with [a] mission of empowering ethnic communities to prosper sustainably by strengthening their value system'.[4] The organization recently opened a museum in Roing, which was inaugurated by Kiren Rijiju, a local Arunachali and the Minister of State (Independent Charge) for Youth Affairs and Sports and Minister of State for Minority Affairs. The museum was established with 'an objective to research and document the rich cultural heritage of North East of India in general and Arunachal Pradesh in particular and find out the commonalities among the different ethnic communities from all over the world' (AC Team 1 2017). Vikram runs the organization along with twelve office holders and board members. They aim to open a research university beside the museum. Their focus is on collaboration with foreign institutes and implementation of student exchange programmes. The student exchange programme is highlighted in the annual report (undated), emphasizing the connections with different indigenous and native traditions of the world. 'Miss Maria Priscilla Alvarado Gomez was the first scholar from Costa Rica attached to RIWATCH to study the traditions of Idu-Mishmis for a period of 3 months in 2008–2009. She found lots of common cultural threads with Natives of Costa Rica and Native Americans of USA' (RIWATCH, n.d.).[5]

RIWATCH is part of the US-based ICCS. It is difficult to ascertain who supports the organization directly, but its networks consist of the Vivekananda Kendra, RSS, and the BJP, alongside many non-Christian indigenous traditions in the region. On its Facebook page, ICCS is described as an organization that 'strives for a world where indigenous cultural heritage and traditions are valued for their intrinsic wisdom to strengthen communities and enrich life'. Conceived in Nagpur (where the RSS headquarters are), Maharashtra, in 1994, first under the guidance of Dr Yaswant Pathak and then Professor Bakhle, ICCS was established in 1996 in Arunachal Pradesh. Dr Pathak, who travelled extensively, was highly influenced in Kenya by the writings of the African theologian John Mbiti's book *African Religions and Philosophy* and sought to establish closer links and intellectual collaboration between India and Africa, which was the initial orientation of the ICCS (Elst 2012, 144). In Nagpur, he established (in ICCS) Indo-African studies, later extending the ICCS to other native traditions, drawing on their close affinity with India (Elst

2012). According to Konrad Elst, Dr Pathak closely followed the writings of Ram Swarup (1920–1998) who was the intellectual pioneer of the project Voice of India (VOI) alongside Sita Ram Goel (1921–2003). The views of VOI against Muslims and Christians are so extreme that, according to Walter Andersen, it makes the RSS appear like a 'conciliatory alternative' (quoted in Nanda 2009, 109).

Since 2003, ICCS has conducted various activities, including conferences and workshops, under the forum 'World Council of Elders of the Ancient Traditions' (WCEAT) (ICCS n.d). Here is a flavour of some of the themes of these and conferences:

> The first international conference was held at Mumbai in 2003 with the theme 'Mitakuye Oyasin – We are all related' ... The second conference was in 2006 at Jaipur with the theme 'Spirituality beyond Religions' ... The third conference was held in 2009 at Nagpur with the theme 'Renaissance of the Ancient Traditions: Challenges and Solutions' ... The theme of this 4th Conference was 'Nourishing the Balance in the Universe'. The event was jointly organized by International Center for Cultural Studies (ICCS), Dev Samskruti Vishwa Vidyalaya (DSVV) and co-sponsored by the Council of Elders Mayas [sic], Xincas and Garifunas, European Congress of Ethnic Religions (ECER) and Children of Mother Earth. A total of 458 delegates from 33 countries including 178 from overseas participated in the conference. (Samvad 2012, 6)[5]

The activities of RIWATCH and ICCS offer a platform for different indigenous communities to share their knowledge and collaborate on an international scale. Centred very much on 'insider' knowledge of indigenous peoples, the activities of these groups gain prominence when they collaborate with the RSS and other Sangh members. In the 2012 conference on 'Nourishing the Balance in the Universe', Dr Mohan Bhagwat, *sarsanghchalak* of the RSS, delivered the keynote address where:

> He praised the efforts and resolve of the Elders in preserving their traditions and cultures. He recalled the priceless treasures of Bharat thought [sic] like 'Live and Let Live', 'Unity in Diversity', 'World is one family' & 'Let us ennoble the world' and remarked that these have extreme relevance today. Universal outlook is the hallmark of Bharatiya thought and the happiness and well-being of everyone is always sought ... (*Samvad* 2012, 8)

The focus of RIWATCH and ICCS is presented as an ecumenical movement, though it is highly focused on a non-Christian and non-Muslim paradigm, where there is an attempt to find a connection between different native traditions – Paganism, Native American, and Hinduism. And this is the idea of Hindutva, Vikram described to me during our meeting. In fact, the centrality of 'nature' and

'MITAKUYE OYASIN – WE ARE ALL RELATED'

how native traditions around the world gravitate around this idea is represented in the 'Fourth Conference and Gathering of the Elders of the Ancient Traditions and Cultures' at the Dev Sanskriti University, Haridwar (March 2012):

> The typical daily schedule started with the demonstration of ceremonies and rituals of the different cultures ... Worshipping Nature was the underlying principle of these cultures and traditions. Though in different ways, they all worshipped the five basic elements of Nature i.e. Earth, Air, Water, Fire and Sky. 'Love Mother Earth' was the message that emanated from all these rituals and religious ceremonies. (Quoted in Elst 2012, 141)

Hindutva, then, is central to the goals of ICCS and RIWATCH in light of the responsibility Hindu traditions have to the world, Vikram tells me:

> If you look at the whole world's cultural heritage, there are only two civilisations that have been running continually for a long time. They are Chinese and Hindu. Others like Egyptian or Incas, they were once born and now they are gone. These traditions, particularly Indian tradition, have the responsibility to help others to identify their own past richness and things. That responsibility we should share.

On its website, ICCS further qualifies this point and adds that 'Hindu society, being the oldest, and arguably most vibrant ancient tradition in the world, which can still be classed, in some sense as a flourishing civilization, naturally takes on the mantle of host'.[6] The initiative of RIWATCH and Vikram's involvement in it speaks to particular issues surrounding the relationship between nature, Mother Earth, and nationalism that is underwritten by what 'indigenous' implies and based very much against a Judeo-Christian (and Islamic) framework.[7] This is a point reiterated in ICCS's most recent conference in Mumbai:

> Elders, like Pat McCabe from the Diné Nation, raised in the Lakota tradition of the Native American peoples, spoke eloquently, while remaining hard-hitting in her keynote address that ancient traditions must come together in a real meaningful sense in order to push back against the socio-economic forces harming the Earth. The emphasis on feminine divine was the set theme, and a special focus was set on protecting, nourishing and living harmoniously with Nature ... The challenge seems clear enough. And the solution is equally as clear – that of a complete overhaul of the socio-political-economic framework in which our societies operate underpinned by a Judeo-Christian narrative.[8]

There are different ways of reading the summary of events described by the ICCS. On the one hand, the importance of 'ancient knowledge' preserved and sustained through the ages among native and indigenous communities is worth acknowledging, with some newspaper headlines even lauding indigenous peoples as the 'best guardians of world's biodiversity' (Hill 2017). Indeed, the movement to record indigenous knowledge has already been highlighted by the United Nations and UNESCO through the phenomena referred to as indigenous knowledge, traditional knowledge, and traditional indigenous knowledge.[9] While these forms of knowledge are seen as a panacea to the worst kinds of modernity and consumerism, the loss of indigenous knowledge is set against the 'reach of technology and Christianity [which brought with it] the alarming prospect of an end of knowledge about ways of life that included unexplored pathways of human progress' (Niezen 2011, 125).

The unintended consequences of such challenging ideas are their reverberations. Different groups, such as Hindutva activists in Northeast India and the ICCS, take up these ideas by targeting a particular Judeo-Christian worldview, further entrenching antagonism. The way Hindutva actors navigate through this quagmire in Northeast India is to work with indigenous religions to revive the pre-Christian gods and lay claims to the soil, not in (secular) Christian terms of dominance but through benevolence, where nature facilitates both loyalty to the nation and ties to 'ancient cultures', an idea, argues Niezen (2011, 124–26), that is not unfamiliar in indigenous peoples discourses. The idea that enables Hindutva to link with the global indigenous ideas of 'ancient cultures' is through Paganism.

In his lecture at the Vivekananda Kendra Institute of Culture (VKIC), anthropologist B. B. Kumar noted: 'Ancestor worship is an essential feature of our religion (generically known as Paganism; a generic term that includes Hinduism)' (Kumar 2015, 33). In its official party text, the BJP reiterates this claim under the heading 'Cultural Nationalism'. The BJP draws on the idea of Pagan, applied to those who worshipped the 'God of the pagans, which in Latin means "locality"' (Bharatiya Janata Party 2005, 94). Pagans are also referred to as 'country-dwellers' or 'heathens'; Paganism was the old religion of pre-Christian Europe. It exists today in many forms, ranging from 'Native Spirituality, Celtic Spirituality, European Traditional Religion, the Elder Faith, and the Old Religion' (Bharatiya Janata Party 2005, 94).

What is important though, the BJP text argues, is that Paganism survived the onslaught of Christianization in Europe and is now undergoing a 'massive revival' in the West, similar to Hindutva, which is also undergoing a revival. The BJP text argues that Paganism relates, crucially, to local gods and ancestors of the land based on the ideas of polytheism, or belief in many deities; pantheism, or that the divine is everywhere; and finally that the divine is expressed as both male and female (Bharatiya Janata Party 2005, 96; *Hinduism Today* 1991). In summing up the basic overlap between Paganism and Hinduism, the BJP text says:

'MITAKUYE OYASIN – WE ARE ALL RELATED'

> In a sense at the basic level Hinduism is a Pagan religion. As Paganism allows for evolution Hinduism too allows for evolution. Since Paganism is belief in many Gods there is generally no fight over Gods. This is the greatest virtue of Polytheism. The highest merit of Polytheism is its capacity to integrate Gods. If Gods can work together, religions can work together. (Bharatiya Janata Party 2005, 97)

Once Hinduism is expressed along these lines, it has the potential to relate with other 'native traditions' that are intimately connected to land. An interview with Prudence Jones of the Pagan Federation by the scholar of religion Michael York in 1991 focuses on this idea of allying with Hinduism. Jones points out that there is an important connection between Hinduism, Shintoism, and Paganism as they are all 'indigenous faiths' and are not dogmatic, like the religions of the book, Islam and Christianity, which are monotheistic – with a 'Supreme Deity who has to be obeyed'. Arguing for the need to organize themselves into one coherent body, Jones even suggests forming a 'Worldwide Council of Indigenous Religions'. She further suggests that like Hinduism, which is native to India, European Pagan religion 'is the native, indigenous religion of Europe' (*Hinduism Today* 1991). For Prudence Jones, there is a clear ideological platform to align the UK Pagan Federation with Hinduism, affording them a larger political profile.

This interview is significant because it has been reprinted in 2005 by the BJP (under 'Cultural Nationalism') in local and national RSS magazines, such as the *Organiser* and *Heritage Explorer*, and has also appeared in the activities of the ICCS. Several of my Sangh informants referred to this interview in recent years. It is often emphasized to demonstrate the struggle of Paganism – because of suppression by Christianity – and its revival as a lesson to Christians who have suppressed their 'ancient cultures'. The revival is seen as a challenge to the Judeo-Christian framework that dominated through imperialism and colonization, and now Hinduism in its resurgence is able to offer support to all indigenous traditions in the world. The common themes that link Paganism, Hinduism, and indigenous religions are animism and kinship with nature (Rountree 2012; Harvey 2005), a discourse that is popular among Western pagan groups whose motto (to quote the first principle of the Pagan Federation) is 'Love for and Kinship with Nature'.

There are two ways in which the discussion surrounding Paganism has developed. First is the discourse over the 'closeness to nature' that scholars (Fisk 2017; Harvey 2005; Rountree 2012) have articulated. They show how most modern Paganism is intimately tied to nature, often articulated as 'animism' – which includes all of 'earth's visible inhabitants'. These inhabitants, that is, 'trees, rocks, rivers, mountains, caves, insects, animals (including humans), fire, snow, particular tracts of land or indeed the whole earth itself (or Herself) – are conscious and en-souled or en-spirited' (Rountree 2012, 308). In these texts, earlier, more negative uses of animism, based on E. B. Tylor's (1871) evolutionary idea – that animism is the basis of primitive religion that gives rise to polytheism and then monotheism – are abandoned for a more positive version that recognizes a world that is 'full of persons, only some of whom are human, and life is always lived in relationship to others' (Harvey 2005, xi).

This 'new animism' can be found in a host of scholars (Bird-David 1999; Harvey 2005; Ingold 2006) and can also be applied to local writers (Kumar 2015; Bhide 2002, 2010; Jamatia 2011) who too are interested in reconstituting the term 'animism'. For instance, Nivedita Bhide, an advocate of indigenous religions of Northeast India, explains that the dictionary definition of 'animism' is the 'attribution of life (soul) to natural objects and phenomena' (Bhide 2002, xx). She holds this as a positive description and links anima and *atman* (soul). She concludes that Hindus believe that *atman* pervades the entire universe: 'if we go by the dictionary meaning of Animism, then all Hindus are animist, too' (Bhide 2002, xx). She believes that the present crisis, where Hindus have been separated from animist tribals, is because of the colonial and missionary strategy of 'divide and convert' (Bhide 2002, xx).

Similarly, the turn towards nativism, with the appeal to roots that Paganism encourages, inadvertently produces other kinds of connections to do with land, identity, and authentic nationalism through 'blood' and 'belonging' (Ivakhiv 2005; Gallagher 2009). In the process of reclamation of land and tradition around a particular set of local symbols and ideas, many nativist traditions in Russia and the Slavic countries (post-USSR), for example, used a mixture of different traditions combined with nativism, Paganism, animism, and Vedic sources of the Aryan race against the Semitic religions. Paganism, for instance, is used as a way to link with 'spiritual Aryanism in Europe' (Gallagher 2009, 585; Ivakhiv 2005, 213; Fisk 2017, 33). Adrian Ivakhiv (2005) argues that these movements are often related to disillusionment with modernity, Christianity, capitalism, and Zionism, characteristic features associated with a loss of identity. In fact, for the Ukrainian Native Believers, Christianity is to be blamed for taking away their original traditions, cultures, and values (Ivakhiv 2005). The solution for the Native Faiths, Ivakhiv suggests, is 'a recovery of the original condition through a rebirth of the remnant forms of tradition and custom encoding those original relationships ... by which human groups once lived in harmony with Nature' (Ivakhiv 2005, 216).

If we are to look at Hinduism as the 'common principle of all native–indigenous traditions of various communities', as Bhide suggests, then there is room to conceptualize the connection among Hinduism, indigenous religions, and Native Faiths in Europe and elsewhere through connections with RIWATCH, WCEAT, and ICCS. This is a connection that Meera Nanda made in her presentation at the European Conference on Modern South Asian Studies at Lund in 2014. She argued that there is a relation between what she calls 'neo-Pagans' and Hindutva through the language of environmentalism, critique of 'Semitic monotheism', and their efforts to find connections between their pre-Christian European gods and Hinduism, the 'living religion of nature' (Nanda 2004). She calls this 'Hindu triumphalism' (Nanda 2009) – a movement that explicitly argues for Hindu superiority, alongside presenting Hinduism, according to the Vedic scholar and an ally of Hindu nationalists David Frawley, as the answer to the 'regeneration of the planet' (quoted in Nanda 2009, 109). Like the discussion earlier, Hinduism is pitted against the monotheistic faiths that are seen as intolerant, totalitarian, and wilfully decimating local cultures in their wake. In contrast, Hinduism is viewed as pluralistic, humanitarian, and the only force that is capable of acting as a catalyst to regenerate European Paganism to fight against the growth of Islam (Nanda 2009, 113).

In his book *Return of the Swastika: Hate and Hysteria versus Hindu Sanity*, Koenraad Elst, a sympathiser of the Sangh, accuses Nanda of overplaying the connection between Hindutva and neo-Pagans. If at all this connection could exist, he says, it is through the WCEAT. This could be the beginning of an international network of similar traditions, he notes (Elst 2015, 52–3). Both Nanda's and Elst's critiques tend to be highly polemical. What is interesting, however, is that Hindutva is making certain 'worlds' possible through its encounter with different indigenous and native movements all over the world. If the basic principle of Hindutva is to do with the soil and the gods and ancestors that inhabit it, then it is possible for its affiliates/adherents to subsume Paganism, nativism, animism, and indigenous traditions. This universalism is, of course, a challenge because many native and indigenous traditions have distinct practices that identify them as such. But by providing a broad canvas upon which anything can be etched, the evolution of Hindutva in the Northeast, through clarifying its identity by engaging with questions of indigeneity and indigenous religions, has created worlds that are possible and potentially universal.

Creating Common Worlds

'Indigenous peoples all [speak many] different languages but in our meetings, we are speaking one language. Our relationship to Mother Earth is identical.'[10] The former Secretary-General of the United Nations, Ban Ki-Moon, quoted these words from a long-time indigenous activist Tonya Gonnella Frichner during the United Nations' first world conference on indigenous peoples in New York in September 2014. Various scholars have observed that nation and culture are kindred concepts related to, or existing in, the 'soil' (Malkki 1992, 29; Clifford 1988). 'Mother Earth' is the ideal metaphor to carry home the message of the soil as it is

> the centre of the universe, the core of their culture, the origin of their identity as a people. She [Mother Earth] connects them [indigenous peoples] with their past (as the home of [their] ancestors), with the present (as [the] provider of their material needs), and with the future (as the legacy they hold in trust for their children and grandchildren). In this way, indigenousness carries with it a sense of belonging to a place.[11]

In the words of the anthropologist Liisa Malkki, '"native", "indigenous", and "autochthonous" have all served to root cultures in soils' (Malkki 1992, 29). This homology is evident in how 'culture' is derived from the Latin for cultivation (Malkki 1992, 29). Here, the metaphor of roots – and soil – continues to pervade much of the thinking of the Sangh, UNESCO, and indigenous peoples. Through my interactions with Abhishek, a senior RSS *pracharak* (full-time worker), it became clear to me that the territorial nation and the metaphysical valence of nation and culture are both marked as universalizing Hindutva.

Abhishek was the main organizer of the RSS *shakha* where the ideas of RIWATCH were on display. During the *shakha*, Abhishek spoke in depth with Vikram, a RIWATCH leader, and gave a talk to the 120 tribal boys who attended it. Abhishek has a PhD from Jawaharlal Nehru University (JNU) in International Relations, focusing on Indonesia. He began to appreciate the extent to which the *Bharatiya* (Indian) culture has influenced the language and culture of Indonesia that is pervasive in many aspects of its history, borrowing Sanskrit concepts such as 'Bhinneka Tunggal Ika' (Unity in Diversity), which became its national motto. He told me that it was because of his work in Indonesia and the Northeast of India that he began to appreciate the 'universalism of Hindutva'. He acknowledged the importance of people like Savarkar, Hedgewar, and Golwalkar as important thinkers for the Sangh, but also reminded me that although one must continue to use 'their methodology' of 'man-making, nation-building', one must also be prepared to 'deconstruct their ideas to reconstruct our country'. Parochial nationalism is therefore antithetical to the growth of the nation, he said. Using the language of humanitarianism, coexistence, and liberalism, ideas one may not immediately associate with Hindutva, he argued for Hindutva, progressing from the individual, to society, nation, the level of internationalism, and culminating in universalism.

Probing a bit further, I asked him, 'How can the universalism of Hindutva be applied somewhere else, say, in China, Europe, or America?' Abhishek answered in one sentence: 'Hindutva is an ideology that is relevant and universal in whichever country that acknowledges the soil as the core indigenous ideology from which everything else has cropped up.' This language envisages encounters that connect and intersect with the wider world. Hindutva worlding is not simply about creating cultures but worlds (Palmer and Hunter 2018). In light of this, Hindutva worlding comes about through its physical grounding and metaphysical resonance – that of the 'Mother Earth'.

There is substantial evidence on the way Mother Earth is used interchangeably with Mother Nature, goddesses, and the national symbol Bharat Mata (Mother India) by the Sangh (and others) (Niezen 2011; Permanent Forum on Indigenous Issues 2010). It is a way to fuse the nation, culture, and soil to Mother Earth. Reminiscent of the discussion regarding RIWATCH, ICCS, and Hindutva, organizations like the Global Indigenous Caucus, in their New York meeting in 2009, issued the statement that 'indigenous peoples of all over the world speak with one voice' (quoted in Niezen 2011, 128). This sort of universal voice, akin to that propounded by RIWATCH through the Hindutva worlding – 'we are all related' – is often heard in the context of environmental issues. The language of 'indigenous spirituality' becomes intertwined with ideas of how to care for 'Mother Earth' and looks towards indigenous peoples' notions of care, stewardship, and guardianship of the world (Niezen 2011, 128–29).[12] Critics, however, warn us of the danger of this view, which is often based around a particular European 'grammar of conquest' (Brosius 2001).

Reacting against the generalized concept of the 'sacred' through his work in Penan, Malaysia, Peter Brosius (2001) reminds us that indigenous peoples actually relate to the world in very specific ways, following a rich vocabulary inherited from the land and their ancestors. The universalizing of indigenous religions minimizes the location-specific, culturally rooted practices of people who relate to local contexts in ways that often make generalization extremely difficult, if not impossible, as academic constructions. But in the realm of political articulations, these haphazard universalizing discourses are highly productive. Local knowledge is often usurped when their plight is taken up by activists to appeal to 'remote audiences' in a language that has global recognition. This world-making, whereby the terms 'sacred' and 'Mother Earth' have powerful resonances, relates to the global circulation of ideas in a way that is generative. In Jamatia's description of indigenous peoples in the Northeast, these ideas take on a comparative salience. He says:

> For countless generations, forest [sic] has been their home; therefore they are the most intimate to the Mother Nature [sic]. They are the simplest people on the earth. They are as holy and pure as the Mother Nature itself ... So for them every portion of the Mother Earth and its creation (Nature) is pure and sacred. (Jamatia 2011, 8)

If we acknowledge, following the anthropologist Tania Li, that identifying as indigenous or tribal is about *positioning*, 'which draws upon historically sedimented practices, landscapes, and repertoires of meaning, and emerges through particular patterns of engagement and struggle' (Li 2000, 150), then we may view Hindutva in a similar light. The positioning of Hindutva and indigenous religions in the Northeast opens up the core issue of identification around similarities – land, nature, animism, and Mother Earth. Li's remarks become relevant insofar as Hindutva is a philosophy of indigeneity. It is hard to see how it could be excluded. Yet it must be stressed that Hindutva activists are not necessarily shouting to be heard when it comes to the UNDRIP, or for them to be recognized as indigenous peoples. But they are aligning, or *positioning*, themselves with indigenous religions precisely to allow them to make certain 'worlds' possible that might easily slip under the radar, in spaces that people might least suspect.

Conclusion

The opening vignette of Modi conducting *bhumi puja*, as he takes the ennobled soil from all over India and plants it firmly within the larger Hindu imagination of what Ayodhya represents, confirms the idea of One India, Great India. This larger political drama enacted with full ritual regalia and accompanying accoutrements also tells a story of how the Northeast, with all its political resistances based on difference, is assimilated and unified, indexed through the soil – earth that shares the small ground.

This chapter investigates how Hindutva activists seek to appropriate the idea of indigeneity by showing how these categories are not simply descriptive but also politically charged. The homology between Hindutva and indigenous, 'of the soil', demonstrates a particular synergy that is both productive and challenging. Paganism, animism, and even UN ideas of indigeneity remind us of how world politics, economies, communications, and cultures are all entangled and inter-related, a friction (Tsing 2005) that continually persists and astounds. Tsing says, 'Cultures are continually co-produced in the interaction I call "friction": the awkward, unequal, unstable, and creative qualities of interconnection across difference' (2005, 4). The difference in ideas and geographical locations immediately comes to mind with Tsing's description of friction that is, however, brought together in varying ways that produce 'cultures'. What is missing in her description is the idea of 'sameness', a technique that argues for the very opposite of 'friction', a well-oiled machine, a harmony. Hindutva is the harmonious echo that produces and aspires to fulfil 'worlds' in which differences are celebrated, and where sameness is the grammar. The image of the soil, and how ideologies crop up from it, provides the lasting finality of Hindutva worldings.

It is challenging because Hindutva makes universal claims about indigeneity, even through UN discourses of indigenous peoples. What happens when dominance and not marginality enters the discourse of indigeneity? In a sense, the point made by James Cox (2007) with regard to the locality of indigenous religions is surely valid here. Even though Cox's definition of indigenous religions might fit in with Hindutva ideas of belonging in India, specific studies of local contexts, as he has done among the Shona of Zimbabwe and the Arrernte of Central Australia, demonstrate that universalizing the local can only be done if the 'local' is taken seriously and studied in its own right. Peter Brosius too is sceptical of the discourse of the 'sacred' – localized and distinct to Penan – when global movements usurp it for universal circulation that may not always compound with local articulations. This is where Hindutva ideologies, through their universalizing claims, connect with Paganism and other native traditions as a universal form of indigenous religion through, paradoxically, its appeal to the local. Not only are ideas of Hindutva challenging the way we think about certain concepts, their global circulations, and indeed their translations, but they are also making certain worlds possible through entering the discourse of indigeneity and indigenous religions. Here, experimental Hindutva thinking, by pursuing national and transnational routes, is fashioning a certain sensibility that demonstrates that theirs is a way of life.

Notes

* Sections of this chapter are revised from my book *The Greater India Experiment: Hindutva and the Northeast* (Stanford: Stanford University Press, 2020).

1 Sangh Parivar activists and ideologues evoke the idea of Bharatvarsh (found in the Sanskrit epic the Mahabharata) covering the area from the 'Indus to the seas' and below the Himalayas (Savarkar 1969, 31–32). This also relates to their idea of 'Greater India' that includes Afghanistan, Pakistan, India, Bangladesh, Sri Lanka, Nepal, Bhutan, Tibet, Myanmar, and, in some cases, Cambodia, Thailand, and Indonesia (see Longkumer 2020).

2 In 1995, the Supreme Court of India deliberated on whether Hinduism/Hindutva is a way of life. In the judgment, it acknowledged the indeterminate nature of these terms – Hindu/Hinduism/Hindutva – and declared that 'it is difficult to appreciate how the term "*Hindutva*" or "Hinduism" *per se* can be assumed to mean and be equated with narrow fundamentalist Hindu religious bigotry ... these terms are indicative more of a way of life of the people' (Jacobsohn 2003, 200–202).

3 All names have been changed.

4 http://sewainternational.org/riwatch/ (accessed on 16 December 2021).

5 Most recently, in February 2018, they organized a conference in Mumbai, titled 'Exploring Divinity through the Feminine in Ancient Cultures'. https://mailchi.mp/85a6ccf8a40a/iccs-us-newsletter-465959?e=082d92ab26 (accessed on 16 December 2021).

6 https://mailchi.mp/85a6ccf8a40a/iccs-us-newsletter-465959?e=082d92ab26 (accessed on 16 December 2021).

7 Hindu nationalists have supported Zionism. They also acknowledge that although Judaism is monotheistic, their god is exclusively for their people and not proselytizing in nature (Elst 2012, 153; Nanda 2009, 108).

8 https://mailchi.mp/85a6ccf8a40a/iccs-us-newsletter-465959?e=082d92ab26 (accessed on 16 December 2021).

9 'A Spiritual Relationship with the Land,' taken from the UNESCO teaching material entitled Living by Indigenous Knowledge. http://www.unesco.org/education/tlsf/mods/themec/mod11.html (accessed on 20 January 2020).

10 'Secretary-General's Remarks at the Opening of the World Conference on Indigenous Peoples', United Nations Secretary-General, 22 September 2014, https://www.un.org/sg/en/content/sg/statement/2014-09-22/secretary-generals-remarks-opening-world-conference-indigenous (accessed on 16 December 2021).

11 This quote is from 'A Spiritual Relationship with the Land' taken from the UNESCO teaching material entitled *Living by Indigenous Knowledge*. http://www.unesco.org/education/tlsf/mods/themec/mod11.html (accessed on 20 January 2020).

12 *Heritage Explorer* published a special issue on the Indian Independence Day (2017): 'Traditional Preservation Systems of Biodiversity in North East Bharat'. It highlights the role traditional knowledge, traditional indigenous knowledge, and traditional ecological knowledge play in preserving the biodiversity of the region: http://www.heritagefoundation.org.in/Download/heritage_explorer/2017/august2017.pdf (accessed on 1 June 2021).

It relates closely to the UNESCO ideas of 'traditional knowledge' to preserve ancient learning and lore, against the worst effects of modernity: http://www.unesco.org/new/en/natural-sciences/priority-areas/link/ (accessed on 16 December 2021).

References

AC Team 1. 2017. 'Kiren Rijiju Inaugurates RIWATCH Museum and Chimari Bridge in Arunachal Pradesh'. *Affairs Cloud*, 23 July. https://affairscloud.com/kiren-rijiju-inaugurates-riwatch-museum-chimari-bridge-arunachal-pradesh/?amp (accessed on 16 December 2021).

Bharatiya Janata Party. 2005. *Evolution of BJP*. Party Document Vol. 8. New Delhi: Bharatiya Janata Party.

Bhide, M. N. 2002. 'Prologue'. In *Traditional Customs and Rituals of Northeast India, Vol I.*, edited by P.C. Sarma, xiv–xxxvi. Guwahati: Vivekananda Kendra Institute of Culture.

———. 2010. 'One as Beautiful Many'. *Quest* 4(1): 54–74.

Brosius, P. J. 2001. 'Local Knowledges, Global Claims: On the Significance of Indigenous Ecologies in Sarawak, East Malaysia'. In *Indigenous Traditions and Ecology: The Interbeing of Cosmology and Community*, edited by John A. Grim, 125–58. Cambridge, MA: Harvard University Press.

Bird-David, N. 1999. '"Animism"' Revisited: Personhood, Environment, and Relational Epistemology'. *Current Anthropology* 40(S1): S67–S91.

Clifford, James. 1988. *The Predicament of Culture: Twentieth-century Ethnography, Literature, and Art*. Cambridge, MA: Harvard University.

Cox, J. L. 2007. *From Primitive to Indigenous: The Academic Study of Indigenous Religions*. Aldershot: Ashgate.

Das, Manosh. 2020. 'Meghalaya: Soil, Water from Jaintia Hills for Ram Temple "Bhumi Pujan"'. *Times of India*, New Delhi, 28 July.

Elst, K. 2012. 'The Gatherings of the Elders: The Beginnings of a Pagan International'. *The Pomegranate* 14(1): 140–58.

———. 2015. *Return of the Swastika: Hate and Hysteria versus Hindu Sanity*. Budapest: Arktos Media Ltd.

Fisk, Anna. 2017. 'Appropriating, Romanticizing and Reimagining: Pagan Engagements with Indigenous Animism'. In *Cosmopolitanism, Nationalism, and Modern Paganism*, edited by Kathryn Rountree, 21–42. London: Palgrave Macmillan.

Gallagher, Anne-Marie. 2009. 'Weaving a Tangled Web? Pagan Ethics and Issues of History, "Race" and Ethnicity in Pagan Identity'. In *Handbook of contemporary Paganism*, edited by M. Pizza and J. R. Lewis, 577–90. Leiden: Brill.

Harvey, G. 2005. *Animism: Respecting the Living World*. New York: Columbia University Press.

Hill, D. 2017. 'Indigenous Peoples Are the Best Guardians of World's Biodiversity'. *The Guardian*, 9 August.

Hinduism Today. 1991. 'Europe's Ancient Nature Worshippers, the Pagans, Call for a Hindu Alliance'. 1 February. https://www.hinduismtoday.com/magazine/february-1991/1991-02-europe-s-ancient-nature-worshippers-the-pagans-call-for-a-hindu-alliance/ (accessed on 16 December 2021).

Ingold, T. 2006. 'Rethinking the Animate, Re-animating Thought'. *Ethnos: Journal of Anthropology* 71(1): 9–20.

Ivakhiv, A. 2005. 'Nature and Ethnicity in East European Paganism: An Environmental Ethic of the Religious Right?' *The Pomegranate* 7(2): 194–225.

Jacobsohn, G. J. 2003. *The Wheel of Law: India's Secularism in Comparative Constitutional Context*. Princeton, NJ: Princeton University Press.

Jamatia, B. B. 2011. *Religious Philosophy of the Janajatis of Northeast Bharat*. Guwahati: Heritage Foundation.

Joshi, N. M. 2000. *Ashwattha*. Chennai: Vivekananda Kendra Prakashan Trust.

Kumar, B. B. 2015. *Social and Cultural Continuum in India with Special Focus on the Northeast*. Guwahati: Vivekananda Kendra Institute of Culture.

Li, T. 2000. 'Articulating Indigenous Identity in Indonesia: Resource Politics and the Tribal Slot'. *Comparative Studies in Society and History* 42(1): 149–79.

Longkumer, A. 2017. 'Is Hinduism the World's Largest Indigenous Religion?' In *The Brill Handbook of Indigenous Religion(s)*, edited by Siv Ellen Kraft and Greg Johnson, 263–78. Leiden: Brill.

———. 2020. *The Greater India Experiment: Hindutva and the Northeast*. Stanford: Stanford University Press.

Malkki, L. 1992. 'National Geographic: The Rooting of Peoples and the Territorialization of National Identity among Scholars and Refugees'. *Cultural Anthropology* 7(1): 24–44.

Nanda, M. 2004. 'Dharmic Ecology and the New Pagan Movement: The Dangers of Religious Environmentalism in India'. Eighteenth European Conference on Modern South Asian Studies, Lund University, Sweden, July.

———. 2009. 'Hindu Triumphalism and the Clash of Civilisations'. *Economic and Political Weekly* 44(28): 106–14.

Niezen, R. 2011. 'Indigenous Religion and Human Rights'. In *Religion and Human Rights: An Introduction*, edited by John Witte and M. Christian Green, 119–34. Oxford: Oxford University Press.

North East Now. 2020. 'Meghalaya: Soil, Water from Jaiñtia Hills Taken to UP for Building Ram Temple at Ayodhya'. Guwahati, 27 July.

Palmer, H, and V. Hunter. 2018. 'Worlding'. *New Materialism*. 16 March. https://newmaterialism.eu/almanac/w/worlding.html.

Permanent Forum on Indigenous Issues. 2010. 'Study of the Need to Recognise and Respect the Rights of Mother Earth'. United Nations, Ninth Session, New York, 19–30 April. http://www.un.org/esa/socdev/unpfii/documents/E.C.19.2010.4%20EN.pdf (accessed on 1 December 2021).

Pollock, S. 1998. 'The Cosmopolitan Vernacular'. *Journal of Asian Studies* 57(1): 6–37.

RIWATCH. N.d. *Research Institute of World's Ancient Traditions Cultures & Heritage*. RIWATCH: Lower Dibang Valley.

Rountree, K. 2012. 'Neo-Paganism, Animism, and Kinship with Nature'. *Journal of Contemporary Religion* 27(2): 305–20.

Samvad. 2012. 'Newsletter'. Delhi, 1–8.

Savarkar, V. D. 1969. *Hindutva: Who Is Hindu?* New Delhi: Hindi Sahitya Sadan.

Tsing, A. 2005. *Friction: An Ethnography of Global Connections*. Princeton, NJ: Princeton University Press.

9

FROM CASTES TO NATIONALIST HINDUS
THE MAKING OF HINDUISM AS A CIVIL RELIGION

Suryakant Waghmore

A Hindu is not a Hindu because he accepts certain doctrines or philosophies, but because he is a member of a caste. (Hinnells and Sharpe 1972)[1]

In November 2019, the above epigraph from Hinnells and Sharpe (1972) was proved right in Karnataka, as the state witnessed another case of caste-related killings when a couple was hacked to death for intercaste marriage. The man belonged to Madar caste and the woman to Lamani caste. While both are listed as Scheduled Castes, or SCs (ex-untouchables) in Karnataka, Lamanis consider themselves to be higher than Madars, and it was the Lamanis who were accused of murdering the couple. Violence among SCs is, however, rare in India. Caste may construct what Frederick Bailey calls 'civility of indifference' in rural India (Bailey 1996), and instances of full-scale intercaste wars are indeed rare. However, transgressions that violate ritual and hierarchical order result in intercaste violence, and ex-untouchable castes are mostly at the receiving end.

In this chapter, I engage with the question of new Hindutva by revisiting an old conflicting distinction set up by Ashis Nandy between Hindutva and Hinduism (Nandy 1991). While Nandy hoped for an end of Hindutva at the hands of Hinduism, the former has not only survived but grown leaps and bounds. A foundational problem with those who place faith in Hinduism for fighting Hindutva is their overlooking of the caste question. I approach new Hindutva by locating caste at the centre of popular Hinduism and thereby distinguishing it from Hindutva. Hindutva has historically pursued a nationalist critique of caste and thus has been part of the Hindu-modernizing/reform process (Bayly 1988). I engage with the contemporary forms of engagement with caste in Hindutva's ideology-building to unravel the making of Hinduism as a civil religion.

Caste, though weakening, continues to substantially define the selfhood of most Hindus in rural and urban India (Waghmore 2018, 2019). Anti-caste discourse is all-pervasive in movements that mobilize around Phule–Ambedkarite ideology and the imagined *bahujan*[2] collective identity (Waghmore 2013). Left movements are also now setting foot into anti-caste politics. Hindu nationalists engage with the problem of caste by resorting to a discourse and politics of Hindu unity and humanism across castes.

I delve into the politics of inclusion and broad-basing in Hindutva by focusing on Tapas, one of the recent and important educational initiatives of Rashtrotthana Parishat (hereafter Rashtrotthana) – affiliated to the Rashtriya Swayamsevak Sangh (RSS) – in Karnataka. Tapas is an initiative in higher secondary education targeted towards brilliant but poor boys aspiring to study engineering at the Indian Institutes of Technology, or IITs (the most prestigious engineering colleges in India). Tapas aims to counter the marketization of education by providing quality education, residence, and coaching to the most meritorious among the poor to enable them to compete without disadvantage in the screening exams for the IITs (All India Joint Entrance Examination – JEE). Based on structured and unstructured interviews and group discussions with key leaders, volunteers of Rashtrotthana, and alumni and students of Tapas, I suggest that Hindutva consistently reinvents itself while competing, learning, and co-opting some other civil solidarities in (India's) civil sphere (Alexander 2006).

The RSS is denied the status of an association in civil society, and Rudolph (2000, 1766) suggests that the RSS does not constitute civil society as it fails to generate social capital for democracy. Following Rudolph may make the RSS appear as a form of uncivil solidarity in the civil sphere. RSS is nevertheless an association and I pursue Hansen (1999), who refers to the RSS and affiliate institutions as 'alternative civil society'. I develop the idea of alternative civil society further to explore the contemporary universal claims and dimensions of ideology building in the RSS – more particularly the making of Hinduism as civil religion.

Complementing the studies that attribute the social service of the RSS to expanding the political base of the BJP, I suggest social initiatives like Tapas point to newer attempts in Hindutva to turn Hinduism into a civil religion. While such an attempt cannot be claimed to be a new phenomenon, changing political and socio-economic conditions along with newer moral and social interventions in the civil sphere demand construction of the Hindu religion as a civil religion. Religion here is fused with nationalism to produce a nationalist Hindu – a higher and better being than the one driven by popular Hinduism of caste. Such a process has meant constructing Hinduism as a civil religion fit for governance and politics in the interest of Hindus but not void of modern and futuristic ideas and possibilities of equality. Both the past and present are innovatively constructed so as to build a nationalist Hinduism that undermines and even criticizes caste distinction and inequality. By strategically undermining caste and simultaneously calling for compassion within Hindus, Hindutva mobilizes towards forming solidarity around nationalist Hinduism based on the ideals of *sewa*. Hindutva thus succumbs to pressures of varied progressive civil currents and responds by co-opting and inventing hybrid forms of social intervention to consolidate Hinduism as a civil religion.

Hinduism as a Civil Religion

On 15 August 2018, Mohan Bhagwat (RSS chief) visited an English-medium school run by Rashtrotthana in Bengaluru, where Tapas is also located. As the chief guest for the Independence Day celebrations, he unfurled the national flag and called for responsibility, sacrifice, and world progress and peace – evoking ideas from Buddha and the Preamble to the Indian Constitution.[3] This was in line with Mohan Bhagwat's Vijaya Dashami speech in 2015 in Nagpur, where a (new) *dharma* was evoked with universal claims based on diverse but certain essential elements of *sewa* and compassion. This included recognition of caste discrimination and Ambedkar's politics of compassion.

> In Shri Guruji's (second chief of RSS) words, Ambedkar's talent was a confluence of *Acharya Shankar's* sharp Intellect and *Tathagat Buddha's* unbounded compassion ... Let us all Hindus unite! Do not compromise with any discrimination. Let us set an example of human brotherhood to the world afflicted by sorrow.[4]

Ambedkar, however, is depoliticized and peripheral in the praxis of the RSS. Caste is not frequently mentioned as a great ethical past, and discrimination on its basis is increasingly recognized as a problem to be dealt with. As Ambedkarite and Mandal movements revolve around the repertoire of caste as structural inequality, Hindutva constructs Hinduism as a civil religion, not necessarily bound by caste anymore,[5] but as a step towards mobilizing various castes in favour of nationalist Hinduism. For Robert Bellah, civil religion need not impinge on private religion, and it is not always invoked in favour of worthy causes (Bellah 1967). Bellah used the idea of American civil religion to refer to 'a set of beliefs, symbols, and rituals that exist alongside of, and rather clearly differentiated from the churches'.

> The American civil religion was never anticlerical or militantly secular ... it borrowed selectively from the religious tradition in such a way that the average American saw no conflict between the two. In this way, the civil

religion was able to build up without any bitter struggle with the church powerful symbols of national solidarity and to mobilize deep levels of personal motivation for the attainment of national goals. (Bellah 1967)

A recent attempt to recover civil religion in contemporary times is made by Philip Gorski (2010). For him, the enemies of civil religion lay in religious nationalism and liberal secularism. In contemporary times, he calls for rescuing civil religion, which could help arrive at a balance between pluralism and solidarity. Excessive solidarity on racial and national basis leads to fragmentation, but civil religion could help bring together realism and hope, which for Gorski is a theological and civil virtue (Gorski 2010). Both Bellah and Gorski bend toward a positive reading of civil religion, and Gorski, in particular, carves out neat compartments of religious nationalism and liberal secularism as those opposed to civil religion. In public life, however, there may be a wide spectrum of civil religion – from worthy causes to regressive social closure, symbols, and rituals (state and non-state) – and its usage by competing groups in competing forms for a sustained inner consolidation within a particular ethnic or religious group. In religiously plural democracies, civil religion may hold the illusory promise of equality for in-group, and civility of indifference and even violence for those outside.

Now let's return to the question of Hinduism versus Hindutva. While Hinduism in its popular practice lacks universal salvation philosophy of solidarity and may seem more like a collection of castes that occasionally unite for political and ritual purposes,[6] Hindutva seeks to actively unite the divided and hierarchically ordered castes under the rubric of Hindu unity. The fear of the 'other' (Muslims and Christians) mostly dominates the repertoires of such mobilization, along with cow protection and localized communal conflicts. A sustained cultural and economic intervention with marginal groups like *adivasis* too has been another important strategy (Froerer 2010). While gaining votes and the trust of marginal groups is the motivation, Hindutva increasingly seeks to make newer and deeper social unity across castes, advocating an ethic of equality and universal brotherhood at the same time.

Broadly civil religion helps us locate the rooted virtues and morals beyond the private form of the religion – in the sphere of politics. The division of religion and politics is a misnomer in India as the state and society continually intersect, and the polity does reflect the ethos of upper caste Hindus. While liberal and post-colonial critics of Hindutva place hope in Hinduism for outdoing Hindutva, we may gain more analytically by framing Hinduism of Hindutva as a national civil religion. The Nehruvian legacy founded national solidarity on secularism, while the actual democratic practice remained embedded in ethnic relations. Secularism was based on certain conventions of civil speech and restraint in the interaction between communities and religious formations – in some ways a colonial model of management of difference that got elevated to state ideology (Hansen 2016).

The RSS and the BJP have subverted secularist nationalism, first, through *strategies of ideology building*, where a diverse set of socio-religious practices was clubbed under the rubric of Hinduism (Jaffrelot 2007). Second, Hindu nationalism draws on older reserves of religious nationalism (as against modern nationalism) that were central to most forms of Indian nationalism (Van der Veer 1994). And finally, Hindu nationalism emerged out of the longest and most successful trajectory of democracy in India – it has succeeded in mobilizing and bringing Hindu consciousness to the fore in public arenas and electoral politics (Hansen 1999). The alternative civil society that the RSS constructs (Hansen 1999) selectively feeds on the other progressive left and liberal civil currents to evolve dynamically and continually consolidate Hinduism as a civil religion.[7]

While 'othering' of non-Hindus continues to be central, I focus here on the politics and morals that drive the processes of inclusion of marginal castes in Hindutva. Christianity and its salvation ideology inspire both the idea and possibility of civil religion. Hinduism, however, is hierarchical and a group-tied religion and Bellah's concept may not be, therefore, easily transferrable. Fitzgerald (1990) provides an insightful distinction between the two meanings of *dharma*. He suggests that *dharma* in the first sense is about ritual order of hierarchy, and in the second sense, it corresponds more closely with Western conceptions of religion/soteriology. Hinduism, for Fitzgerald, is fundamentally a group-tied religion and even attempts of the second sense of *dharma* (salvation philosophies) end up being 're-absorbed again in hierarchical totality, sometimes as a caste group' (Fitzgerald 1990, 113).

To compliment Gorski (2010), I suggest that civil religion need not be against religious nationalism and that the making of civil religion may itself be a political process – Ambedkar's conversion to Buddhism and his construction of a Buddhism suitable for compassionate social democracy is a case in point (Fuchs 2001). A competition may thus ensue on claiming the best of civility and civil religion between and within competing ethnic and religious groups. As we will see in the following sections, national Hinduism of Hindutva claims to be more tolerant and inclusive and thus more civil than any other religious communities (Muslims and Christians).

Despite its growth, Hindutva has limited cultural and ideological resources to unite Hindus, and prominent repertoires (include othering of Muslims and the construction of a golden past) face the challenge of popular Hinduism as it continues to be embedded in multiple hierarchies of class, gender, and caste. Further, new urbanism promotes individualism and newer freedoms that may not want to be embedded in either caste- or group-driven religious solidarity. Caste association and politics create competitive groups and cultures that are not always conducive to constructing a nationalist Hindu identity. In the newer context of mobility, urbanism, incipient individualism, and rampant caste competition, Hindutva works towards constructing Hinduism as a civil religion, which is open to science, education, equality, world peace, and, more importantly, driven by the ethic of sacrifice. All of these are evoked as part of a glorious past. In the next section, I will elaborate on how Hindutva wears an increasingly accommodative, futuristic, and compassionate coat. It continues to be anti-West (Christianity) and anti-Islam (Muslims), but a new discourse of equality and humanism works towards constructing Hinduism as a civil religion.

Locating Caste and Rashtrotthana in Karnataka

Party politics in Karnataka revolves around two dominant castes: the Vokkaligas and the Lingayats – the former is dominant in south Karnataka and the latter in north Karnataka. Both Lingayats and Vokkaligas moved away from Congress after Devaraj Urs radically promoted non-Lingayat and non-Vokkaliga leaders from the Other Backward Classes (OBCs). H. D. Deve Gowda emerged as the leader of Vokkaligas in Karnataka, and the Lingayats gradually moved towards the BJP after the Janata Dal (Secular) (JDS) came to be identified with Vokkaligas (Shivasundar 2012).

The BJP has been able to garner significant support from the Lingayats, making Karnataka the first state for its success in south India. The present chief minister of Karnataka, Basavaraj Bommai, is a Lingayat and B. S. Yediyurappa, the former chief minister of Karnataka, too was a Lingayat, and Lingayats mostly vote in favour of the BJP. However, since 2016, progressive currents within Lingayats in north Karnataka have actively mobilized and claimed an independent and a new Lingayat religion, which is different and even opposed to Hinduism. Hinduism is framed by dissenting Lingayats as a religion governed by caste hierarchy and inequality, whereas the new Lingayat religion is based on ideals of equality and inclusion that rejected Vedas – both poles apart. This move was supported by the Congress and opposed by the RSS–BJP.

Rashtrotthana was formed in 1965 out of volunteerism (*sewa*) of the RSS. It was founded by M. C. Jayadev (1932–2017), a Lingayat, who led the organization until the mid-1990s. Jayadev joined the RSS during his college days. He resigned from his job as a manager at Hindustan Garage Motors to devote himself fully to the RSS (and later Rashtrotthana) and the larger project of nation-building. He was a very important Lingayat voice in the RSS and is said to have been a strong supporter of the BJP leader and fellow caste-man B. S. Yediyurappa. In 2011, when Yediyurappa was in competition with a Brahmin worker of the Sangh for the chief minister's post, M. C. Jayadev stood by him – dividing the RSS along caste lines (Shankar 2011). Caste is latent in the daily workings of Rashtrotthana and the RSS, and it manifests in divisive form among the workers and leaders mostly because of politics-induced caste polarization. However, M. C. Jayadev's voluntary spirit and selflessness for the cause of the Sangh and nation until the end of his life are sources of inspiration for workers in Karnataka and beyond, including Prime Minister Narendra Modi.

Rashtrotthana grew significantly under M. C. Jayadev and is now one of the most important social organizations in Karnataka. Though the RSS and affiliated organizations are largely controlled and run by Brahmins, non-Brahmin workers like M. C. Jayadev too have contributed significantly to the RSS over the years. The increased support among Lingayats for the BJP during the past two decades may undermine the role the RSS has played in enrolling non-Brahmins, particularly Lingayats, in the Hindutva fold.

As we will see in the following sections, workers in the RSS and Rashtrotthana underplay caste and mostly disengage with it in their everyday functioning as a narrative of Hindu unity dominates. However, as mentioned earlier, the RSS is not void of caste dynamics, which manifests overtly when political leaders clash or compete for power within the BJP. M. C. Jayadev was a mentor to the Lingayat leader B. S. Yediyurappa and supported him in 2011, even when Yediyurappa faced corruption charges. On the other hand, Brahmins leaders within the RSS supported Anant Kumar in an intercaste rivalry that ensued within the BJP in 2011 (Shankar 2011). Party politics is of deep interest to all workers of the RSS, and it was obvious especially in times of political crisis. While I was pursuing fieldwork in July 2019, the BJP had managed to attract MLAs from the alliance government of JD(S)–Congress, leading to its fall. Senior workers of Rashtrotthana were keenly following the developments minute-by-minute on their phones as the crisis unfolded and the JD(S)–Congress government delayed the vote of confidence. Politics (BJP) was, however, morally distinguished from the religious nationalism of the RSS. A senior *pracharak* (full-time RSS worker) commented, 'Guruji used to always say, politics is like bathroom and if you enter there's always a strong possibility that you will slip and fall.' Here, slipping and falling imply losing one's morals and ethics and falling into the impure world of corruption and seduction of power. Leaders like Narendra Modi were seen as few and exceptional – a character built out of the RSS foundations.

Rashtrotthana – The Cultural Organization and Professional Non-Governmental Organization (NGO)

Presently, Rashtrotthana runs several projects that broadly cover health, education, livelihood, and culture, and religious nationalism is the ideological force behind all its initiatives. While Rashtrotthana initially began as a movement to produce literature for Hindu awareness and unity, over the years, it has emerged as a major social, educational, and cultural organization in Karnataka. This has been achieved with significant support from successive governments, corporate and individual donations, and the ideological commitment of RSS workers. In Bengaluru alone, Rashtrotthana has two major English-medium schools (there are twenty-five schools in Karnataka and most of these are Kannada-medium schools), a major blood bank and thalassemia day care and dialysis centre,[8] *goshala* (shelter for indigenous cows), Yogic Sciences and Research Institute, and a well-equipped publishing house that publishes books and booklets[9] on important Hindu personalities[10] who embodied the ethic of sacrifice for the nation.

The impressive infrastructure is mobilized through donations. For instance, the blood centre is built on land (currently estimated to be over INR 250 million) donated by Jayantilal Nagarlal Shah and the land for the Central Board of Secondary Education, or CBSE, school at Thanisandra was donated by M. C. Modi. Modi was a Gandhian and eye surgeon in Bangalore known for his numerous free eye surgeries. When in power, 'individuals' within the Congress too have extended state support over years (the Yoga building in 1972 gained from such support and similarly land was provided for the Nandagokula[11] orphanage). Over the years, Rashtrotthana has built networks with corporate bodies and generous individuals who have supported its cultural and social endeavours.

Education is one of the main areas of Rashtrotthana's interventions. In Karnataka, the Lingayats and the Vokkaligas extend their economic and political influence into the academic sphere, founding and controlling several educational societies and institutions – other castes have also followed this pattern. However, Vokkaligas in southern Karnataka and Lingayats in northern Karnataka dominate the academic sphere (Patil 2007). Rashtrotthana thus is a small player as compared to Lingayat and Vokkaliga networks. However, it seeks to compete with several other institutions and market forces that undermine the (Hindu) tradition and culture. Rashtrotthana counters its marginal position through repertoire and strategies that weave together a discourse of economic justice, recovery of Hindu heritage, compassionate and sacrificial ethics – broadly framing and consolidating Hinduism as a civil religion. Below I discuss the case of Tapas to elaborate.

FROM CASTES TO NATIONALIST HINDUS

Tapas – Inclusive Gurukul

The IITs are considered premier institutes of engineering education in India, and admission to these institutes is sought after by the new and old middle classes. Admission to the undergraduate programmes is through the national competitive JEE. Success in this exam, however, is more a function of coaching, and coaching companies charge anywhere between INR 4 and 6 lakh annually. Coaching begins as early as seventh or eighth grade and is well beyond families with limited means and income. Workers and founders of Tapas maintained that the Tapas project is aimed at reaching out to the most meritorious among the poor in Karnataka and making coaching available to them.

The term 'Tapas' draws from 'tapasya',[12] and its motto was decided in keeping with the NGO-ized discourses, 'reaching the unreached'. Founders emphasize the need for providing quality education to the poor, irrespective of caste and religious considerations.[13] The idea was borrowed from Super 30, an educational coaching programme for the poor run by Anand Kumar in Bihar. Super 30 is known for its exceptional success, and Anand Kumar has received several national and international awards. A Bollywood movie too was made on his story. In 2010, he was awarded the Yashwantrao Yuva Puraskar by the Akhil Bharatiya Vidyarthi Parishad (ABVP) in Bangalore. Drawing from Kumar's intervention, Dinesh Hegde (CEO of Rashtrotthana) and M. P. Kumar[14] pursued the idea to create Tapas. As compared to Super 30, Tapas was to have better standards of residence, food, and infrastructure for its students, while being rooted in Hindu culture. Anand Kumar's voluntary spirit and liberal innovation were to be transformed into a Hindu voluntary ethic. Tapas also benefitted from considerable corporate and state support as Rashtrotthana is itself like a large corporatized NGO. Dinesh Hegde is not very comfortable with the designation of CEO, for he had begun his time in RSS as a volunteer in the 1980s.

M. P. Kumar initially mobilized funds from information technology (IT) workers in the Bay Area in California to support Tapas, while Rashtrotthana used the infrastructure available at its campus Thanisandra. Kumar also negotiated with the leadership of a coaching company BASE (Be Ahead with Sustained Excellence) to provide free coaching to students selected at Tapas. BASE agreed to provide free coaching as part of their corporate social responsibility (CSR) activity; they also helped Rashtrotthana hold state-wide entrance tests to select the best among the economically deprived.

While there is a class basis for providing education to the poorer students so that they can make it to the elite IITs, it was also coupled with the idea that the poor could preserve culture and contribute to nation-building better as opposed to the well-off who study at the IITs and mostly leave the country. Gajanan Lokhande who works in the corporate sector and volunteers actively and coordinates administrative and intellectual endeavours of the Parivar (Sangh) on education explained:

> Our main idea is to uplift, reach the unreached – the children who are highly talented but who cannot afford the education of highest form. Most of the children are from rural and humble background ... We are transforming three generations. By getting one child here, we are transforming the students life, parents life. We bring the marginalized into mainstream and our hope is that they will contribute to nation building ... Almost 95 percent of IIT graduates go abroad. They indirectly help, of course. We want these students to directly help in nation building. Bring people who are not in the current education system, bring them in [mainstream], transform them and put them into nation building activity.

While Gajanan believed that quality education should be made available to all free of cost and education at Rashtrotthana was in accordance with UNESCO's ideal of rooting education in culture and the *panchamukhi shikshana* of old *gurukul* form was therefore relevant (physical, emotional, psychological, intellectual, and spiritual development).

Besides education, culture is also taught to the students at Tapas. The economically well-to-do urbanized were seen as more inclined to Western values – almost beyond redemption. Advertisements for state-wide tests and admission eligibility to Tapas are mailed to major government schools and posted online, as well as published in some selected newspapers. Only those with an annual income level below INR 150,000 are eligible to apply. Following the state-wide screening test, workers of Rashtrotthana pay home visits to shortlisted candidates to ensure that their income levels are indeed below INR 150,000.

Coaching with Samskara

Tapas annually admits around thirty students for pre-university college. Of the students who joined between 2017 and 2019, 50 per cent were from the high castes, followed by 41.3 per cent OBCs and 8.7 per cent SCs. None were from the Scheduled Tribes, or STs. The selected students are put through a test of ten days to see if they can survive the rigorous *dinachari* (daily schedule based on Ayurveda) that is central to life at Tapas. The *dinachari* is engraved on the walls of the Tapas building.

The daily schedule is organized to provide an environment of 'discipline' and 'purity' as such a socio-cultural environment is considered necessary for academic achievement. The nationalist monk Swami Vivekananda's ideals of renunciation and service to the nation further provide the foundations for the coaching education at Tapas. The *dinachari* begins at 4.30 a.m. and involves yoga, *bhajan*s, and prayer along with studies. Activities like yoga, *bhajan*s, celebrations of Hindu festivals, and *desi* (indigenous) games are said to provide and strengthen the foundation of *sewa* (service to motherland) among the students of Tapas. The ideal of nationalist voluntary service is also cultivated through the occasional RSS *shakha*s at Tapas.

Following a generous grant from the public sector Oil and Natural Gas Corporation (ONGC), Tapas moved to a new building at Banashankari Campus. Tapas is now well equipped with a library, labs, study rooms, classrooms, dining room, kitchen, and shared living facilities for students. Pictures of Goddess Saraswati, Bharat Mata, and Om adorn the classroom walls and pictures of Indian scientists and national heroes adorn the corridors. At the entrance is a large picture of Swami Vivekananda and on the side is a tree of success with photos of students of Tapas who have made it to the IITs, thus constructing Tapas as a space of scientific education and simultaneously a reservoir for nationalist Hinduism.

Students on the campus follow 'tapasya' in actuality. They have limited contact with their families and the outside world and have no access to the Internet or smartphones. Trips outside are limited to those planned for exposure (including the IITs and the *goshala* run by Rashtrotthana). *Shakha* meetings (RSS assembly) are organized weekly or fortnightly and constitute critical socio-cultural engagement for students. Students shared that the *shakha*s help them appreciate and live as a Hindu collective through games, lectures, worship, slogans, and songs. Successful past students and other personalities with Hindutva orientation regularly visit Tapas to motivate students and emphasize the need for culture and *sewa*. Along with coaching, students imbibe knowledge about the cultural heritage, military power, and past economic might of the Hindu nation.

Warden as Mother and Education with Samskara

Despite its focus on providing coaching, Tapas is organized more on the *gurukul* (residential) form of education. Instead of a warden, Tapas has Rukmini (aged fifty) as *mataji* (mother), who used to be an active member of the ABVP in her undergraduate years and served as secretary of the Vidyarthini section. Rukmini has a mother-like relation with all students of Tapas, and she follows up on their lives and careers both during and after Tapas, helping them in educational and familial matters. The thick social network of Rashtrotthana with other social organizations is used to help students in all possible forms.

Rukmini is from the Vokkaliga caste and is a paid employee. Her husband and her son (an engineering graduate) are not members of the RSS, but they support her engagement with the Rashtrotthana. Rukmini explained the need to inculcate *samskara* among students along with formal (Western) education: 'Flower is education, the smell of the flower is *samskara* ... both are integrated ... you would not like a smell-less flower ... no one in society would like a person without *samsakaras* ... learning is important and with learning *samsakaras* is most important.'

Samskara, in actual terms, involves singing *bhajans* and prayers in the morning and evening, along with practising meditation and yoga. *Bhajans* are sung twice a day. Students also pray before every meal. The prayers include 'Mathruvandana, Brahmanada', meditation and *shanti* mantra, which are said to relax the mind and help improve concentration, attention, devotional feeling, and respect towards (our) tradition and culture. Singing of 'Vande Mataram' is also a routine at Tapas. For students, it evokes happiness and a sense of patriotism.

Gowtham R, a first-year student at Tapas, shared:

> Singing 'Vande Mataram' makes me feel very patriotic and happy. It makes a shiver run down my body. I feel immense source of happiness and pride when I sing it. I am so happy to be here in Tapas because it helps me love my country more than I could till now.

Samskara also means respecting elders at home and senior workers at Tapas. It is common for the alumni and present students to touch the feet of workers at Tapas. The embodiment of these daily rituals contributes to taking pride in the history and culture of Hindu-India and a political consciousness about invasion of India – both medieval and colonial India – that caused the decay of Indian (Hindu) society and culture. Rudip, a student from the Vokkaliga caste, completed his education at Tapas and now studies at one of the prestigious IITs. He recalled how *karyakartas* (RSS workers) would talk about the nation, 'our' duties towards it, patriotism, and the impact it had on him:

> Earlier [before joining Tapas] I used to celebrate festivals, but now I know why we celebrate festivals. Earlier history was only Mahatma Gandhi and Jawaharlal Nehru – now I know Shivaji and Chandrashekar Azad ... Before joining Tapas, when there were surgical strikes [against Pakistan in 2016], I simply read that in the newspaper and left it at that. But the air strikes [Balakot in 2019], we used to read every detail in the newspaper.

After joining Tapas, practising yoga and singing *bhajans* helped Rudip build a spiritual self, and the attack on Pakistan became a matter of nationalist pride and excitement for him. Hinduism had become a national and nationalist religion that was part of the banal and every day. The most memorable days at Tapas for him were also celebrating festivals like the Ganesh Chaturthi, for the collective effort that was put into decorating and cooking by students. Hinduism had been turned into a national civil religion with a heightened sense of political and religious consciousness coupled with Hindu unity. Rudip had discovered Hinduism afresh; it involved preserving the old but also giving up the old – a sublated Hinduism.[15]

Sublated Hinduism: From Hinduism of Caste to Hinduism as a Civil Religion

Sublation in Hegelian dialectic is both negation and preservation of an earlier form, and it is neither synthesis nor irony (Palm 2009). The evolution of Hinduism into a civil religion in Hindutva discourses is thus part of the dialectic within Hinduism. As suggested earlier, the citizenship discourses and anti-caste politics in Phule–Ambedkarite movements frame the Hinduism of caste as one opposed to freedom and citizenship rights of marginal groups, and this discourse has now spread from southwest to northwest India. The making of Hinduism into a civil religion in Hindutva discourse is thus a necessity both for local politics and global cosmopolitan claims.

Khudeshvany (aged twenty) too experienced and understood sublated Hinduism at Tapas. His parents run a provision store and stay in a rented house in Bengaluru. He could not get admission in any of the IITs and now studies computer science at PES Mandya. He continues to carry the spirit of Hindu unity and equality with him. Influenced by the ideological and cultural education he gained at Tapas, he is critical of caste divisions and conflict in Karnataka. Khudeshvany is a Vannikula Kshatriya, a caste that is listed as OBC in Karnataka. Besides coaching for IIT–JEE, Tapas introduced Khudeshvany to the 'greatness of Indian *sanskriti*' (culture) that has been 'lost' over the years, making India an 'insignificant' power in the world. The projection of the past, though invented, does not make this invention less effective; rather, the invented version is tailored to present-day needs and sensibilities.

'Outside there is caste,' said Khudeshvany, 'something that we need to counter.' He distinguishes the popular Hindu religion outside from the civil form of Hindu religion he learnt at Tapas. This Hinduism is different from the one he grew up with at home. While most rituals and festivals match, the earlier form of Hinduism was without any consciousness for him. 'Our calendar is *panchanga, sanskruti* [culture] is the right path and the main motto of *shakha*s was unity,' shared Khudeshvany. The making of (non-caste) Hindu self and its unity with Hindu nation (past and present) points to a new form of sublated Hindu consciousness tied to neither caste nor individualist orientations. Such Hindu consciousness also counters the alienation that caste may bring, especially for castes considered marginal and low. Khudeshvany hopes to join politics and correct the wrongs.

What B. R Ambedkar had thought and what are we doing? Politics is selfish. Politicians have ignored drought. Only Narendra Modi is working for 18 hours. We need youth force [but] they are distracted. [We need to] [f]ill patriotism in each of them. I will work for 5–6 years in IT and join politics.

Khudeshvany's nationalist Hinduism is not purely Brahminic; the RSS is strategically allowing some de-Brahminisation as part of the project of building Hinduism as civil religion. Khudeshvany, for instance, did not like the food much at Tapas; he is fond of meat (but not beef), something that was not allowed during his two years of residence at Tapas. Occasionally when he stepped out to meet his parents, he would enjoy his favourite meals. Living at Tapas for two years did not alter his diet preference, and the workers of Rashtrotthana also do not insist on vegetarianism outside of Tapas.

In the everyday functioning of Rashtrotthana, and more particularly Tapas, the hierarchy of caste is replaced with the hierarchy of respect, seniority, and submission to authority within the movement and the historical narratives it is based on. None of the present students that I talked to from marginal castes complained of discrimination along caste lines. This is decidedly different from popular Hinduism. Such a version of inclusion is indeed not egalitarianism; it is rather an alternative version of hierarchy that promises a reversal of estrangement embedded for non-pure castes in popular Hinduism.

Another student, Rajinappa, the 'star' alumnus of Tapas, belongs to Scheduled Caste. His photo is on the tree of success that one notices on entering the Tapas building. Rajinappa was raised by his single mother. His two-room *kaccha* house is like any other low-class poor Hindu house, with pictures of the Hindu gods and goddesses Saraswati, Lakshmi, and Ganesh decorating the living room. Rajinappa now studies aeronautical engineering at one of the leading IITs. The Reddys are the dominant caste in his village, and the SCs are still not allowed entry into some of the village temples. When visiting this village, I nudged a full-time senior Brahmin worker of Rashtrotthana about this practice in the village. The worker turned sociological, 'Reddys are used to power, they cannot tolerate prosperity of SCs.' As suggested by Schultz (2013), Hindutva is seen by some upper caste Hindu *kirtankars* as anti-Hindu because of its reformist takes on caste practices and the system. Rajinappa, on the contrary, prefers Rashtrotthana and Tapas as against the Hinduism of Reddys in the village. Rajinappa is part of the small group of RSS students who get together on the IIT-Bombay (Mumbai) campus. He has also not turned vegetarian but continues to be a nationalist Hindu, aware of the problems of the Hindu religion and hopeful of the possibilities that Hinduism as a civil religion offers under Hindutva.

FROM CASTES TO NATIONALIST HINDUS

Yoga with English and Hindu Manushyata *[Humanism]*

Yoga is constructed as a secular form, and an affiliate arm of Rashtrotthana actively promotes yoga in government schools. Tapas has a rigorous yoga regime for students. Murlihar Murthy (aged sixty-four) is a retired schoolteacher and has been an RSS worker for thirty-three years. Murlihar now volunteers to teach yoga and provide counselling to students at Tapas. When I asked Murlihar Murthy his caste, before answering the question, he told me, 'In RSS, *nau jati helodilla*' (we don't share caste). Murlihar Murthy is a Lingayat, and his brother, presently district *sanghchalak* in Davangere, is also a committed worker of the RSS. Murlihar and his family have donated 8 acres of land to Rashtrotthana in Davangere. Not that caste divisions do not persist in Rashtrotthana or the RSS, but it is urged to think beyond caste in the interest of religion and nation. Brahmin, Lingayat, or Vokkaliga workers would thus not hesitate to eat at the homes of SC and OBC students alike.[16] This invariably influenced students who found meaning in celebrating the unity and greatness of Hindu culture as opposed to caste-centred solidarities.

While yoga is secularized, English is not castigated anymore, and the limits of celebrating Sanskrit are almost realized. Abandoning its earlier stance regarding the use of the English language, the RSS is now using and co-opting English for the further consolidation of Hindutva. Literature and brochures are published in English and Kannada extensively both for mobilizing funds and for lay readers. As the importance of English in education grows, the educational wing of Rashtrotthana too has consistently evolved to start English-medium schools, sometimes evoking opposition from elderly *pracharak*s. Arunji, a full-time worker of the RSS and Rashtrotthana in his early sixties, explained the need and compulsion to go with English: 'Aap zinda hain toh kuch kar sakte hain humare shastro main bhi bola hain' (Even the *shastras* emphasize the need to be alive to do something [ignoring English would mean our annihilation]).

At Tapas, while the formal education is imparted in English through BASE coaching, there are also efforts to provide extra classes for improving communication in English. This does not, however, undermine the focus on teaching *sewa* or cultural nationalism. Rather, a global discourse of humanism rooted in Hinduism is evoked. Khudeshvany recalled *manushyata* (humanism) as one of the key learnings at Tapas and criticized the obsession with making money: 'Increasingly now people are giving up *manushyata* and running after money. In *shakha*s they tell [teach] us about the need to return to *manushyata* …'

Manushyata is strictly Hindu as it involves valorising and celebrating Hindu culture and tradition. For Khudeshvany, it was also a reminder that 'Western' practices are alien and could erase Hindu selfhood: 'January 1st is not our [Hindu] new year, in our Hindu culture January 1st is not our new year [reiterates]. Our new year is on *Yugadi* ...'

The form of humanism that the students learn is based on the unification and homogenisation of students as Hindus. This is a broader consolidation and may be mildly opposed to Hindu cosmopolitanism revolving around caste in urban spaces (Waghmore 2019) and Hindu politeness in rural polity (Waghmore 2018) that are rooted in caste. The young men from different castes at Tapas live together, learning rituals and culture, history, and science to evolve as nationalist Hindus. Neither the daily life nor the ethos is void of hierarchy here; however, a new hierarchy about 'respect' to *pracharak*s (mostly Brahmins), national heroes, and religious–national symbols is evoked. Such sentiment is not necessarily anti-caste but does create a political solidarity of Hindus beyond caste.

Tapas may seem substantially advanced as compared to Hinduism-centred nationalism that is routinized in school education (Benei 2008). Its repertoires draw on the discourse of class and economic justice along with reclaiming the glorious Hindu past. While Rashtrotthana has grown with help from public and private donations, Tapas has drawn on corporate and public resources, small capitalists, and the voluntary spirit of workers to provide *gurukul*-style private coaching to the poor but meritorious students from different castes. Beyond caste – a larger community of Hindus is sought to recover the glorious past crushed by invaders (Muslims and British) – an alternative civil society is constituted (Hansen 1999) that is not totally uncivil and is functioning within the competitive currents of the local civil sphere.

Alternate Civil Society and Hinduism as a Civil Religion

Rashtrotthana and Tapas constitute the alternate civil society of the RSS and affiliate organizations (Hansen 1999), and together they strive towards reimagining Hinduism as a civil religion. The alternate civil society now intersects with the mainstream liberal and secular civil society occasionally. For instance, in June, both English and Kannada newspapers in Bengaluru report the success of students at Tapas who secure admissions to the IITs and other prestigious regional engineering colleges. Tapas thus appears as a good Samaritan committed to the cause of poor but talented students. Through its corporate, non-government, and government networks, Tapas is a project of Rashtrotthana that straddles the progressive spaces of economic justice while being firmly rooted in nationalist Hindu traditions. Students who join engineering colleges also continue their affiliation with the RSS at these institutes or form new collectives if the RSS student groups do not exist.

FROM CASTES TO NATIONALIST HINDUS

Hinduism as a civil religion is a nationalized religion, one where the territory of India and a 'thin' and abstracted notion of Hinduism are merged to create a new common space that can mediate between the localized communities of sects and castes. The initiative of Tapas points to the evolving nature of the RSS and its civil projects in keeping with the educational demands and desires of the younger generation. Students learn to cross the boundaries of caste and embody a spirit with marked rituals and practices of nationalist Hinduism. Hinduism is learnt as an accommodative and civil religion for all Hindus, and Hindu *manushyata* is evoked to counter Westernization and internal 'divisions'.

The making of Hinduism as a civil religion also points to a new Hindu consciousness among the lower and marginal castes, which counters the estrangement popular Hinduism creates. While liberal Hindus hope to use Hinduism to counter Hindutva, Hindutva is slowly countering the ills of the Hindu religion by framing and promoting Hinduism as a national civil religion. Caste, however, is not just localized but integral to the metaphysics of Hinduism, and Hinduism as a civil religion continues to find it difficult to overcome caste.

Notes

1   Despite their volume being geared towards presenting Hinduism as a world religion, Hinnells and Sharpe (1972) also recognize the power of caste and its centrality in defining Hindu subjecthood (Fitzgerald 1990).
2   'Bahujan' literally means majority and was popularized by Kanshiram throughout India to mobilize the bottom 85 per cent of non-pure castes.
3   Full speech can be accessed from www.youtube.com/watch?v=IfICIgMg4As (accessed on 20 September 2019).
4   Accessed from *Samvada*. English translation of the speech is available. https://samvada.org/2015/news/mohan-bhagwats-rssvijayadashami-speech-2015/ (accessed on 16 October 2020).
5   See Malvika Kasturi's scholarship on reforming *dana* by Sanatan Dharma Sabha as part of their project of revitalising *sanatana dharma* to craft citizenship, nationalism, and modern civil society (Kasturi 2010). Malvika Kasturi suggests that the boundaries of the 'Hindu public' here were delimited by *varnasrama dharma* as the working members of this public with the greatest rights were upper caste Hindus (133).
6   For Tocqueville, Islam represented an *aristocratic civil religion* and Hinduism was an uncivil religion (petrifying effect, civilization stops itself before belief, piety without morality, immaterialism, turns followers into pacifists); see Kelly (1995). Tocqueville seems to sum up Hinduism as a religion of superstition and among Indian thinkers, Ambedkar was a major sceptic and making of a genuine 'Hindu public' was simply impossible for him.

7   Such measures range from support for intercaste marriages, pro-labour discourses, and stepping back from aggressive vegetarianism and beef ban (Andersen and Damle 2018).

8   On the day of my visit to the centre, I observed several Muslim patients. The head of Rashtrotthana informed me that close to 40 per cent of beneficiaries at the Thalassemia Centre were Muslims.

9   These include people like Bala Gandharva, Ramana Maharishi, Obavva, Tulsidas, and several others.

10 This is not the standard range of north Indian eminent Hindus who represent the RSS's idea of national self-sacrifice and includes some local personalities like Bala Gandharva, Ramana Maharishi, and Obavva.

11 As per Hindu mythology, Krishna and his brother Balram were brought up by King Nanda in Gokul as their lives were at risk from their evil uncle, Kansa. The name of the orphanage symbolizes foster parents' place (Nanda–Gokul).

12 'Tapasya' refers to meditation, austerity, and self-discipline that monks resort to for *moksha*. The students too are expected to achieve a similar focus and self-discipline towards their goal of making into the IITs.

13 Only one Muslim student has studied at Tapas; he is now pursuing engineering at the National Institute of Technology, Suratkal.

14 Names of some respondents in this essay have been changed. M. P. Kumar is the founder and CEO of Global Edge Software. A former member of the ABVP, though not a full-time worker, he volunteers considerable time planning and supporting activities of Rashtrotthana. His company also provides an annual donation of around INR 2 million for the everyday operational costs of Rashtrotthana.

15 I thank Thomas Blom Hansen for helping me build on Hegelian dialectic and its analytical utility in theorizing nationalist Hinduism as a civil religion.

16 However, while we were visiting the home of the only Muslim alumnus of Tapas, none of the workers ate or drank at his place.

References

Alexander, J. 2006. *The Civil Sphere*. New York: Oxford University Press.

Bailey, F. G. 1996. *The Civility of Indifference: On Domesticating Ethnicity*. New Delhi: Oxford University Press.

Bayly, S. 1998. 'Hindu Modernisers and the "Public" Arena: Indigenous Critiques of Caste in Colonial India'. In *Swami Vivekananda and the Modernisation of Hinduism*, edited by W. Radice, 93–137. New Delhi: Oxford University Press.

Bellah, R. N. 1967. 'Civil Religion in America'. *Daedalus* 96(1): 1–21.

Benei, V. 2008. *Schooling Passions: Nation, History, and Language in Contemporary Western India*. Stanford, California: Stanford University Press.

Fitzgerald, T. 1990. 'Hinduism and the "World Religion" Fallacy'. *Religion* 20(2): 101–18.

Froerer, P. 2010. *Religious Division and Social Conflict*. New Delhi: Social Science Press.

Fuchs, M. 2001. 'Religion for Civil Society? Ambedkar's Buddhism and the Imagination of Emergent Possibilities'. In *Charisma and Canon: Essays on the Religious History of the Indian Subcontinent*, edited by Vasudha Dalmia, Angelika Malinar, and M. Christof, 250–73. Oxford: Oxford University Press.

Gorski, P. 2010. 'Civil Religion Today'. Association of Religion Data Archives Guiding Paper Series. http://www.thearda.com/rrh/papers/guidingpapers/Gorski.pdf (accessed on 1 December 2021).

Hansen, T. B. 1999. *The Saffron Wave: Democracy and Hindu Nationalism in Modern India*. New Delhi: Oxford University Press.

———. 2016. 'Secularism, Public Passion and Public Order in India'. In *Contesting Secularism: Comparative Perspectives*, edited by A. B. Sorensen, 207–32. London and New York: Routledge.

Hinnells, J. R., and E. J. Sharpe. 1972. *Hinduism*: Oriel Press.

Kasturi M. 2010. '"All Gifting Is Sacred": The Sanatana Dharma Sabha Movement, the Reform of Dana and Civil Society in Late Colonial India'. *Indian Economic and Social History Review* 47(1): 107–39. doi:10.1177/001946460904700104.

Kelly, C. 1995. 'Civil and Uncivil Religions: Tocqueville on Hinduism and Islam'. *History of European Ideas* 20(4–6): 845–50.

Jaffrelot, C. 2007. *Hindu Nationalism*. Princeton, NJ: Princeton University Press.

Nandy, A. 1991. 'Hinduism versus Hindutva: The Inevitability of a Confrontation'. *Times of India*, 18 February.

Palm, R. 2009. 'Hegel's Concept of Sublation'. Institute of Philosophy. Leuven, Katholieke Universiteit Leuven. PhD: 198.

Patil, S. H. 2007. 'Impact of Modernisation and Democracisation on a Dominant Community: A Caste Study of Lingayat Community in Karnataka'. *Indian Journal of Political Science* 68(4): 665–84.

Rudolph. S. 2000. 'Civil Society and the Realm of Freedom'. *Economic and Political Weekly* 35(20): 1762–69.

Schultz, A. 2013. *Singing a Hindu Nation: Marathi Devotional Performance and Nationalism*. New York: Oxford University Press.

Shankar, B. V. S. 2011. 'Now Caste Politics Takes Centre Stage'. *Mid-day*, 21 April.

Shivasundar. 2012. 'BJP in Karnataka: Between the Devil and the Deep Blue Sea'. *Economic and Political Weekly* 47(17): 25–27.

Van der Veer, P. 1994. *Religious Nationalism: Hindus and Muslims in India*. Berkeley: University of California Press.

Waghmore, S. 2013. *Civility against Caste: Dalit Politics and Citizenship in Western India*. New Delhi: Sage.

———. 2018. 'From Hierarchy to Hindu Politeness'. In *Waning Hierarchies, Persisting Inequalities: Caste and Power in 21st Century India,* edited by S. Jodhka and J. Manor, 113–39. Delhi: Orient Blackswan.

———. 2019. 'Community, Not Humanity: Caste Associations and Hindu Cosmopolitanism in Contemporary Mumbai'. *South Asia: Journal of South Asian Studies* 42(2): 375–93.

10

WHEN HINDUTVA PERFORMS MUSLIMNESS
ETHNOGRAPHIC ENCOUNTERS WITH THE MUSLIM RASHTRIYA MANCH

Lalit Vachani

> If we (Hindus) worship in the temple, he (the Muslim) would desecrate it. If we carry on bhajans and car festivals (*rath yatras*), that would irritate him. If we worship cow, he would like to eat it. If we glorify woman as a symbol of sacred motherhood, he would like to molest her. He was tooth and nail opposed to our way of life in all aspects – religious, cultural, social, etc. He had imbibed that hostility to the very core. (M. S. Golwalkar, second Supreme Commander of the RSS; 1966: 122)

> Islam means security and peace, but today Islam is associated with violence, terror and fundamentalism. Is it not the responsibility of all of us to project the right face of Islam by tearing away this 'naqab' (mask) of terror, violence and fundamentalism? (K.S. Sudarshan, fifth Supreme Commander of the RSS; 24 December 2002 – Foundation Day of the Muslim Rashtriya Manch)

In 2002, India's premier Hindu nationalist organization, the Rashtriya Swayamsevak Sangh (RSS), formed a new affiliate, the Muslim Rashtriya Manch (MRM, or Muslim National Forum), dedicated to the cause of Muslim outreach. Why would the RSS feel the need to form and control an affiliated organization of Indian Muslims? Who is the ideal Muslim citizen as imagined and configured by the RSS? And why would Indian Muslims want to be associated with the RSS?

This essay focuses on the seemingly paradoxical phenomenon of Muslim outreach by the RSS. It draws upon my recent research/film documentation of the MRM, described 'as an independent Muslim organization that receives guidance from the RSS',[1] and which was set up in 2002 by the RSS *sarsanghchalak* (supreme commander) K. S. Sudarshan.

I show that the establishment of the MRM has been influenced by goals of political agenda-setting, reframing, and legitimation where the RSS–BJP foregrounds the MRM to present versions of various anti-Muslim Hindu-majoritarian projects such as the Triple Talaq Bill – Muslim Women (Protection of Rights on Marriage) Bill – the revocation of Article 370 in Kashmir, and the building of the Ram Temple in Ayodhya. In recent months, the MRM has also been used to legitimize the anti-constitutional and discriminatory Citizenship Amendment Act (CAA) and justify the arrests of young Muslim anti-CAA student activists over flimsy charges in the aftermath of the February 2020 Delhi riots.

Does the formation of the MRM in 2002 reflect a genuine attitudinal change on the part of the RSS in its imagination of Indian Muslims? I argue that this is not the case. The RSS consistently demonstrates a deeply ambivalent relationship towards its offshoot, the MRM. Muslims from the organization are not expected to participate in core RSS activity such as attending the daily sessions of *shakha*. Muslim representation in the MRM is largely symbolic and performative with Muslims joining the organization largely for instrumental reasons. Drawing from my recent filming/research, I also suggest that despite the language of outreach, Muslim citizens are not the intended target audience of the MRM project. It is not about bringing new Muslim converts to Hindutva. Instead, MRM's main work is representational and performative. It is about staging visible scenes and moments of 'Muslim participation' and 'inclusive Hindutva' for the media, and performing sedate, palatable (vegetarian), preferred Muslimness for the RSS rank and file and the broader Hindu population – scenes and moments where *visibly* Muslim people promote vegetarianism, rescue cows, proclaim support for the Ram temple, and attack other Muslim opposition and student leaders (Asaduddin Owaisi, Sharjeel Imam, Umar Khalid, and so on) for their inauthenticity and disloyalty to the Hindu nation.

Research Contexts

The essay draws on three filming and research trips that I conducted in Delhi between July and December 2018, and another film shoot that immediately preceded the May 2019 Indian national elections. Other than the MRM convenors and spokespersons I met over these trips, I also filmed and interviewed a former member of the MRM in East Delhi and several Muslim residents in the *galis* (streets) of Old Delhi in the neighbourhood of Kashmere Gate. In large part, this *gali* ethnography was to ascertain and verify the truth claims of MRM representatives and their frequent assertions that the majority of Indian Muslims had benefited from their policies and were either active supporters of the MRM or were joining the organization in large numbers.

In addition, I describe and analyse in detail two events that were staged by the MRM to understand how Hindutva performs 'Muslimness': an MRM public rally for the construction of the Ram Temple that was held in December 2018 and a semi-private meeting of MRM *ulema* just before the May 2019 national elections that aimed to enlist religious clerics in the MRM and secure a larger share of the Muslim vote for the BJP. I also draw on my earlier documentary film work on the RSS (1993, 2002) from a time that predates the MRM's existence, to reference the pre-existing and pervasive Hindu nationalist discourse on the Muslim as outsider and internal threat who must be reined in and domesticated by undergoing processes of *Bharatiyakaran* (Indianization).

The Incomplete Muslim Citizen-Subject

Since its inception in 1925, there has been a remarkable consistency and continuity of ideology in the RSS's configuration of the Indian Muslim. The consolidation of Indian Muslims as a political community in the context of the colonial-era Khilafat movement, followed by the forging of Hindu–Muslim solidarity during the non-cooperation movement launched by the Congress in 1920, deeply troubled the RSS founder K. B. Hedgewar, for whom the Muslim community was an existential threat. 'The *yavana*-snakes reared on the milk of Non-Cooperation were provoking riots in the nation with their poisonous hissing,' he observed about Muslims (Bhishikar 1991, 25). A few years later, the communal riots of 1923 in Nagpur provided the impetus for the formation of the RSS (Basu et al. 1993; Jaffrelot 1999; Hansen 1999; Kanungo 2003; Noorani 2019). Thus, the perception of the Muslim as the threatening other was very much the *raison d'être* of the RSS, while the Nagpur riots of 1927, when RSS *swayamsevaks* who had received training at the RSS *shakha* repelled a Muslim mob, were seen as a vindication of militant Hindu *sangathan* (organization) under the RSS.[2]

Veer Savarkar's foundational ideology of Hindutva was central to the formation of the RSS and Hedgewar's conception of Indian Muslims. Rejecting the Congress view of inclusive territorial nationalism, the essential principles of Savarkar's Hindu nationalism were based on exclusion, and were designed as a political construct to consolidate Hindus. With primacy given to territory and culture in this world view, authentic and complete citizen-subjects had to be Hindu and bear allegiance to the Hindu nation as their *pitrabhumi* (fatherland), *matrubhumi* (motherland), and, crucially, their *punyabhoomi* (holy land). In contrast, Muslims and Christians were necessarily incomplete and suspect citizen-subjects as their *punyabhumi* lay elsewhere:

> For though Hindusthan to them is Fatherland as to any other Hindu, yet it is not to them a Holyland too. Their holyland is far off in Arabia, or Palestine. Their mythology and Godmen, ideas and heroes are not the children of this soil. Consequently, their names and their outlook smack of a foreign origin. Their love is divided. (Savarkar 1923, 112)

This construction was developed further by M. S. Golwalkar, for whom Hindus were not settlers descended from the Aryans but the original, indigenous inhabitants of this land. Golwalkar's definition of the Hindu nation and the citizen-subject was based on the criteria of belonging as defined by the unities of race, religion, language, culture, and geography, and consciously shifted the focus from territorial nationalism to cultural nationalism. This strategic reformulation allowed Golwalkar and the RSS to define Muslims and Christians as 'the foreign races':

> From this standpoint, sanctioned by the experience of shrewd old nations, the foreign races in Hindusthan must either adopt the Hindu culture and language, must learn to respect and hold in reverence Hindu religion, must entertain no idea but those of the glorification of the Hindu race and culture, i.e. of the Hindu nation, and must lose their separate existence to merge in the Hindu race; or may stay in the country, wholly subordinated to the Hindu Nation, claiming nothing, deserving no privileges, far less any preferential treatment – not even citizen's rights. (Golwalkar 1939, 27)

Further in the text, Golwalkar professes to be an admirer of 'German race pride' and applauds Germany's purging of the Jews as 'an expression of the highest form of race pride' and 'a good lesson for us in Hindusthan to learn and profit by' (Golwalkar 1939, 89).

With the growing public profile of the RSS and its political wing, the Bharatiya Jan Sangh, from the 1970s onwards, there has been a concerted attempt to soften the image of Golwalkar as the incendiary ideologue of the RSS and author of the racist and communal *We or Our Nationhood Defined*.[3] In addition, there have also been attempts within the RSS fold to resuscitate Golwalkar as a visionary who believed in religious pluralism (Jeelany 1971; Sinha 2006). But a close analysis of the excised and redacted writings of Golwalkar reveal that while the language has become more temperate, the essential issues that define the Indian Muslim as an incomplete citizen-subject continue to dominate the discursive canon of Hindu nationalism[4] and are carried forward in the everyday activities of the RSS.

As a parallel exercise in refurbishing the image of the RSS, revisionist histories have emphasized how RSS leader Balasaheb Deoras developed friendships with

Muslim leaders while they were imprisoned together during the Emergency, how the RSS and the Jamaat-e-Islami shared the same grievances and a common programme of opposition against the Congress, and how the RSS (as further testimony to the changing times) had opened its doors to minorities in 1977, enabling them to join the RSS *shakha* (Kelkar 2011, 140–41; Anderson and Damle 2018, 98). While filming the RSS in Nagpur in September–October 1992, I had asked to meet the Muslims and Christians who attended the RSS *shakha* and was assured that we would be introduced to some of them. But this never happened over the course of our shoot – our RSS minders always made some excuse about the absence of Muslim and Christian *swayamsevak*s at the *shakha*. However, while filming RSS children, youth, and *pracharak*s in the context of the Ram Janmabhoomi mobilization, we did witness up-close the hostility of the RSS towards Indian Muslims (Vachani 1993). In 2000 and 2001, when I returned to film the RSS, the anti-Muslim diatribes of my RSS interlocutors had only become more strident. In his Vijayadashami (RSS Founders Day) public speech in 2000, the RSS *sarsanghchalak* K. S. Sudarshan railed against the Semitic religions Christianity and Islam, their insularity, and their retrograde conversion practices:

> Islam and Christianity are the two Semitic religions that believe in one God, but they divide humanity in two groups. Christianity says, 'there are the Christians and the disbelievers are Heathens'. Islam says, 'the believers are Muslim, and the rest are *kafirs* (infidels)'. And for these religions the assimilation of one by the other is essential for world peace. And now look at the history of havoc and the bloodshed unleashed by Islam and Christianity.... (K.S. Sudarshan in Vachani 2002)

While Sudarshan reserved his strongest critique for the conversion practices of the Roman Catholic church replete with allegations about the violent, contemporary practices of the Jesuits, he also sought the formation of a nationalist, *swadeshi* church that could expel the foreign churches from India, and in a familiar refrain once again called on Indian Muslims to perform *Bharatiyakaran* or to 'Indianize' their Islam in the manner of Indonesian Muslims.[5]

At the beginning of the new millennium, the RSS had over the seventy-five years of its existence demonstrated remarkable continuity in depicting the Indian Muslim in one of two primary modes.[6] The first presented the Muslim as a foreigner or outsider, not of this land, disloyal or hostile to Hindus. The second presented the Muslim as someone whose forefathers were Hindu, but who on account of coercion or constraint had to convert to Islam. This converted Muslim refused to assimilate or accept the cultural heroes of this land as defined by the RSS. This figure of the yet-to-be-assimilated Muslim was therefore always suspect and inferior – at best, he was only capable of attaining a second-class citizenship. Further, this incomplete Muslim citizen-subject was said to be in urgent need of remoulding, of Indianization or *Bharatiyakaran*. This is the subject and the task that the MRM would address.

Origins of the MRM

> The RSS is a true friend of the Indian Muslim. We are Hindustani Muslims, our DNA is Hindu. (Mohammad Afzal, National Convenor of the Muslim Rashtriya Manch, December 2018)

Why did the RSS feel the need to float its Muslim affiliate at the end of 2002? There is an urgent need to see the creation of RSS front organizations such as the MRM as a double-edged response to a perceived crisis and as political opportunity. I suggest that the formation of the Muslim Rashtriya Manch (initially formed as the Rashtriya Muslim Andolan – Ek Nayi Raah) was expedited as a safety-valve, or as 'political prophylactic' because of a deep sense of anxiety that the RSS experienced post-2002 Gujarat riots when a number of national and international fact-finding commissions of inquiry and international human rights groups unequivocally indicted the Sangh Parivar and the Narendra Modi regime of enabling the Gujarat pogroms and provoking violence against Indian Muslims.[7] By foregrounding a new relationship with Muslims and by creating Muslim representation within the organization, the RSS attempted to deflect criticism and insulate itself from these new political challenges. The MRM was established on 24 December 2002. According to its website, this was at the behest of 'a group of nationalist Muslims and functionaries of the RSS'. Widely acknowledged as the brainchild of the fifth *sarsanghchalak* of the RSS, K. S. Sudarshan, the first meeting of the MRM occurred at the house of journalist Muzaffar Hussain and his wife, Nafisa Husain, then a member of the central government's National Commission for Women. Official accounts tell us that the meeting was attended by Sudarshan himself, RSS ideologue M. G. Vaidya, senior RSS functionaries Indresh Kumar and Madan Das, the president of the All India Imam Council, Maulana Jameel Iliyasi, Maulana Wahiduddin Khan, the Shahi Imam of Fatehpuri Masjid, Maulana Mukarram, and several Sufi Muslims, educationists, and other intellectuals.[8]

While Sudarshan was the driving force behind the MRM in its early years, his protégé in the RSS, Indresh Kumar, assumed organizational control later. Formally, Indresh Kumar is the *margdarshak* (patron/guide) of the MRM. The MRM website and the MRM volunteers frequently refer to him as their 'messiah'. An RSS *pracharak* who wields a great deal of power, Kumar is part of the Akhil Bharatiya Karyakari Mandal (ABKM), the centralized, all-powerful decision-making body of the RSS.

He was initially accused of being part of the Hindutva saffron terror network, and in 2010, was implicated in the Malegaon, Samjhauta Express, and Ajmer Sharif blasts (Reghunath 2014, 2015; *Firstpost* 2016). The RSS closed ranks in supporting Kumar and organized protests in his defence. Eventually, no charges were filed against him by the National Investigative Agency (NIA). Indresh Kumar's current writings project his new image as an apostle of peace (Kumar 2015, 2016). His aura or charisma within the MRM is reminiscent of a cult and is in stark contrast to the banal, repetitive nature of his speech-making at public fora. As Felix Pal notes, he is extremely powerful and can bestow positions of influence on people close to him, which undoubtedly contributes to this aura (Pal 2020).

The rationale for the foundation of the MRM is explained thus:

> During the freedom movement, the Congress continued to pamper the Muslims to achieve Hindu–Muslim unity as pre-requisite to gain freedom. At the same time some leaders were spewing venom of hatred against them widening the gap between the two communities. While, Congress' policy of appeasement resulted in vivisection of our '*Madar-e-Vatan*,' the 'Hate Muslim' policy further expanded the already existing gap between the two 'brothers'. (Pachpore 2016a)[9]

According to the MRM's official narrative, this conflict between the politics of appeasement and the politics of hatred necessitated a *third way* that recognized that Muslims shared the same ancestry, culture, and traditions as the Hindus. Over time, Indian Muslims had lost their way and there was a need to bring them out of their minority status and into the mainstream, and to 'make them realize this underlying current of unity-in-diversity'[10] (Pachpore 2016a; Muslim Rashtriya Manch Website 2016). Mohammed Afzal,[11] the national convenor of the MRM, recalled the speech Sudarshan made on 24 December 2002: 'The real meaning of Islam is peace, then why is it that Islam is only known as the face of terror. You must work to show us the true face of Islam.'

Having constructed this artificial binary about the two faces of Islam, and having straitjacketed the Indian Muslim as immutable, hostile to peace, and anti-national, the RSS project of remoulding the Indian Muslim could begin in earnest.

I had presumed that the making of the 'new *Musalmaan*' would take the usual RSS form of disciplining the body and 'character building' for MRM volunteers at the site of the *shakha*, but Afzal told me that this was not a requirement:

> Indreshji (Kumar) told us: You are freed from the need to wear RSS knickers, the need to attend RSS *shakha*. You don't need to come to the RSS. But go and work in your community and take the RSS message to your *ulema* (religious leaders).

The RSS decision to separate Muslim bodies from Hindu ones preserves the status quo and ensures that there is no bodily contact or physical and social interaction between Hindus and Muslims at the RSS *shakha*. It has the heuristic benefit of continuing a time-honoured, deeply communal, and pedagogical system of indoctrination of Hindu boys and young men at the *shakha* without disrupting the codes of otherness that are central to its propagation. This social distancing from Muslims within an organization that has Muslim outreach as its main focus is suggestive of the RSS ambivalence about the MRM project. Walter Anderson and Sridhar Damle have documented that within the organization there are significant differences of opinion about the existence of the MRM. While one school of thought within the RSS approves of its brand of nationalist Muslim who can legitimate Hindutva projects, another school of thought within the RSS continues to be suspicious of any association with Muslims, and prefers strategies of Hinduization (as opposed to *Bharatiyakaran*/Indianization) and reconversion (*ghar wapsi*) in dealing with Indian Muslims (Anderson and Damle 2018, 101).

Instead of socialization via the *shakha*, the MRM engages in several other activities that I discuss in detail below, all of which highlight the intrinsically performative character of its project.

Creating Representation: The Making of the RSS Ulema

> Under the guidance of Sudarshanji and Indreshji, we began our work with the ulema. We travelled the length and breadth of the country by public transport. It was a big struggle, but we convinced the ulema to give up the Islam of Terror and embrace the Islam of Peace.
>
> We were successful. Sudarshanji told us in 2007, 'I thought that this work would take fifteen years, but you have done it in five years.' (Mohammad Afzal, MRM National Convenor, October 2018)

One of the main aims of the RSS's Muslim outreach project is to create an entirely new, alternative religious clerisy that can displace and supplant the existing national organizations that represent Indian Muslims such as the All India Muslim Personal Law Board (AIMPLB), Babri Masjid Action Committee (BMAC), the Jamaat-e-Islami Hind, and the Jamiat-Ulema-e-Hind.

Maulana Suhaib Qasmi is a key member of the MRM and one of its ten Muslim convenors (nine are Sunni; one is a Shia Muslim).[12] He is the founder of the Jamaat Ulema-e-Hind (JUH),[13] a Sunni organization that supports the RSS and the BJP. Qasmi studied at the Islamic seminary Darul Uloom in Deoband for ten years and has been with the BJP since 1996. In 2002, he joined the MRM and formed the JUH in 2006. The JUH formally merged with the BJP in 2011. Qasmi explained that the JUH works actively to prepare a workforce of younger *ulema* that could legitimize and underwrite RSS–BJP projects, thus creating an alternative Muslim clerisy to challenge traditional Muslim political and religious bodies:

> Islam is run on the basis of two seats of power: the *masjid* and the *madarsah*. The Congress had completely hijacked these spaces. It is only in the past ten-fifteen years because of the efforts of Sudarshanji and Indreshji that we now have younger *ulema* who are willing to work for Hindu–Muslim unity and for the nation… The Jamiat-e-Ulema-Hind, the Jamaat-e-Islami had worked with the Congress and Left parties to divide Hindus and Muslims[14]. But now the JUH is breaking these barriers, as we believe in *Ganga–Jamuni Tehzeeb*.[15]

The function of the Hindu nationalist Muslim *ulema* is to provide religious legitimacy and political heft to the MRM in carrying out Hindutva projects that oppose the traditional power centres of Indian Islam. In the past, this has taken the form of setting up *parivar sulah kendras* (family reconciliation courts) in opposition to the Sharia courts (*Darul Qaza*) proposed by the AIMPLB[16] to deal with legal issues of *triple talaq* and *nikah halala*.[17] Alternatively, the *ulema* might help sanction a grand *namaz* and Quran recitation at the River Saryu in Ayodhya to support the construction of the Ram temple with 1,500 clerics performing *wazu* (ablutions).[18] There are also negative acts of prohibition and opposition. For instance, in 2011, the MRM *ulema* opposed the position of the Jamiat-Ulema-i-Hind that had declared the singing of 'Vande Mataram' to be against the tenets of Islam. MRM *ulema* have also issued or secured alternative *fatwas* that support RSS–BJP pet projects such as banning cow slaughter. Their official publication *Gai aur Islam* (Cows and Islam, Khan et al. 2015, 21–22) compiles a list of *fatwas* over the years that have appealed to Muslims to avoid the slaughter of cows. A good example is the 2015 *fatwa* secured specifically for the publication of *Gai aur Islam* from the Iranian Grand Mufti and Shia cleric, Ayatullah Alawi Gurgani:

> Fatwa Question: If the slaughter of cows is banned and the cow is considered a sacred animal in India, what is the appropriate action for Muslims?
>
> Fatwa Answer: If the slaughter of cows is banned and there is a possibility of discord or violence over this, then Muslims should avoid cow slaughter.

Rewriting Quranic Scripture, Reinterpreting Islam the RSS Way

> They have been taught that either you are a Muslim, or you are a kafir (infidel). And if you are a kafir, they have every right to destroy you. When

they have this ideology, how can they live with us? This attitude will change, it will have to change. Perhaps, their scriptures will need to be changed. (Vinayak Rao Phatak, RSS *sanghchalak*, Nagpur; Vachani 1993)

On 5 June 2017, Indresh Kumar attended an *iftar* party at Jamia Millia Islamia University organized by the MRM. In his speech to an audience of primarily MRM members, he announced that Muslims must stop eating *gosht* (meat) during Ramzan. Later, Kumar clarified that he was urging Muslims to give up eating beef and not goat meat.[19]

Indresh Kumar further pronounced that his words had religious sanction and that the Quran prohibits the eating of beef. In an interview with rediff.com (S. Ashraf 2017), he elaborated, 'Gosht bimari hai, doodh aur ghee shifa aur ilaaj hai' (Cow meat spreads illnesses, whereas milk and ghee are healthy and a cure for diseases). Asked about the source of this information, Kumar claimed that this was written in the Quran and is part of the *Hadith* (sayings of Prophet Muhammad). The importance of the cow to Islam could be gauged from the Quranic chapter, 'Surah-e-Baqar' (The Cow), he went on authoritatively. Kumar asserted that there is no mention of cow slaughter in this chapter and that cow slaughter is not permitted in Mecca or Medina, nor in most Western countries, as beef is poisonous meat and a well-known source of disease. This sensational announcement after the *iftar* party at Jamia Millia Islamia was amplified by the Hindu nationalist press and mainstream television, as Indresh Kumar and other MRM spokespersons gave numerous interviews to journalists to discuss the finer points of this revelation.[20]

Kumar's statement was met with derision and disbelief by my Kashmere Gate *gali* interlocutors:

> Rahman: What is this mischief? I may not eat beef in deference to my Hindu brothers' sentiments. But does he really think Muslims will believe that this is written in our scriptures?
>
> Asif: Is he a *Haji*? He should talk to me, as I am someone who has gone on the Haj recently. I would tell him that you get all kinds of meat in Mecca and Medina, including beef. You can buy beef in packets and you can also buy it fresh in the open market. (Video interview, December 2018)

As Ajaz Ashraf (2017) shows, Kumar's claims are unfounded. The 'Surah-e-Baqar' does not consider the heifer or the calf as a sacred animal, and there is no reference in the text to its flesh being poisonous. He points out that Kumar may have mistaken the use of the word 'goh' (monitor lizard) for 'gau' (cow) in the *Hadith*, where the Prophet declines to consume the meat of the monitor lizard when it is offered to him. According to Ashraf, such scriptural intervention by Indresh Kumar might reflect great ignorance but is also suggestive of a hidden agenda:

WHEN HINDUTVA PERFORMS MUSLIMNESS

> Given the ease of global connectivity, it is incredible that Kumar should twist facts, and invent them. But there is a method to his strategy: it is to address a large segment of Muslims in India who read the Quran in Arabic but do not understand the language. The illiterate among them cannot even access translations of the Quran to understand its meanings. They simply learn by rote the verses for the purpose of prayer. So, when they hear a leader like Kumar claim that the Quran bans cow slaughter or the chapter of Al-Baqara is on diseases, there is a possibility they might believe him or get confused. (A. Ashraf 2017)

While Ashraf's argument is compelling, I suggest that at the present moment the primary goal of the MRM is not to change the consciousness of the Indian Muslim. Instead, the MRM aims to set political agendas and themes for public discussion, and stage scenes and circulate images primarily for consumption by the Hindu nation and the RSS rank and file.

These themes and images graphically connote the remoulding of the incomplete Muslim citizen-subject that is the central mission of the RSS. Examples include images of Indresh Kumar leading a group of Muslim men as they hold hands and chant 'Bharat Mata ki Jai' (Victory to Mother India/Hail Mother India) and 'Vande Mataram' (I bow to thee, Mother), or when they follow his lead by enthusiastically repeating the slogan, 'Hum Imam-e-Hind Ram ki kasam khatey hain, Mandir wahin banayenge' (We swear by the Imam of Hind, Ram that we will build the temple there [in Ayodhya]).

Scenes of vegetarian Muslim *gaurakshaks* nurturing cows, Muslims engaging in symbolic sacrifice by cutting goat-shaped cakes on Bakr-Id instead of participating in the tradition of animal sacrifice, Hindu women tying *rakhi*s on the wrists of Muslim men during Raksha Bandhan, or Muslims and Hindus playing Holi together are among the instances of the MRM's performative syncretism that showcase the docile, domesticated, and non-threatening Muslim subject in the service of the Hindu nation.[21]

These images of *Hindutva performing Muslimness* circulate in worlds that are marked by a very different everyday reality for Indian Muslims, who are at the receiving end of multiple forms of violence deployed by the Hindutva regime and its vigilantes. These acts that range from beef lynchings and police attacks on Muslim universities, to the organization of anti-Muslim riots in Delhi and the arrest of Muslim student leaders aim to disenfranchise Muslims and relegate them to the status of secondary citizens in overt and violent ways.[22]

LALIT VACHANI

Staging Events I: Bharatiya *Muslims for the Ram Mandir*

On 16 December 2018, the MRM organized a public rally in Delhi to call for the building of the Ram temple in Ayodhya. Initially, the plan was to stage a massive rally of 25,000 people at the sprawling Ramlila public grounds. But eventually the ambitions were scaled down to one of manageable proportions by organizing the event at the smaller Jantar Mantar protest site.[23] The aim of the rally was to show that nationalist, patriotic Muslims were in favour of building the Ram temple. By staging this event, the MRM hoped to influence the state, the Supreme Court, and the opposition parties to expedite the construction of the temple.

The rally was clearly stage-managed, and the majority of the audience of approximately 500 persons was organized.[24] Our film team arrived at the venue an hour before the scheduled beginning and were able to document the gathering crowds. We observed BJP *mahila morcha* (women's wing) workers accompanying small groups of veiled women to the seating area. Busloads of young men began to arrive at the Jantar Mantar protest zone about an hour before the rally's scheduled beginning, closely watched over by MRM leaders and minders. One bus arrived from Uttarakhand, and its leader introduced himself to us as Masoom Ali, an MRM and BJP coordinator from Haridwar district. Ali confirmed that he had organized his group for the rally and that they had come to show their support for the 'Ram Mandir and for *Ganga–Jamuni Tehzeeb* [syncretic culture] of the only nationalist party, the BJP'. But as our team began to interview Ali, he was immediately silenced by the organizers of the rally who were keeping vigil behind us. 'Don't mention the BJP!' Ali was warned. I was gently berated by Girish Juyal, the MRM rally organizer,[25] 'Why are you interviewing him? Please only speak to our authorized spokespersons.'

Initially, I was perplexed by this attempt at censorship and control. After all, Ali was praising the BJP and showing support for the construction of the Ram temple, so what could be the problem? But after speaking to the authorized spokespersons and filming them in interaction with other journalists and TV reporters, I realized that the MRM was attempting to project this rally for the Ram Mandir as a spontaneous gathering of nationalist Muslims without political affiliations to the Hindu nationalist groups that were lobbying for the Ram temple. When my initial interviewees confirmed that the RSS and the BJP had organized and staged this event, the organizers were disturbed that this information was shared with me and felt the need to prevaricate by masking their own involvement in this staging.[26]

The authorized representatives enlisted to speak to the media were Mohammed Afzal, Yaser Jilani,[27] and Maulana Suhaib Qasmi, all of whom attempted to project the rally as one in which Muslims had spontaneously and independently congregated, with the MRM providing a cultural platform for this expression. No organizational or political affiliations to the Sangh Parivar were mentioned. These attempts by MRM spokespersons Yaser Jilani and Mohammad Afzal to disguise the actual circumstances of the rally and its links to the RSS–BJP took on absurd overtones where even a reporter from the pro-Hindutva Zee TV grew increasingly impatient over the course of his interview:

> Afzal: They (other political parties) only do vote-bank politics.
>
> Zee Reporter: And you don't do vote-bank politics?
>
> Afzal: We don't do it, and we never have... we are independent...
>
> Jilani: We are a social organization, and we try to bring society together...
>
> Zee Reporter: But you support the BJP?
>
> Jilani: A nationalist organization like ours has nothing to do with any political party. Our only aim is to build the Ram temple. [At this point, the exasperated Zee News reporter abruptly cut the interview.]

The high point of the rally was the entry of the MRM's 'messiah', Indresh Kumar. To much fanfare and the repeated chanting of 'Madr-e-Watan, Hindustan!' (Long live Mother India!) Kumar offered benign blessings to the gathered crowd while MRM workers and leaders (almost all Muslim) rushed to touch his feet.

As Muslim MRM speakers and religious clerics addressed the crowd with a series of short speeches, Kumar continued to give interviews to the media crews gathered at the site, completely ignoring what the MRM leaders were saying in a telling indication of the lack of importance of Muslim voices within the MRM.[28] During these short interviews, Kumar reiterated the spontaneous and apolitical nature of the event. Pressed on how the aims of the rally fitted in with the core electoral promise of the BJP to build the Ram temple, Kumar snapped at the journalist from the India Today/Aaj Tak news channel,[29] 'Don't politicize everything. This is a spiritual awakening of Indian Muslims who have come here of their own free will. It is their independent decision to have the Ram temple.'

Kumar's speech to the assembled crowd focused on the imperative to immediately build the Ram temple and was replete with creative fabrication. For instance, in his account, the membership numbers of the MRM had increased exponentially, so as to be scarcely believable. According to Kumar, hundreds of thousands of Muslims had joined the 'movement' on 24 December 2002. The MRM had organized meetings with around 2.5–3.5 million people and now had a membership of 'two to four crores' (20–40 million).[30]

Along with these exaggerated numbers, Kumar also gave new meanings to several familiar concepts. In a novel departure from the conventional use of the term 'minority', traditionally used to refer to Muslim and Christian communities, Indresh Kumar interpreted the word to mean 'marginalized'. By terming Indian Muslims *alpsankhyak* (the minority community), Kumar claimed that the Congress and the Left parties had consigned Muslims to live a life on the margins. But after years of marginalization, Indian Muslims now wanted to belong and become part of the mainstream. Therefore, Kumar asserted, Indian Muslims had rejected the politics of 'minorityism' to assemble in this spontaneous gathering to build a grand temple for Ram.

Another arresting innovation was the use of Islamic symbolism and mythology to describe the Hindu god Ram as Imam-e-Hind[31] (the ruler of India) and as one of 124,000 messengers of Allah.[32] In contrast, the Mughal emperor Babur was described as a *shaitan* (devil) who stole *khudah* (God) away from Muslims by illegitimately breaking a temple to build the Babri mosque.[33]

Kumar ended his speech with a description of the utopian Ramrajya that the Ram temple would bring:

> There will be an end to illiteracy. There will be no hunger and no poverty
> There will be no domestic violence, and no rape
> There will be an end to communal violence, caste politics and untouchability
> There will be no pollution, and no filth.
> We will learn to love again.
> Let's end the fighting, let's build our Ram temple.

While a familiar scene in the pageant of Hindu nationalism, what stood out in this rendition was the sight of a visibly Muslim audience listening with rapt attention to this vision of Ramrajya. Ensuring that these images would be captured and circulated by the media was one of the main tasks of the event organizers. They did not seem to be concerned with whether the audience was engaged or whether the speeches resonated with the crowd at the site. Instead, they were preoccupied with the correct messaging of the event to the media teams assembled there (including ours), and to ensure that the acts of Muslim outreach by the MRM and the RSS were being properly communicated to the wider audience of the Hindu nation.

Staging Events II: *The* Ulema *and the Muslim Vote*

On 5 May 2019, just a week before the Indian general elections, the MRM organized a Rashtriya Ulema Sammelan (national religious leaders' meeting) at the Ghalib Institute in New Delhi. This was intended to be a congregation of 'nationalist-minded *ulema*', to appeal to them to urge Muslims to vote for the BJP in the upcoming elections.[34]

WHEN HINDUTVA PERFORMS MUSLIMNESS

The presentation styles and overall ideological approach at this event differed markedly from the Ram temple rally of December 2018. Unlike the media and public spectacle of the Ram temple rally, the *ulema* meeting was a closed event and was, therefore, not widely covered by the mainstream media. There was only one television crew from the state-affiliated news agency ANI, which recorded an interview with Indresh Kumar at the venue (Figure 10.1). The relative freedom from the constraints of calibrating a message for the mass media may explain some of the features of the *ulema* event that I describe below.

Indresh Kumar began by referencing the Ram temple rally of 16 December with blatant fabrication. During the event, we had documented the MRM spokespersons and Kumar describing the rally as an 'apolitical' event in which nationalist Muslims had spontaneously congregated to petition for the building of the Ram temple. At the *ulema* meeting six months later, however, Kumar added a twist: he now described the meeting as one where Muslims had spontaneously congregated and taken a very *political* decision to vote for the BJP in the 2019 Indian elections!

> On the 16th of December 2018 thousands of Indian Muslims from all over the country got together and said that this time we will reject the politics of hatred. We will make the BJP win, and we will be a part of the new government. Our vote for the BJP will be expressed at the booth and we will show our willingness to participate in the new government.

Figure 10.1 Indresh Kumar interviewed by ANI at the Rashtriya Ulema Sammelan (5 May 2019)

Source: Lalit Vachani.

Contradicting his earlier stand on the pejorative and discriminatory use of the term *alpsankhyak* by the Congress and the Left that prevented the Indian Muslim from becoming part of the mainstream, Kumar himself now repeatedly used the word *alpsankhyak* to refer to Indian Muslim minorities. In both his speech and his interview with the ANI journalist, which we recorded, Kumar detailed the achievements of the Modi-led BJP government in providing career opportunities and social welfare benefits for the *alpsankhyak* community. Deploying a variant of the widely criticized theme of 'minority appeasement' with which the Sangh Parivar attacks the Congress Party, Kumar told the assembled audience that the present BJP government had given more to Muslims than had any previous Congress government. Even if all targets had not been achieved, a beginning had been made, and more goods would follow, he promised. Therefore, if Muslims did not want to be left out of the social welfare net, they must vote for the BJP.

Addressing the *ulema* attending the meeting, Indresh Kumar was less conciliatory and more threatening:

> I have seen many of your faces before, when you were doing the work of the Devil (*shaitan*). Some have now come around to us, but I believe a few of you continue to do the work of the Devil ...
>
> Well, the BJP government will come to power on the 23rd of May, with or without your support. You can choose to join us, beat the *dhol*, and distribute *ladoos*. Or you can remain in your *galis* feeling miserable and sad... if you want to prevent yourself from entering the gates of heaven (*Jannat*) and you wish to go to hell (*Jahannam*), who can stop you?[35]

In his study on the outreach to Indian Muslims during the 2014 Indian election, Mohammad Reyaz (2019) asks whether the overtures that were made to Indian Muslims by the BJP were not an alternative form of minority appeasement – a charge that the BJP has used *ad nauseam* to attack the Congress. In this context, Indresh Kumar's speech to the *ulema* and assembled Muslims, reinforced by his interview to ANI, was both appeasement and threat. While appealing to the good sense of the Muslims in the audience to vote for the party that could provide them with basic amenities, Kumar was also reminding them how bad things could get if they were outside the safety net that could be provided by the MRM, the RSS, and the BJP. In essence, this was the third way proposed and implemented by the MRM and Indresh Kumar. The *ulema* meeting was not a manifestation of the politics of hatred, nor was it entirely about the politics of appeasement. Rather it showcased a politics of persuasion commingled with threat, a veritable carrot-and-stick approach in an attempt to win the Muslim vote.

Like the Ram temple rally, the crowd at the Rashtriya Ulema conference also appeared to have been managed. I observed that the *ulema* in attendance were primarily young religious scholars from small towns in Uttar Pradesh. The Muslims who constituted the general audience had been brought there from Old Delhi and the Nizamuddin West area. A young woman in a veil who was called on stage to recite a few verses from the Quran approached us with a request: 'I came here because of my *majboori* (compulsion). Please don't show this on TV. I will be embarrassed, and my friends and family will be upset with me if they see me at a Manch meeting.'

Our film team observed that the majority of the crowd sat separately from the main organizers of the MRM and their guests and families, and that they appeared to be there for the free snacks and dinner. Later, my *gali* interlocutors confirmed that crowds for MRM events were organized by invitation and sometimes by payment. In a cynical aside, Taufik asked me, 'Who is behind the veil?' Ghyasuddin elaborated that there had been events where veiled Muslim women had been paraded by the MRM, when it was later discovered that they were wearing the *kalava* (sacred Hindu thread). 'No Muslim woman would ever wear a *kalava*. So now you will understand why they [the MRM] have very little credibility with us!'

Sewa and the Street

In his study of Hindu nationalist electoral mobilization strategies, Tariq Thachil (2014) demonstrates how in favourable conditions, elite parties like the BJP are able to retain their core constituency voters while garnering the votes of the poorer sections of society by facilitating basic social services at the grassroots level. In the context of the MRM, some Muslim intellectuals and scholars have expressed a similar concern: the poorer and backward sections within the Muslim community might gravitate to the MRM because of the social welfare services it can provide (Ali 2017).

Arguing that the MRM was the first organization to work closely with Muslims for their social and economic uplift, its national media coordinator and BJP spokesperson Yaser Jilani outlined an impressive, albeit generic, set of social welfare schemes that the organization offered. These include delivering pensions to widows and divorced Muslim women, launching an *anaj* bank scheme for subsidized distribution of food grains, ensuring access to public health for poor Muslim families, education for children,[36] scholarships for Muslim youth, assistance in getting election and Aadhaar identification cards made for the disenfranchised and the poor (Video interview, 17 December 2018).

However, upon closer look, Jilani's assertion that the MRM's schemes were attracting Muslims to the organization appeared to be high on rhetoric and low on delivery. As Felix Pal has recently shown, the social welfare claims-making of the MRM is overstated, especially with regard to its claims to provide pensions for divorced Muslim women. Pal also discovered that the much-publicized grain banks had been outsourced to several RSS-affiliated organizations, and the MRM was not involved in the delivery mechanisms (Pal 2020). My *gali* interlocutors corroborated these findings. They did not know about most of these social welfare initiatives or anyone who had benefited from any of the schemes:

> Ghyasuddin: If they had reached out to us, then only they would know the problems of the *qaum* (community). But they have never approached us.
>
> Asif: I know that they (MRM) are a front of the RSS, and we are scared of the RSS.
>
> Therefore, I would not approach them with my problems in any case.
>
> Taufik: I think it is *sewa* (welfare) only for themselves, or for their family members and friends. (Video interview, May 2019)

Shoaib Khan, an ex-convenor of the organization, was scathing in his critique of the welfare schemes coordinated by the MRM. I met Khan in August 2018 at his office in East Delhi. Khan runs a public dispensary and health centre that caters to poor, working-class Muslims. When the Narendra Modi-led BJP election campaign reached out to the Muslim community in 2014 with its 'Sabka Saath, Sabka Vikas' (Solidarity with All, Development for All) electoral pitch,[37] Khan was impressed. Disillusioned with the Congress party, Khan believed that the BJP election messaging was sincere and saw it as a good opportunity to do social work and give back to the community. He had no hesitation in joining the MRM. But even as Khan rose swiftly to the position of convenor of the MRM, he rapidly grew disillusioned:

> I had wanted to intervene in the field of education and health to help poor, lower-caste slum-dwellers and working-class Muslims. But I realized that *sewa* for the MRM was in name only. They were simply not interested in the social upliftment of the community.
>
> This health centre (where we are meeting) ... this is the result of my planning and is what I had hoped to do with the MRM. But they were not interested. Show me one important school or hospital for Muslims that they have built. (Video interview, 15 December 2018)

For Khan, the bulk of MRM work was to provide 'photo-opportunities for RSS–BJP projects', such as building the Ram temple. The breaking point of his relationship with the MRM was an event that showed Khan that the RSS was so embarrassed by its association with the MRM that ultimately it was not even willing to acknowledge it.

Khan told us about the RSS-sponsored *iftar* party that was to be held at the Parliament Annexe on 2 July 2015. After the controversial comments about the violence in Kashmir that had recently been made by the special invitee, the Pakistani High Commissioner Abdul Basit, the MRM hastily withdrew its invitation to Basit. But this was not enough. The RSS leadership, which was facing criticism from within the organization, distanced itself from the sponsorship of the event, publicly declaring that the MRM was the sole organizer of the *iftar* party and that it had nothing to do with it:[38]

> Here we were on the frontlines, doing everything that the RSS wanted. And they were not even willing to accept us, to acknowledge us. This hypocrisy got to me, and it left a bitter taste. It was only a matter of time before I left. (Video interview, 15 December 2018)

Khan, however, noted that there are many people who will continue to join the MRM:

> There are two kinds of people who join. There are those who are in trouble, and then there are those who want self-gain and profit. They think, it is their government in power. We can benefit financially, and get ahead. And as you know, our community is in a precarious position. (Video interview, 15 December 2018)

As Pal shows, the majority of Muslims who join the MRM do so for instrumental reasons, and not because they agree ideologically with the RSS: 'Muslims join the Manch to punish traditional Muslim centres of authority, in the pursuit of reward, following Indresh Kumar or to guarantee their personal security in a Hindu nationalist India' (Pal 2020, 285).

As this essay has shown, the primary aim of the MRM is performative and not persuasive vis-à-vis the Muslim constituency that it ostensibly addresses, and is a performance meant primarily for the Hindutva and RSS media sphere. MRM performances are of several kinds. Thus, one set of performances showcase Muslim representation and support for issues that form the core political agenda of the RSS–BJP, such as the movement to build the Ram temple at Ayodhya.

Others showcase scenes of performative syncretism and behavioural changes on the part of Muslims, with Muslims seen to participate in Hindu cultural events like Holi and Raksha Bandhan, to protect and nurture cows, to change their dietary habits and publicly give up animal sacrifice.

A third set of performances stage an alternative history of the RSS relationship with Muslims. Claiming itself as the authentic agent of *Ganga–Jamuni tehzeeb*, the MRM appropriates a cultural tradition that the RSS has always historically rejected. Further, the MRM inverts and projects a communal praxis to the Congress and the Left parties. In the process, it attempts to absolve the RSS–BJP from a history of communal rioting and present culpability in engineering and legitimizing violence against Muslims, such as in the Delhi riots of February 2020.

Thus, the MRM literally provides a *manch*, or a stage, for the RSS. Its displays are carefully designed and staged to be recorded and circulated by the Hindu nationalist press corps and on social media. In form and content, these performances address the imagined Hindu nation rather than the *gali* Muslim or the Muslims who were assembled for the Ram temple rally. In this sense, the MRM provides crucial source material and stories for mediatized forms of Hindu nationalism.

Conclusion

On 16 January 2020, the MRM held a meeting at the Constitution Club in New Delhi with the aim of sensitizing the *ulema* about the contentious CAA. The MRM wished to reassure the *ulema* that the act was not discriminatory and that it would not adversely affect the Muslim community. While the meeting was in progress, it was disrupted by a handful of anti-CAA protestors who raised slogans against the act and the MRM leaders for supporting it. They were roughed up by MRM volunteers in the assembled audience and subsequently handed over to and arrested by the Delhi police.

The framing of this event for mainstream media and social media channels followed the same pattern of deception, exaggeration, and fabrication as the earlier events that were staged for the media by the MRM. Although this footage was recorded by multiple media channels that conclusively showed that the protestors had engaged only in peaceful actions such as shouting slogans (*Scroll.in* 2020; *Economic Times* 2020), the MRM spokesperson Yaser Jilani framed the event as 'an attempt on the life of the messiah, Indresh Kumar with the "Vadra-Congress"[39] and opportunistic leaders like Ahmed Patel and Ghulam Nabi Azad responsible for the action'. Jilani's interview to the openly jingoistic and pro-BJP television channel Republic World then went on to attack the peaceful protestors who had gathered at Shaheen Bagh to protest the CAA. They were described as people 'who had sold the integrity of Islam for Rs. 500 and a few platefuls of Biryani' (Jilani) and those 'who were defiling sacred Hindu symbols like the swastika at the Shaheen Bagh protests' (Republic World 2020).

A few weeks later, in a video interview to another Hindu nationalist channel Pyara Hindustan (2020), the JUH leader Maulana Suhaib Qasmi attacked Muslim leaders like Asaduddin Owaisi, student leaders Sharjeel Imam, Umar Khalid, and Kanhaiya Kumar, and the Congress and the Aam Aadmi Party (AAP), accusing them of fomenting the anti-CAA protests. This interview followed the same pattern as the earlier one that I have described, with an equally aggressive TV reporter and the interviewee (Qasmi) jointly lamenting 'the anti-national forces that were intent on dismembering the nation'.[40]

In a hyper-real, post-truth universe of alternative facts and 'emotional truths' (Hansen 2017), where a partisan and jingoistic mainstream media works overtime to discredit any form of opposition or dissent, the MRM has proved to be a particularly useful front organization for the RSS in foregrounding its various anti-minority, Hindu majoritarian projects like building the Ram temple, supporting the State in its attack on Kashmiri Muslims, or in promoting the CAA. By foregrounding self-generated images of the 'good' Muslims as prescribed by the RSS – docile, law-abiding, Muslim Ram-*bhakt*s who strive to protect cows, are vegetarian by choice, obsequious to Indresh Kumar, Narendra Modi, and the RSS—the MRM discredits the 'bad' Muslims and legitimizes attacks on them: those who are already at the receiving end of daily violence and cow vigilantism, the inspirational Shaheen Bagh peaceful protestors, the brave Muslim students of Jamia Millia Islamia University and Aligarh Muslim University who were at the forefront of the anti-CAA protests in 2019, and other ordinary Muslims who simply refused to accept the yoke of secondary citizenship as imagined by the RSS–BJP.

Notes

1 Video interview with Mohammad Afzal, National Convenor of the MRM, October 2018.

2 For a detailed account and analysis of the 1927 Nagpur riot and the method by which the RSS pre-empted and instigated the violence while maintaining a facade of self-defence, see Basu et al. (1993, 18–20).

3 Some accounts by RSS ideologues attempt to deny that Golwalkar had primary authorship, arguing that the work was not written by him (Frawley 1998) or that it was an abridged version of G. D. Savarkar's *Rashtriya Mimansa – Arthat Hindusthan ka Rashtreeya Swaroop* (Sinha 2006). Alternatively, some say that it was an 'immature work' written when Golwalkar was not yet the *sarsanghchalak* of the RSS and, therefore, not representative of the RSS viewpoint. Further revisionist writings suggest that since the book predates the Nazi 'final solution' by a few years, comments like 'purging of the Jews' merely refer to the removal of the Jews from office, the stripping of their citizenship and/or their emigration from Germany; alternatively, the text merely sought equality of all religious communities before the secular law of the land and the curtailing of 'privileges' for the minorities (Elst 1999; 2006). For a comprehensive critique of how the Sangh Parivar ideologues have prevaricated in their attempt to dissociate from the incendiary text, see Islam (2017, 54–62; 2018, 10–11).

4 For example, in *Bunch of Thoughts* (1966), Golwalkar claims that 'the hostile elements within the country pose a far greater menace to national security than the aggressors from outside'. For Golwalkar, these 'internal threats' were the Muslims, Christians, and

Communists. Referring to Muslims and Christians, Golwalkar invokes the spirit of Savarkar:

> But the question before us now is, what is the attitude of those people who have been converted to Islam or Christianity? They are born in this land, no doubt. But are they true to their salt? Are they grateful to this land which has brought them up? ... Do they feel it a duty to serve her? No! Together with the change in their faith, gone is the spirit of love and devotion for the nation ... They have also developed a feeling of identification with the enemies of this land. (Golwalkar 1966, 111–12)

5   Sudarshan was invoking Golwalkar who repeatedly undermines the flawed and anti-national Indian Muslim by comparing him with the idealized, exemplary Indonesian Muslim who reveres Hindu deities, has studied the Ramayana, and retains a deep sense of pride in his Hindu culture and heritage (Golwalkar 1966, 133, 256, 264). See also Sinha (2006).

6   Paola Bacchetta describes these two categories in class terms with the former, the foreign invaders designated as upper class, and the Muslims who converted from Hinduism as being of lower caste origin. Bacchetta mentions a recently formed third category: the 'Hindu-Muslims'. As we will discuss, this would be the ideal Muslim subject as imagined by the RSS in forming the MRM – one whose conduct would be consistent with the normative ideals prescribed by Hindu nationalism and who could be assimilated back into the Hindu nation. Bacchetta also emphasizes how the RSS imagines Muslim men as excessively sexual and hyper-masculine, 'a projection of promiscuity and aggression that the British had earlier assigned to lower-caste Hindus, and diverts its anger towards them' (Bacchetta 2018, 387). The project of domesticating and reining in the 'new *Mussalman*' under the auspices of the MRM represents the course correction envisaged by the RSS.

7   See, for example, the Concerned Citizens Tribunal reports of May and October 2002; the National Human Rights Commission Report (31 May 2002); Amnesty International Memorandum to the Indian government (28 March 2002); the Human Rights Watch report (April 2002); the USCIRF (U.S. Commission on International Religious Freedom) Hearings, and the report on the Gujarat communal violence (May–June 2002). For more details about these reports and fact-finding tribunals, see Engineer (2003) and the Coalition against Genocide reportage list: https://www.coalitionagainstgenocide.org/reports.php (accessed on 5 January 2022).

8   There is no mention of the BJP in formal accounts of the meeting. But Mohammed Afzal, the national convenor of the MRM, told me that senior BJP leaders L. K. Advani and Sushma Swaraj were also present at the meeting.

9   Interestingly, these two flawed approaches to the 'Muslim problem' are re-framed by RSS leader and MRM patron Indresh Kumar as the *minority appeasement of Muslims by Mahatma Gandhi* and the *Hate Muslim policies of the Hindu Mahasabha* (MRM website; emphasis mine). It is significant to note that the RSS completely absolves itself of any kind of complicity or culpability in this conception of the 'other' or its participation in past incidents of anti-Muslim violence. It is almost as if Godhra and the ensuing Gujarat

pogroms of 2002 in which the Sangh Parivar was the primary instigator of violence had never occurred.

10 The MRM thus reproduced the familiar Nehruvian slogan in its founding narrative. As I will discuss subsequently, several secular and pluralist tropes in popular circulation that predate the Nehruvian era unity-in-diversity theme (for example, *Ganga–Jamuni tehzeeb*, *mili-jhuli sanskriti*, *Hindu–Muslim bhaichara*) are also appropriated, inverted, and projected by the RSS. The opposition forces (the Congress and the Left parties) are frequently accused of fomenting communal violence and depredations on the Muslim community, while the RSS–BJP is projected as emancipating the community by showing Muslims the true, peaceful path of Islam and by visibly and publicly demonstrating instances of Hindu–Muslim syncretism.

11 Mohammad Afzal was the protégé of the senior BJP Muslim leader Sikandar Bakht and was therefore naturally drawn to the MRM since its inception. He described the work of the MRM as 'the bridge' between the RSS and Muslims. 'The RSS did not trust Indian Muslims and Muslims did not trust the RSS. The MRM was able to get them to understand each other' (interview with Mohammad Afzal, October 2018).

12 Suhaib Qasmi and Kokab Mujtaba are the two religious clerics, with the title of national convenor (Maulana) who are part of the MRM committee. Kokab Mujtaba is the Shia face of the MRM.

13 I first met Suhaib Qasmi at the MRM Ram temple rally on 16 December 2018. As he introduced himself and handed me his visiting card, I was confused at reading the name of his organization – Jamaat Ulema-e-Hind. The name is derived from the established Muslim organization, the Jamiat-Ulema-e-Hind, which was founded in 1919, participated in the Indian nationalist movement, believes in a composite culture, and is deeply suspicious of the motivations of the Sangh Parivar. The borrowing of the name of this organization is designed to confuse and is suggestive of a clever method of purloining religious capital for immediate political mobilization. When I asked him about this, Qasmi did not deny that the naming of his organization was intentional.

14 Qasmi's critique of the Congress and the Left parties extended to allegations of inciting communal riots for political gain. No evidence or detail was provided to back up these claims.

15 Video interview with Suhaib Qasmi, May 2019. *Ganga–Jamuni tehzeeb* refers to the syncretic culture of the doab regions of north-central India, representing the fusion of Hindu and Muslim cultural and religious elements. It is also sometimes referred to as India's composite culture, or *mili-jhuli sanskriti*. See Mohammada (2007), Roy Burman (1996), Virmani (2007), and Safvi (2014).

The MRM is presented as the authentic repository of *Ganga–Jamuni tehzeeb*, a claim which is never backed up by any evidence and is circulated repeatedly by senior MRM functionaries on social media. In this way, the RSS uses its front organization to appropriate, invert, and reinvent a past that they have historically always felt threatened by, and rejected. For details on the RSS–BJP ambivalence towards, and eventual rejection of composite culture, see Noorani (2019).

16 For more details about the tussle over Muslim personal law between the MRM and the AIMPLB, see *MyNation* (2018) and *NewsBharati* (2018).

17 A practice in which a woman after being divorced by *triple talaq*, marries another man, consummates the marriage, and gets divorced to be able to remarry her former husband. The incidence of *triple talaq* and *nikah halala* is minuscule in India, but the political benefits of legislation to criminalize the practice have been immense for the RSS family in projecting itself as the defender of Muslim women's rights.

18 This grand *namaz* eventually did not take place. While the RSS had initially endorsed the display of inter-religious camaraderie facilitated by the MRM, it changed its stand when Hindu seers protested against holding this event. The RSS claimed that it was not involved in the organization of the *namaz*, and the event was cancelled (*Scroll.in* 2018; *Swarajya* 2018).

19 Kumar claimed that the word for goat meat is *maas* (Times Now 2017). However, in regular parlance, both *gosht* (Urdu) and *maas* (Hindi) refer to goat meat. Since *gosht* is commonly thought of as goat meat, some media channels quite logically broadcast the story that the RSS expected Indian Muslims to turn vegetarian. Indresh Kumar blamed the 'intentional mischief mongering' media for this controversy. However, this ideal of the vegetarian Indian Muslim is not without precedent – in 2016 and later, again in 2018, the MRM put out a call that Muslims 'should give up their bad habits of animal sacrifice and cut a goat shaped cake as symbolic sacrifice to commemorate Bakr-Id' (Pachpore 2016a; PTI 2017; *DNA* 2017; NewsX 2017; Outlook Web Bureau 2017; *The Print* 2018a). In general, it appears that the RSS would prefer its nationalist Muslims to be vegetarian. As a last resort, they may consume meat as long as they eschew beef.

20 The majority of television channels that are sympathetic to Hindu nationalism tend to accept such statements at face value. However, not all channels were willing to suspend palpable disbelief. 'It seems that the RSS claims to know more about Islam than established Muslim clerics,' said an incredulous Akshay Tandon, the anchor of a news show on the NewsX channel (NewsX 2017). Other channels were even more critical, with the feisty executive editor of the digital website *Newslaundry*, Atul Chaurasia, attempting to debate the issue with Indresh Kumar. This did not go down well with Kumar, who walked off in a huff, abruptly terminating the interview while it was being recorded (*Newslaundry* 2017).

21 In December 2018, we filmed a group of Muslim men nurturing and feeding cows at the Hanuman Mandir, an event organized by the Gau Parkosht (Cow Division) of the MRM. See Kumar (2016) on Raksha Bandhan and a video of him playing Holi with Muslims (YouTube 2015). See also, Virag Pachpore on an eco-friendly Bakr-Id (Pachpore 2016b) replete with the symbolic goat cake sacrifice, and the feeding of grass and jaggery to cows. These staged events have an active afterlife as source material for wider social media consumption and are publicized to the Hindu nation via WhatsApp, Facebook, and Twitter. As part of an MRM WhatsApp group, I receive regular updates about such events. The same information was later disseminated by allied WhatsApp groups, such as the ones coordinated by the Muslim Gauraksha Dal and the Rashtriya Ekta Muslim Manch. Individual MRM volunteers would further circulate these newsfeeds

via WhatsApp and Facebook. Such events are also publicized by RSS publications like *Panchjanya* and *Organiser* and form a crucial part of the wider social media ecology and the communication strategies of the RSS.

22 The images of the 'good Muslims' that I describe are matched by the heavily edited, manipulated, morphed, and manufactured images of the 'bad Muslim' shown stealing or slaughtering cows, preying on Hindu women, spitting on fruits and vegetables in a bid to infect Hindu bodies, or provoking violence against the Indian state with incendiary speech-making. These images are also actively circulated and disseminated on Hindu nationalist WhatsApp groups to dehumanize Muslims, and to incite and justify further acts of state and vigilante violence against them. For a good forensic investigation of one such case, see Patel and Zubair (2020).

23 MRM volunteers told me that their plans changed once the VHP decided to schedule their large rally for the Ram temple at the Ram Lila grounds (*Economic Times* 2018), exactly a week before the MRM had planned their event. It was decided that it would be redundant to stage another rally on the same grounds a week later. Clearly, the VHP sponsored event was also considered much more significant than the one the MRM had planned under its banner.

24 The organization of the political rally and its audience is common during elections. However, this rally was unusual as it was not held in an electoral context. It is reminiscent of the pattern by which the RSS organizes crowds with minute planning and then masks the organizing principle in an attempt to show that the mob has assembled spontaneously (Vachani 2017).

25 Girish Juyal is an RSS *pracharak* and the national organizing convenor of the MRM. He coordinates all campaigns of the MRM and is the most powerful person in the MRM after Indresh Kumar, with whom he works closely. He prefers to keep a low profile within the MRM but kept a watchful eye on our team as we went about interviewing MRM workers. In 2020, Juyal continued in his organizational role with the MRM. But he was now also convenor and founder member of a new outfit – the Jai Bharat Manch, which explicitly worked on the issue of the CAA, to assure Muslims that the act was not discriminatory and to discredit the anti-CAA protests (LiveBharatNews 2020).

26 See also Chaudhuri (2018) and *The Print* (2018b) on how the MRM projected Muslim women as supportive of building the Ram temple while hiding their affiliations to the Sangh Parivar.

27 Yaser Jilani is the national media coordinator of the MRM and the youthful, smooth, and suave face of the organization as he appears regularly on mainstream television. He is also the official spokesperson for the BJP.

28 The cosmetic value of the Muslim members in the MRM is self-evident in the visual composition and the framing of photographs for mass media consumption and social media circulation. The photograph and video invariably centre Indresh Kumar, with the MRM Muslims making up the periphery of the frame or the background behind Kumar.

29 In his interactions with journalists, Indresh Kumar appears to favour the pro-Hindu nationalist press and television channels like Zee TV, Republic TV, and Times Now

while displaying a disdain for the secular or centrist mainstream press. Equally, the pro-Hindutva press and TV channels give an inordinate amount of coverage to the MRM – for instance, Zee TV was broadcasting live at regular intervals during the Ram temple rally. For Kumar, the preferred mode of journalism is one where the journalist accepts information uncritically and publishes it in its entirety. He does not take kindly to repartee or questioning and tends to get irritable and aggressive when interrupted.

30 See Pal (2020) who records similar findings of exaggerated membership estimates. The figure of 10,000 active MRM members was mentioned by several volunteers and appears to be a much more realistic estimate. See also Raza (2014).

31 This title was bestowed on Ram by Allama Iqbal, the future national poet of Pakistan. Iqbal created this honorific title Imam-e-Hind in 1908 to rally Muslims and Hindus to participate in the nationalist movement around the inspirational figure of Ram (Saquib 2016).

32 The Quran mentions names of only twenty-five messengers, allowing space for this imaginative insertion by the MRM.

33 In another hyper-real moment of political grandstanding, Indresh Kumar insisted that the mosque was never demolished in 1992 since it was never a mosque. Instead, a temple was demolished by Babur at Ram's birthplace, and this urgently needed to be rebuilt. MRM volunteers are proud that it was a Muslim architect, K. K. Muhammad who discovered Hindu relics under the structure of the Babri mosque. For a critique of the investigation at the excavation site in 2003, and the preconceived notions, shoddy methodology, and dubious evidence of the temple construction below the mosque presented by the ASI, see Varma and Menon (2010).

34 The attempt to secure the Muslim vote continued even though some of my MRM interlocutors admitted that it would be difficult to get Muslims to vote for the BJP, especially in light of the near-complete absence of BJP Muslim candidates in the 2019 elections. For all the MRM's rhetoric of wanting to bring Indian Muslims to the 'mainstream', the BJP has an abysmal record of providing political representation for Muslims in both state assembly and parliamentary elections. The BJP does not select Muslim candidates as part of its core election strategy as Muslims tend not to vote for the BJP anyway. Further, there is a perception that selecting Muslim candidates will alienate the core Hindu support of the BJP. In many ways, this is the central conundrum of attempting to create minority electoral representation within Hindu majoritarian politics. The BJP political machinery adopts tactics based on creating anti-Muslim sentiment and communal polarization to consolidate the Hindu vote. With a focus on 'winnability', the BJP election machinery has reduced and almost done away with any form of dependency on the Muslim vote (see Jha 2017; Jaffrelot 2019a, 2019b).

35 Indresh Kumar uses a mixture of Hindi and Urdu (with occasional, strategic use of Arabic to demonstrate his 'reading' of the Quran) to address his audience. He frequently laces his speech with metaphors that present his audience with the choice of *Jannat–Jahannam* (Heaven–Hell) and with threats of divine retribution. In this telling, the incomplete Muslim subject must maintain constant vigil against the *shaitan ka rasta* (the path of the Devil). Depending on whim and contingency, these *shaitani* (devilish) forces are

variously ascribed to the non-RSS–BJP *kattarwadi* (fundamentalist) *ulema*, the Congress and the Left parties, anti-CAA Shaheen Bagh protestors, and Pakistan.

36 Jilani enthusiastically mentioned the *beti bachao, beti padhao* (save daughters, educate daughters) initiative. However, this is not exclusively an MRM campaign but one that was introduced by the Ministry of Women and Child Development in 2015. He was also particularly proud of the slogan that the MRM had introduced for its educational outreach to the community: *aadhi roti khayenge, bachchon ko padayenge* (we will eat half a *roti*, but we will educate our children).

37 For a detailed account of the BJP outreach to Muslims over the 2014 election campaign, including efforts by the MRM to advertise Modi to the community, see Reyaz (2019).

38 For more details on the *iftar* party controversy, see Andersen and Damle (2018, 92–94) and Kartikeya 2017). The distancing of the MRM by Hindu nationalist groups occurs frequently. On 12 July 2018, the MRM planned a grand *namaz* accompanied by Quranic recitation on the banks of the River Saruyu in Ayodhya. With 1,500 Muslim clerics due to participate, the plan was to send a message of peace and brotherhood in support of the Ram temple and was initially supported by the RSS. When Hindu seers protested against holding this event, the RSS claimed it was not involved and the event was cancelled (*Scroll.in* 2018; *Swarajya* 2018). The distancing of the RSS from the MRM is often strategic. Every TV broadcast that showcases the MRM taking up a core RSS–BJP issue invariably has Indresh Kumar or another RSS–BJP leader stressing that the MRM consists of 'independent Muslims' voicing their opinion. See also the description and analysis of the Ram temple rally earlier in this essay.

39 The 'Vadra-Congress' is a term coined by the right-wing, pro-BJP TV anchor Arnab Goswami and is used as a codeword to attack the Congress party on the grounds of nepotism and corruption. Robert Vadra is a businessman who is married to Priyanka Gandhi of the Congress party. He was accused by opposition parties of receiving undue favours in making various land deals under the previous Congress regime. While these charges of corruption have not yet been legally substantiated, the BJP constantly uses the threat of investigation to put Congress and its leaders on the defensive.

40 In videos sent to me by my interlocutors, MRM personnel attacked the Tablighi Jamaat sect for infecting Indians with the Coronavirus (also see *Organiser* 2020), and justified the arrests of the anti-CAA, Muslim student leaders Gulshifa Fathima, Meeran Haider, Umar Khalid, and Sharjeel Imam as being responsible for causing the February 2020 Delhi riots.

References

Ali, M. 2011. 'RSS, VHP, Friends of Muslims: Muslim Rashtriya Manch'. *TwoCircles.net*, 17 February. https://www.altnews.in/viral-video-of-muslim-vendor-licking-fruits-is-from-mps-raisen-falsely-linked-with-spreading-coronavirus/ (accessed on 5 January 2022)

Andersen, W., and S. Damle. 2018. *The RSS: A View to the Inside*. Delhi: India Viking.

Ashraf, A. 2017. 'Holy Cow: RSS' Indresh Kumar Lied about What the Quran Says about Cow and Beef. But Why?' *Scroll.in*, 12 June. https://scroll.in/article/840362/holy-cow-rss-indresh-kumar-lied-about-what-the-quran-says-about-cow-and-beef-but-why (accessed on 5 January 2022).

Ashraf, S. F. 2017. 'RSS Leader: "Gosht" Is Cow Meat, Quran Prohibits Eating It'. *Rediff.com*, 7 June. https://www.rediff.com/news/interview/rss-leader-gosht-is-cow-meat-quran-prohibits-eating-it/20170607.htm#:~:text=At%20an%20iftaar%20At%20the,eating%20gosht%20a%20'disease' (accessed on 5 January 2022).

Bacchetta, P. 2018. 'Queer Presence in/and Hindu Nationalism'. In *Majoritarian State: How Hindu Nationalism Is Changing India*, edited by A. Chatterjee, T. Hansen, and C. Jaffrelot, 151–73. London: Hurst and Company.

Basu, T., P. Datta, S. Sarkar, T. Sarkar, and S. Sen. 1993. *Khaki Shorts and Saffron Flags: A Critique of the Hindu Right*. New Delhi: Orient Longman.

Bhishikar, C.P. 1991. *Keshava Sangha Nirmata*. Nagpur: Suruchi Prakashan.

Chaudhuri, P. 2018. 'Media Analysis: RSS-affiliated Org Reported as 'Muslim women' Supporting Ram Mandir in Ayodhya'. *AltNews*, 27 November. https://www.altnews.in/media-analysis-rss-affiliated-org-reported-as-muslim-women-supporting-ram-mandir-in-ayodhya/ (accessed on 5 January 2022).

DNA. 2017. 'Sacrifice Bad Habits, Cut Goat Cake This Bakrid, Says RSS Muslim Wing'. *DNA*, 30 August. https://www.dnaindia.com/india/report-sacrifice-bad-habits-cut-goat-cake-this-bakrid-says-rss-muslim-wing-2541722 (accessed on 5 January 2022).

Economic Times. 2018. 'VHP Holds Massive Rally for Ram Temple at Delhi's Ramlila Maidan'. 9 December. https://economictimes.indiatimes.com/news/politics-and-nation/watch-thousands-gathered-in-delhi-for-vhp-rally-for-ram-temple/videoshow/67010689.cms (accessed on 5 January 2022).

———. 2020. 'Anti-CAA Slogans at RSS' Ulema Meet; Delhi Police Detains 8 People'. 17 January. https://economictimes.indiatimes.com/news/politics-and-nation/anti-caa-slogans-at-rss-ulema-meet-delhi-police-detains-8-people/articleshow/73316648.cms (accessed on 5 January 2022).

Elst, K. 1999. 'Was Guru Golwalkar a Nazi?' The Koenraad Elst site. https://www.youtube.com/watch?v=2SfM4_deF_g (accessed on 4 December 2021).

———. 2006. 'Disowning Golwalkar's We'. https://www.academia.edu/14793753/Disowning_Golwalkars_We (accessed on 5 January 2022).

Engineer, A. A. 2003. *The Gujarat Carnage*. New Delhi: Orient Longman.

Firstpost. 2016. '"Irrefutable" Evidence Against RSS Leader in Malegaon Blast, Says AAP'. *Firstpost*, 19 May. https://www.firstpost.com/politics/evidence-against-rss-indresh-kumar-malegaon-blast-case-aap-2788478.html (accessed on 5 January 2022).

Frawley, D. 1998. 'The Fascist Identified'. *Organiser*, May 31.

Golwalkar, M. S. 1939. *We, or Our Nationhood Defined*. Nagpur: Bharat Publications.

———. 1966. *Bunch of Thoughts*. https://www.thehinducentre.com/multimedia/archive/02486/Bunch_of_Thoughts_2486072a.pdf (accessed on 5 January 2022).

Hansen, T. 1999. *The Saffron Wave: Democracy and Hindu Nationalism in Modern India*. New Delhi: Oxford University Press.

———. 2017. 'Babri Masjid and Its Aftermath Changed India Forever'. *The Wire*, 7 December. https://thewire.in/communalism/babri-masjid-aftermath-changed-india-forever (accessed on 5 January 2022)

Islam, S. 2017. *Golwalkar's We or Our Nationhood Defined*. New Delhi: Pharos Media.

———. 2018. *RSS: Marketing Hindutva as Fascism*. New Delhi: Pharos Media.

Jaffrelot, C. 1999. *The Hindu Nationalist Movement and Indian Politics, 1925 to the 1990s*. New Delhi: Penguin Books.

———. 2019a. 'A De Facto Ethnic Democracy? Obliterating and Targeting the Other, Hindu Vigilantes, and the Ethno-State'. In *Majoritarian State: How Hindu Nationalism Is Changing India*, edited by A. Chatterjee, T. Hansen, and C. Jaffrelot, 41–67, London: Hurst and Company.

———. 2019b. 'BJP's Rise Has Meant a Shrinking Number of Muslim Lawmakers in India'. *The Wire*, 26 March. https://thewire.in/rights/christophe-jaffrelot-majoritarian-state-muslims-parliament (accessed on 5 January 2022)

Jeelany, S. 1971. 'Shri Guruji's Talk with Dr. Saifuddin Jeelany: A Noted Muslim Scholar'. RSS Facebook Page, February 1971. https://m.facebook.com/nt/screen/?params=%7B%22note_id%22%3A816459282513309%7D&path=%2Fnotes%2Fnote%2F&refsrc=deprecated&_rdr (accessed on 5 January 2022)

Jha, P. 2017. *How the BJP Wins: Inside India's Greatest Election Machine*. New Delhi: Juggernaut Books.

Kanungo, P. 2003. *RSS's Tryst with Politics: From Hedgewar to Sudarshan*. New Delhi: Manohar.

Kartikeya, C. 2017. 'RSS Is Lying: Muslim Rashtriya Manch Is as Much an RSS Outfit as BJP'. *Catch News*, 10 February. http://www.catchnews.com/politics-news/rss-is-lying-muslim-rashtriya-manch-is-as-much-an-rss-outfit-as-bjp-1467992819.html (accessed on 9 April 2020).

Kelkar, S. 2011. *Lost Years of the RSS*. New Delhi: Sage Publications.

Khan, M. F., S. Quraishi, and A. Singh, 2015. *Gai aur Islam*. New Delhi. Gaurakhsha Parkosht, Muslim Rashtriya Manch.

Kumar, I. 2015. *Duniya ko Prem aur Shanti ka Sandesh*. New Delhi: Muslim Rashtriya Manch.

Kumar, I. 2016. *Vishwa ka Manveeyah Parv – Rakshabandhan*. New Delhi: Rashtriya Ekta Mission.

LiveBharatNews. 2020. 'Jai Bharat Manch Varanasi dwara Nagarikta Sanshodhan Kanoon par Paricharcha ka Ayojan' *LiveBharatNews*, 10 February. https://www.youtube.com/watch?v=SqzaVK12Cc8 (accessed on 5 January 2022).

Mohammada, M. 2007. *The Foundations of the Composite Culture in India*. Delhi: Aakar Books.

Muslim Rashtriya Manch Website. 2016. 'About Us: Muslim Rashtriya Manch'. 13 January. http://muslimrashtriyamanch.org/Encyc/2016/1/13/About-us.aspx (accessed on 5 January 2022).

MyNation. 2018. 'It's Sharia Courts vs Parivar Centres as RSS Muslim Wing Takes on AIMPLB'. 8 August. https://www.mynation.com/news/sharia-courts-sangh-parivar-rss-muslim-aimplb-pd53vi (accessed on 5 January 2022).

NewsBharati. 2018. 'MRM Launches Third Parivar Sulah Kendra in U'khand'. 10 November. https://www.newsbharati.com/Encyc/2018/11/10/MRM-launches-third-Parivar-Sulah-Kendra-in-U-khand.html (accessed on 5 January 2022).

Newslaundry. 2017. 'NL Interviews: Why Run Away from an Interview, Mr Indresh Kumar?' 14 July. https://www.youtube.com/watch?v=M6wlCDVi8Zc (accessed on 5 January 2022).

NewsX. 2017. 'RSS Muslim Wing's Appeal to Shun Animal Sacrifice, Says Animal Sacrifice Is Bad Like Triple Talaq'. 31 August. https://www.youtube.com/watch?v=GD09im2QqAc (accessed on 5 January 2022).

Noorani, A. G. 2019. *The RSS: A Menace to India*. New Delhi: LeftWord.

Organiser. 2020. 'Muslim Rashtriya Manch Demands Strict Action against Tablighi Jamaat'. 9 April. https://www.organiser.org/Encyc/2020/4/9/Muslim-Rashtriya-Manch-Demands-Strict-Action-Against-Tablighi-Jamaat.html (accessed on 9 April 2020).

Outlook Web Bureau. 2017. 'Animal Sacrifice During Bakrid Is Bad Practice Like Triple Talaq: RSS Muslim Wing'. *Outlook*, 30 August. https://www.outlookindia.com/website/story/animal-sacrifice-during-bakrid-is-bad-practice-like-triple-talaq-rss-muslim-wing/300987 (accessed on 5 January 2022).

Pachpore, V. 2016a. 'Muslim Rashtriya Manch: Rekindling Hindu Muslim Synergy'. *Organiser*, 27 June.

———. 2016b. 'Report: Eco-Friendly Eid'. *Organiser*, 19 September.

Pal, F. 2020. 'Why Muslims Join the Muslim Wing of the RSS'. *Contemporary South Asia* 28(3): 275–87. DOI: 10.1080/09584935.2020.1776219.

Patel, J., and M. Zubair. 2020. 'Video of Muslim Vendor's Unhygienic Handling of Fruits Falsely Linked with Spreading Coronavirus'. *AltNews*, 8 April https://www.altnews.in/viral-video-of-muslim-vendor-licking-fruits-is-from-mps-raisen-falsely-linked-with-spreading-coronavirus/ (accessed on 5 January 2022).

Pyara Hindustan. 2020. 'Muslim Nationalist Maulana Qasmi Great Speech on Anurag Thakur Owaisi CAA Shaheen Bagh Sharjeel Imam'. 29 January.

Raza, D. 2014. 'The Saffron Muslim'. *Hindustan Times*, 19 January.

Reghunath, L. G. 2014. 'The Believer: Swami Aseemanand's Radical Service to the Sangh'. *The Caravan*, 1 February. http://www.caravanmagazine.in/reportage/believer (accessed on 5 January 2022).

Reghunath, L. G. 2015. 'What Swami Aseemanand Had to Say about the Role of Senior Leaders from the RSS in Attacks Such As the Malegaon 2008 Blasts'. *The Caravan*, 25 June. https://caravanmagazine.in/vantage/how-senior-leaders-rss-aided-and-instigated-perpetrators-attacks-such-malegaon-2008-blasts (accessed on 5 January 2022).

Republic World. 2020. '"Pre-planned Attack on Indresh Kumar by Vadra-Congress Agents", Alleges Yaser Jilani'. 17 January. https://www.republicworld.com/india-news/politics/pre-planned-attack-on-indresh-kumar-by-vadra-cong-agents-remarks-yas.html (accessed on 5 January 2022).

Reyaz, M. 2019. 'Hindutva's Reach Out to Muslims in the 2014 Elections'. In *The Algebra of Warfare-Welfare: A Long View of India's 2014 Election*, edited by I. Ahmad and P. Kanungo, 242–71. New Delhi: Oxford University Press.

Roy Burman, J. J. 1996. 'Hindu–Muslim Syncretism in India'. *Economic and Political Weekly* 31(20): 1211–15.

Safvi, R. 2014. 'Understanding Ganga–Jamuni Tehzeeb: How Diverse Is the "Indian Multiculturalism"'. *DNA*, 15 June. https://www.dnaindia.com/analysis/standpoint-understanding-ganga-jamuni-tehzeeb-how-diverse-is-the-indian-multiculturalism-1995684 (accessed on 5 January 2022)

Saquib, S. 2016. 'As Politicians Made Ram "Hindu", Indian Muslims Lost Their "Maryada Purshotam"', The Wire, 11 October. https://thewire.in/communalism/politicians-made-ram-hindu-indias-muslims-lost-maryada-purshotam (accessed on 5 January 2022)

Savarkar, V. D. 1923. *Hindutva: Who Is a Hindu?* Bombay: S. S. Savarkar, 1969.

Scroll.in. 2018. 'Uttar Pradesh: RSS Affiliate Will Host Namaaz Along Saryu River in Ayodhya on July 12, Say Reports'. *Scroll.in*, 11 July. https://scroll.in/latest/886094/uttar-pradesh-rss-will-host-namaz-along-the-saryu-river-in-ayodhya-on-july-12-say-reports (accessed on 5 January 2022).

———. 2020. 'Citizenship Act Protestors Shout Slogans at RSS Muslim Wing's Pro-CAA Event, Detained'. *Scroll.in*, 16 January. https://scroll.in/latest/950110/citizenship-act-protestors-raise-slogans-at-rss-muslim-wings-pro-caa-event-detained (accessed on 5 January 2022).

Sinha, R. 2006. *Shri Guruji and Indian Muslims*. Nagpur: Suruchi Prakashan.

Swarajya. 2018. 'Ayodhya: Namaz on Saryu Bank Cancelled After Protests by Seers'. 12 July. https://swarajyamag.com/insta/ayodhya-namaz-on-saryu-bank-cancelled-after-protests-by-seers (accessed on 5 January 2022).

Times Now. 2017. 'RSS Leader Says Meat Is a Disease Post Iftar Party, Stokes Controversy'. https://www.timesnownews.com/india/video/rss-leader-indresh-kumar-prophet-mohammed-quran-iftar-ramzan/62471 (accessed on 5 January 2022).

Thachil, T. 2014. *Elite Parties, Poor Voters: How Social Services Win Votes In India*. Cambridge: Cambridge University Press.

The Print. 2018a. 'Muslim Affiliate of RSS Cuts Goat-shape Cakes Symbolising Sacrifice on Bakrid'. 23 August. https://theprint.in/politics/muslim-affiliate-of-rss-cuts-goat-shape-cakes-symbolising-sacrifice-on-bakrid/103973/ (accessed on 5 January 2022).

———. 2018b. 'RSS Ropes in Muslim Women to Push for Ram Temple in Ayodhya'. *The Print*, 6 February. https://theprint.in/report/rss-ropes-in-muslim-women-to-push-for-ram-temple-in-ayodhya/33901/ (accessed on 5 January 2022).

Vachani, L. 1993. *The Boy in the Branch*. Documentary. A Wide Eye Film for 'SOUTH', Channel 4 TV, UK.

———. 2002. *The Men in the Tree*. Documentary. Wide Eye Film.

———. 2017. 'The Babri Masjid Demolition Was Impossible without RSS Foot-Soldiers Like These'. *The Wire*, 8 December. https://thewire.in/communalism/rss-sangh-parivar-babri-masjid (accessed on 5 January 2022).

Varma, S., and J. Menon. 2010. 'Was There a Temple under the Babri Masjid? Reading the Archaeological 'Evidence'.' *Economic and Political Weekly* 45(50): 61–72.

Virmani, S. 2007. *Had-Anhad* (Bounded-Boundless). Documentary. www.kabirproject.org (accessed on 5 January 2022).

YouTube 2015. 'Indresh Kumar Playing Holi with Muslims'. https://www.youtube.com/watch?v=UKt10aMij7w (accessed on 5 January 2022).

VIOLENCE

11

VIOLENCE AFTER VIOLENCE
THE POLITICS OF NARRATIVES OVER THE DELHI POGROM*

Irfan Ahmad

It was not only human lives that were annihilated during the days of political violence unleashed in the northeastern localities of India's capital New Delhi in late February of 2020. Words, too, were/are being massacred in (mis)characterizing that violence. Analytically, at stake is this fundamental issue: without correct naming, we can understand neither the violence nor its past or future. It is not mere verbal gymnastics; naming is critical to the diagnosis of the problem as also to its prevention. Indeed on naming rests, in many ways, life as well as death. To safeguard the chastity of language, and my own ethical integrity, I will, therefore, not call the violence in Delhi a riot, as it was widely called then as well as subsequently. Let me name it what it truly is: a pogrom.

This essay anthropologically explores the crucial subject of the politics of naming over longue durée. In so doing, it puts forward an original argument (see later) that seldom has much of social science literature made, definitely not in the ways enunciated, executed, and demonstrated here. This argument is derived from as well as extends my larger monographic work on political violence (Ahmad forthcoming). Given the space limit and specific aims of this essay in the present volume, it is not feasible to lay bare full detail of my claim here. In part, this is also because the regnant doxa my argument is positioned against is not limited to a specific field of inquiry, discipline, or a set of authors. My contention instead pertains to the very ubiquitous nationalist epistemology to which almost every discipline, field, or most authors pledge their affiliation, albeit not identically (Ahmad 2011). This nationalist epistemology as a knowledge/power matrix with Hindu Orientalism as its lynchpin is, moreover, international. Academic knowledge in 'post-colonial' India is heavily indebted to and informed by what I call Hindu Orientalism, a set of practices and repertoires, which draws on, updates, and recasts historical European Orientalism (especially its branch of Indology) to organize intellectual production, circulation, and dissemination under the overarching banner of nationalism (Ahmad 2021a). Theoretically, nationalism is thus not an antithesis of Orientalism (Breckenridge and van der Veer 1993). As co-constitutive, they instead work as a pivot of knowledge in general, including about 'riots' and 'communal violence'. In the tradition of *Begriffsgeschichte* (rendered as 'the history of concepts' [Richter 1995][1] but used here in the frame of political anthropology; see later), an examination of concepts and terms at the heart of this knowledge – riot and communal violence are amongst them – is thus essential. Although the sources of my argument are complex, stemming as they do from by weaving many theoretical–methodological traditions together and conducted beyond the purview of a particular discipline, by the time readers have finished this essay, the merit of its argument will hopefully become evident.

This essay is arranged into three sections. In the first section, I outline my argument in critical engagement with recent literature on communal violence and riots, especially the work of Ward Berenschot and Sudha Pai and Sajjan Kumar. The next brief section presents an alternative genealogy of riots in India in a comparative framework. To illustrate the argument about the politics of naming acts of political violence as riots, I dwell on the 1989 Bhagalpur violence to show how and why it was termed a 'riot' despite credible evidence suggesting it was a fitting case of a pogrom. This argument is further illustrated through the detailed case study of the 2020 Delhi political violence in the third section. In the Conclusion, I summarise the essay's main argument. Here I also reflect on nationalism as a gigantic machine, which transforms humans qua humans into Chinese, Egyptian, Germans, Indians, or Italians such that visible in its mirror are only terrifying shadows of besieged humanity in a desperate quest of itself.

The Argument

In two steps, the argument unfolds as follows. First, there is a hidden politics that the name 'riot' performs. It institutes a false equalization that flattens the gigantic power inequality between Hindus and Muslims, and in a single stroke makes them both equally capable and responsible for riot, itself wrongly viewed as between two communities. This false equalization stands on a pervasive but incorrect idea that a 'balanced' approach entails condemning both minority and majority communalism, which supposedly mirror each other. Given this notion of resemblance, in the book *The Algebra of Warfare–Welfare*, I call this received wisdom the 'ditto theory'

VIOLENCE AFTER VIOLENCE

(Ahmad 2019). Ditto refers to resemblance. Its perfect example is a thread of tweets posted on 26 February by television journalist Rajdeep Sardesai: 'Political Hindutva vs radical Islam has created a volcanic situation [in Delhi].'[2] Sardesai's tweet was only a 'nuanced' version of the ruling Bharatiya Janata Party's (BJP) Amit Malviya, who, with no evidence, dubbed it a 'violent Islamic onslaught' (*The Telegraph* 2020). Views like Sardesai's inform academic Ashis Nandy's too. A journalist asked him a question that already contained its answer: 'How do you see Delhi riots from a Hindu versus Muslim perspective since it wasn't one-sided?' Pat came Nandy's reply: 'Yes, it was from both sides' (Tandon 2020).

To establish the terminological accuracy of pogrom is to simultaneously interrogate the descriptor 'riot' and examine the manifold assumptions of ditto theory that undergird it and from which the term riot emanates. My insistence on the (in)accuracy of the term 'riot' should not be taken as a mere linguistic squabble. Following the tradition of *Begriffsgeschichte* inquiry, my interest in 'riot' or 'pogrom' as terms is neither simply philological nor lexical. In my reading, concepts and categories not only index 'reality out there', they also organize, coordinate, condition, and direct reality. That is, concepts bear dynamic relationships to the political–cultural structure. It follows that concepts in themselves say very little unless we map out the wider horizon of the political in which they are deployed. Notably, concepts acquire their efficacy and potency conjunctionally, contrastively, and relationally. For instance, 'despotism' has one meaning when juxtaposed against 'liberty' and quite another when posited against 'anarchy' (Richter 1995, 10; Ahmad 2009a, 14). Aided by methodological–conceptual insights from *Begriffsgeschichte*, my second argument is that there is a prior theory of violence rooted in the composition and history of nationalism and almost independent of incidents of violence. An academic theory or argument about 'communal' or 'Hindu–Muslim' violence presupposes and partakes in that epistemology rather than simply collect 'data' about specific cases of violence as an 'objective' scholar or analyst. What, then, is that nationalist epistemology?

The first major source of what I am calling a nationalist epistemology is the Orientalist text written by the British soldier-writer William Watts, a member of the Calcutta Council who had participated in the 1757 Battle of Plassey. The defeat of the Nawab of Bengal Siraj-ud-Daulah in the battle led to the installing of colonial rule. To legitimize the British rule, Watts depicted Muslims as outsiders (as were the British themselves) and Hindus as 'native Indians'. He also described Muslims as 'fierce, oppressive, very rapacious' and Hindus as 'mild, subtle, frugal' (quoted in Sen 2002, 100). These descriptions were readily embraced by Hindu reformers and proto-nationalists like Ram Mohan Roy (Dhar 1987). Over a century later, the colonial scribe W. W. Hunter replayed this equation between Islam and 'fanaticism'

(Hunter 1871). The entwined notions of Muslims as outsider and fanatic equally informed discourses such as H. L. V. Derozio's (d. 1831), deemed as an advocate of 'liberal' nationalism, 'free thinking' (Mondal 2020, 21) and 'rationalist philosophy' (Banerjee 2014, 36). His poem 'The Enchantress of the Cave' echoes this British ideology.[3] Without locating it in the longer history as I have done here and writing about violence in post-independence India, Julia Eckert argues how India's laws assume a prior motive and theory of violence. This theory posits that violence by Muslims is premediated and emanates from religious 'fanaticism', while violence by Hindus is a 'natural reaction'. As an example, she refers to the alleged attacks by Muslims on the Sabarmati train at Godhra station, killing fifty-seven Hindus inside a coach in 2002. As the attackers were non-evidentially taken to be Muslims, they were tried under the new anti-terrorism law, whereas the subsequent 'retaliatory' violence against Muslims (which killed around 3,000) by Hindus were dealt with under the Indian Penal Code. To Eckert, 'there was the perception of a growing double standard in Indian law or of a *dual law* that judged Muslim violence and protest as terrorism and Hindu violence as "natural reaction" or spontaneous "outburst"' (Eckert 2012, 330, emphasis in original).

These two interconnected contentions laid out earlier – the ditto theory according to which both Hindus and Muslims are equally responsible for 'communal' violence in which the state acts as a neutral arbiter and that there is a prior theory of violence in which Islam is seen as a fanatic religion and Hinduism as tolerant and meek – set my argument apart from nearly all the dominant arguments about 'Hindu–Muslim violence'. Surveying the literature on communal violence, in his important book *Riot Politics*, Dutch anthropologist Berenschot classifies it under six separate approaches: primordialist, ideological, instrumentalist, constructivist, social–psychological, and relational. He calls his own approach relational, the distinction of which, however, remains as obfuscating as the assumed neat separation of the six approaches from one another. To state the obvious, they also overlap. Importantly, in philosophical terms, primordialist too is a social construction in the same way as social–psychological is no less ideological. In the frame of this essay's argument, elements of both ditto theory and the nationalist epistemology about the prior theory of violence variously inform all six approaches. Clearly, this claim needs to be demonstrated, which I cannot do here because of word constraints. What I can do is show how Berenschot's own text, written with reference to influential works on violence by Paul Brass, Ashutosh Varshney,[4] Paul Wilkinson, and others, displays it.

Justifying the choice of the word 'riot' to describe the 2002 anti-Muslim political violence in Gujarat, Berenschot says that he sees no differences between 'smaller outbursts of violence between Hindus and Muslims that take place every year' and 'the exceptional one' that the 2002 Gujarat one was because in either case 'riots are never fully spontaneous'. When examined closely, this argument implodes. In the same paragraph I have quoted from earlier, he says that 'spontaneity and unruliness' mark a riot. Logically, then, neither what he calls the normal yearly violence nor the exceptional one like the 2002 violence should be called riots. Instead of calling both political violence, he calls them riots against his own definition. The contradiction does not end there. He states that 'pogrom' and 'genocide' are 'rhetorical terms'; hence he would call the 2002 Gujarat political violence a 'riot', not a 'pogrom'. It is not that he is against the term 'pogrom' per se. Elsewhere, and unlike Veena Das,[5] he writes that the 1984 violence against Sikhs was 'essentially a ... pogrom'. This is a correct (and ethical) formulation. But what is the logic (or constraint) to withdraw the term 'pogrom' in the case of 2002 anti-Muslim violence in Gujarat? This would be justifiable if readers are told about the difference between the two. They are not. Astonishingly, while he finds 'pogrom' rhetorical, he shows no serious discomfort with the term 'terrorism', which Narendra Modi, the then chief minister of Gujarat, used to describe the burning of the train coach that killed over fifty Hindus.

As he proceeds, Berenschot's conceptual muddiness comes to its full glare. While he calls 'pogrom' and 'genocide' 'terms', for him 'riot' is a mere 'word'. What are the reasons to maintain this position? To me, the most important one appears to be an unawareness of *Begriffsgeschichte*, which distinguishes concepts and terms (following philosopher Martin Hollis [1994], I use them as interchangeable) from words (Richter 1995, 9). Additionally, I see no reason to use 'rhetorical' negatively as Berenschot does. Indeed, as an anti-positivist writer (and an underground poet), I value rhetoric. Furthermore, contrary to his own claim about 'riot' as a 'word' rather than a term, the latter is so critical that he organizes his whole book around it, so much so that he views India in terms of 'riot-affected' and 'riot-free' areas (Berenschot 2011, 9, 11, 19).

The evident analytical imbroglio in his text is on account of the fact that Berenschot subscribes to and enacts, inadvertently or otherwise, the ditto theory. It is no coincidence that to show anti-Muslim violence, as nationalist epistemology has, as a tale from 'both sides', he subtitled the book 'Hindu–Muslim Violence in the Indian State'. Early on, in the Preface, he tells readers: 'On 27 February 2002, a new round of horrific Hindu–Muslim violence erupted in Gujarat' (Berenschot 2011, viii). Mark the ditto theory at full play here in that it was an act of violence from both sides: Hindus and Muslims. Also notice the word 'erupt'. In the *Oxford English Dictionary*, 'erupt' as a verb signifies natural, unplanned processes such as volcano or coming of teeth through gums. As a noun, 'eruption' is 'the bursting forth (of water, fire, air, etc.) from natural or artificial limits'. Was the 2002 anti-Muslim violence of such a nature? The cited text in Berenschot's book, like its subtitle, however, betrays his own argument and data.

Berenschot's argument is that far from being spontaneous, riots are products of networks of actors 'engaged in the organization and instigation of violence'. And these networks comprising politicians, state authorities, the police, party workers, activists, and criminals 'shape the mobilization and instigation that take place during communal riots' (Berenschot 2011, 189). Notably, the networks are not formed during or just before the riots; they exist independently and long before the riots 'as everyday facilitation by political actors of the interaction between state institutions and citizens'. Here Berenschot insightfully identifies two mechanisms: brokerage and patronage, which, respectively, mean exchange of information and access to state resources between citizens and state institutions (Berenschot 2011, 11). The book's blurb tersely articulates the argument as follows: 'The author reveals how ... various types of rioters – from politicians, local criminals, Hindu-nationalist activists to neighbourhood leaders and police officials – organize and perpetrate violence.' Since riots are not spontaneous but, as he himself says, organized by prior networks and the agents in their organization and perpetration are not only civilians but police too, to use the term (not a word) 'riot' is grossly misleading. Yet he uses it. This is because, in addition to not undertaking a comparative examination of the term, for instance, between India and Western nation-states (as I do later), he participates in its specific usage to validate and reproduce the Indian nationalist epistemology.

The ditto theory as integral to nationalist epistemology appears in the Conclusion that begins by describing a meeting between two youth groups, Hindu and Muslim, in the Isanpur market of Ahmadabad where Berenschot did fifteen-month-long fieldwork after the 2002 pogrom. Accompanied by the ethnographer, the Hindu group led by Mahesh visited the market to meet Rajabhai, leader of the Muslim group. Mahesh introduces Rajabhai to the anthropologist as 'a famous local Muslim don'. In this brief encounter, Mahesh tells Berenschot that 'during the riots he [Rajabhai] was very active attacking us Hindus'. Apparently, Rajabhai approves of Mahesh's comment, adding that they nonetheless continue to be brothers. Berenschot then writes: 'In this book I have focused on the processes of mobilization and instigation through which people like Rajabhai and Mahesh end up in clashing mobs' (Berenschot 2011, 187). Needless to say, the figures of Mahesh and Rajabhai here serve as representatives of Hindus and Muslims engaged equally in communal violence. This ethnographic staging of the encounter, however, raises several questions: does Rajabhai have the same political power as Hindu politicians possess in Ahmadabad or Gujarat? Does he or his community members exercise the same influence in the judiciary, bureaucracy, media, the police, and other departments? Indeed, are these state institutions not biased against and hostile to Muslims? Are the socio-economic and educational capitals of Mahesh and Rajabhai as metonyms of Hindu and Muslim communities of the same level and value? Are not Muslims, as shown by the government-appointed Sachar Committee (absent from Berenschot's index; see Hansen 2007), heavily marginalized in nearly every vital domain of life, most significantly in the economy, government services, and police force?

The portrayal of Mahesh and Rajabhai as figures representing Hindus and Muslims with equal power, resources, and influences thus violates the reality observed by the ethnographer himself to end up paying homage to the ditto theory at the core of nationalist epistemology. A telling illustration of this nationalist epistemology is Berenschot's uncritical embrace of the term 'post-Godhra violence'. Recall the notions of Islam as a fanatic and of Hinduism as a tolerant religion. Recall too the notions operative among state agencies (broached through Eckert's work) that violence by Muslims emanates from religious 'fanaticism' and is premediated, while violence by Hindus is simply a 'natural reaction'. My point is that the unqualified usage of 'post-Godhra violence' amounts to replaying Modi's nationalist justification of the anti-Muslim pogrom as a reaction to the Godhra violence for which Muslims were non-evidentially held responsible but the truth of which 'we shall never know' (Sundar 2004, 153).

My critique of Berenschot, hence the distinction of my argument, also stands valid vis-à-vis *Everyday Communalism: Riots in Uttar Pradesh*, co-authored by Sudha Pai and Sajjan Kumar. Obviously, these two works are different. While Berenschot describes his approach as 'relational', Pai and Kumar call theirs 'constructivist'. Unlike Berenschot's work which stands in the classical tradition of long-term sustained ethnographic work in one location, Pai and Kumar's work is based on short-term fieldwork in four districts of Uttar Pradesh (UP): two each in east (Gorakhpur and Mau) and west UP (Muzaffarnagar and Shamli). Within each district, they selected many villages and towns where 'riots were severe'. The similarity is that both focus on a specific state: Gujarat and UP. Temporally, Pai and Kumar focus on developments since the 2000s marking 'the resurgence ... of Hindu–Muslim riots' (Pai and Kumar 2018, 1, 23, 31, 33). Taking this resurgence as 'a "new" saffron wave', their principal proposition, after Paul Brass's argument about an 'institutionalized riot system', is that there is 'an institutionalized everyday communalism (IEC)'.

Specific to their 'model' is the point that riots are no longer urban as they have spread to villages too. They also note the increasing participation of Other Backward Classes and Dalits in Hindutva politics and riots. Important to this new wave is the propagation of 'Subaltern'/'non-Brahminical Hindutva' and the orchestration of low-intensity, local (not pan-state) riots. The term 'subaltern Hindutva' requires some comments. From a social science framework, using 'subaltern' as a noun is misleading, even an act of symbolic violence. An appropriate word is its verbal form, 'subalternated', which shows the process leading to the condition of being a subaltern. The term 'subaltern Hindutva' also reminds me of 'subaltern fascism' used by Kannan Srinivasan in a volume edited by Jairus Banaji that comparatively discusses fascism in India and Europe (Srinivasan 2013, 99–34). My point is that an engagement with Srinivasan and Banaji, none of whom figures in the book, would have made their argument about IEC only stronger had they clarified why they preferred to call it 'subaltern Hindutva', not 'subaltern fascism'. This becomes even more important, for fascism is nothing else but a face and form of nationalism, the assumed observe of which, communalism, is the analytical core of their book. Aiming to acquire power through religious polarization, the engine of the IEC, Pai and Kumar observe, is the Rashtriya Swyamsevak Sangh (RSS) and BJP. Why do the RSS and BJP want to acquire power, however? They want power 'to establish a permanent anti-Muslim bias as the platform of contemporary "Hindutva" and legitimize it as normal in the eyes of the people' (Pai and Kumar 2018, 2–3, 5, 26, 249).

For the purpose of this essay, the terms 'riots' and 'communalism' both remain under-examined, even unexamined, especially the former. This problem is only compounded because of the book's focus on the 'new' wave but without a thorough relation made with 'riots' prior to the 2000s. The non-scholarly use of the term 'riot' thus is unable to account for the 1980 anti-Muslim Moradabad political violence in which the Provincial Armed Constabulary opened fire on 40,000 Muslims while they were offering the 'Eid prayer'. Journalist M. J. Akbar called it 'a cold-blooded massacre of Muslims', pointing out especially that it was not 'a Hindu–Muslim riot'. Yet, in the same chapter, he called that violence a 'riot' (Akbar 1988, 33). But Akbar is no academic. Integral to academic work are standards of analytical consistency and terminological coherence, which are simply absent here. Not only do Pai and Kumar describe the so-called low-intensity, local political violence as riots, they also take, as does Berenschot, the 2002 Gujarat pogrom as 'riots' (Pai and Kumar 2018, 2).

The case of the Moradabad massacre unsettles the claim of Pai and Kumar on two counts. First, they take the Congress party as 'secular' and BJP–RSS as 'communal' (more on this later). It is because of this sealed separation between the two that they see the rise of 'communal mobilization' as an upshot of the 'collapse' of the Congress in the 1980s (Pai and Kumar 2018, 14; cf. Ahmad 2016). At that time of the Moradabad massacre, the party in power was, however, the Congress, not the BJP. Likewise, agents inflicting violence on Muslims were not civilian rioters but the police. In short, what they call 'riot' is beyond party politics, and its actors are not only civilians but also the state functionaries.

As for the term 'communalism', their treatment of it is theoretically unsatisfactory, if not thoroughly impoverished. A thoughtful discussion on communalism and nationalism, when it concerns Muslims as Pai and Kumar's book does, has to account for interventions, inter alias, by Ayesha Jalal and Gyanendra Pandey. Both Jalal and Pandey appear in the text; however, the specific writings by them that squarely address this issue are absent (Pandey 1999; Jalal 1997). Jalal and Pandey differently show that communalism is not the obverse of nationalism but a category invented by the latter to quarantine itself and stigmatize the politics enacted by Muslims. Viewed from this perspective, using the term 'communalism' is itself a problem rather than a solution. Furthermore, Pai and Kumar conduct no theoretical inquiry into 'nationalism' (see the Conclusion on this) whose signatures are 'riots' and 'communal violence'. Without going into this matter any further, a close reader cannot but notice everyday communalism in the very prose of Pai and Kumar. Like several others, they see north India, including UP, 'as the Hindi heartland' (Pai and Kumar 2018, 10). Is there no language other than Hindi there? And if north India has been a key centre of Urdu, why not call it the Hindi–Urdu heartland instead? Culturally, language is as important as the party politics and electoral arithmetic with which Pai and Kumar are more concerned. My point about Urdu is that contrary to the popular idea of language as a bare vehicle of thought, language is also thought. This everyday communalism is differently present in Berenschot too. Taking India/Gujarat as Hindu, in his prose are phrases such as 'Muslim locality' and 'Muslim-dominated localities', but logical analogous description like 'Hindu-dominated localities' is almost non-existent (Berenschot 2011, 15). The description of north India as the Hindi heartland belongs to the nationalist epistemology. In order to grasp the working of that nationalist epistemology vis-à-vis the phenomena of "riots" and their understandings, we begin where it all started: British colonial politics.

Genealogy of 'Riots' in India

Like 'communalism', 'riot' in India has a peculiar meaning. Outside India, a riot generally refers to unplanned violence by civilians against the state or its symbols or overt allies. To sociologist Loukia Kotronaki and political scientist Seraphim Seferiades, a common feature of all riots is the 'unexpected, convulsive nature of their outburst'.[6] David Waddington, a British sociologist of riots, maintains that rioters are civilians, and their violence is directed primarily against the police and only rarely against the public (Waddington 2015, 423).

Consider three recent examples of riots in Western countries: the 2005 riots in France (BBC News 2005; Fassin 2006), the 2008 riots in Greece (Kaplan 2018), and the 2011 riots in England (Somaiya and Burns 2011). In all these cases, riots were sparked by the killing of youth by the police. For instance, in Greece, it was the killing in Athens of a fifteen-year-old student, Alexis Grigoropoulos, by the police that led to three weeks of rioting. In England, it was the murder by the London Police of Mark Duggan, a twenty-nine-year-old African-Caribbean man, which ignited riots that spread to a number of cities. In none of these cases did the police aid, join, and side with the rioters.

In contrast, riot in India has historically been viewed between two communities. As historian Gyanendra Pandey observes, British colonialism considered itself a neutral ruler whose job was to maintain law and order by preventing clashes between myriad not-yet-modern communities, especially the Hindus and Muslims (Pandey 1989, 132–68). In the eyes of the British, Hindus and Muslims clashed against each other because of their respective religions and primordial sentiments. In other words, there was an instinctive hostility between Hindus and Muslims which defied any political rationality or the tenet of the so-called reason. In this theory, undoubtedly, there was justification for colonial rule. Left to themselves, so went the assumption, these communities would endlessly fight against each other, and British rule alone could guarantee peace. That is, the British state was neither the cause of nor a party to the so-called Hindu–Muslim violence but only its spectator or regulator.

With the anti-colonial movement, especially early twentieth century onwards, the nationalist movement too reproduced colonial assumptions. This manifested itself, for one, in the notion of Hindu-versus-Muslim communalism, the two mirroring each other. However, there was another assumption that nearly encompassed everything else: while Muslims had communalism, Hindus had only nationalism. Pandey demonstrates this, again so tersely, in the ubiquitous category of 'nationalist Muslims', but there is the stark absence of its logical correlate: 'nationalist Hindus' (Pandey 1999). By virtue of merely being Hindu, every Hindu was naturally deemed to be a nationalist, whereas Muslims were taken, again naturally, as communal, unless they proved that they were loyal and obedient nationalists.

After India's independence, the 'post-colonial' state stuck to the colonial theory of Hindus and Muslims fighting against each other. This theory allowed the state to claim its neutrality and absolve itself of any role in generating or sustaining the 'Hindu–Muslim' conflict. In short, the ditto theory, traceable to colonialism and readily embraced and continued by the independent state, informs all accounts of communal violence since 1947.

The ditto theory – that it is not the state but the two communities that are (equally) responsible for Hindu–Muslim violence – prevailed well into the 1980s, a period which scholars recognize as marking a new phase of 'riots'. The 1989 Bhagalpur 'riot' best exemplifies this theory. Despite enough evidence of the complicity of the police and civil administration in the large-scale killings, it was called, and continues to be called, a riot. That rioting does not include only killing, looting properties, and pillaging sources of livelihood but also destroying its evidence is a separate, though connected, matter.

The most conservative figure of the people killed in the Bhagalpur violence, as documented in its 1990 report *Bhagalpur Riots* by the People's Union for Democratic Rights (PUDR) is 1,000. Muslims formed 93 per cent of these victims (People's Union for Democratic Rights 1990). A direct outcome of the Ramshila and Shilanyas processions (Chopra and Jha 2014) taken by the Sangh Parivar – a collective term used for India's anti-minorities Hindu right-wing coalition – to build a Ram temple in place of the sixteenth-century Babri Masjid (mosque) in Ayodhya, the pogrom was not limited to the city; it engulfed more than a dozen villages. Killing and looting lasted not for days or weeks but for months. Begun on 24 October 1989, the pogrom continued well into the new year. For the first time, as a teenage student at BN College, Patna University, Bihar, and living in Patna's Sultanganj *mohalla* (area), I experienced curfew and what it meant to live in terror in the wake of the Ayodhya campaign that later in 1992 illegally destroyed the Babri Masjid. I will return to this biographical aspect at the end.

The then chief minister of Bihar expressed the ditto theory as follows. In a statement (Pandey 1992, 38) to reinstate normalcy, he spoke of the destruction of religious places of both Hindus and Muslims even as there was not a shred of evidence of any damage caused to a Hindu shrine or temple. Likewise, the documentary on the Bhagalpur violence by journalist Nalini Singh, shown on national television Doordarshan, struck equivalence between Jamalpur and Logain, sites of violence against Hindus and Muslims, respectively. Four persons were killed in Jamalpur, while 110 people were massacred in Logain. Criticizing the glaring biases in her documentary, Abdur Rahim, a professor of media studies at Osmania University, later noted how Singh showed Hindus as exceptionally 'tolerant' (Rahim 1991, 7).

Even the PUDR report replayed the ditto theory when, contrary to details in its own findings, it described the Bhagalpur violence as 'riots' which 'broke out between Hindus and Muslims'.[7] The descriptor 'riot' was an ideological imposition because the people that the PUDR spoke to did not call it so. Thus, one seventy-year-old called it 'qatl-e-ām' (massacre), stating pointedly: 'nowadays the police kill and loot' (PUDR 1990, 38).

The 2020 Delhi Pogrom in Its Details

More than thirty years after the Bhagalpur pogrom, Sardesai, the 'liberal' television journalist – I wonder if he still calls himself secular – termed the Delhi violence a riot. In the tweets mentioned earlier, he wrote: 'This is a Hindu Muslim riot in which BOTH communities have been involved in terrible acts of violence.' Sardesai's capitalization of 'both' stems less from his purported knowledge of the 'ground reality' of Delhi and more from the language of the majoritarian politics even the PUDR is beholden to. He added: 'Tough to say who "started" it.'

Think about the mammoth power inequality between Hindus and Muslims, and the open incitements of anti-Muslim violence by leaders of the BJP. If the certitude in Sardesai's tweet that there was 'a Hindu Muslim riot' in which both were equally involved was not innocent, so was his doubt about who initiated what he called a riot. In the same thread, Sardesai posted another tweet: 'Political Hindutva vs radical Islam has created a volcanic situation.' Note the bizarre logic of equivalence. What evidence did Sardesai have about his insidious invention of radical Islam? Even within this invention aimed to hurriedly score equalization, there was a stark asymmetry. The corresponding phrase for political Hindutva is political Islamism, not radical Islam. Thus, it should be radical Hinduism versus radical Islam. By not using political or Islamism in the case of Muslims, Sardesai made *Islam* as a faith and tradition radical, whereas he analytically protected Hinduism from Hindutva. The next sentence of the same tweet[8] took the equivalence to a laughable extreme: 'The slightest trigger, be it Shaheen Bagh like road protest or incendiary speech, is enough to lead to an eruption [of riot].' If by an incendiary speech he meant that of Anurag Thakur, a junior minister in the country's federal government, or Kapil Mishra, a former BJP lawmaker in Delhi, notice the unjust move in which the women-led peaceful protest of a disempowered collectivity in Shaheen Bagh[9] was put on the same plane as anti-Muslim hate speech by male chauvinist members of a ruling party wielding power with almost no accountability.

On 28 February, Ashutosh, a journalist and former politician from the Aam Aadmi Party (AAP) who ran the news portal *SatyaHindi.com*, did a show (Aashutosh 2020) to reveal the 'truth of riot' (*danga*) in India. He cited many examples of violence – Ahmedabad, Aligarh, Bhagalpur, Hashimpura, Maliyana, Gujarat (2002), and Muzaffarnagar (2013). Unlike the 1984 Delhi violence, which he rightly called the 'massacre of Sikhs', he made no mention of Muslims as he used the term *danga* for violence in all the above-mentioned places. He told his viewers that his inquiry had made it clear that 'the conflict between both communities has deepened' and 'both have prepared themselves' for a 'war' (*jañg*). Though once he issued a disclaimer that he blamed neither Hindus nor Muslims, the example of 'preparation' he gave concerned only Muslims.

Ashutosh referred to Tahir Hussain, a local Muslim leader belonging to the AAP, at whose house petrol bombs were allegedly found. He also mentioned Shahrukh, who brandished a pistol at a constable. He did not state the source of his information, let alone judge its veracity. For instance, *Newslaundry* ran a remarkably informed piece interrogating the evidence in framing Hussain (Sharma 2020). Exonerating the police of any role in its enactment, Ashutosh not only scripted the 'riot' as between Hindus and Muslims but, through his select examples, he showed Muslims as aggressors and Hindus as victims. Such is 'the truth' behind Ashutosh's show and his news portal, which in English means TruthHindi.com. Can one say that it is truth worshipping power rather than questioning it, even gently?

This is not to say that all Muslims are saints, though one wishes they were. Of course, they too took to killing. Like the Bhagalpur pogrom in which 93 per cent of those killed were Muslim and 7 per cent were Hindu, in the Delhi pogrom too, there were Hindus among the killed. In a city where Muslims are 12 per cent of the population, they constitute 71 per cent of the victims (Ellis-Petersen and Rahman 2020). Beyond the dehumanizing ethnic counting of the victims, I submit that the violence in Delhi, considering all its asymmetrical power configurations – organization, goals, role of the administration, and the mainstream media – qualifies as a pogrom on three counts. First, as noted earlier, unlike a riot the key feature of which is its *convulsive* nature, what happened in Delhi was *purposive* and in no way spontaneous. This distinction between convulsive and purposive is an important one to distinguish riot from pogrom. However, the two should also be analysed as spectrum and continuum because something that began as a riot can potentially turn into a pogrom. What is more, the description 'spontaneous' may not be intrinsic to the phenomenon itself but also can and often be a strategic label to present what is planned to appear as spontaneous. This label, especially in relation to the 'mob' violence, shields perpetrators from identification and, eventually, punishment. To give a historical example, as noted by historian Leonidas Hill, Joseph Goebbels and Adolph Hitler did their best to make the 1938 anti-Jewish pogrom 'appear spontaneous' (Hill 1996, 103, 107). If I seem to belabour this point too much, it is also because I want to lay Yogendra Yadav's claim to rest. Calling the Delhi violence 'riot', Yadav, psephologist-turned-politician, described it as 'auto-triggered' (Yadav 2020). This seems nothing else but pure mysticism, Yadav-style.

Paul Brass, an outstanding scholar of political violence in India, has busted the myth of spontaneity and instead called communal violence 'institutionalized riot systems' (Brass 1996, 12ff). What turns a riot into a pogrom, he writes, is 'when it can be proved that the police and the state authorities more broadly are directly implicated in a "riot" in which one community provides the principal or sole victims …'(Brass 1996, 26). Since the killing does not happen in a vacuum, Brass stresses to account for the 'atmosphere' that precedes a pogrom (Brass 1996, 8–9). The atmosphere is not simply a precondition but a cause of it. This precisely is the second reason to name the violence in Delhi a 'pogrom'.

A pogromist atmosphere existed well before the actual pogrom. The proximate atmosphere was the countrywide democratic, peaceful protest against India's new citizenship law[10] that many justifiably criticized for being discriminating against Muslims. Having first ignored resistance, the BJP, in league with its allies in various sectors of the polity, began to portray it as 'anti-national'. In the right-wing dictionary, anti-national does not mean socio-economic policies that cripple the most ordinary people but the unfounded, inimical notion of being 'pro-Pakistan', directed mainly against Indian Muslims. Not just junior functionaries but the top brass of the party-government, including Prime Minister Narendra Modi and Home Minister Amit Shah, themselves hinted at the protests being 'anti-India and pro-Pakistan' (Subrahmaniam 2020).

Anurag Thakur, the federal minister, displayed this politics of enmity when in an election rally earlier he had openly incited the crowd to kill Muslims by raising the slogan, 'Dēsh kē ghaddārōñ kō/gōlī mārō sālōñ kō' (which translates close to 'shoot the bastards/the nation's traitors') (Basu 2020). It was in the wake of Thakur's incitement that a seventeen-year-old Hindutva activist, linked to many rabidly Islamophobic elements, went to the Jamia Millia Islamia (a central university in New Delhi) to terrorize the protesters there. He brandished his pistol and opened fire at the crowd, prancing insouciantly towards the police, who simply watched on. Soon, Kapil Gujjar, a supporter of Modi, barged into the protest camp in Shaheen Bagh and fired shots. Gujjar proclaimed that 'only Hindus will prevail' in India (Sikander 2020).

Barely 15 miles away from Delhi, in Ghaziabad, Yati Narsinghanand, the head priest of the Devi Temple, made umpteen violent statements to eliminate Muslims as well as Islam. Narsinghanand is a leader of the Hindu Swabhiman and president of the Akhil Bharatiya Sant Parishad. Maintaining that 'Islam must be removed to save humanity', he spoke of a 'final war against Muslims' (Menon 2020). He also applauded Kapil Mishra, the former BJP lawmaker, who alone 'stood for Hindus against Jihadis in Delhi'.

Narsinghanand praised Mishra for his speech in which he, standing beside the deputy commissioner of police, decried the anti-citizenship law protestors and threatened that if the police did not end the protest, he and his men would do so (Bal 2020). That Mishra made this speech in the presence of the commissioner, who rather than act against him obediently listened to him, was revealing. A day after Mishra's speech, the pogrom began. When the distraught people called the emergency 100 number, it went unanswered for up to three days and nights (*The Wire* 2020). The absence of the police in the theatre of violence was likewise noticeable. This was one of the key findings of a report (*The Wire* 2020) based on visits to violence-affected areas, including Bhajanpura,

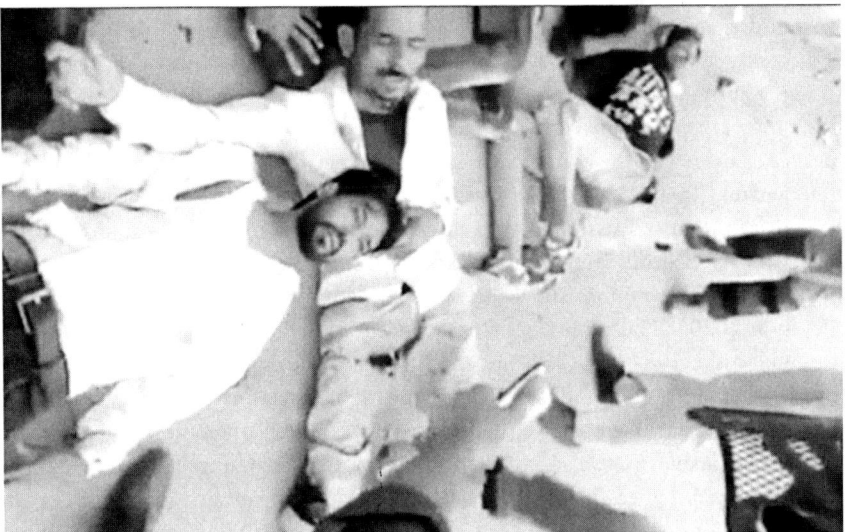

Figure 11.1 Screengrab of a viral video during the Delhi pogrom showing five severely injured men lying on a street while being beaten by men in police uniform and forced to sing the national anthem. All the injured were Muslim; one of them, Faizan, died on 27 February, two days after the incident.

Source: The Polis Project, https://thepolisproject.com/violence-after-violence-the-politics-of-narratives-over-the-delhi-pogrom/#.XvMnkudS-Uk (accessed on 13 August 2021).

Chand Bagh, Gokulpuri, Chaman Park, Shiv Vihar, Main Mustafabad, Bhagirathi Vihar, and Brijpuri.

When and where present, the police, instead of acting against the killers, attacked the unarmed, helpless people. For instance, the police kicked nine-month-pregnant Parveena in her stomach, beat her with a baton, and insultingly hurled the following: 'Yē lō āzādī' (Here, take your freedom; *The Patriot* 2020). This was the police's 'revenge' against the protestors (see Figure 11.1), many of whom had raised slogans for freedom – such as from discriminatory policies and an unjust system as well as for fairness, equality, dignity, and justice. The complicity and culpability of the police were further evident from the brazen ways in which the mob, while coercing Muslims to chant the Hindu slogans, for instance, of Jai Shri Ram, shouted, 'long live the police' and 'it is our administration, they are with us, it is our law' (*The Patriot* 2020). To wipe out evidence, the police also broke CCTV cameras (Kamdar 2020). Right in front of the police station in Bhajanpura, a Muslim *mazār* (mausoleum–shrine) of a saint was set on fire (Mishra 2020).

Third, a key aspect of a pogrom is that its target is not an individual or an undefined collectivity but a specific group. While the *Oxford English Dictionary* defines pogrom as 'an organized massacre ... of any body or class',[11] according to the *Webster's Third New International Dictionary*, it is 'an organized massacre and looting of helpless people, usually with the connivance of officials, specifically, such a massacre of Jews' (Bergmann 2003, 352). Linguistically Russian and derived from the anti-Jewish violence in Tsarist Russia, pogrom is now applicable to many a context. To the definitions of pogrom targeted at a class and people, Brass adds 'community'.

Many credible reports show the targeted nature of attacks on Muslims (Ellis-Petersen 2020). The report cited earlier (*The Wire* 2020) noted that the attack resembled the 1984 anti-Sikh and the 2002 anti-Muslim Gujarat pogroms: 'The death toll is far less, but the targeting is truly frightening – where one shop is burnt, but the two adjacent shops on either side are not.' Along with homes and businesses, places of worship were also attacked, some more devastatingly than others. The religious character of the pogrom and its sheer scale are also evident from the destruction or desecration of over ten mosques, a shrine, and a cemetery. Leaving everything behind, when a single mother managed to flee a site of carnage with her children, the violent mob chased her threatening: 'we will catch you and make you give birth to Shri Ram's progeny' (*The Patriot* 2020). During the nights of terror, slogans of Jai Shri Ram (Hail Lord Ram) and 'Dēsh sē nikālō sālōñ kō, ghaddārōñ kō' (Throw out the bastards, the traitors from the country) reverberated throughout. It is evident how the mob in cahoots with the police killed specific people, destroyed their properties and sources of livelihood (see Figure 11.2) – key elements of pogrom.

Figure 11.2 A handicraft shop gutted during the anti-Muslim pogrom in New Delhi, late February 2020

Source: The Polis Project, https://www.thepolisproject.com/read/violence-after-violence-the-politics-of-narratives-over-the-delhi-pogrom/ (accessed on 13 December 2021).

Furthermore, the targeting was distinctly religious in a double sense. Chanting religious slogans, the attackers presented themselves as religious. Likewise, they targeted the victims by identifying them by their religion, including by hurling slur words like *katuyē* (the circumcised; *The Patriot* 2020). When Susheel Manav of *Janchowk*, a Hindi news portal, went to Maujpur to report, the Hindu crowd asked him why he visited the Hindu area, and not the area of *mullē*, an insulting word for Muslims. Soon the crowd began to beat him. The beating continued even after he showed his identity cards with his Hindu name. As the armed crowd thickened, one person took out his pistol, loaded it, and aimed at Manav. A terrified Manav kept shouting, 'Like you all, I am also a Hindu.' The assault, however, continued until he was stripped to determine if he was a Hindu – uncircumcised. Having ascertained his Hindu identity, he was allowed to leave at the instruction of the police, which had by then reached the scene. In Manav's own account (Manav 2020), the attackers did not flee on seeing the police. They calmly stayed put there, joyfully conversing with one another.

Conclusion: Dwarfed Humans

Recall the appeal for normalcy by Bihar's chief minister after the 1989 Bhagalpur pogrom. Without any evidence, he had spoken of the destruction caused to religious places of both Hindus and Muslims. To enact the same logic of equalization at the heart of the ditto theory, which this essay has hopefully deconstructed with evidence and an alternative analysis, in the 2020 Delhi pogrom, the BJP-aligned media spread the news of a temple 'forcibly occupied' and 'attacked' by 'frenzied Islamist fundamentalists'. Thanks to the investigative journalism by *Newslaundry*, the fakeness of this propaganda was brought to the public attention (Tiwari and Kumar 2020).

The principal aim of this essay was to examine the pervasive but unsustainable notions of Hindu–Muslim violence as 'spontaneous'. In contrast, I have argued why the violence in Delhi should be called a 'pogrom', not a 'riot'. Our failure to use accurate labels amounts to our participation in the continuation of analytical–symbolic violence after the acts and facts of bodily violence – the sheer annihilation of innocent lives. My choice of Bhagalpur and Delhi as case studies is intentional. Against the widespread view of the 'secular' Congress party under which the Bhagalpur pogrom happened and the communal BJP, which presided over the 2020 Delhi pogrom, I demonstrated how pogroms as a phenomenon operate beyond party politics conducted under a nationalist and nationalizing consensus. In marked contrast to most writings in academia as well as outside, my fundamental argument is that there is a prior theory of violence rooted in the structure, thought, and history of nationalism which takes Islam as fanatic and Hinduism as meek and tolerant. Rather than examine this prior theory through 'facts' and details of political violence on the ground, the latter is adjusted or molested to maintain and prolong the former. Following Talal Asad, I have examined the nationalist epistemology that undergirds explanations of political violence, including the terms and concepts utilized therein, 'through its shadows' (Asad 2003, 16). That is, how the scholar Ashis Nandy who has written a book on the illegitimacy of nationalism (Nandy 1994) too subscribes to nationalism in his explanation of the 2020 anti-Muslim political violence in Delhi, calling it a riot rather than a pogrom and describing it as having taken place 'from both sides'. This essay also challenges another dualism. In an article, Sushant Sareen of the Observer Research Foundation seemed to suggest, as did Yadav earlier, that the riot in Delhi simply 'broke out' (Sareen 2020). Replaying the ditto theory, he also dismissed the truth outright, saying it depended on which of the two sides one stood. In contrast, my submission is that the truth, if bravely searched for, stands above the dualism of two sides, beyond which Sareen is too scared to see.

Finally, considering the historical trajectories of most nation-states, I am convinced that truth will remain a momentous casualty, and bloodshed almost an everyday reality, as long as we do not think beyond the dark prison house that nationalism – with its constitutive xenophobia and internal enmity – has become. In the deadly game of nationalism routinely played out between us-nationalists and them-anti-nationals, between us-Hindus and them-Muslims, let us pause to ask if there are any humans among us.

After the Bhagalpur pogrom, I visited the Urdu bookshops in Patna's Sabzi Bagh to see a book of poems by Manāzir Āshiq Hargānvi, a professor at Bhagalpur University. Titled *Āñkhōñ dēkhī* (Eye-witnessed), it was a tale in free verse of violence visited upon Bhagalpur.

> *Ādmī bahut hī bavna hō chuka haiy*
> *Apnī lambāī ka jūta ehsās bī bāqī nahiñ bacha*
> Humans have become so dwarfed,
> Even the illusion of tallness is no more.

Deadly nationalism transforms humans into nationalized machines in figures such as Indians, Germans, Italians, and Chinese. And visible in its mirror are only terrifying shadows of a bruised humanity desperately in search of itself. Is it too much to say, then, that the dwarfed humans that Hargānvi poetically alluded to are the murderous products of ethnifying nationalism? It is too little, perhaps.

Anguished by the recurring 'riots', Munawwar Rana (1952), another noted Urdu poet, took them as integral to the very breathing ambience to the extent that even the gush of fragrance in the atmosphere seemed to be imbued with the smell of camphor, which in Urdu is called *kāfūr*. Rhyming as *kāfūr* does with Bhagalpur, Rana took the latter as the paradigm of the condition of almost every city in India, if not the whole world.

> *Har ēk khushbū ka jhoṅka ab hamēṅ kāfūr lagta haiy*
> *Kisī bhī shahr sē guzrēṅ vō bhāgalpūr lagta haiy*
>
> To us, even the gush of fragrance now seems like camphor
> Whichever city we pass by, it appears like Bhagalpur.[12]

Clearly, Bhagalpur as the paradigm of political violence took place before the pogrom of Bhagalpur too, as it did afterwards, for instance, in the state-mediated violence of Delhi in 2020. Though no one exactly knows the precise contours of the future, the notion of paradigm as broached by Giorgio Agamben[13] allows us, at least in part, to have a sense of the time ahead.

Notes

* This essay is a significantly revised version of the original published by The Polis Project on 28 March 2020. See https://www.thepolisproject.com/read/violence-after-violence-the-politics-of-narratives-over-the-delhi-pogrom/ (accessed on 1 December 2020).

1 A key figure in the development of Begriffsgeschicbte is Reinhart Koselleck; see his *Futures Past: On the Semantics of Historical Time* (2004 [1978]).

2 Sardesai later deleted his tweet, but a screenshot of it was tweeted by Mohammad Reyaz, a professor at Kolkata's Aliah University. @journalistreyaz, 'So @sardesairajdeep Finally Woke up on the Fourth Day and after a Day-Long Tour has Declared that "Tough to Say Who Started it". He further Believes that "Political Hindutva Vs radical Islam has created a Volcanic Situation,"' *Twitter*, 26 February 2020, https://twitter.com/journalistreyaz/status/1232731054517215234 (accessed on 17 January 2022).

3 The poem is cited in Akbar (2021).

4 For a critique of Varshney, see Ahmad (2009b).

5 In her many writings spanning a decade, Das consistently has called the 1984 anti-Sikh violence 'riots'. See Das (1990, 345, 347ff., 1995a, 22, 1995b).

6 Cited in Waddington (2015, 423).

7 This is how the blurb of the report titled *Bhagalpur Riots* by PUDR (1990) describes the anti-Muslim violence.

8 See @journalistreyaz cited earlier.

9 Name of a locality in New Delhi near Jamia Millia Islamia University, Shaheen Bagh, where a women-led protest against the discriminatory Citizenship Amendment Act continued for months, came to signify the countrywide protest against the federal regime

presided over by BJP's Narendra Modi. On the importance of Shaheen Bagh protest as a phenomenon, see Ahmad (2020b, 2021b, 2021c).

10 On the Citizenship Amendment Act, see Ahmad (2020a).
11 Cited in Bergmann (2003, 352).
12 This translation from Urdu, as also the earlier ones, is mine. For rules of transliteration from Urdu/Hindi, readers can see Ahmad (2017).
13 The notion of paradigm – neither inductive nor deductive – appears in many of Agamben's works. For instance, see Agamben (1998, 2009).

References

Aashutosh. 2020. 'Ankit Sharma ko Kyun Maare Gaye 400 Bar Chaku?' *SatyaHindi.com*, 28 February. https://www.satyahindi.com/videos/ankit-sharma-stabbed-400-times-in-delhi-riots-jafrabad-107796.html (accessed on 17 January 2022).

Agamben, G. 1998. *Homo Sacer: Sovereign Power and Bare Life*, trans. Daniel Heller-Roazen. Stanford: Stanford University Press.

———. 2009. *The Signature of All Things: On Method*, trans. Luca D'Isanto with Kevin Attell. New York: Zone.

Ahmad, I. 2009a. *Islamism and Democracy in India: The Transformation of Jamaat-e-Islami*. Princeton: Princeton University Press.

———. 2009b. 'The Secular State and the Geography of Radicalism'. *Economic and Political Weekly* 44 (23): 33–38.

———. 2011. 'Anthropology of Nationalism, Nationalism of Anthropology: Notes on the Idea and Practice of Indian Anthropology'. Paper at the Anthropology Colloquium, Macquarie University, Sydney, Australia.

———. 2016. 'Between Mourning and Melancholia: Religion and Politics in Modern India'. *Journal of Religious and Political Practice* 2(3): 348–57.

———. 2019. 'Introduction: Democracy and the Algebra of Warfare–Welfare'. In *The Algebra of Warfare–Welfare: A Long View of India's 2014 Election*, edited by Irfan Ahmad and P. Kanungo, 1–54. New Delhi: Oxford University Press.

———. 2020a. 'Citizen Amendment Act Is Confirmation of India as a Hindu Nation-State'. Berkley Center for Religion, Peace and World Affairs, 9 March. https://berkleycenter.georgetown.edu/responses/citizen-amendment-act-is-confirmation-of-india-as-a-hindu-nation-state (accessed on 17 January 2022).

———. 2020b. 'Shaheen Bagh Protest Challenges BJP Govt's Brand of Populism, Is Generative of New Vision of Democracy'. *First Post*, 4 February. https://www.firstpost.com/india/shaheen-bagh-protest-challenges-bjp-govts-brand-of-populism-is-generative-of-new-vision-of-democracy-7976271.html (accessed on 17 January 2022).

———. 2021a. 'Hindu Orientalism: The Sachar Committee and Over-representation of Minorities in Jail'. In *The Politics of Muslim Identities: South and Southeast Asia*, edited by Lulia Lumina, 115–44. Edinburgh: Edinburgh University Press.

———. 2021b. 'Shaheen Bagh Is Not an Event of the Past, It Is an Interrupted Future – Part I'. *Maktoob*, 12 March. https://maktoobmedia.com/2021/03/12/shaheen-bagh-is-not-an-event-of-the-past-it-is-an-interrupted-future-part-i/ (accessed on 17 January 2022).

———. 2021c. 'Shaheen Bagh; an Interrupted Future: Irfan Ahmad's Essay – Part II'. *Maktoob*, 13 March. https://maktoobmedia.com/2021/03/13/shaheen-bagh-an-interrupted-future-irfan-ahmads-essay-part-ii/ (accessed on 17 January 2022).

———. Forthcoming. *Terrorism in Question: Toward a Decolonial Anthropology*.

Akbar, M. J. 1988. *Riot after Riot: Reports on Caste and Communal Violence in India*. Delhi: Penguin.

———. 2021. 'An East Bengal in West Bengal'. *Open Magazine*, 12 March.

Asad, T. 2003. *Formations of the Secular: Christianity, Islam, Modernity*. Stanford: Stanford University Press.

Bal, H. S. 2020. 'Why Delhi Police Did Nothing to Stop Attacks on Muslims'. *New York Times*, 3 March. https://www.nytimes.com/2020/03/03/opinion/delhi-pogrom.html (accessed on 17 January 2022).

Banerjee, S. 2014. 'A Brief History of South Asia'. In *South Asia in the World: An Introduction*, edited by Susan Wadley, 22–65. Oxford: Oxford University Press.

Basu, S. 2020. 'Jamia Millia Shooting: Making of a Hindutva Terrorist'. *The Diplomat*, 3 February. https://thediplomat.com/2020/02/jamia-millia-shootout-making-of-a-hindutva-terrorist (accessed on 17 January 2022).

BBC News. 2005. 'Many Held as French Riots Spread'. 5 November. http://news.bbc.co.uk/1/hi/world/europe/4407688.stm (accessed on 17 January 2022).

Berenschot, W. 2011. *Riot Politics: Hindu–Muslim Violence in the Indian State*. London: Hurst.

Bergmann, Werner. 2003. 'Pogroms'. In *International Handbook of Violence Research*, edited by Wilhelm Heitmeyer and John Hagan, 351–67. Dordrecht, The Netherlands: Springer.

Brass, P. 1996. 'Introduction: Discourses of Ethnicity, Communalism, and Violence'. In *Riots and Pogroms*, edited by Paul Brass, 1–55. London, New York: Palgrave Macmillan.

Breckenridge, C. A., and P. van der Veer. 1993. 'Introduction'. In *Orientalism and the Post-colonial Predicament: Perspectives on South Asia*, edited by Carole Breckenridge and Peter van der Veer, 1–19. Philadelphia: University of Pennsylvania Press.

Chopra, S., and P. Jha. 2014. *On Their Watch: Mass Violence and State Apathy in India, Examining the Record*. Gurgaon: Three Essays Collective.

Das, V. 1990. 'Our Work to Cry, Your Work to Listen'. In *Mirrors of Violence: Communities, Riots and Survivors in South Asia*, edited by Veena Das, 345–394. Delhi: Oxford University Press.

———. 1995a. 'Anthropological Knowledge and Collective Violence: The Riots in Delhi, November 1984'. *Anthropology Today* 1(3): 4–6.

———. 1995b. *Critical Events: An Anthropological Perspective on Contemporary India.* Delhi: Oxford University Press, 1995.

Dhar, P. N. 1987. 'Bengal Renaissance: A Study in Social Contradiction'. *Social Scientist* 15(1): 26–45.

Eckert, J. 2012. 'Theories of Militancy in Practice: Explanations of Muslim Terrorism in India'. *Social Science History* 36(3): 321–45.

Ellis-Petersen, H. 2020. 'Inside Delhi: Beaten, Lynched and Burnt Alive'. *The Guardian*, 1 March. https://www.theguardian.com/world/2020/mar/01/india-delhi-after-hindu-mob-riot-religious-hatred-nationalists (accessed on 17 January 2022).

Ellis-Petersen, H., and S. A. Rahman. 2020. '"I Cannot Find My Father's Body": Delhi's Fearful Muslims Mourn Riot Dead'. *The Guardian*, 28 February. https://www.theguardian.com/world/2020/mar/06/how-can-i-go-back-delhi-fearful-muslims-mourn-riot-dead (accessed on 17 Januray 2022).

Fassin, D. 2006. 'Riots in France and Silent Anthropologists'. *Anthropology Today* 22(1): 1–3.

Hansen, T. B. 2007. 'The India That Does Not Shine'. *ISIM Review* 17: 50–51.

Hill, L. 1996. 'The Pogrom of November 9–10, 1938 in Germany'. In *Riots and Pogroms*, edited by Paul Brass, 89–113. London, New York: Palgrave Macmillan.

Hollis, M. 1994. *Philosophy of Social Science: An Introduction.* Cambridge: Cambridge University Press, Revised Edition.

Hunter, W. W. 1871. *The Indian Musalmans: Are They Bound in Conscience to Rebel against the Queen?* London: Trubner & Company.

Jalal, A. 1997. 'Exploding Communalism: The Politics of Muslim Identity in South Asia'. In *Nationalism, Democracy and Development: State and Politics in India*, edited by Sugata Bose and Ayesha Jalal, 77–103. Delhi: Oxford University Press.

Kamdar, M. 2020. 'What Happened in Delhi Was a Pogrom'. *The Atlantic*, 28 February. https://www.theatlantic.com/ideas/archive/2020/02/what-happened-delhi-was-pogrom/607198/ (accessed on 17 January 2022).

Kaplan, R. 2018. 'Those Greek Riots'. *The Atlantic*, December. https://www.theatlantic.com/magazine/archive/2008/12/those-greek-riots/307225/ (accessed on 17 January 2022).

Koselleck, R. 2004 [1978]. *Futures Past: On the Semantics of Historical Time*, trans. Keith Tribe. New York: Columbia University Press.

Manav, S. 2020. 'Ab Shishr Hi Iss Mulk Mein Humara Pehchaan Patra Hai' *Janchowk*, 26 February. https://janchowk.com/pahlapanna/how-susheel-manav-attacked-know-whole-story/ (accessed on 17 January 2022).

Menon, A. 2020. 'Dasna Priest Called for "War on Islam" in Run-Up to Delhi Violence'. *The Quint*, 5 March. https://www.thequint.com/news/politics/narsinghanand-saraswati-hindutva-delhi-violence-muslims-dasna-ghaziabad (accessed on 17 January 2022).

Mishra, M. 2020. 'Chand Bagh ki Muslim Basti, Saamne Teen Sau Dangai aur Ek Bhi Khakhidhari Nahi'. *Janchowk*, 28 February. https://janchowk.com/art-cultur-society/chand-bagh-muslim-area-three-hundred-rioters-no-police/ (accessed on 17 January 2022).

Mondal S. 2020. 'Revisiting Hindu Nationalism: Perspective of Bankimchandra'. *Journal of Indian Council of Philosophical Research* 37:19–30.

Nandy, A. 1994. *The Illegitimacy of Nationalism: Rabindranath Tagore and the Politics of Self*. Delhi: Oxford University Press.

Pai, S., and S. Kumar. 2018. *Everyday Communalism: Riots in Uttar Pradesh*. Delhi: Oxford University Press.

Pandey, G. 1989. 'The Colonial Construction of "Communalism": British Writings on Banaras in the Nineteenth Century'. In *Subaltern Studies VI: Writings on South Asian History and Society*, edited by Ranajit Guha, 132–68. New Delhi: Oxford University Press.

———. 1999. 'Can a Muslim Be an Indian?' *Comparative Studies in Society and History* 41(4): 608–29.

Pandey, P. 1992. 'In Defense of the Fragment: Writing about Hindu–Muslim Riots in India Today,' *Representations* 37: 27–55.

People's Union for Democratic Rights. 1990. *Bhagalpur Riots*. Delhi: PUDR.

Rahim, A. 1991. 'The Role of Media in Communal Conflict: A Situational Analysis of Socio-religious Crisis in India'. Paper presented at the AMIC–SIDA Seminar on the Role of the Media in a National Crisis, Colombo, 15–17 May. http://citeseerx.ist.psu.edu/viewdoc/download?doi=10.1.1.1001.6299&rep=rep1&type=pdf (accessed on 17 January 2022).

Richter, M. 1995. *The History of Social and Political Concepts*. New York: Oxford University Press.

Sareen, S. 2020 'No One Caused Delhi Riots?' *DailyO*, 2 March. https://www.dailyo.in/politics/delhi-riots-shaheen-bagh-communal-riots-kapil-mishra-north-east-delhi-anti-caa-protests-caa-jamia-nagar-muslims/story/1/32529.html (accessed on 17 January 2022).

Sen, S. 2002. *A Distant Sovereignty: National Imperialism and the Origins of British India*. London: Routledge.

Sharma, A. 2020. 'Indian Media Has Made Tahir Hussain the Face of Delhi Riots. What's the Evidence?' *Newslaundry*, 28 February. https://www.newslaundry.com/2020/02/28/indian-media-has-made-tahir-hussain-the-face-of-delhi-riots-whats-the-evidence (accessed on 17 January 2022).

Sikander, Z. 2020. 'No More Riots. In Modi and Amit Shah's New India Shooters Are Becoming the Norm'. *The Print*, 3 February. https://theprint.in/opinion/no-more-riots-in-modi-and-amit-shahs-new-india-shooters-are-becoming-the-norm/358029/ (accessed on 17 January 2022).

Somaiya, R., and J. F. Burns. 2011. 'Rioting Widens in London on 3rd Night of Unrest'. *New York Times*, 8 August. https://www.nytimes.com/2011/08/09/world/europe/09britain.html (accessed on 17 January 2022).

Srinivasan, K. 2013. 'Subaltern Fascism'. In *Fascism: Essays on Europe and India*, edited by Jairus Banaji, 99–134. Gurgaon: Three Essays Collective.

Subrahmaniam, V. 2020. 'India's Muslims Are Punished for Asking to be Indian'. Al Jazeera, 7 March. https://www.aljazeera.com/indepth/opinion/india-muslims-punished-indian-200306190342176.html (accessed on 17 January 2022).

Sundar, N. 2004. 'Toward an Anthropology of Culpability'. *American Ethnologist* 31(2): 145–63.

Tandon, A. 2020. 'Ashis Nandy: It's Very Difficult to Go Back to Pre-violent Days after You've Once Participated, Killed'. *The Tribune*, 8 March. https://www.tribuneindia.com/news/features/ashis-nandy-its-very-difficult-to-go-back-to-pre-violent-days-after-youve-onceparticipated-killed-52702 (accessed on 17 January 2022).

The Patriot. 2020. 'Venom of Communal Hatred Spares None'. 7 March. https://thepatriot.in/2020/03/06/venom-of-communal-hatred-spares-none/ (accessed on 17 January 2022).

The Telegraph. 2020. 'BJP Voice Spews Hate Regarding the Delhi Violence'. 26 February. https://www.telegraphindia.com/india/bjp-voice-spews-hate-regarding-the-delhi-violence/cid/1748697?ref=miscrecommended-stry-1 (accessed on 17 January 2022).

The Wire Staff. 2020. 'Delhi Riots: Emergency Services Were Unresponsive for up to 72 Hours, Says Fact Finding Report'. *The Wire*, 29 February. https://thewire.in/communalism/delhi-riots-fact-finding-report (accessed on 17 January 2022).

Tiwari, A., and B. Kumar. 2020. 'Media Fact-check: Did a Muslim Mob "Forcibly Occupy" a Temple in North East Delhi?' *Newslaundry*, 6 March. https://www.newslaundry.com/2020/03/06/fact-check-did-a-muslim-mob-forcibly-occupy-a-temple-in-north-east-delhi (accessed on 17 January 2022).

Waddington, D. 2015. 'Riots'. In *The Oxford Handbook of Social Movements*, edited by Donatella Della Porta and Mario Diani, 423–38. London: Oxford University Press.

Yadav, Y. 2020. 'Delhi Riots Neither Designed by Modi Govt, Nor Islamic Conspiracy. It's Far More Dangerous'. *The Print*, 26 February. https://theprint.in/opinion/delhi-riots-neither-designed-by-modi-govt-nor-islamic-conspiracy-its-far-more-dangerous/371544/ (accessed on 17 January 2022).

12

DEVELOPMENT
INDIA'S FOUNDATIONAL MYTH

Mona Bhan

On 5 August 2019, the Bharatiya Janata Party (BJP) government, headed by Narendra Modi, unilaterally abrogated Articles 370 and 35A of the Indian Constitution to repeal Kashmir's semi-autonomous status in India and undermine its United Nation (UN)–mandated right to self-determination through a free and impartial plebiscite. Of course, Kashmir's semi-autonomous status was in place against the backdrop of an Indian occupation that has made it the most militarized place in the world. Many Indians considered Articles 370 and 35A to be an obstruction to Kashmir's integration into India and celebrated the BJP government's decision as a bold step to correct a seven-decade-long 'historic blunder' that, they claimed, had impeded Kashmir's growth and development and 'promoted separatist' sentiments in the Valley (BBC News 2019). India's violent annexation of Kashmir was framed as a benevolent step to 'usher in a new dawn' in the region through Indian investments – at par with other states in India – and build a more peaceful and prosperous region (*Economic Times* 2019; Shringla 2019). A few months after the abrogation, while the residents were silenced by an unprecedented media and communication blackout and forced to remain caged inside their homes through curfews and shutdowns, Indian investors met in various cities of the country to carve out new investment opportunities in the region in mining, pilgrimage tourism, real estate, housing, and hydropower. In a PowerPoint slide from an investment summit held in Bangalore a few weeks after the abrogation, Article 370 was drawn as a concertina wire, which symbolized its oppressive grip over Kashmir, and represented India's historic failure to integrate the region, which according to government officials, had 'lagged' behind every other state in India (Parker 2019). Vast numbers of Indians celebrated Modi as the *vikas purush* (development man), convinced that Article 370 had stymied development in Kashmir and held it hostage for seven decades.

Despite the fact that Kashmir has routinely performed better compared to other Indian states on many socio-economic indicators such as education, poverty, life expectancy rates, and wealth distribution patterns, thanks in large part to land reforms of the 1950s, the myth of its underdevelopment has persisted in the Indian consciousness for decades (Vishwadeepak 2019). India's myth of development gained even more traction after 5 August when it was reinvented as Hindu India's burden to salvage a Muslim territory, a script that aligned perfectly well with settler-colonial narratives that have long sold exploitation as liberation while wishing local populations out of existence. Indeed, I argue that the myth of development is a foundational myth that has since India's formation in 1947 fed on colonial caricatures of Kashmiris as helpless and economically backward to legitimize the shifting politics and identity of the Indian nation-state – first as a nominal secular nation under the Congress government and now as an authoritarian Hindu *rashtra* under the BJP. Indeed, as I will demonstrate, Kashmir was key to the constitution of the Indian nation's secular credentials and is critically important to the project of refiguring India as a Hindu nation. Without Kashmir, the very idea of India – whether in its secular incarnation or its majoritarian Hindu avatar – stands on shaky grounds. Notwithstanding Kashmir's centrality to India's existential identity, it is the myth of the region's dependence on the country that has persisted and informed a range of political experiments over time. From using development as a counterinsurgency strategy to win hearts and minds to deploying it as a tool of depopulation and settler colonialism, India has, for decades, relied on development to justify its illegal control and occupation of Kashmir (Bhan 2014a). Now under Modi's regime, development has become an instrument of a demographic war against Kashmir's Muslim-majority population – a project of 'political and economic integration' designed to dress up India's war against Kashmiri lives as a humanitarian project. And yet, India's development experiments in the region have for years induced fears of displacement and depopulation, along with weakening people's economic and ecological resilience. In other words, for many in Kashmir, particularly those riverine communities who live on the disputed Line of Control (LoC) and suffer the consequences of India's mega-dams, development has for decades meant the threat of depopulation. To them, hydropower development is a settler-colonial project long in the making designed to transform their homes into a militarized frontier.

Settler Colonialism and the Myth of Dependence

For decades, the Indian government invoked colonial tropes of defence and protection to deny Kashmiris their sovereignty. They represented Kashmir as a potential victim of the hawkishness of China and Pakistan; it was India's defence infrastructure that protected the region from predatory international players, they claimed. At the same time, the perception of Kashmir's economic backwardness – its status as a resource-starved region, or a 'begging bowl' – was another justification used by the Indian state to undermine its prolonged struggle for freedom and sovereignty. The rationale offered was that Kashmir was 'heavily dependent on New Delhi for its funds, more than any other state in India', a dependence which, according to mainstream Indian views, 'call[ed] into question its demands of autonomy or even azadi' (Jain 2011). Even for Kashmir's politicians who sided with India to uphold its charade of democracy, it was an 'uncomfortable' exercise to visit Delhi with a 'begging bowl every year' asking the prime minister for finances to run the state's economy (Jain 2011; Bhan 2014b).

Yet Kashmir's inflated budget allocations were spent on sustaining its defence infrastructure and supporting extractive power companies such as the NHPC, India's premier hydropower corporation, which is in the business of building dams on the region's contested rivers. For instance, in 2006, when India's former prime minister Manmohan Singh announced an INR 240 billion package for Kashmir, INR 180 billion went to the NHPC, while the remaining funds were spent on roads and infrastructure (Jain 2011). India's announcements of big economic packages for Kashmir, declared Haseeb Drabu, ex-director of J&K Bank, were at best fraudulent exercises (Jain 2011). When Jammu and Kashmir's state government demanded ownership over Kashmir's hydropower projects, which offered minimal benefits to the erstwhile state, Indian media narratives called the effort a 'misplaced bout of economic activism' (Jain 2011). They foregrounded governance issues such as Kashmir's 'rampant power theft' and inefficient 'transmission and distribution' infrastructure, as well as the paucity of local skilled workers, to distract from more fundamental questions about Kashmiri political and ecological sovereignty, and India's status in the territory as an occupying power. Kashmiris were expected to prove their economic mettle before they could be deemed worthy of political rights and freedoms. In the meantime, between 2001 and 2015, the NHPC earned INR 194 billion from hydropower projects in the state (Nayak 2016).

The abrogation of Articles 370 and 35A, and more recently the new regulations around domicile status, are meant to facilitate Indian settlements in Kashmir and transform Kashmiri Muslims into a disenfranchised minority in their homeland. This usurpation of their homes, land, rivers, mountains, and meadows have made longstanding questions about the region's political, economic, and ecological sovereignty even more critical. At the same time, these illegitimate laws, while trying to render an international dispute as an internal matter, have revealed the hypocrisies of Indian narratives that built a case for the Indian occupation using

Kashmir's manufactured dependence on India. Indeed, the origins of these narratives long predate the current right-wing BJP government. However, what is remarkably different about the Modi regime is the brazenness and impunity with which it has implemented its settler-colonial policies and extractive infrastructure in Kashmir, triggering fears of depopulation and massive exploitation of its land and waterscapes by a colonial state.

Modi government's unabashed proclamation of its settler-colonial agenda – and the dizzying speed at which it is being implemented – reveals that the rhetoric of inclusive and equitable development is a ruse to hide the RSS's vision for Kashmir's permanent solution, which is to rid Kashmir of its Muslim majority and transform it into a predominantly Hindu state. Indeed, soon after the abrogation of Articles 370 and 35A, the Vishwa Hindu Parishad (VHP) prodded the government to rebuild 435 Hindu temples that had been 'demolished' by Kashmiri militants (*The Print* 2019). For long, the popular agenda of the VHP and several right-wing citizen groups has been to restore Kashmir's Hinduness which, they claim, harkens back to the 'pre-Mahabharata era', and 'makes every Indian (read Hindu) a stakeholder' in the contest over Kashmiri territory (*Pune News*). If under the Congress, Kashmir – the only Muslim-majority state in the Indian federation – was indispensable for India's existential identity as a secular republic, reconfiguring Kashmir as Hindutva's last frontier is foundational to building a Hindu *rashtra*. At the time of Partition, and decades after that, Kashmir was used to prop up India's international, albeit flawed, reputation as a secular polity. With the ascent of Hindu majoritarianism in India, Kashmir became the battleground to redefine the core of Hinduness, as well as India's religious and political identity as a Hindu territory. That the meanings attached to Kashmir in the Indian imaginary can vary from being a vehicle to tout its secular credentials to being a proof of its success in saffronization reveals how India has always depended on the territory for its self-definition. The cost is borne by Kashmiris, for whom home, habitation, and belonging, particularly after August 2019, have become tenuous categories as they grapple with the aftermaths of new laws that are meant to alter the region's demographics and reconfigure it as a Hindu homeland. The myth of Kashmir's dependence on India is therefore a delusion nurtured by deep existential crises anchored firmly in India's birth out of a colonial experiment.

While previous Indian governments invoked development's 'healing touch' to hide the systemic violence of military occupation on Kashmiri bodies and landscape, Modi's development initiatives are couched in the language of '*naya* Kashmir' (new Kashmir), resonating with the threat of depopulation and the mass eviction of Kashmiri Muslims from their homeland (News 18 India 2019). In the months following the abrogation, Kashmir's local economy suffered a loss of USD 2.3 billion (*Indian Express* 2019). Hundreds of start-ups experienced huge setbacks because of the internet blackout, and unpicked apples rotted in the orchard towns and villages of Shopian and Sopore. The abrogation of Articles 370 and 35A accelerated Kashmir's militarization while simultaneously facilitating the extractive logics of accumulation. Since August 2019, the Indian government has encouraged the piecemeal auctioning of Kashmir's land and resources to private Indian investors through online bidding contracts in which Kashmiris cannot participate in the absence of 4G internet connectivity. Indian syndicates are using their 'financial muscle power' to outcompete Kashmiris and to utilize the government's 6,000-acre land bank to set up multiplexes, film production centres, information technology (IT) parks, and medical complexes (Wani 2020). In addition to these efforts, the government's enthusiasm around the opening up of multiplex cinema theatres, banned by militant outfits in the 1980s at the beginning of the armed *tehreek*, and the identification of sixty-seven spots for the sale of liquor in the Valley are seen as purposeful moves to offend local religious and cultural sensibilities, and enforce India's vision of cultural homogenization. In the meantime, Kashmiris experience heightened raids and surveillance, a series of militarized lockdowns, and deadly encounters in which their homes are razed to the ground, and children, men, and women are detained in prisons in Kashmir and India through punitive laws such as the Public Safety Act (Shameem 2020).

While the Hindu *rashtra*'s '*naya* Kashmir' vision brazenly deploys new development and domicile laws to eliminate Kashmiri Muslims from their homeland, depopulating Kashmir's strategic landscapes has been an ongoing feature of Indian development praxis for a long time. As Mirza Saaib Bég, a Kashmiri lawyer points out, 'Modi has not transformed India; he has merely unmasked it' (Bég 2020). For Kashmiris, thus, the rise of Hindu majoritarianism is not a transformation of India's core values, as argued by many liberal Indians, but simply a brazen display of what was already a constitutive element of the Indian polity. Earlier Indian regimes, too, held on to Kashmiri territory against people's wishes using a mix of military force and fraudulent elections to silence a Muslim-majority region and violently repress their political freedoms. Likewise, India's development interventions – whether framed as benevolent measures meant to win hearts and minds or as tools to enforce cultural homogeneity – have ended up strengthening India's military occupation of Kashmir and paved the way for its ongoing settler-colonial project.

Development as Depopulation

For decades, Kashmiris have experienced land grabs, massive displacements, glacial melting, land and water scarcity, and ecological catastrophes such as floods and earthquakes because of militarized development projects such as highways, railway lines, and hydropower dams. In Gurez and Bandipora where I have been conducting ethnographic research since 2012, a 330-megawatt dam on the contested waters of the River Kishanganga has displaced multiple villages while dispossessing people of their land, river, and forests. The villagers describe the Kishanganga dam as a national security project despite the successive Indian governments' attempts to showcase it as a development package designed to generate jobs and employment. They complain how legal statutes were used to criminalize community resistance and, in Bandipora in particular, anti-terror laws such as the Public Safety Act (PSA) were used to clamp down on union activism and people's resistance to land grabs.

Riverine communities in Gurez, living in villages along the LoC, considered hydropower development to be an instrument to rid the mountain valley of its indigenous population and transform it into an empty borderland. For them, the Indian government's assurances that the dam would submerge only two villages did not alleviate concerns about the dam irreversibly transforming the local weather and eventually making the place uninhabitable. Such concerns intensified after 2016 when Modi weaponized Kashmir's rivers against Pakistan, threatening to unilaterally revoke the transboundary Indus Waters Treaty after the Uri attack in which twenty-two Indian soldiers were killed, allegedly in a planned attack by Pakistan.

Since then, and particularly after August 2019, Modi's attempts to claim Kashmir's rivers have intensified as the BJP government announced its plans to 'expedite' the construction of hydroelectric projects, deemed 'strategically important' within the context of Chinese investment in the China–Pakistan Economic Corridor (CPEC), a USD 64 billion infrastructural project focused on building roads, highways, and energy infrastructure in parts of Pakistan, Azad Kashmir, and Gilgit Baltistan. According to Indian commentators, CPEC could reduce India's access to resources and weaken its territorial claims over the disputed region.

In 2016, Modi threatened to revoke the Indus Waters Treaty to 'exploit to the maximum' the waters of the western rivers of the Indus basin. Hindu ideologues have called the treaty India's *brahmastra* against Pakistan, comparing it to the destructive potential of the mythic weapon used in several Hindu mythological wars such as the Mahabharata. After the Pulwama attack on 19 February 2019, which killed forty Indian soldiers, Nitin Gadkari, the Union Water Resources Minister, announced that Pakistan would not get 'a single drop of water' even from the eastern rivers of the Indus basin, over which Pakistan has full consumptive rights according to the provisions of the treaty. In one stroke, Gadkari claimed that like Kashmir's territory, its waters, too, were India's integral part.

It is important, however, to look beyond the rhetoric of water wars and acknowledge Hindutva's ultimate project in Kashmir. The River Indus is tied to Hindu re-imaginings of Kashmir as a land of Hindu antiquity. Even the word 'Hindu' comes from the Sanskrit word Sindhu and represents to many Hindus a male warrior God (Bhan 2021). Claiming Kashmir's rivers that flow into Pakistan as repositories of Hindu history is meant to rewrite Kashmir's union with India as a fait accompli. It is the BJP's ultimate attempt at *ghar wapsi* (return to home) – a series of RSS- and VHP-initiated forced interventions to 'reconvert' Muslims and Christians to Hinduism. In this case, the logic of *ghar wapsi* is applied to Kashmir's rivers, as their waywardness and dissidence is tamed through dams that alter their flows so that they cannot be allowed to serve as links between warring nation-states. Hindu ideologues want to reclaim these rivers to correct the historic wrongs of an international water treaty.

In my interviews from 2012 to 2018, riverine communities expressed urgent concerns that the Indian state wanted to unleash the powers of the dam to transform Gurez into a *terra nullius*, an empty borderland, by flooding the villages of Badwan, Khopri, Wanpora, Tragbal, and Bakhtoor. According to the Indian army, there were frequent 'infiltrations' from across the border in Tragbal and Bakhtoor, and in recent years, many Indian soldiers and militants have been killed in deadly encounters. Gurezis have known all too well that for India, Gurez is primarily a border, a 'virgin territory', where the priorities of national security trump everything else, including the lives, homes, and livelihoods of its inhabitants. Under the veneer of their symbiotic relationship with the Indian military, therefore, lay the difficult realization that since 1947 Gurezis had been 'imprisoned' in their own valley. The Indian military's dense and ubiquitous presence in Gurez made rebellion difficult, if not impossible. Furthermore, frequent shelling along the LoC since the late 1980s had made it impossible to live safely and prompted many villagers to relocate to Bandipora and Srinagar. Although relocated families maintained dual residence, the perception among government and military officials that Gurez was already depopulated made it even easier to imagine it as an empty landscape. Hence, despite official assurances that the dam would displace only two villages, Gurezis were convinced that the consequences would be worse. They worried that India was planning to stick to its earlier plans to displace nine Gurezi villages which Pakistan's legal interventions with the Hague Permanent Court of Arbitration had delayed. Large swathes of the Gurez valley would be depopulated and rendered empty. Even prior to the abrogation of Article 370, Indian development interventions had transformed Gurez into a sacrificial zone, where dams became an instrument to depopulate a 'strategic frontier' of its indigenous population.

Despite their struggles, riverine communities claim a *khudmukhtar* (independent) river cannot be restrained for too long. Nor can the dam dictate its seasonal rhythms or its whims and fancies. 'The river empties out when it has to in September, and it lets our women cross so they get firewood from the forests. Even our goats can cross the entire stretch in September and October to graze in higher altitude pastures', I was repeatedly told. At the same time, the gushing river connected riverine communities with places and people beyond the LoC. The river's vibrancy shaped material and affective links that India's development projects could not erase. Its dissent flows, people hope, would reconfigure national geographies and carve out new and yet unrealized potentials for freer Kashmiri futures.

References

BBC News. 2019. 'Article 370: What Happened with Kashmir and Why It Matters'. 6 August. https://www.bbc.com/news/world-asia-india-49234708 (accessed on 15 December 2020).

Bég, M. S. 2020. 'With India Changing Domicile Law, Kashmir's Indigenous Population Faces Risk of Dispossession, Possible War Crime'. 27 June. The Polis Project (accessed on 14 July 2021).

Bhan, M. 2014a. *Counterinsurgency, Democracy, and the Politics of Identity in India: From Warfare to Welfare?* London: Routledge.

———. 2014b. 'Morality and Martyrdom: Dams, Dharma, and the Politics of Work in Indian Occupied Kashmir'. *Biography* 37(1): 191–224.

———. 2021. 'Infrastructures of Occupation: Mobility, Immobility, and the Politics of Occupation in Kashmir'. In *Kashmir and the Future of South Asia*, edited by S. Bose and A. Jalal, 71–90. London and New York: Routledge.

Economic Times. 2019. 'Revocation of Article 370 Will Usher in a New Dawn in J&K: PM Modi'. 9 August. https://economictimes.indiatimes.com/news/politics-and-nation/narendramodi-live-update-revocation-of-article-370-will-usher-in-a-dawn-of-development-in-jk/articleshow/70591359.cms (accessed on 11 December 2019).

Indian Express. 2019. 'Kashmir Economy Suffered Loss of Rs. 17,878 Cr in 4 Months after Article 370 Abrogation'. 17 December. https://indianexpress.com/article/india/kashmir-economy-suffered-loss-four-months-after-article-370-abrogation-jk-6172096/ (accessed on 12 February 2020).

Jain, S. 2011. 'Kashmir: The Economics of Azadi'. NDTV. 8 November. https://www.ndtv.com/india-news/kashmir-the-economics-of-azadi-468032 (accessed on 24 March 2020).

Nayak, V. 2016. 'RTI Reveals NHPC Earned Rs. 194 Billion from Hydel Projects in J&K between 2001–2015 While MOU Requires Working Out a Method for Transfer of Projects Back to J&K'. Commonwealth Human Rights Initiative. 21 April. https://www.humanrightsinitiative.org/blog/rti-reveals-nhpc-earned-rs194-billion-from-hydel-projects-in-jk-between-20012015-while-mou-requires-working-out-a-method-for-transfer-of-projects-back-to-jk (accessed on 24 January 2021).

News 18 India. 2019. 'PM Modi "Very Confident" of Building Naya Kashmir, Says Top Entrepreneurs Keen to Invest in J&K'. 12 August. https://www.news18.com/news/india/modi-very-confident-of-building-naya-kashmir-says-top-entrepreneurs-keen-to-invest-in-jk-2267081.html (accessed on 22 March 2020).

Parker, C. 2019. 'India's Clampdown on Kashmir Continues'. *Washington Post*, 13 August. https://www.nytimes.com/2019/09/19/opinion/india-pakistan-kashmir-jammu.html (accessed on 24 March 2020).

Pune News. 'India 4 Kashmir – Common Indians Initiate Movement to Reclaim Kashmir'. https://www.punekarnews.in/india-4-kashmir-common-indians-initiate-movement-to-reclaim-kashmir/ (accessed on 15 March 2021).

Shameem, B. 2020. 'Destroying Houses in Kashmir: A Collective Punishment'. 4 June. *Newsclick*. https://www.newsclick.in/Destroying-houses-in-Kashmir-Collective-Punishment (accessed on 13 March 2021).

Shringla H. V. 2019. 'India Is Building a More Prosperous Kashmir'. *New York Times*, 19 September. https://www.nytimes.com/2019/09/19/opinion/india-pakistan-kashmir-jammu.html (accessed on 20 April 2020).

Jaishankar, S. 2019. 'Changing the Status of Jammu and Kashmir Will Benefit All of India'. *Financial Times*, 24 September. https://www.ft.com/content/4f0e297a-d3bd-11e9-8d46-8def889b4137 (accessed on 24 March 2020).

The Print. 2019. 'Article 370 Done, Now VHP Wants Govt to Build Temples Destroyed by Militants in Kashmir'. 8 August. https://theprint.in/india/article-370-done-now-vhp-wants-govt-to-build-temples-destroyed-by-militants-in-kashmir/274353/ (accessed on 24 March 2020).

Vishwadeepak. 2019. 'Economist Jean Dreze: Article 370 Helped Reducing Poverty in Jammu and Kashmir'. *National Herald*, 9 August. https://www.nationalheraldindia.com/india/economist-jean-dreze-jandk-more-developed-than-gujarat-special-status-helped-reducing-poverty (accessed on 22 April 2020).

Wani, F. 2020. 'Mining Bids Not Going to Kashmiris'. *New Indian Express*. 29 June. https://www.newindianexpress.com/nation/2020/jun/29/mining-bids-not-going-to-kashmiris-2162778.html (accessed on 26 March 2021).

13

PRATIKRIYA, GUILT, AND REACTIONARY VIOLENCE

*Parvis Ghassem-Fachandi**

In late February and early March 2002, the city of Ahmedabad in Gujarat descended into a pogrom. Hindu activists were returning from the temple town of Ayodhya, a popular pilgrimage site outside the state, in an overcrowded train. They had gone there to support the building of a Hindu temple to Lord Ram on the site of a former Muslim mosque, which had been destroyed by activists ten years earlier. The train stopped briefly in Godhra. After an altercation between Muslim station vendors and Hindu activists, stones were thrown onto the train, which stopped again outside the station. Then two coaches of the train caught fire. Many passengers were killed. In the days and weeks following the incident, the Muslim community of Gujarat became the target of a state-wide pogrom. In cities like Ahmedabad, Muslims faced economic boycotts, attacks on their residential neighbourhoods, destruction of their property, and the indifference or complicity of the police in these acts. Hundreds of Muslim shrines and mosques were attacked, burnt, and razed to the ground. Mass rape, arson, and deadly violent attacks by large, organized crowds and gangs armed with swords took place in front of a gaping, knowing, and partly approving or even participating public.

This event is commonly referred to as the 'Gujarat riots'. The passage from *pogrom* to *riot* constitutes an act of reduction that does two things at once. It integrates a particular event into a series of preceding events, eliminating its specificity.[1] Furthermore, the term 'riot' complicates the assertion of culpability because it invokes two equal communities mutually attacking one another. Pogroms, by contrast, are organized events following a planned objective characterized by a psychological mobilization that far exceeds the immediate group of actors in a riot. There is no concept in Gujarati that can be assimilated semantically to the term *pogrom*, though there are many words that allow for the rendering of *riot* (Ghassem-Fachandi 2012, 60).²

When the state had barely begun recovering in May, Uma Bharati, the then Union Minister for Youth and Sports, responded to a query by a journalist why the 'riots' had been so exceptional. She responded: 'The rise of intolerance among Hindu youth and the fact that they are unapologetic about such inhuman acts is a cause of great concern. That such elements – even if small in number – exist among Hindus is terrible. They must be destroyed from the roots' (*Times of India* 2002a, 10).³ A few weeks later, commentator Mahesh Daga wrote about the bewilderment of the well-known violence expert and police consultant K. P. S. Gill in the same newspaper. Like Bharati, Gill expressed consternation at 'the apparent lack of remorse' by ordinary Hindus and the extreme levels of brutality unleashed against the Muslim minority in the state. Confirming this understanding, Daga asked what might explain 'this cynical disregard for the sanctity of human life, especially among a people who otherwise pride themselves on their non-violence, pacifism, and need one add, vegetarianism?' (*Times of India* 2002b, 10).⁴

The oddity in these platitudinous exchanges is what they bring into play without becoming explicit: the suggestion that in past communal violence, violent actors were more apologetic about inhuman acts committed. Gujarat has witnessed extreme forms of communal violence in the late 1960s, mid-1980s, and at both ends of the 1990s. It is rather absurd that a 'riot expert' like Gill would be astonished about the lack of remorse by perpetrators. Daga points out that such absence is what characterizes instances of ethnic violence generally. In ethnic violence worldwide, victims are held responsible for becoming targets, and perpetrators fall short of either developing or acknowledging retroactive feelings of guilt. Bharati and Gill seem to suggest that there exists a 'normal' case in which violent actors were somewhat less violent or at least felt bad about what they did afterwards. Significantly, Muslims are never mentioned, nor the nature of the violence unleashed against them. In this, the statements by Bharati and Gill succeed in passively confirming a stable stereotype. If it was unusual for Hindus to engage in such extreme behaviours, by implication, it was not so for Muslims, who in Gujarat are closely associated with violence.⁵

This essay describes a non-Muslim response to the pogrom and its aftermath that is segmented in time and unfolding in a particular context. Since 2002, Gujarat has lingered under a shadow of adumbrated guilt with all its productive or unproductive possibilities.⁶ While it remains unclear to what extent the case I describe can be considered reparative action, I nonetheless turn to a context that I believe is underrepresented in scholarship on Hindutva. The reason for this seems to be that in many ethnographic contexts, explicit reference to any form of political discourse, especially Hindutva, is either strictly avoided or altogether lacking. The explicit mention of Hindutva politics in everyday life summons conflict and hence is often either deliberately dodged or unconsciously avoided. The ideology that now dominates state politics is not often offered into the open discussion but retains a subterranean presence. I insist, however, that this discourse is indirectly referenced and acknowledged. In my description and interpretation, I address guilt in two ways, as external attribution and as reactive feeling manifesting in circuitous ways in social relationships.

Elision of Guilt and Reactionary Violence

When I first began fieldwork in Gujarat in the mid-1990s, past episodes of Hindu–Muslim violence were rarely openly discussed. Upon inquiry, I was rather quickly accused of summoning the tensions I, in fact, wanted to learn about. What scholars had written found no resonance in the minds of my interlocutors. A veil of silence lay over such issues, and foreigners were not supposed to be introduced to them. Even in later years, I experienced much resistance to the discussion in diverse contexts: among an urban educated Brahmin class of professors at Gujarat University where I studied language as much as in rural Gujarat among farmers largely considered 'illiterate'. Communal violence was acknowledged but dismissed as an aberration, the machinations of corrupt politicians and criminal gangs. It did not reflect who Gujaratis thought they were despite the fact that many were living witnesses of previous rounds of violence. Given the state's history, this avoidance behaviour seems in retrospect to be a concerted form of denial. What exactly was this denial avoiding?

The tale that Gujarat was a comparatively peaceful state is a cover story that Gujaratis, including many Muslims, tell themselves and others to this day. This story is sustained in no small measure with references to Mohandas K. Gandhi, a son of Gujarat and considered the symbolic father of the Indian nation. As a figure of identification, Gandhi, in many ways, constitutes the state's global moral face. For the longest time, this figure provided a convenient mask with which Gujaratis represented their state to the world and, more significantly, to themselves, despite the raging ambivalence they felt towards this figure. This also explains Daga's reference to vegetarianism, as in India dietary abstention is more apodictically associated with non-violence than in Europe.

The experience of the 2002 anti-Muslim pogrom made me aware of how ensconced this routine avoidance had become and how convoluted emotions rebelled against the inner moral command emanating from Gandhi. The days of violence in Ahmedabad were filled not only with fear, shame, and shock but also with enthusiastic participation, enjoyment, awe and fascination. The psychological mobilization for violence resulted in miscellaneous forms of complicity. The tales that Gujaratis told themselves about themselves no longer made much sense.

The Gujarat pogrom seemed to follow a script that was anticipated, yet surprisingly took everyone by surprise.[7] Violence after the Godhra incident was predictable, given the history of communal conflagration in Ahmedabad and the country at large. Construed as a provocation of Hindus by Muslims, the incident demanded a rebuttal. But then, as a local stereotype goes, a Hindu is by nature passive, more coward than a bully.[8] This understanding is a product of a sense that Gujarat as a state was characterized by a rational, economic ethos attributed to affluent merchant groups (*vepari*), associated with vegetarianism, non-violence, and a particularly forward-looking peaceful character and culture.[9]

What occurred was nonetheless unusual because, as far as communal violence goes, the Gujarat pogrom exceeded in severity most of what urban residents had witnessed in their lifetimes. The alleged constitutional disadvantage of Hindus, when confronted by aggression, became an opportunity for the Hindu nationalist organizations to fulfil their promise to defend the Hindu community against Muslims in a delegation of violent labour. It is these organizations that committed the worst atrocities during the pogrom. When Uma Bharati and K. P. S. Gill oddly referred to 'Hindu youth' and 'ordinary Hindus' lacking remorse they elided the fact that most atrocities were carried out by, or under the supervision of, these organizations. They had been mobilizing, recruiting, training, and planning for years, including among those sections of society that have suffered generations of discrimination and exclusion (such as Dalits and *adivasis*). That omission is, hence, not an innocent oversight but a decisive displacement characteristic of the entire public discussion after the pogrom.

The most powerful man at the helm of the state at the time of the pogrom, Chief Minister Narendra Modi, had at his disposal the entire state machinery, the administrative apparatus, the intelligence services, the police and security forces, and close relations with the entire edifice of Sangh Parivar institutions (the family of Hindu organizations that espouse Hindutva ideology such as the Rashtriya Swayamsevak Sangh [RSS], Vishva Hindu Parishad [VHP], and Bajrang Dal). It was from this mighty position that Modi, three days into the anti-Muslim violence, employed the term *svabhavik pratikriya* (natural reaction) to describe the anti-Muslim pogrom. This expression, uttered long before the incident in Godhra was understood or the post-Godhra violence had ended, suggests a particular relation of guilt to agency.

More than a description, *pratikriya* (reaction, counteraction) provided an interpretative frame for the unfolding violence. It combined the theme of revenge and retribution with the image of an automatic mechanism suggesting the detachment of ritual procedure: a *pratikriya* is always preceded by a *kriya* (an act or a deed). If the Godhra incident was the deed, the initial *kriya*, the pogrom was but its response, a counteraction to undo the bad deed. The translation of the expression into English was 'Every action has an equal and opposite reaction', referencing Newton's third law of physics. One should see here the invocation of the idea of an immediate karmic retribution. Why Muslims in Ahmedabad and central provinces should be at the receiving end of such retribution, as the alleged acts were committed in the town of Godhra, was never sufficiently explained. Such details did not matter at the time, nor do they today. Muslims were collectively held responsible for acts that the vast majority of them had never perpetrated. They were held guilty collectively and, as minority, they had to be taught a lesson. The Gujarat pogrom was interpreted as providing that lesson. Hindus had to overcome their constitutional cowardness in a supposed act of defence of their religion, their women, and their country.

Furthermore, by stressing detachment in the context of organized violence, agency was seriously obscured. By *natural*, a sort of inevitability was suggested as if organized collective violence was akin to a twitch following a pinch, an unavoidable and innocent impulse. While Muslims in Ahmedabad were held guilty for acts they had not perpetrated, violence perpetrated in the name of a general Hindu anger or fury (*Hindu krodh*) was deemed an innocuous reflex (Eckert 2010, 159–61; Sundar 2004, 153–55). In other words, Hindus had reacted in anger but were not guilty. If *karma* strikes, there is no agency and hence no culpability. Muslims, however, were held collectively responsible. Their suffering was the expression of karmic retribution, invoking the automatic causality of *pratikriya* (reaction, counteraction). While the expression 'natural reaction' captured well how many Gujaratis legitimized the violence, it entirely misrepresented the facts of the pogrom. In this way, guilt became obfuscated for reasons of narrative coherence. What needed to remain coherent was the myth that Hindus never launch the first attack, and are by nature calm and defensive, passive, or fearful. At the same time, if provoked, they could explode and vanquish their enemy with one big swoop. The image invoked was that of Lord Shiva, whose anger once awoken could make even the mighty Himalaya tremble (Makawana 2002, 11–17; see also discussion in Ghassem-Fachandi 2012, 185–212).

The term *pratikriya* was quickly picked up and widely used to refer to the pogrom. Other idiomatic expressions also circulated on the street, such as *karvu j pade* ('It must be done'), which suggested a decisive imperative to violence. In this way, the Gujarat pogrom was accompanied by a distinctive collective atmosphere or mood for which the German term *Stimmung* seems the most adequate (Borneman and Ghassem-Fachandi 2017, 105–35).[10] During the violence, on the basis of false information in vernacular newspapers and rumours, men on the street believed that Muslims had abducted Hindu girls for reasons of *enjoi*.[11] Terminologies that were used for killing exceeded usual vocabularies and suggested a sacrificial script summoning an imagery suffused with neo-Vedic terminology and a strange tendency to imagine and describe violent acts in pornographic detail (Ghassem-Fachandi 2012, 66–78, 2017, 156–59).

The general psychological mobilization for violence was clearly palpable at sites where I ventured. Similar observations can be gleaned in various fact-finding reports. Common people were emboldened to engage in forbidden things such as looting and stone-throwing, and at other sites, rape and murder by organized gangs (Ghassem-Fachandi 2012, 31–57, 93–122). During the days of violence, one ubiquitous writing on city walls read: 'It is an open secret, the Modi government is with us.' The sentence was usually written in Hindi, one of India's official languages ('Ye to andar ki baat hai, Modi sarkar hamare sath hai'), but occasionally also in Gujarati. The pronoun 'us' (*hamare*, literally 'our') here referred to Hindus, while the sentence implicitly addressed Muslims, the section of society that was being collectively harmed. It expressed most blatantly how Gujaratis affirmed the criminal passivity of the police during the pogrom, the strong pro-Hindu bias of state administrators and services, as well as government officials and ministers. The expression *Ye to andar ki baat hai*, which I have here translated as 'It is an open secret' also means 'It is insider knowledge' or 'It is said,' suggesting a more conspiratorial twist. It expresses a general understanding that the government is complicit in the unfolding of events.

The consequence was a permissive atmosphere in the street that despite all feelings of impudence or effrontery can only be described as suffused with sizzling excitement. At an improvised tea stall on Ashram Road not far from what used to be Shiv Cinema (all venues were closed because of curfew), a group of middle-aged men stood around a woman sitting on the ground selling tobacco, *pan* (betel leaf with areca nut), and plastic water pouches. I approached the group. The woman had set up the makeshift shop on the pavement to earn a few bucks, flouting the general lockdown in the city. I joined the men, feeling safer in their company than alone and bought a single cigarette. I wanted to overhear their discussion and engage in a dialogue. The men spoke to one another in a joking manner, fooling around the way groups of men often do when they have time on their hands. Silently standing on the side, I smoked and nodded, but they ignored me. Disappointed at their disinterest, I planned to move along and find another corner to observe a city unhinged. But then a man on a bicycle passed with two overlarge filled cloth bags hanging on both sides of his steering wheel. It was a washerman (*dhobi*), apparently transporting his customer's freshly laundered clothes. He wore a large beard and a skullcap that identified him as a Muslim. He approached relatively slowly and did not speed up his gait when rolling past us.

Busy with one another, the men did not see him at first. Once they noticed him, however, I witnessed the quick atmospheric transformation into a sort of frenzy. It took a moment to build but finally arrived at a dangerous climax. This happened fast. One man raised both arms, lamenting loudly into the air, complaining how a Muslim dared to show his face under the open sky on this day. The cyclist turned his head and offered a faint smile while calmly pedalling on with his heavy load. Another of the group asked for a phone and called an acquaintance. After a few minutes, a small van arrived. I was dumbfounded by the quick turn of events. The men boarded the van gesticulating wildly, driving off in the direction of the Muslim cyclist. Clearly, they wanted to harm or discipline the man. I do not know what happened afterwards. This then was the sort of 'anger' invoked to explain and legitimize urban violence. Such groups of men were neither the organized goons of extremist Hindu organizations like the RSS, VHP, Shiv Sena, or Bajrang Dal that were roaming the streets killing and destroying at will, nor government officials or underclass criminal groups. These were regular citizens channelling to one another feelings of indignation. They were authorizing themselves to engage in hooligan behaviour, taking pleasure in opposition to Muslims. What responsibility do such actors carry for surfing the permissive mood of the moment?

In 2002, most city residents I spoke to saw a clear involvement of the Gujarat government in the pogrom. This acknowledgment was made with a sense of pride and moral rectitude, not embarrassment or sorrow. Many individuals tended later to straight out deny these forms of emotional participation, and I sometimes had the impression that they were sincere; that is, they were indeed no longer entirely aware of their earlier statements and behaviours. This, together with the participation of subaltern communities in attacks, constituted the reason for the brazen expression of triumphalism by Sangh Parivar leaders after the pogrom, the family of Hindu organizations, as well as the magnitude of humiliation for Muslims.

The long-term effects of this questionable development are elaborated in a recent observation by author Amrita Shah in her publication *Ahmedabad, A City in the World* (2015, 1–28). In this well-written description of life in the contemporary city, the author accompanies a middle-aged Muslim named Meraj to his former home in Asarwa-Chamanpura in northeast Ahmedabad, which was attacked and emptied of Muslims in 2002. After years in a relief camp, Meraj moved to the large Muslim neighbourhood of Juhapura and picked up the pieces of his broken life. One day he longs to return to his former home to show the author where he used to live, where his family lost their shop and possessions during the pogrom. While visiting Chamanpura and drinking tea in an adjacent home, a former Hindu neighbour's relative holds forth about the need to teach Muslims a lesson in 2002. Meraj does not become incensed or show annoyance at the man's exhortations. In fact, to the author's surprise, he nods and agrees with him. Sensitive to the oddity of what she witnesses, Shah is disturbed about Meraj's submissive acquiescence. In the plot structure of the pogrom, Muslim victims like him feature merely in the role of tragic collateral damage in retribution deemed karmic, automatic, and necessary because of the black sheep of Muslim society.[12]

I fear that this sort of interaction is a rather common affair in Ahmedabad today. I know many Muslims who for years now circumvent all contact with Hindus and hesitate to apply for jobs in Hindu areas or businesses to avoid humiliating and volatile experiences. These evasions disadvantage them even further in an already discriminatory context. A new hierarchy has established itself in the city. Locals refer to this hierarchy by employing an English idiom: the city was characterized by the distinction between an 'H-class' and an 'M-class'. The letters are colloquial abbreviations for Hindu and Muslim, respectively, referring to the aggregate binary. The word for distinction that is usually employed in the Gujarati vernacular is *bedbhav* (discrimination), a word also used in the context of caste distinction (*te bedbhav rakhe che*, 'he keeps distinction,' that is, he will not drink tea with me).

It is in such a context of growing mutual alienation that a surprising message reached me one day a few years ago while I was living in Fatehvadi, Juhapura, the same ghetto in the southwestern corner of Ahmedabad in which Meraj had found his new home after the 2002 cleansing. In a village not far from Sanand town, the news went, there lived a Bharvad,[13] a Hindu, who was building a Muslim shrine, a *dargah*, on his own ancestral land. This was unusual news, and it spread fast among the people with whom I was working. Many originally hailed from the rural areas surrounding Sanand and thus were immediately curious about this man. It is not uncommon for Hindus to visit or sometimes even officiate at a Muslim shrine. It is rarer for Muslims to officiate at Hindu shrines – although I have run into such cases also over the years.[14] It is, however, rather curious for a Hindu to build a Muslim shrine from scratch and on his own initiative. The days of royal patronage of religious institutions is but a faint memory if such facts are remembered at all. If anything, Muslims today associate Hindus with the demolition of their religious heritage, be it the Babri Mosque in Ayodhya in 1992 or the shrine of Vali Gujarati and others in Ahmedabad in 2002.

At the time, it was said that this Bharvad was building the shrine on what had formerly been Muslim land but had been sold for a low price. This piece of information rang true for most residents present. It made immediate sense because many Muslims living in Fatehvadi had hailed from villages where their fathers had been forced to sell their small plots of land for a pittance a generation ago. This is why they had migrated to the city where they gathered in ghettos after recurring bouts of urban violence displaced them time and again. Now, these lost lands were suddenly worth manifold the price of prior years. *What would have happened if my father had not sold the land?* was a recurring question.

But the story of the Muslim shrine built by a Hindu turned out to be a bit different. I met Kalubhai Bharvad in Ahmedabad where he regularly works, while his residence remains in the village. I did not have his phone number but got the information that he was working as a night guard (*chowkidar*) on the grounds of the Ahmedabad Municipal Fruits and Vegetable Market. One night, I ventured there with two friends for a surprise visit. While climbing up the metal stairs to an empty office on the deserted grounds, we heard agitated voices in an intense discussion echoing in the dark. Kalubhai Bharvad was talking to another night guard, a much younger man, who was listening intently. He once in a while bombarded Kalubhai with questions. Kalubhai told of strange appearances at the vegetable market that he had recently witnessed. After this first encounter, Kalubhai generously invited me to visit him in his home village and promised to show me the Muslim shrine he was building.

'Give Me My Land Back!'[15]

Kalubhai Bharvad is a man in his mid-forties, or so he thinks. It is common for rural folks not to know their exact age. Muscular and compact, he has a pleasant air about him infused with much frenetic energy. Everyone greets him when he passes, walking in quick, determined steps. Villagers seem to appreciate him: his neighbours, work colleagues, caste brethren, and other acquaintances. Although vibrant, he displays no other particular features that are unique except one. When Kalubhai's legs rest, his mouth picks up the pace and speaks with the same rapidity as his legs when moving. Each time I visited him, he appeared somewhat annoyed that he had to interrupt whatever he was saying at the time in order to properly receive me as local protocols demanded.

Accustomed to speaking quickly, he rolls one word into another and utters sentences without interruption for a long while, often overwhelming his audience with allusions and repeating what he said shortly before. When I first tried to speak to him, I found myself mostly defeated. The impenetrable and continuous humming, overlaid by a strong local idiolect, allowed no clear identification of verbs and nouns, the end or beginning of sentences, leaving me with too limited a comprehension. I decided he was racing in mumbling. It was as if he had to hurry to crowd as much as possible into one sentence, into one single breath, into one long monotonous sound. What did he just say?

PRATIKRIYA, GUILT, AND REACTIONARY VIOLENCE

I admit this was a humbling experience, as I have been working in Gujarat for years, including in rural areas such as this village. And I was more or less proud of my linguistic abilities. Now I had to allow myself the expense of two research assistants to catch the intricacies of what he told me without fatiguing or even irritating him through frequent follow-ups while questioning. Kalubhai appeared to seek connections between occurrences and suspended meanings, which he liked to anchor and bring home to the main narrative arc. He needed the suspense as it held his mind on a constant edge. Given his quick associative pace, I did not regret that decision. Both my assistants, although native speakers and from opposite ends of Ahmedabad's social universe, acknowledged difficulties in understanding Kalubhai's phonology, which made me feel a bit better. 'He speaks funny,' one of my assistants, Munavar, commented dryly.

Kalubhai's oddity is not the result of a handicap but more a reflection of the generosity of his natural audiences, consisting almost exclusively of local farmers, who apparently enjoyed and understood his references and allusions. Often themselves quite monosyllabic, they had gotten used to his way of singing a story in his humming mumble. When we first met, after what seemed like a brief moment of real surprise that someone like me appeared at his nightly job, Kalubhai immediately took my presence as preordained and weaved it into his general narrative (disappointing me as I wanted to hear about the apparitions). Me, I was initially surprised because I expected a man in traditional attire. Bharvads are known to be conservative dressers, which for Western eyes often appears exotic. Kalubhai, however, looked much less flamboyant and more like a grocer or accountant than a shepherd.

Falling into a sequence of entangled stories over the course of several visits, Kalubhai eventually narrated to me the events and dreams that prompted him to begin constructing a Muslim shrine on his ancestral land in his residential village, being himself a Hindu. Some of these discussions were held in private, with only his wife and my assistants present; others were in larger groups of villagers that showed curiosity to watch Kalu sing to a foreigner and be entertained. In this written text, the story will appear more systematic than how it was relayed to me, which is an unavoidable side-effect of integrating a spoken, meandering, and associative oral rendering into a narrative textual form with a page limit: descriptive exposition on paper.

It began with unfortunate events and a series of accompanying dreams and visions, which Kalubhai alternately calls *sapna* (dream) and *drashti* (vision). The dreams began approximately seven years ago – about the same time Sanand irreversibly became a boomtown. At this time, things in Kalubhai's life did not fare too well. Family members got sick and almost died; another had an accident.

Kalubhai started having dreams that woke and shook him up violently during the night. Those habitually sleeping near him became alarmed, and some refused to be at his side at night.[16] This was followed by periods of sleeplessness and general uneasy tension. A saintly figure calling himself Peer began appearing in his dreams, sternly demanding the return of his land. Says Kalubhai: *Peer shu kidhu? Mara jagia api do, keh* ('What did the Pir say? He said, "Give me my plot"').

Note the imperative tone of voice, unembellished and direct. Kalubhai repeats this command often when he speaks, more often than it is possible to reproduce in a written text. It is as if there should be no doubt, no ambiguity in the listener what the spectral entity was asking for. In front of his co-villagers, Kalubhai speaks in a similarly blunt way. Sometimes he will use the word 'plot' or 'space' (both *jagia*), sometimes 'land' (*jamin*), indicating that which must be returned. In the logic of the story Kalubhai is relating, he is at this point not yet aware of the fact that the saintly or divine figure appearing in his dreams is a Muslim.

Kalubhai knew that his paternal grandfather (*dada*) had illicitly enlarged his traditional agricultural plot, the one Kalu had inherited from his father, by encroaching on adjacent land. On that adjacent land, which he refers to as 'neutral' (he means 'without an owner'), once stood what he calls a cenotaph (*paliyo*). Stone cenotaphs are strewn all over the rural landscape of central and north Gujarat, stretching all the way into Rajasthan (Lehmann 2003). They are usually associated with the deeds of heroic local figures detailed in local legends. They include equestrian Rajput knights defending cows or the kingdom from marauders or women who chose to immolate themselves on their husband's funeral pyre in chastity and sacrifice. His grandfather razed the stone and enlarged his land by appropriating the unused part. Until recently, Kalu had not thought much of it as illegal encroachment on adjacent or neighbouring land is a common rural practice. But then, unfortunate events began to happen, and Kalu became attentively focused on these past transgressions.

Later, villagers affirmed this estimation to me. It was business as usual to encroach on neighbouring and adjacent agricultural land. Everyone would do it, as long as they could get away with it. Land and real estate registries in rural India are legendary for being knotty institutions. Information about land ownership is hazily recorded and can easily be manipulated through corrupt machinations. Encroachment constitutes a form of unscripted rural practice that is as common as it is kept secret and silent. Occasionally, land disputes can culminate into violent conflicts, often between close relatives such as cousins or brothers. A while later, the figure appeared again in Kalu's dreams and gave him an ultimatum saying that in *sava mahina*, that is, in exactly five weeks, he *must* give back the plot, the place which his grandfather had encroached. In a third dream, finally, a face appeared and spoke: *Hu Pir chhu, keh! Mara jagia mane api do!* ('I am a Peer', he said! 'Give to me my plot!')

This time, it was the face of a small boy with a green turban. In the dream, the child began dancing and jumping wildly all over the place. For the first time, Kalubhai responded to the command: 'I will give your land back, trust me.' But the boy, instead of an answer, spread the fingers on one of his hands real wide. The fingers elongated unnaturally until the veins popped up from under its flesh and finally seemed to separate from one another in a horrific vision. Kalubhai was terrified. The image of limbs that stretch beyond any natural length is a typical characteristic of nightmarish apparitions associated with malevolent ghosts (*bhut*) in Gujarat. I have heard similar descriptions of ghostly appearances, which are usually hard to bear and described as a disturbing nightmarish ordeal. Kalubhai took the warning to heart.

Not understanding exactly who this unsettling figure might be but sufficiently troubled by the warning, Kalubhai began planning for the building of a temple to Ramdev Peer Bhagwan on his land, a locally known deity.[17] He naturally assumed that the nightly apparitions were of a Hindu divinity. The word *peer* is often used in written Gujarati for what is considered a Hindu deity, but even more commonly the word *pir* denotes the presence of a Muslim shrine.[18] At the specified place, where the ancient stone had once stood, on the land he had inherited from his father and grandfather, Kalu made preparations to ritually install the picture of Ramdev Peer. Together with his cousin, he went to an appropriate shop to buy a small marble temple for housing the icon.

Then something strange happened. The shop owner, instead of welcoming the business, reacted with an inexplicable hesitation. Encouraging Kalubhai to sleep over his decision, he told him to go home and see the next day. That was no ordinary behaviour for a sales merchant, Kalu explained. Warned by the shop owner's strange behaviour, for which Kalu could give no satisfactory explanation, the entity manifested itself again in Kalubhai's head the next morning and addressed him most forcibly: *Beta, hu mandir ma na hoi, hamara dargah hoi, keh. Me dargah na Pir chhe, keh* ('"Son, I am not in temple, we rest in dargah," he said. "I am a Pir of the dargah," he said').[19]

Now Kalubhai understood that these visitations were from a *Muslim* Pir, whom he began addressing as Pir Dada ('Grandfather Pir'). There was no other name at this time that he could have used. Kalu explained to me that he did not know much about Islam or Muslim shrines. But in the local villages of surrounding areas, Muslim shrines belong as much to the local sacred landscape as the ubiquitous mother goddess shrines or Ram and Hanuman temples. However, this village never had a Muslim shrine in living memory. Indeed, at the time of Kalubhai's grandfather, when the small stone was visible on the borders of his agricultural fields, villagers referred to it as *paliyo* (cenotaph) or simply *pattar* (stone). It was situated next to a tree, which somehow was associated with the stone. But there was no shrine built at that time, and to date it remains unclear whether the entity dwelling there had ever been considered Muslim in the past.

But that was now to change. The news of Kalubhai's dreams sparked various memories among his rural neighbours and co-residents. Villagers suddenly remembered that in the olden days the spot around the tree was called the place of Chinthariya Pir – *chinthra* for rags. Visitors would bring pieces of used, colourful cloths and attach them to the tree as a form of *mannat* (vow).[20] Villagers began telling Kalubhai that many years ago a white horse had been seen galloping in this area. Some claimed that it moved about alone through the brush. Others saw a rider on the horse, a large male figure with a long beard and handsome features wearing a turban (*pagdi*).[21] Some confirmed seeing strange things moving about in the dark. Soon enough, Kalubhai saw the figure in his dreams in these very details as it addressed him: *Hu Chinthariya Pir chhu ane hu Makkahna panch pir paikino ek chhu* ('I am Chinthariya Pir and I am one of the Five Pirs of Makkah').[22]

The Pir rode on a white horse and carried a flame in his hand. Residents of the village told me that the flame had, in fact, often been seen at night: a light moving in the dark through the fields in different directions but always stopping at the approximate location of the shrine. This then was Chinthariya Pir, the author of Kalubhai's visions and nightly dreams.[23]

The shrine whose infancy I witnessed four years ago when I began this ethnographic work is now a large structure with corrugated ceilings and balustrades. It looks humble but sophisticated enough to withstand many years to come. It forms a high cement platform in the middle of nowhere: surrounded by brush and adorned by a large tree located between agricultural fields of castor oil fruit (*erenda*). The tree has grown large, littered with hundreds of colourful pieces of ripped cloth from old wear like *saris*, *kurtas*, *salwar kameez* – material reminders of issues, ailments, and desperate wishes. There is no paved road or possibility to reach this shrine in any comfortable manner besides walking past fields and through thick underbrush. During the monsoon, the shrine is barely accessible except by wading through long stretches of muddy water.

The surprising speed with which Kalubhai Bharvad has been able to furnish a proper Muslim shrine with limited funds speaks of the effectiveness of the local register in which he is playing. Soon Kalubhai invited Alkhubhai, an elderly Muslim from the Qureishi community of a neighbouring village, to officiate as *mujavar* (caretaker) at the shrine, which is now officially named Chinthariya Pir Dada Dargah. In a dream, Kalubhai beheld that Alkhu's grandfather used to officiate to the forgotten Pir and that Alkhu was actually born not in a neighbouring village, as he himself had thought, but in Kalu's village and only afterwards was taken to the former to be raised. Kalubhai contacted Alkhubhai and told him this information from his dreams. They both relate to one another as old familiars and friends.

Alkhubhai now visits the shrine every Thursday (Figure 13.1). It is the day when Kalubhai falls possessed (*hajri*) and draws a small local audience, limited to surrounding villages and rural areas. Alkhu told me, he initially knew nothing about being a shrine caretaker before Kalubhai's invitation. He had to learn everything from scratch and was impressed that he could do this at such an advanced age. It seems that he has become positively contaminated by Kalubhai's energy and enthusiasm.

Figure 13.1 Shrine caretaker at Chinthariya Pir Dargah, Spring 2019
Source: Photo by author.

Conclusion

Why did the question of culpability never properly emerge in public discourse after the pogrom? One reason was Narendra Modi's political will to shape the electorate into a permanent Hindutva majority.[24] While the death of victims during the pogrom was deemed tragic, Hindu anger was ultimately rationalized by identifying a prior crime committed in Godhra that offered moral legitimization for all that had followed. Construing the pogrom as a mere reaction to the Godhra incident confirmed the truth of Hindutva moral narratives that define Hindus as hapless victims of Muslim aggression since the arrival of Islam on the subcontinent. The aftermath of the pogrom was an obdurate morass of political scheming, public lying, and factual obfuscation. Aided by the powerful influence of Hindu nationalist organizations in the state, Gujarat settled after the pogrom for weeks into a zombie-like disposition, simultaneously shocked and fascinated by the naturalized unfolding of surreal events. The general silence of many Gujaratis crept up on me like a paralyzing fog, lodging itself into my own speech, eventually blurring the memory of many I spoke to, twisting tongues into many a make-believe and finally obscuring everything that had been so obvious. What could have been an honest reckoning became a farce.

Modi pre-empted the time for Gujaratis to express sorrow or regret. The state itself orchestrated no mourning, which might have led to reflection on forms of culpability and complicity. Instead of introspection and a reckoning, while Muslim relief camps were still operating, the chief minister began campaigning for elections to be held within months of the violence – in December 2002 – timing that the Election Commission of India criticized severely at the time. In this way, the Gujarat pogrom and its murky aftermath became the midwife to the political success of Narendra Modi, which is why he can never properly address or denounce the events. The pogrom permanently stained his political career and whatever his political triumph, he will never be able to whiten this bloody spot.

During and especially after the violence, Modi did not try to conceal his Hindu nationalist bias. This changed the rules of the game for India at large after he later became prime minister. In Gujarat, he was the chief minister who need not apologize because the pogrom defined what he considers a mere matter of fact: minority Muslims are at the mercy of majority Hindus. He would not defend Muslims against the violence of the majority. With this, he displayed openly what had been implicitly acknowledged for a long time and the reason why many considered him an authentic arbiter of truth. This was a significant departure from the rhetorical contortions of prior generations of state politicians, who tried to mould their communal strategies to fit democratic form and pay lip service to Mahatma Gandhi.

PRATIKRIYA, GUILT, AND REACTIONARY VIOLENCE

According to Ashis Nandy, the murder of Gandhi was a collective communiqué in which many participated, not least Gandhi himself (Nandy 1991, 70–98). Modi confirmed the sense that Gandhi must be killed again, in the present. The Gandhi that Modi needed Gujaratis to get rid of was the troubling hesitation and doubt in their minds that had blocked them from blatantly affirming a majoritarian Hindu dominance. Hindus were to emerge from the pogrom free to choose violence, free of the superego's torturous grip. Modi transformed the ambivalence many Gujaratis felt for this figure into a form of Hindu righteousness and indignation. If Gandhi had invoked ancient Hindu ideals such as non-violence (*ahimsa*) to renounce violent action, the new dispensation defined Hindus as vulnerable exactly because of their intimate association with the very same non-violence. This vulnerability needed an organized, violent Hindu response. This was achieved with a delegation of violent labour to Hindu nationalist organizations who after the pogrom went mostly unpunished, the leaders not held responsible, their institutional structures unaltered. The propaganda flyers, the statements by local politicians, the rumours, and misrepresentations – nothing was taken back, nothing was addressed, reflected, or set right. There was no sense of accountability achieved for the events of the pogrom. Modi simply shifted gear and most Gujaratis followed suit.

This new strategy marked the beginning of Modi's meteoric rise onto the national stage more than a decade after the Gujarat pogrom, where he had already shown himself in sync with the mood of the majority of voters. He consequently has won every election in which he campaigned. In Ahmedabad, the absence of a discourse on guilt has petrified the relation between the two aggregate categories, Hindus and Muslims, even further. It has now created the 'H' and the 'M-class' of citizens, a hierarchy as noxious as the one between caste-Hindus (*savarna*) and those traditionally excluded from the moral Hindu order (*avarna*), untouchables. The logic of the former is significantly connected to the logic of the latter in that this new hierarchy is to replace and substitute for the older division between caste Hindu and outcaste. In this new moral order, individuals who show remorse have not been able to transform such retrospective feelings into effective political opposition (Jasani 2020, 676–77). Guilt integrated into a landscape of memory might have avoided this development as, under the right circumstances, it can foster pro-social effects conducive to the expression of regret and responsibility, and articulate a general concern for justice (Baumeister, Stillwell, and Heatherton 1994).

In this essay, I have described one ethnographic context in which the identification of guilt becomes possible, while it remains to be seen if it will be productive. Kalubhai Bharvad denies any meaning that invokes contemporary politics (*rajkaran*) or sociological facts such as the agrarian order of land acquisition and alienation, the marginalization of the minority community or the events of the pogrom. Yet

Chinthariya Pir appears in his dreams and gives direct commands, which are almost exact replicas of what local Muslims say when they realize the gravity of the loss of agricultural land in Sanand district. It remains to be seen whether this shrine will grow or wither away in the immediate future. To date, it is strongly associated with only one man. It has so far not been challenged by village or district authorities, nor were there any attempts to appropriate the shrine by Hindutva agitators or activists, which would alienate local Muslims.

What is certain is that Kalubhai's shrine takes us back to a prior loss. It manifests the need to make Muslims present again, indeed, to *give them back their place*. The shrine of Chinthariya Pir represents an attempt to reconstitute the chain that links aggregate categories allegorically. It reconstitutes the complicated local concatenation of worship, belief, and co-presence to one another that characterizes the unique character of Indian cultural traditions. After waves of violence, Hindutva agitation, a political takeover, and a hyped development agenda that has run aground, these links have been severed. Kalubhai reinstates the chain by implicating his own father and grandfather in a transgression that could have easily gone unnoticed. But he makes their transgressions count in the present. They express a specific generational guilt in a somatic form through disease and possession states in which land that belonged to a supernatural entity is reclaimed and in which this ambiguous figure becomes ultimately defined as a proper Muslim Pir. What is most astonishing in this gradual development is the support Kalu receives from members of the village community who actively participate in associating, remembering, and imagining a bearded equestrian figure, holding a light in the dark. While Kalu might be considered an odd fellow, to my knowledge, no one really opposed him or tried to sabotage his ambitious project.

The Pir does not speak to Kalubhai as a friend or ally but as a stern figure of authority making demands, threatening, and even taunting him. He gives him orders that are difficult for a Hindu to fulfil. And yet Kalubhai submits, which impresses his village audience and visiting Muslims from neighbouring villages or slum areas in Ahmedabad adept at discerning fake from authentic moments of religious sublimity. What is the agency of this commanding voice? Who is speaking? It is hard to avoid the conclusion that Kalubhai speaks against all odds with the voice of a collective superego, a voice demanding the recognition of a trans-generational guilt vis-à-vis Muslims. And although, like most ethnographic expositions, this one too ends as an unfinished story whose further unfolding must be awaited, one cannot avoid the impression that in the contemporary political climate, there lies an element of atonement in Kalubhai's eager willingness to submit to a Muslim Pir.

In 2019, while on a trip from Ahmedabad to Kalubhai's village, I asked my friend Habibabhai about Hindutva, a question I had not asked him for a long while. I wanted to know what it is to him after twenty-five years of BJP rule in Gujarat, nearly seventeen years after the pogrom. As a Muslim living in the state at the margins of a large city, he personally had witnessed the violence of 2002. His survival story comes with many gruesome tales and experiences from which he never properly recovered. It seemed to me that he was the perfect person to ask. After pondering briefly, accustomed to my many questions, he gave me one of his shortest answers ever: 'What is Hindutva? All are united, but Muslims remain separate ...'[25]

The religion of Hindus and Muslims was *sanklayelu*, intertwined or interconnected (also *jodayelu*). In Gujarati, a *sankal* is a chain, the individual members of which are locked to one another forming a concatenation. They cannot be separated without causing harm, without losing their function of binding together local communities into a unity. Land stands metaphorically for the ancestral place of Muslims in Gujarat, for their link in the chain: their intimate belonging to the state. If they migrated from rural areas into the city, they did so out of a dire need in years past because their plots of land yielded too little to survive. In cities like Ahmedabad, waves of violence have again displaced them into ghettos and slums. Muslims have lost their origins, their place in the chain. Kalubhai's busy voice seems to want to retrieve this missing link.

Notes

*   I thank Dr Razak Khan for kindly reading an early brainstorm draft of this essay in my absence at a conference on Understanding New Hindutva in Göttingen, Germany, organized by Professor Dr Srirupa Roy in 2018. I also thank the Zentrum Interdisziplinäre Forschung (ZiF) in Bielefeld for a generous fellowship year in Bielefeld from 2018 to 2019. Especially, I want to thank S. A. Pathan, Salman K., and Prachi Dublai for reflections, comments, and much-needed help with translations during on-site ethnographic fieldwork on Chinthariya Pir Dargah in Gujarat during the wild spring of 2019. Without their energetic enthusiasm and intellectual wit, this text could not have been completed any time soon. Finally, I want to thank Anja Mayer, a German ethnographer and moviemaker, who accompanied me to Kalubhai's village in prior years. She provided much needed visual material and engaged in many invaluable discussions.

1   Many large and small violent events in Gujarat are routinely called 'riots', although the empirical events differ in form and motivation widely. Despite indicating excess, the term *riot* suggests something familiar about reoccurring conflicts in neighbourhoods in mostly urban areas. The term *pogrom*, by contrast, does not allow for such relegation to commonplace. The events of 2002 were nothing but exceptional in every way, not in the least in the perception of those who witnessed and participated in them. This exceptionality is mostly denied today.

2   Usually translated as devastation or destruction, the word 'pogrom' derives etymologically from the Russian *grom* meaning 'thunder', *gromit* 'to thunder, to destroy without pity'. The *Oxford English Dictionary* (1987) defines pogrom as 'an organized massacre for the destruction or annihilation of any body or class'.

3   The interview was conducted by journalist Smita Gupta. Uma Bharati is a Hindu nationalist and currently the national vice president of the Bharatiya Janata Party (BJP), the ruling party of India.

4   The 'Kalinga effect' in the title refers to the remorse and contrition often attributed to Mauryan Emperor Asoka after the Battle of Kalinga in 265 BCE. The war is said to have made such an impression on the emperor that he devoted his life to *ahimsa* (non-violence), albeit only after he had vanquished his enemies.

5   This automatic association of Muslims with violence has many complexities that are particular to societies traditionally characterized by caste distinction where forms of displacement and projection have replaced older forms of complementarity. I cannot deal with these questions here. An understanding of these projections and how they affect intersubjective dynamics must include a consideration of Muslim diet (meat and beef-eating), forms of worship (ritual animal sacrifice), coming-of-age rites (circumcision), and the widespread stereotypical assumption that Muslims share a general mental inclination towards enjoyment and carelessness (Kakar 1995, 138). For a more patient exploration of some of these themes, see Ghassem-Fachandi (2012).

6   Cf. Nag (2002, 10).

7   The formulation is taken from Sudhir Kakar (1995, 51).

8   This stereotypical expression is very commonly used in Gujarat and elsewhere in India and can be traced to a text by Mohandas K. Gandhi, who wrote, '... the Mussalman as a rule is a bully, and the Hindu as a rule is a coward.' Cf. Gandhi (1924). Also see Ghassem-Fachandi (2019, 83–98 and Kakar (1995, 438).

9   Such psychological idealization is not singular or unusual in the context of sectarian, communal, or ethnic violence in India but rather endemic and fundamentally characterizes it. For an exploration of idealization in communal mobilization in India, compare with Kakar (1995).

10 In local idioms, the collective mood was indicated by terms such as *vaataavaran* or simply *stithi*, as if denoting weather conditions. The Gujarati term *hava* (wind, air, as in 'violence is in the air') was equally used and approximates the German expression 'Es liegt in der Luft' (*te havaamaa chhe*, 'It lies in the air'). Rubina Jasani (2020, 676) mentions the term *mahoul* (environment).

11 *Enjoi* is idiomatic Gujarati taken from the English word 'enjoy' and employed in a Gujarati sentence with a local logic. The word became widely popular among non-English speakers in the 1990s as the Coca Cola commercial *Enjoy!* entered India. During pogrom violence, men on the street employed the term to denote forms of pleasure in violent actions, such as rape and bodily mutilation, which they attributed to Muslims (Ghassem-Fachandi 2012, 74).

12 It is unclear to me whether Meraj would have acquiesced quite in the same manner had he not been sitting in a Hindu home of a residential area cleansed in 2002 and in the presence of an outside guest (the author). In my experience, what and how one speaks about past violence in Ahmedabad is determined by the immediate context in which one finds oneself. Meraj would likely have reacted differently had the man spoken thusly in Meraj's new home in a Muslim area. This does not contradict Shah's insightful observation of a bizarre and disturbing scene.

13 A Bharvad is a member of a community whose traditional occupation was taking care of animals (shepherd caste herding livestock).

14 These cases should be distinguished from the attempts at reconversion of Muslims and Christians in the *ghar wapsi* campaigns by Hindu nationalist organizations, which peaked in 2014, twelve years after the pogrom.

15 'mane mari jamin pachhi apo'.

16 In Gujarati villages, it is common for larger groups of men to sleep together during the night in a barn or even outside on cement platforms near a temple or shrine at a village square.

17 This choice of this Hindu folk deity is very significant but cannot be elaborated here for reasons of brevity. Note that it is somewhat astonishing that Kalubhai did not immediately understand the apparition of the boy to represent a Muslim. It makes sense, however, in light of the tradition of Ramdev Peer. For a fascinating discussion of Ramdev Pir (or Peer), the saint's relation to the Meghval community, to Islam and Ismailism, see the scholarly work of Dominique-Sila Khan (2003, 60–94).

18 Cf. Dominique-Sila Khan (2003, 97–124). Note that in spoken and written Gujarati, the words *pir* and *peer* are indistinguishable. Many villagers in this particular context are illiterate or read and write rarely.

19 A *dargah* is a Muslim shrine, the mausoleum of the dead Muslim saint, that is, a Pir.

20 The tree onto which colourful pieces of cloth are attached when making a vow is a common site in rural Gujarat. Not exclusive to one particular religious community, the practice is not mentioned in any classic religious text. The 'rag uncle' is a traditional figure and must have a long unwritten history in folk tradition (Daya 1990 [1848], 19–21). I have seen many such trees over the years and suspect that most villages in Gujarat have one in their immediate surrounding vicinity.

21 This description fits depictions of Ramdev Peer as much as various Muslim saints. It also resembles other apparitions of elongated bearded figures that often appear in mosques that Muslims regularly mention to me. These latter apparitions are referred to as 'white djinns'. They visit mosques to pray during the night. People respectfully avoid them because their anger can have serious consequences. While a form of spirit being, they are not malevolent by nature but pious.

22 Dominique-Sila Khan (2003, 63) mentions the current hagiography in which a Hindu Ramdev defeated five Muslim Pirs from Mecca 'who were forced to admit that he was more powerful than they'. In Kalubhai's version, we see a transformation typical for the

flexibility of folk tradition, where Ramdev is constructed as one of the five Pirs and not their rival.

23 So far, no one has been able to explain to me who or what the five Pirs of Mecca are. They appear in the mythology of Ramdev Peer, the Hindu deity. Ramdev Peer is depicted with a beard and sitting on a horse indistinguishable from the other five Pirs (or is maybe even part of the five?). Cf. Dominique-Sila Khan (2003, 65).

24 For a discussion of the Hindu majoritarian ascendency in recent years, see Chatterji, Hansen, and Jaffrelot (2019, 1–15).

25 In Gujarati: 'Hindutva etle shu? Bada ek, musalman alag …'

References

Baumeister, R. F., A. M. Stillwell, and T. F. Heatherton. 1994. 'Guilt: An Interpersonal Approach'. *Psychological Bulletin* 115(2): 243–67.

Borneman, J., and P. Ghassem-Fachandi. 2017. 'The Concept of *Stimmung*: From Indifference to Xenophobia in Germany's Refugee Crisis'. *Hau: Journal of Ethnographic Theory* 7(3): 105–35.

Chatterji, A. P., T. B. Hansen, and C. Jaffrelot (eds.). 2019. *Majoritarian State: How Hindu Nationalism Is Changing India*. London: Hurst & Company.

Daya, D. 1990 [1848]. *Demonology and Popular Superstitions of Gujarat*. Translated by A. K Forbes. New Delhi: Vintage Books.

Eckert, J. 2010. 'Kultur und Schuld: Narrative der Verantwortung'. In *Zurechnung und Verantwortung: Tagung der Deutschen Sektion der Internationalen Vereinigung für Rechts- und Sozialphilosophie* vom 22–24(134): 155–168

Gandhi, M. K. 1924. 'Hindu–Muslim Conflict, Its Causes and Cure'. *Young India*, 29 May.

Ghassem-Fachandi, P. 2012. *Pogrom in Gujarat: Hindu Nationalism and Anti-Muslim Violence in India*. Princeton University Press.

———. 2019. 'Reflections in the Crowd: Delegation, Verisimilitude, and the Modi Mask'. In *Majoritarian State: How Hindu Nationalism Is Changing India*, edited by Angana P. Chatterji, Thomas Bom Hansen and Christophe Jaffrelot, 83–98. London: Hurst & Company.

Jasani, R. 2020. 'Violence, Urban Anxieties and Masculinities: The Foot Soldiers of 2002, Ahmedabad'. *Journal of South Asia Studies* 43(4): 675–90.

Kakar, S. 1995. *The Colours of Violence*. New Delhi: Viking Penguin Books India.

Khan, D. S. 2003 [1997]. *Conversions and Shifting Identities. Ramdev Pir and the Ismailis in Rajasthan*. New Delhi: Manohar

Lehmann, N.M. 2003. 'Über den Tod hinaus: *Sati*, das Ideal and Kshatriya Ehefrau'. In *Selbstopfer und Entsagung im Westen Indiens* (mit Andrea Luithle). Vorwort von Prof. Dr. Georg Pfeffer. Hamburg: Verlag Dr. Kovac.

Makawana, K. (ed.). 2002. *Godhra Hatyakand, Kalamno Dharma ane Adharma*. Kishor Rajkot: Pravin Prakashan.

Nag, K. 2002. 'The Guilty of Gujarat: No One to Police the Police'. *Times of India*, Ahmedabad edition, 1 June.

Nandy, A. 1991. *At the Edge of Psychology*. Calcutta: Oxford University Press.

Shah, A. 2015. *Ahmedabad: A City in the World*. London: Bloomsbury.

Sundar, N. 2004. 'Toward an Anthropology of Culpability'. *American Ethnologist* 31(2): 145–63.

Times of India. 2002a. 'Terror Within'. Ahmedabad edition, 29 May.

———. 2002b. 'Psyche of the Aggressor: No Kalinga Effect in Gujarat'. Ahmedabad edition, 13 July.

CONTRIBUTORS

Irfan Ahmad is a political anthropologist and senior research fellow at the Max Planck Institute, Göttingen, Germany. Author of two monographs and editor of three volumes, he is the author, most recently, of *Religion as Critique: Islamic Critical Thinking from Mecca to the Marketplace* (2017) and the editor of *Anthropology and Ethnography Are Not Equivalent* (2021). Earlier, he taught at Australian and Dutch universities. He contributes to various discussions in Indian and international media.

Ritajyoti Bandyopadhyay teaches History at the Indian Institute of Science Education and Research (IISER) Mohali, India. He is also a permanent module fellow of the Merian–R. Tagore International Centre of Advanced Studies 'Metamorphoses of the Political' (ICAS:MP).

Amrita Basu, the Paino Professor of Political Science and Sexuality, Women's and Gender Studies at Amherst College, is the editor or co-editor of seven books and the author of two monographs, including *Violent Conjunctures in Democratic India* (Cambridge University Press, 2015).

Mona Bhan is the Ford Maxwell Professor of South Asian Studies and Associate Professor of Anthropology at the Maxwell School, Syracuse University. Bhan is the author of *Counterinsurgency, Development, and the Politics of Identity: From Warfare to Welfare?* (2013) and the co-author of *Climate without Nature: A Critical Anthropology of the Anthropocene* (2018). She is also the co-editor of *Resisting Occupation in Kashmir* (2018) and a member and co-founder of the group Critical Kashmir Studies Collective.

CONTRIBUTORS

Parvis Ghassem-Fachandi was born in the former 'West-Berlin' in a divided Germany and spent his early childhood in Montréal, Paris, and Berlin. He is the author of *Pogrom in Gujarat: Hindu Nationalism and Anti-Muslim Violence in India* (2012).

Thomas Blom Hansen is Professor of Anthropology at the Stanford University. He is the author of *The Saffron Wave: Democracy and Hindu Nationalism in Modern India* (1999), *Wages of Violence: Naming and Identity in Postcolonial Bombay* (2001), *Melancholia of Freedom: Social Life in an Indian Township in South Africa* (2012), and *The Law of Force: The Violent Heart of Indian Politics* (2021).

Arkotong Longkumer is Senior Lecturer in Modern Asia at the University of Edinburgh and Senior Research Fellow at the Kohima Institute, Nagaland. He is the author of *The Greater India Experiment: Hindutva and the Northeast* (2020), co-author of *Indigenous Religion(s): Local Grounds, Global Networks* (2020), and co-editor of *Neo-Hindutva* (2019).

Srirupa Roy is Professor and Chair of State and Democracy, Centre for Modern Indian Studies, at the University of Göttingen and a co-director of the Merian–Tagore International Centre of Advanced Studies (ICAS:MP). She is the author of *Beyond Belief: India and the Politics of Postcolonial Nationalism* (2007) and co-editor of *Violence and Democracy in India* and *Visualizing Secularism and Religion: Egypt, Lebanon, Turkey, India* (2012).

Ashwin Subramanian completed his MA at the Centre for Modern Indian Studies, University of Göttingen, and joined the doctoral program in Anthropology at Harvard University in the autumn of 2021.

Lalit Vachani is a documentary filmmaker and research scholar at the Centre for Modern Indian Studies, University of Göttingen. His documentaries include *The Salt Stories* (2009), which follows the trail of Gandhi's Salt March in Narendra's Modi's Gujarat; *An Ordinary Election* (2015), an in-depth study of an Indian election campaign; and *The Boy in the Branch* (1993) and *The Men in the Tree* (2002), which document the ideology and the growth of the RSS and Hindu nationalism.

Suryakant Waghmore is Professor of Sociology at the Department of Humanities and Social Sciences, Indian Institute of Technology Bombay (IITB). He is the author of *Civility against Caste* (2013) and co-editor of *Civility in Crisis* (2020).

INDEX

4G services, 118, 126n24

Aadhaar Bill, 32
Aadhaar (unique identification) number, 32
Aam Aadmi Party (AAP), 28, 49, 121–122, 238, 262
'abstract Muslim,' 15
Afzal Guru, hanging of, 32
Agricultural Produce Market Committees (APMC), 55
Akhand Bharat, 12, 20
Akhil Bharatiya Itihas Sankalan Yojana, 26
Akhil Bharatiya Vidyarthi Parishad (ABVP), 31–32, 49, 62, 67, 108, 113, 124n15, 207, 209, 216n14
Akhlaq, Mohammad, 30
Aligarh Muslim University, 48
Allahabad, renaming of, 43
All India Majlis-e-Ittehadul Muslimeen (AIMIM), 168, 170, 175, 177n15, 178n17
All India Railwaymen's Federation (AIRF), 49
   nationwide strike against the privatization of the Indian Railways, 49

Amnesty International India, 56
Ananta Aspen Centre, 75, 89
'ancient atavisms,' 2
anti-CAA protests, 125n18
anti-CAA protest sites, Hindu right-wing mobs attack on, 50
'anti-India' slogans, 31
anti-Muslim rhetoric of 1969, 14
anti-national Muslims, 16
anti-Romeo squads, 123n5
Anti-Terrorism Squad (ATS), 28
armed irregulars, 166
Article 35A of the Indian Constitution
   constitutional status of, 79
   parliamentary resolutions abrogating the status of, 45
   for protecting Kashmiris' rights to land ownership and permanent residency, 66
Article 370 of the Indian Constitution
   abrogation of, 56, 68, 275, 281
   constitutional status of, 79
   impact on development of Kashmir, 276
   legal challenge to, 100n17
   parliamentary resolutions on, 45

INDEX

revocation of, 66, 119, 220
special status for Kashmir, 16, 126n26
articulation of Hindutva, 5, 10–11, 14, 97, 130, 145, 158, 160, 193, 195
Astha Bharati, 36
Asthana, Rakesh, 38
Atmanirbhar Bharat (Self-reliant India), building of, 52
atrocities against Dalits, cases of, 34
Auditor-General, 6
Aurangzeb Road, renaming of, 30
authoritarian populism, 1, 5, 10, 97
Ayodhya–Babri Masjid verdict, 119
Azad, Chandrasekhar (Raavan), 38, 42, 125n18

backsliding, democratic, 4
Bahujan Samaj Party (BSP), 109, 125n17
Bailey, Frederick, 199
Bajrang Dal, 48, 109, 287, 290
Balakot air strikes, 44–45
Begriffsgeschichte, 252
Bhansali, Sanjay Leela, 35
Bharatiya Gau Raksha Dal, 62
Bharatiya Janata Party (BJP), 188–189, 253, 302n3
　abrogation of Articles 370 and 35A of the Indian Constitution, 275
　assembly election, 28
　fostering of Hindu–Muslim tensions, 59
　Hindu nationalism, 1, 72
　in 2014, 5, 6, 25
　promise of *achhe din* (good days), 26
　relation with RSS, 183
　setback in the Delhi legislative 'Turning to Roots, Rising to Heights' theme, 84
　under Narendra Modi, 275

Unnao rape case, 39, 41, 51
victory in Assam state elections, 33
　in West Bengal, 131
　winning of seats in Lok Sabha, 158
Bharat Petroleum Corporation Limited (BPCL), 45
Bharat Sanchar Nigam Limited (BSNL), 45
Bhima Koregaon violence, 41, 52, 57, 125n18
Bhim Army, 36, 38, 56, 114, 125n18
Bhushan, Prashant, 38, 43
'black laws' of anti-terrorism, 8
black money, 34
Bohra community, 171
Border Security Force (BSF), 43
border tours, 83
Bunch of Thoughts (1966), 239n4

Caravan magazine, 25, 57, 107, 117–118, 126n22
Carnegie Endowment for International Peace's international network, 75, 96
caste-free spaces, 12
castes of Hinduism, 199–201
　alternate civil society, 214–215
　coaching with *samskara*, 208–209
　Hinduism as civil religion, 201–204
　locating caste and Rashtrotthana in Karnataka, 204–205
　Rashtrotthana, 206
　relation with Hindutva, 199–200
　sublated Hinduism, 211–212
　Tapas project, 207–208
　warden as mother and education with *samskara*, 209–211
　yoga with English and Hindu *manushyata*, 213–214

309

INDEX

Central Bureau of Investigation (CBI), 6, 34
Central Information Commission, 6
Central Reserve Police Force (CRPF), 44
Central Vigilance Commission, 6
Central Vista elite, 96–97
Centre for Social and Economic Progress (CSEP), 98n2
ChalChitra Abhiyaan, 107–108, 117, 118, 120, 123, 125
Chameli Devi Jain Award for Outstanding Woman Journalist, 107
Chauhan, Gajendra, 7, 29
check-and-balance institutions, 6, 8
Chief Justice of India (CJI), 26, 133
Child Labour Prevention Act, 37
Citizenship Act (1955), 20n1
Citizenship Amendment Act (CAA), 16, 20n1, 44, 47, 67, 79
   all-India *bandh* (strike) against, 113
   passing of, 47
   sit-in protest against, 48
Citizen's Religious Hate Crime Watch, 63
'city of gates,' from the, to the notorious city, 160–163
'civility of indifference' in rural India, 199, 202
civilizational power, 9, 83–86, 84–89, 87
   See also Hindutva establishments
clash of civilizations, 84
Coal Mines (Special Provisions) Act (2015), 29
Coastal Regulation Zone Notification (2019), 47
communal charge, of history, 163–168
communalism, problem of, 3
communal violence breaks, in Muzaffarnagar, 25
Communist Party of India (CPI), 40, 121, 131, 166
Compensatory Afforestation Funds Act (2016), 34
Concerned Citizens Tribunal, 240n7
Confederation of Indian Industries (CII), 75
Constitutional Amendment Bill, 124th, 43
construction of communalism, 3
cooperative federalism, promotion of, 28
corruption, issue of, 26, 34, 66, 205, 245n39
COVID-19 pandemic, 18–19
cow belt, 18
cow slaughter, issue of, 30
Criminal Procedure Code, 56
Custodian of Enemy Property, 18

Dabholkar, Narendra, 30, 38
Dadri lynching (2015), 64–65
Dalit celebrations, at Bhima Koregaon, 16
Dalit Sarvaiya community, 33
Dalit settlements, of Shabbirpur village, 36
Dalit violence in Una (2017), 38
Dassault Aviation (France), 28, 40
Dassault Rafale procurement case, 28–29, 40, 43, 47
Deendayal Research Institute (DDRI), 75
Delhi pogrom (2020), 50, 56, 117, 220, 238, 245n40, 253, 261–267
Delhi Riots: Conspiracy Unravelled, 53
democracy, bogeymen of, 9
democratic authoritarianism, 1
demonetization, policy of, 34
Directorate of Revenue Intelligence (DRI), 37

INDEX

Dismantling India: A 4 Year Report, 25
Doklam crisis, 37, 38
domicile laws, in Jammu and Kashmir, 17
Dr A. P. J. Abdul Kalam Road, 30

economically weaker sections, 43, 114–115
Election Commission of India, 6, 63, 298
Elgar Parishad case (2020), 42, 53, 57
Enemy Property Act (1968), 18
Enemy Property (Amendment and Validation) Bill (2016), 35
epistemic communities, 73
European Commission's Lorenzo Natali Media Prize (2011), 107

Factories Act, 37
Faizabad, renaming of, 43
Farmers (Empowerment and Protection) Agreement of Price Assurance Act, 55
Farmers' Produce Trade and Commerce (Promotion and Facilitation) Act, 55
farmers protest, against agrarian crisis, 36, 37
Farm Services and the Essential Commodities (Amendment) Ordinance, 55
Film and Television Institute of India (FTII), Pune, 7, 29
Finance Bill (2016), 33, 35
Ford Foundation, 29
Foreign Contribution (Regulation) Act (2010), 33, 63
forest lands, protection of, 34
Forum for Integrated National Security (FINS), 77, 80, 100n13
Forum of Integrated Security, 89

'gaps and ambiguities' of democracy, 8
Gau Raksha Samiti, 109

Geelani, S. A. R., 32
ghar wapsi (homecoming) campaigns, 28, 64, 226, 281, 303n14
ghettoization of Muslims, 152
Global Hunger Index (GHI), 57
Gogoi, Akhil, 44, 48
Gogoi, Ranjan, 39, 46, 51, 126n25
Golwalkar, M. S., 84, 142, 183, 192, 222, 239n4
good governance day, 8
Goods and Services Tax (GST), 37
Greater India experiment, The, 13
Greenpeace India, 28, 31
gross domestic product (GDP), 19, 54
gross enrolment ratio (GER), 54
Group of Intellectuals and Academicians (GIA), 50
Gujarat riots (2002), 13, 27, 33, 224, 284
Gurgaon, renaming of, 34

Hadiya's marriage, legality of, 40
Hall, Stuart, 10
Hate Crime Watch, 25, 63
Hathras rape victim, 56
Hedgewar, K. B., 84, 183, 192, 221
Hindu anger, 13–16, 288, 298
Hindu Dharma Sena, 28
Hindu Ekta Manch, 39
Hindu fighting force, 162
Hindu–Muslim solidarity, during the non-cooperation movement, 221
Hindu nationalism, 1–4, 10–12, 18, 61, 68–69, 72–75, 77, 79, 84, 88, 94, 96, 97, 100n16, 107, 159, 175–176, 184, 203, 221, 232, 242n20
Hindu nationalist violence, 59, 61–64
  populism and religious nationalism, 65–68

INDEX

state–societal linkages, 64–65
Hindustan Aeronautics Limited (HAL), 28
Hindutva, 199
  affiliations, 82, 103n44
  politics, 108
Hindutva and indigeneity, in northeast India, 181–183
  creating common worlds, 191–194
  culture, nationalism, and indigeneity, 184–191
  local grounds, global networks, 183–184
Hindutva and Muslimness, 219–220
  Bharatiya Muslims for the Ram mandir, 230–232
  incomplete Muslim citizen-subject, 221–224
  origins of the MRM, 224–226
  research contexts, 220–221
  rewriting Quranic scripture, reinterpreting Islam, 227–229
  RSS Ulema, 226–227
  sewa and the street, 235–238
  Ulema and the Muslim vote, 232–235
Hindutva establishments, 72–74
  right-wing think tank worlds, 74
    agendas and activities, 80–83
    central vista elite, 96–97
    civilizational power, 84–89
    lineages and contexts, 74–77
    networks and opaque publicities, 89–90, 93–96
    organizational locations and connections, 78–80
    terminology, 77–78
Hindutva project, 2–3, 9, 13, 18, 73–74, 89, 226–227

Hindu Yuva Sena, 38, 126n
Hindu Yuva Vahini, 35, 109
'Howdy Modi!' rally, at Houston, Texas, 46
Human Rights Watch, 30
Hyderabad Central University (HCU), 108, 124n15

Imam, Sharjeel, 49, 52, 220, 238
inclusion of Hindutva, 5, 11–13, 26, 200, 203–204, 212
India Ideas Conclave, 84–90, 91–92, 93, 100n15
Indian Air Force (IAF), 40
Indian Christians, attack on, 37
Indian Council for Social Science Research (ICSSR), 36
Indian Council of Historical Research (ICHR), 26
Indian Council of World Affairs (ICWA), 98n2
Indian *dharmocracy*, 86, 102n
Indian Penal Code (IPC), 62, 254
Indian right-wing think tanks, 77–78, 89
India Policy Foundation, 76, 82, 95
India's foundational myth, 275–276
  development as depopulation, 279–282
  Settler colonialism, 276–279
Indic Thoughts festival, 87
Indra Sawhney verdict, 44
Indus Waters Treaty, 280
Institute for Defence Studies and Analyses (IDSA), 98n2
institutional forbearance, 9
intercaste violence, 199
international elite integration, 90
International Labour Conference, 96

INDEX

International Press Freedom Award, 107
intra-bureaucracy transfers, 6

Jaish-e-Mohammed terror camp, 44
Jammu and Kashmir Reorganization Act, 45
'JAM' (Jan Dhan-Aadhaar-Mobile) trinity, 26
'Janata Curfew,' 51
Jannayak Janta Party (JJP), 46
Jawaharlal Nehru University (JNU) Students' Union, 31, 59, 93, 95, 124n15
'#JusticeforSushantSinghRajput,' 55

Kalburgi, M. M., 30, 38
'Kalinga effect,' 302n4
Karni Sena, 35
Kashmir, special status for, 16
Kathua rape case, 39
Kautilya Fellows Programme, 82, 101n20
Kendriya Vidyalayas, 27
Kerala's Sabarimala temple case, 42
Khalid, Umar, 31, 52, 55, 220, 238
Khan, Pehlu, 35, 64
Khilafat movement, 221
Kovind, Ram Nath, 37, 51
Kumar, Kanhaiya, 31, 62, 238
Kumar, Megha, 14
Kumbh Mela, 19, 58, 83
Kurt Schork Award in International Journalism, 107

Lamani caste, 199
Lankesh, Gauri, 30, 38, 116, 126n21
lateral entry, in civil services, 6
law and order failures, 14
law-making, form of, 16

Leone, Amulya, 50
Life Insurance Corporation (LIC), 45
Line of Actual Control (LAC), 53
long-distance nationalism, 18
love jihad, 25, 63, 65, 108, 110
Lutyens elite, 90, 97

Madar caste, 199
mahagathbandhan (grand alliance), 31
Maharashtra Anti-Terrorism Squad (ATS), 28
Mahatma Gandhi National Rural Employment Guarantee Scheme (MNREGS), 32
Majoritarian State, 4, 150
Maratha–Kunbi caste cluster, 172
Marathwada Chamber of Commerce, 171
Marathwada Mukti Sangram (MMS), 161
Marathwada Regional Development schemes, 171
massive religious festivals, 19
matrubhumi (motherland), 221
'mediatization' of new Hindutva, 18
metropolis, majoritarian, 130–132
   civil war and an interrogation, 132–140
   common sense of majoritarian city, 144–147
   instance 1, 147–148
   instance 2, 148–150
   instance 3, 151–152
   majoritarian city, 140–144
Mevani, Jignesh, 33, 38, 114, 120, 125n18
middle India, social segregation and everyday Hindutva in, 158–160
   'city of gates' to the notorious city, 160–163

INDEX

communal charge of history, 163–168
community capitalism and the consolidation of upper caste power, 171–175
social and spatial dynamics, 168–171
Mines and Minerals (Development and Regulation) Amendment Bill, 33
Minimum Support Price (MSP), 55
Ministry of Human Resource Development (MHRD), 26
Ministry of Social Justice and Empowerment, 27
Misra, Dipak, 39, 42
Modi, Narendra, 3, 4, 7, 50, 60–61, 205, 212, 287, 298–299
    abrogation of Articles 370 and 35A of the Indian Constitution, 275
    announcing of national lockdown to curb the spread of COVID-19, 51
    'Atmanirbhar Bharat' initiative, 52
    CAA–NRC issue, 119
    as chief minister of Gujarat, 34
    Dassault fighter jets deal, 29
    declaration of 'victory' over COVID-19 pandemic, 19
    demonetization, policy of, 34
    denial of visa by the USA, 27
    Donald Trump's visit to New Delhi, 67
    foundation for the controversial Ram Temple in Ayodhya, 181
    free cooking gas (LPG) connections to families living below the poverty line, 32
    Hindu nationalist violence, 61–64
    idea of 'Ek Bharat, Shreshtha Bharat,' 182
    inauguration of Sardar Vallabbhai Patel statue, 42
    involvement in the 2002 Gujarat riots, 27, 224
    launch of
        Pradhan Mantri Jan Dhan Yojana, 26
        Pradhan Mantri Ujjwala Yojana, 32
        Swachh Bharat Abhiyan, 27
    leadership style, 66
    nationalist justification of the anti-Muslim pogrom, 257
    'naya Kashmir' (new Kashmir) initiative, 278
    plot to assassinate, 39, 124n16
    populist and religious nationalist commitments, 66
    Ram Mandir Bhoomi Pujan, 54
    rise to power, 13
    'Sabka Saath, Sabka Vikas' initiative, 236
    second term as India's prime minister, 45
    settler-colonial agenda, 278
    Unnao rape case, 39
    victory in the 2014 Lok Sabha elections, 27
    as *vikas purush* (development man), 276
    visit to France, 28
    Wing Commander Abhinandan Varthaman case, 44
    withdrawal of farm laws, 58n2
money bills, 8, 32, 35, 42
Mont Pèlerin Society, 89
Most-Favoured Nation (MFN), 44
Mughalsarai Railway junction, renaming of, 43
Muslim community and opponents of Hindutva, 16
Muslim mobs, threats of, 15

INDEX

Muslim Rashtriya Manch (MRM), 12, 219, 224–225

Nagpur riots (1923), 221
'Namaste Trump' rally, 50
Nandy, Ashis, 199, 253, 268, 299
national agenda, development of, 28
National Crime Records Bureau (NCRB), 62–63
National Democratic Alliance (NDA), 26, 61, 108
National Democratic Progressive Party (NDPP), 40
National Education Policy (NEP), 54, 116
National Eligibility Test (NET), 30
National Institution for Transforming India (NITI Aayog), 5, 27–28, 99n8
National Investigation Agency (NIA), 40, 124n16
Nationalist Congress Party (NCP), 46
National Judicial Appointments Commission (NJAC) Act, 6, 26
national lockdown, during COVID-19 pandemic, 51–52, 54, 68, 124n9
National Narcotics Control Bureau (NCB), 53
National Population Register (NPR), 47, 67
National Register of Citizens (NRC), 46, 66
National Sample Survey Office (NSSO), 44
National Security Act (NSA), 38, 42, 110, 124n10
National Security Convention, 89
Navsarjan Trust, 34
Nehru Memorial Museum and Library (NMML), 30, 93

New Delhi Municipal Council (NDMC), 30
New Hindutva, 1
  articulation, 10–11
  demand-side, 2
  inclusion, 11–13
  modulations and moving targets, 18–20
  moment of arrival, 4
  populists in power, 4–5
  rule, 5–9
  supply-side, 2
  timeline from September 2013–October 2020, 25–57
  understanding, 2–4
  and the 'UP model,' 107–122
  violence, 13–18
nikah halala, 227, 242n17
Nizam's rule, 11, 166, 168
  Marathwada Mukti Sangram (MMS), 161
  police action for ending, 160
  shift in political power, 169
non-Brahmin caste movements, 125n17
non-resident Indians (NRI), 26
nun gang rape case (2015), 28

Observer Research Foundation (ORF), 75, 268
'Occupy UGC' protest, 30
Oil and Natural Gas Corporation (ONGC), 45, 209
Operation Polo (1948), 164
ordinary Hindus, 17, 19, 285, 287
Other Backward Classes, 111, 125n17, 204, 257
Padmavat (film), 35
'pagan' belief systems, 12

315

INDEX

Pakistan's Most-Favoured Nation (MFN) trade clause, 44
Pansare, Govind, 28, 30, 38
Parliament attacks (2001), 32
partition, in 1947, 11
patriotic tourism, 83
People's Union for Civil Liberties (PUCL), 25
pink revolution, 64
pitrabhumi (fatherland), 221
police encounter killings, rise in, 35
populism and religious nationalism, 65–68. See also Hindu nationalist violence
populists in power, 4–5
post-colonial theory, 2
Pradhan Mantri Jan Dhan Yojana, 26, 32
Pradhan Mantri Ujjwala Yojana, 32
Prasar Bharati, 6, 93, 95
Press Club of India, 32
prime minister's office (PMO), 36
Principal Economic Advisor, 87
pro-BJP WhatsApp groups, 62
public–private partnerships, 43
Public Safety Act (PSA), 46, 279–280
public sector enterprises (PSE), 45
Punjab State Legislative Assembly, 57
punyabhoomi (holy land), 221

racial fear, 10
racial pride, 10
Rafale fighter jet procurement case, 47
Raisina Dialogues, 89
Ram Mandir Bhoomi Pujan, 54
Rao, Varavara, 42, 43, 53, 55, 57, 124n
Rao, Y. Sudershan, 26, 40
Rapid Action Force (RAF), 112
Rashtriya Swayamsevak Sangh (RSS), 2, 59
  in Arunachal Pradesh, 12
  ideologues, 6
  ideology of Hindutva, 221
  raison d'être of, 221
  role of, 7
  swayamsevaks, 221
reactionary violence, 284–286
  'give me my land back!', 292–297
  guilt and reactionary violence, 286–292
Reddy, Kishan, 50–51, 55
religious minorities, 13, 20n1, 47, 59, 61, 68, 79, 125n17, 126n27
Reserve Bank of India (RBI), 33
Right to Fair Compensation and Transparency in Land Acquisition, Rehabilitation and Resettlement (Second Amendment) Bill, 29
riots in India
  Ahmedabad (1969), 14
  in August 1946, 11, 140, 143
  Babri Mosque demolitions (1992), 148
  Bhagalpur (1989), 252, 260–261
  Calcutta (1947), 11, 143
  Calcutta (1964), 143, 146
  Delhi (2020), 50, 56, 117, 220, 238, 245n40, 253, 261–267
  genealogy of, 259–261
  Gujarat (2002), 27, 109, 224, 301
  Hindutva politics and, 257
  ideological effects of, 15
  Jamia Millia Islamia University (2015), 52
  Muzaffarnagar (2013), 26, 108
  Nagpur (1927), 221
  protest against CAA, 68

316

INDEX

Shamli riots (2013), 25
by spreading rumours, 59

Sabarmati Express, burning of, 38
Sahara–Birla papers, 34
Samasta Hindu Aghadi, 39
'Samvad Global Hindu Buddhist Initiative,' 89
Samyukta Kisan Morcha (SKM), 58n2
Samyukta Maharashtra Samiti (SMS), 161
Sanatan Sanstha, 28, 38
Sangh Parivar, 3, 5, 7, 31, 75, 77–78, 79, 96, 182, 195n1, 224, 231, 234, 241n13, 261, 287, 290
Sangh social mobilizations, 8
Sarabhai's Report on the Communal Situation and Riots in Calcutta (1950), 143, 155n12, 155n13
Sardar Sarovar Dam, 46
Sardesai, Rajdeep, 253, 261–262
Sarhad ko Pranam, 83
Scheduled Castes (SCs), 41, 125n17
post-Matric scholarship regulations for, 125n20
Scheduled Castes and the Scheduled Tribes (Prevention of Atrocities) Act, 41–42, 114, 125n19
Scheduled Tribes (STs), 41, 125n17
post-Matric scholarship regulations for, 125n20
secessionist and separatist activities, in Jammu and Kashmir, 57
Securities and Exchange Board of India (SEBI), 5
sedition laws, 8
settler colonial project, 16–17, 276, 278–279
sexual violence, 14, 25, 108

Shah, Amit, 27, 45, 47, 53, 62, 79, 80, 119, 126n
Shaheen Bagh sit-in protest, 48
Shaheen Education Institute, in Bidar, Karnataka, 49
Shamli riots (2013), 25
Shiv Sena, 11, 13, 46, 53, 159, 162–164, 169–170, 172, 175, 290
Smart Cities Mission, 29
social and spatial dynamics, everyday Hindutva, 168–171
social boycott, of Christians, 37
Sohrabuddin Sheikh encounter killing case (2014), 27
Special Investigation Team (SIT), 53
state-societal linkages, 64–65. *See also* Hindu nationalist violence
Statue of Unity, 42, 84
St Sebastian Church, fire accident (2014), 27
Student Islamic Organization (SIO), 52
Sunni Waqf Board, 46, 126n25
'super spreader' events, 19
Supreme Court of India, 6, 25–26, 29, 31–32, 34, 38–42, 44, 47, 50, 57, 68, 125n19, 126, 230
surgical strike
against 'black money' and 'corruption,' 34
film on, 118
against militants across the LoC, 34
against Pakistan, 210
Swachh Bharat Abhiyan (Clean India Mission), 27
Swadeshi Jagran Manch, 42, 76
Swamy, Stan, 57
Swamy, Subramaniam, 33, 79
Syama Prasad Mookerjee Research

INDEX

Foundation, 76–77, 80, 95, 100n13, 100n15, 100n16

Tablighi Corona, myth of, 19
Tablighi Jamaat, 51, 54, 245n40
Terrorist and Disruptive Activities (Prevention) Act (TADA), 123n4
Think Tank Index, 75, 99n7
Think Tanks and Civil Society Program (TTCSP), 99n7
Track 1.5 diplomacy, 77
Trilateral Commission, 90
Trinamool Congress (TMC), 131, 153n2
triple *talaq*
  practice of, 38, 45, 227, 242n17
  Triple Talaq bill (2019), 80, 220
Trump, Donald, 4, 46, 50, 67
'Turning to Roots, Rising to Heights' theme, 84

undernourishment in India, 57
United Progressive Alliance (UPA)-II, 28
University Grants Commission (UGC), 30
Unlawful Activities (Prevention) Act (UAPA), 35, 45, 110, 124

Unlawful Activities (Prevention) Amendment Bill, 45
Unnao rape case, 39, 41, 51
'Urban-Naxal-Jihadi' network, 50, 53
urban naxals, 16, 50, 53
Uttar Pradesh's (UP's) public buses colour, 8

varnashramadharma, 86
Vemula, Rohith, 31, 108
village councils, 34
violence, politics of, 13–18, 251–252. See also riots in India
  argument, 252–259
Vishwa Hindu Parishad (VHP), 12, 35, 278
Vivekananda Foundation, 82
Vivekananda International Foundation, 76, 85, 89, 95, 99n7, 100n13

Working People's Charter, 25
World Economic Forum, 19, 90
World Press Freedom Index, 56
World Watch Monitor, 37